Social History of Africa

LAW IN COLONIAL AFRICA

Social History of Africa
Series Editors:
Allen Isaacman and Luise White

David William Cohen and E. S. Atieno Odhiambo
Burying SM
(forthcoming)

Myron Echenberg
Colonial Conscripts:
The Tirailleurs Sénégalais *in French West Africa,*
1857—1960

Kristin Mann and Richard Roberts (editors)
Law in Colonial Africa

Belinda Bozzoli
(with the assistance of Mmantho Nkotsoe)
Women of Phokeng:
Consciousness, Life Strategy, and Migrancy
in South Africa, 1900—1983
(forthcoming)

LAW IN COLONIAL AFRICA

edited by
Kristin Mann
Richard Roberts

HEINEMANN
Porstmouth, NH

JAMES CURREY
London

Heinemann Educational Books, Inc.
361 Hanover Street
Portsmouth, NH 03801–3959

James Currey Ltd
54b Thornhill Square, Islington
London N1 1BE

ISBN 0–435–08053–9 (Heinemann cloth)
ISBN 0–435–08055–5 (Heinemann paper)
ISBN 0–85255–652–7 (James Currey cloth)
ISBN 0–85255–602–0 (James Currey paper)

First published 1991.

Library of Congress Cataloging-in-Publication Data
Law in colonial Africa/edited by Kristin Mann and Richard Roberts.
    p.   cm. — (Social history of Africa series)
    Includes bibliographical references and index.
    ISBN 0–435–08053–9. — ISBN 0–435–08055–5 (pbk.)
    1. Law — Africa — History and criticism. 2. Rule of law — Africa — History.
    3. Colonies — Law and legislation — History. I. Mann, Kristin, 1946–   II. Roberts,
    Richard, 1949–   III. Series. LAW
    349.6 — dc20
    [346]   90–25784
                                                 CIP

British Library Cataloguing in Publication Data
Law in colonial Africa. — (Social history of Africa)
    1. Africa. Law. History
    I. Mann, Kristin 1946–   II. Roberts, Richard   III. Series
    342.0096

ISBN 0–85255–652–7
ISBN 0–85255–602–0 pbk

Cartography by Adrienne Morgan.
Cover design by Jenny Greenleaf.
Text design by G&H Soho Ltd.
Printed in the United States of America.
91 92 93 94 95 9 8 7 6 5 4 3 2 1

CONTENTS

Notes on Contributors   vi

Preface   viii

Conference Participants   x

Maps   xi

I   INTRODUCTION

   1   Law in Colonial Africa *Richard Roberts and Kristin Mann*   3

II   PROPERTY AND THE ACCUMULATION OF WEALTH

   2   Paradigms, Policies, and Property: A Review of the Customary Law of Land Tenure *Martin Chanock*   61

   3   The Rise of Taiwo Olowo: Law, Accumulation, and Mobility in Early Colonial Lagos *Kristin Mann*   85

   4   From Giving and Lending to Selling: Property Transactions Reflecting Historical Changes on Kilimanjaro *Sally Falk Moore*   108

III   LAW, POWER, AND AUTHORITY

   5   The Jurisdiction of Muslim Tribunals in Colonial Senegal, 1857–1932 *Dominique Sarr and Richard Roberts*   131

   6   The Dynamics of Collaboration and the Rule of Law in French West Africa: The Case of Kwame Kangah of Assikasso (Côte d'Ivoire), 1898–1922 *David Groff*   146

   7   Tswana Government and Law in the Time of Seepapitso, 1910–1916 *Simon Roberts*   167

   8   The Case of Faama Mademba Sy and the Ambiguities of Legal Jurisdiction in Early Colonial French Soudan *Richard Roberts*   185

IV   LITIGANTS, COURTS, AND LEGAL STRATEGIES

   9   Theft, Homicide, and Oath in Early Twentieth-Century Kano *Allan Christelow*   205

   10   Law in African Borderlands: The Lived Experience of the Yoruba Astride the Nigeria-Dahomey Border *A. I. Asiwaju*   224

   11   "A Case for the Basoga": Lloyd Fallers and the Construction of an African Legal System *David William Cohen*   239

Index   255

NOTES ON CONTRIBUTORS

A. I. Asiwaju, Department of History, University of Lagos, has published widely on the impact of colonial boundaries on African history. His publications include *Western Yorubaland under European rule, 1889–1945: A comparative analysis of French and British colonialism* (1976) and *Partitioned Africans: Ethnic Relations Across Africa's International Boundaries, 1884–1984* (1985). He is currently a commissioner of the National Boundary Commission, Nigeria.

Martin Chanock teaches in the Department of Legal Studies, School of Social Sciences, LaTrobe University. He is the author of *Unconsummated union: Britain, Rhodesia and South Africa, 1900–45* (1977) and *Law, custom, and social order: The colonial experience in Malawi and Zambia* (1985) and is currently engaged in a major study of law and society in South Africa.

Allan Christelow, Department of History, Idaho State University has published widely on both North and sub-Saharan Africa history. His works include *Muslim law courts and the French colonial state in Algeria* (1985). He is currently completing a translation and annotation of a series of *shari'a* court records from Kano as part of the African Historical Sources project.

David William Cohen is Professor of Anthropology and History and Director of the Program of African Studies Center, Northwestern University. He has written widely on the social and cultural history of East Africa, including *Womunafu's Bunafu: A study of authority in a nineteenth century African community* (1977) and together with E. S. Atieno Odhiambo, *Siaya: The historical anthropology of an African landscape* (1989). His latest work, *Burying SM*, on the S. M. Otieno case in Kenya, 1986–87, also with Atieno Odhiambo, will appear in the Heinemann Social History of Africa series.

David Groff is Director of the Portland Campus and assistant director of continuing education at Linfield College in Oregon. He has published a wide range of articles on social and economic history of the Assikasso region of the Côte d'Ivoire.

Kristin Mann, Department of History, Emory University has published *Marrying well: Marriage, status, and social change among the educated elite in colonial Lagos* (1985). She is currently completing a study of the social transformation of nineteenth century Lagos.

Sally Falk Moore is a Professor of Anthropology at Harvard University. Among her publications are two books on legal anthropology, *Law as process: An anthropological approach* (1978) and *Social facts and fabrications: 'Customary' law in Kilimanjaro, 1880–1980* (1986). She has conducted fieldwork among the Chagga of Tanzania.

Richard Roberts, Department of History, Stanford University has published widely on the economic and social history of the Western Sudan. His work includes *Warriors, merchants, and slaves: The state and the economy in the Middle Niger Valley, 1700–1914* (1987) and an edited volume with Suzanne Miers, *The end of slavery in Africa* (1988).

Simon Roberts, Department of Law, London School of Economics, has conducted research among the Kgatla and Ngwaketse of Botswana and has published widely on law and legal anthropology. His publications include *Order and dispute: An introduction to legal anthropology* (1979) and with John Comaroff *Rules and processes: The cultural logic of dispute in an African context* (1981).

Dominique Sarr taught in the Faculté de Droit, Université de Dakar until his untimely death in 1988. During his short career, he published a series of important articles on law in colonial Senegal.

PREFACE

Armed with copies of records from the Lagos Supreme Court, Kristin Mann led a discussion in Richard Roberts's African Social History Workshop at Stanford University in April 1985. Mann had originally turned to court records as part of a prosopographical study of Lagos's early educated elite, and was in 1985 exploring them as a source of information about the social transformation of Lagos in the second half of the nineteenth century. Roberts, too, was working with a court case; the administrative law hearing investigating the alleged abuses of power by a king in French West Africa. Concerned about the limits of oral and other archival sources as repositories of data about the lived-experience of Africans during the colonial period and fired by the rich and detailed information in court records about the daily lives of ordinary Africans, Mann, Roberts, and the Stanford students probed the possibilities and problems of court records as a new frontier of scholarship on African social history. As we pored over the Lagos Supreme Court cases, our discussion kept returning to the little we knew about colonial law and courts, about methods of working with court records, and about the intersection of African legal, social, and cultural change.

Out of the workshop grew a conference which brought together social historians, legal anthropologists, and legal scholars working, often in the early stages, on law in colonial Africa. The goals of the conference were to assess the state of knowledge in the three disciplines, explore the contributions that each could make to the others, and stimulate research on African legal, social, and cultural history. A widely publicized call for papers and a thorough canvassing of the field netted participants from Africa, Australia, Great Britain, and North America who were working exclusively on Anglophonic or Francophonic Africa or on South Africa. Despite concerted efforts, we were unable to elicit contributions from scholars studying the Portuguese, German, or Belgium colonies.

The papers presented at the three-day conference, held at the Humanities Center at Stanford University in April 1988, explored a stunningly wide and diverse array of intellectual problems and research strategies. We regret that it was impossible to include all of the papers in the present volume. Forced to select, a number of criteria guided our difficult and sometimes arbitrary decisions about what to include and what to leave out. First, we decided to exclude the papers on South Africa, owing to the fact that it has been politically independent since 1910, although it has pursued a peculiar form of colonialism inside and outside its borders, and to the unique influence on South African legal history of Dutch-Roman law. Next, we chose to privilege papers based on analysis of court or other little-used legal records. Finally, we selected papers that focused on the interrelated themes of law, property, and accumulation; law, power, and authority; and litigants, courts, and legal strategies.

International conferences are expensive undertakings. We are deeply grateful for a Research Planning Activity Grant from the Joint Committee on Africa of the Social Science Research Council and the American Council of Learned Societies, which transformed a fantasy into a possibility and encouraged us to seek additional sources of funding. Generous support from Emory University, the Hewlett Fund of Stanford University, and the Humanities Center at Stanford University brought the conference to fruition. A grant from the Ford Foundation enabled three West African scholars to participate in the event. We wish to thank all of the conference participants, listed following this preface, for their valuable contributions to our undertaking. We particularly acknowledge our intellectual debt to Martin Chanock and Sally Falk Moore, whose seminal books on the history of law in colonial Africa appeared in 1985 and 1986, respectively, and greatly enriched our thinking about the project. We thank Martin Chanock, Martin Klein, Richard Rathbone, and the African Social History series editors, Allen Isaacman and Luise White, for carefully reading an earlier draft of the manuscript. Their thoughtful criticism markedly improved the anthology. Finally, we have appreciated the enthusiastic support and patient understanding of John Watson, president of Heinemann Educational Books. Responsibility for the limitations of the volume rests, of course, with us alone.

Kristin Mann and Richard Roberts
November 1990

CONFERENCE PARTICIPANTS

Richard Abel, School of Law, University of California-Los Angeles

A. I. Asiwaju, Department of History, University of Lagos

Martin Chanock, Department of Legal Studies, School of Social Sciences, LaTrobe University

Alan Christelow, Department of History, Idaho State University

David William Cohen, Departments of Anthropology and History, Johns Hopkins University

Ann Dunbar, African-American and African Studies Program, University of North Carolina-Chapel Hill

Anne Griffiths, Department of Scots Law, Faculty of Law, University of Edinburgh

David Groff, Continuing Education, Linfield College

Bogumil Jewsiewicki, Département d'Histoire, Université Laval, Québec. His paper was read in his absence.

H. M. Joko-Smart, Faculty of Law, University of Sierra Leone

Martin Klein, Department of History, University of Toronto

Deborah Mack, Department of Sociology and Anthropology, Lake Forest College

Kristin Mann, Department of History, Emory University

Sally Falk Moore, Department of Anthropology, Harvard University

Sean Redding, Department of History, Amherst College

Richard Roberts, Department of History, Stanford University

Simon Roberts, Department of Law, London School of Economics

David Robinson, Department of History, Michigan State University

Dominique Sarr, Faculté de Droit, Université de Dakar

William Worger, Department of History, Stanford University.

Marcia Wright, Department of History, Columbia University. Her paper was read in her absence.

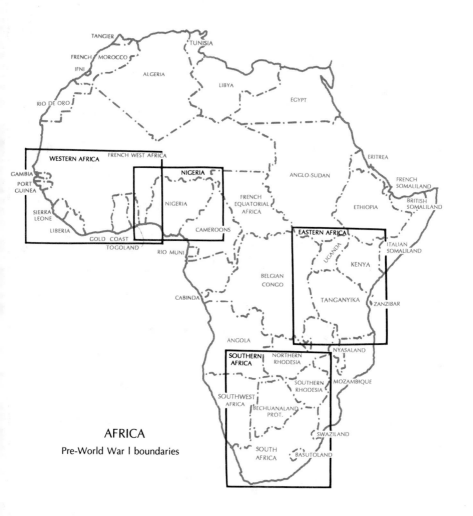

TANGIER

TUNISIA

FRENCH MOROCCO

IFNI

ALGERIA

LIBYA

EGYPT

RIO DE ORO

WESTERN AFRICA

FRENCH WEST AFRICA

ERITREA

GAMBIA

NIGERIA

FRENCH
SOMALILAND

PORT
GUINEA

ANGLO-SUDAN

NIGERIA

FRENCH
EQUATORIAL
AFRICA

BRITISH
SOMALILAND

SIERRA
LEONE

ETHIOPIA

LIBERIA

GOLD COAST

CAMEROONS

TOGOLAND

EASTERN AFRICA

RIO MUNI

ITALIAN
SOMALILAND

UGANDA

KENYA

BELGIAN
CONGO

CABINDA

TANGANYIKA

ZANZIBAR

ANGOLA

NYASALAND

SOUTHERN
AFRICA

NORTHERN
RHODESIA

MOZAMBIQUE

SOUTHERN
RHODESIA

SOUTHWEST
AFRICA

BECHUANALAND
PROT.

AFRICA

Pre-World War I boundaries

SWAZILAND

SOUTH
AFRICA

BASUTOLAND

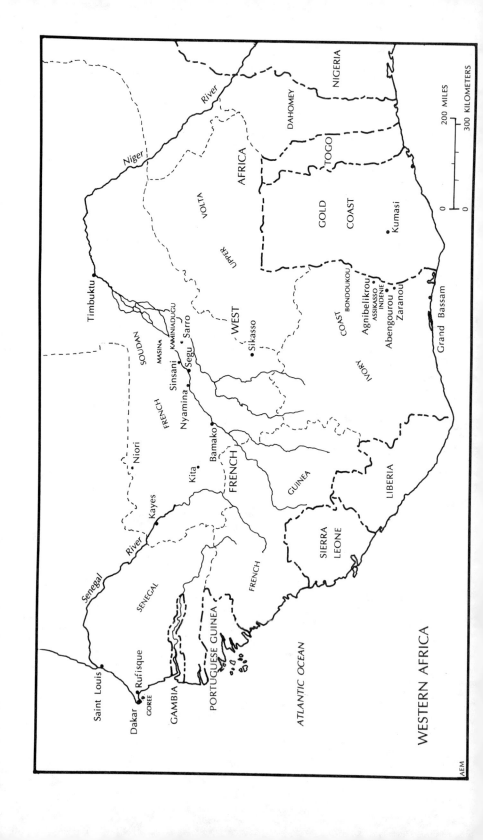

WESTERN AFRICA

NIGERIA

DAHOMEY

TOGO

WEST AFRICA

GOLD COAST

Kumasi

Niger River

VOLTA

UPPER

Timbuktu

SOUDAN

MASINA

KAMINIADUGU

Sinsani
Segu
Sarro

Nyamina

FRENCH

WEST

Sikasso

COAST

BONDOUKOU
Agnibelikrou
ASSIKASSO
INDENIE
Abengourou
Zaranou

Grand Bassam

IVORY

Niori

Bamako

FRENCH

Kita

GUINEA

LIBERIA

Kayes

Senegal River

SENEGAL

SIERRA
LEONE

FRENCH

Saint Louis

Rufisque

Dakar

COREE

GAMBIA

PORTUGUESE GUINEA

ATLANTIC OCEAN

200 MILES

300 KILOMETERS

0

0

AEM

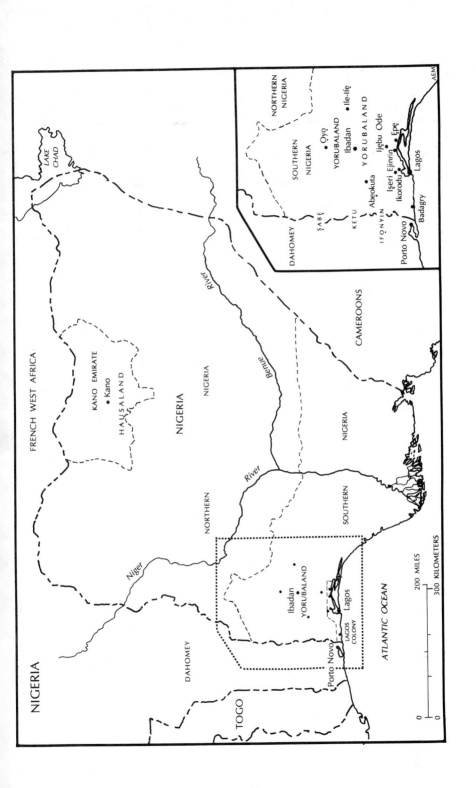

NIGERIA

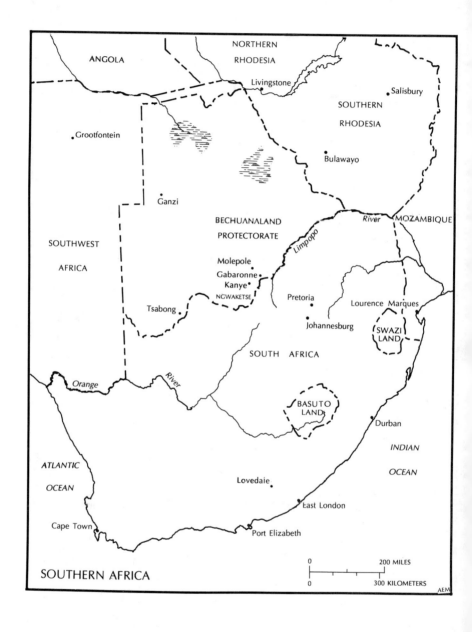

SOUTHERN AFRICA

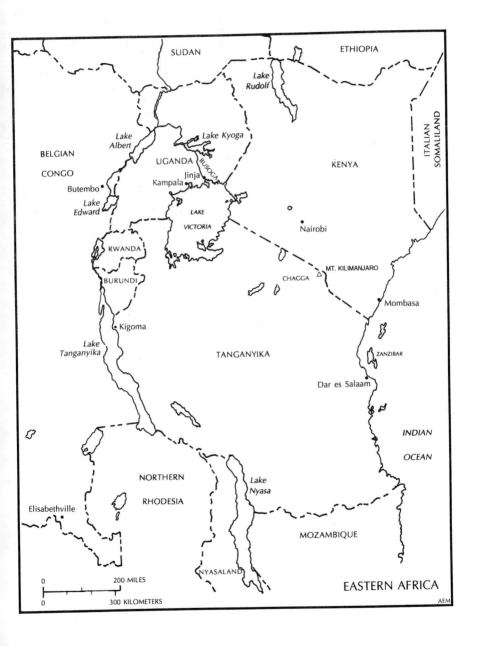

SUDAN

ETHIOPIA

Lake Rudolf

BELGIAN

CONGO

Lake Albert

Lake Kyoga

UGANDA

Jinja

Kampala

BUSOGA

KENYA

Butembo

Lake Edward

LAKE

VICTORIA

Nairobi

ITALIAN SOMALILAND

RWANDA

BURUNDI

Kigoma

CHAGGA

MT. KILIMANJARO

Mombasa

ZANZIBAR

Lake Tanganyika

TANGANYIKA

Dar es Salaam

INDIAN

OCEAN

Elisabethville

NORTHERN

RHODESIA

Lake Nyasa

MOZAMBIQUE

NYASALAND

0   200 MILES

0   300 KILOMETERS

EASTERN AFRICA

AEM

PART I

INTRODUCTION

1

Law in Colonial Africa

RICHARD ROBERTS AND KRISTIN MANN

Law was central to colonialism in Africa as conceived and implemented by Europeans and as understood, experienced, and used by Africans. Laws and courts, police and prisons formed essential elements in European efforts to establish and maintain political domination. They were instrumental as well in reshaping local economies to promote the production of exports for European markets and the mobilization of labor for African and European enterprises. Colonialism sought to impose a new moral as well as political and economic order, founded on loyalty to metropolitan and colonial states and on discipline, order, and regularity in work, leisure, and bodily habits (Cooper 1987; Martin 1987; Atkins 1988; Cooper 1990; Comaroff and Comaroff 1990). By regulating such things as health, sanitation, leisure, and public conduct, law played a vital role in moral education and discipline. Finally, Europeans believed that they were in Africa for the local peoples' own good. The idea of rule of law seemed to them to provide evidence of this fact, and it powerfully legitimized colonial rule.

During the colonial period, law formed an area in which Africans and Europeans engaged one another — a battleground as it were on which they contested access to resources and labor, relationships of power and authority, and interpretations of morality and culture. In the process, Africans encountered the realities of colonialism, and both they and Europeans shaped the laws and institutions, relationships and processes, and meanings and understandings of the colonial period itself. Under colonialism, moreover, Africans used law as a resource in struggles against Europeans. Legal rules and procedures became instruments of African resistance, adaptation, and renewal, as well as of European domination. Law not only affected nor was it only affected by engagements between Africans and Europeans. Struggles among Africans were central as well. In his study of the judicial process among the Barotse, Gluckman (1955:21) remarked, "The Lozi, like all Africans, appear to be very litigious. Almost every Lozi of middle age can recount dispute after dispute in which he has been involved." Gluckman's observation begged such important questions as the nature and meaning of litigation. It reminds us, however, that in the colonial period Africans met one another on the legal battlefield far more often than they did

3

Europeans. The legal discourses and debates, disputes and conflicts among Africans were as important as those between Africans and Europeans in shaping the colonial social order.

The making of customary law in colonial Africa reveals with particular force and clarity the encounter between Africans and Europeans and among Africans themselves. Customary law, regarded by some Europeans as immutable tradition, evolved out of the interplay between African societies and European colonialism. European understanding of precolonial African systems of law and authority and African collaboration with colonial systems of law and government led to the invention of tradition in Africa and its foundation in customary law and local institutions such as chieftaincy and courts. Although Europeans did not see it, their efforts to build colonialism on indigenous authority and tradition confronted processes of change and conflict. In Africa, as elsewhere in the world, laws reflected the imperatives of changing economic, political, and social circumstances and were both transforming and transformed over long stretches of time. At the time of European conquest, in most African societies there was no single, unchanging tradition. There were, instead, contested and continuously reconstituted traditions, best understood as clusters of rules, moralities, expectations, and conflicts, which gave rise to changing regulatory practices.

Identifying chiefs and incorporating them into colonial law and government meant supporting one claimant over others and privileging one form of authority with its linked moral and political ideas over many alternative forms. The invention and eventual codification of custom solidified fluid cultural and legal ideas and relationships into reproducible rules. The litigiousness to which Gluckman referred expressed conflicts unleashed in the colonial period when the quest for tradition simultaneously multiplied competing claims to resources, labor, and authority, yet solidified productive and power relationships. The stakes in these conflicts were high; at issue were control of resources and labor and structures of power and authority. The importance and ubiquity of struggles over authority, resources, and labor help explain the remark by the High Court of Uganda, which heard appeals from lower courts concerning claims and counterclaims for positions of authority, about "these tiresome Busoga headmanship cases" (quoted in Cohen, Ch. 11).

Because of its centrality to colonialism, law provides an excellent window through which to view the colonial period. Examining this rich but neglected topic casts fresh light on the structures of colonialism: its laws, institutions, and procedures. It also exposes to view the pivotal relationships of the colonial era — between Africans and Europeans and among Africans themselves — which very often they lay at the heart of legal conflict. Beyond this, studying law illuminates the economic and political processes central to colonialism, because the reordering they engendered was commonly contested in the legal domain. The study of law thus allows us to explore in new ways enduring problems in colonial historiography. But it also raises for investigation a number of new questions. The discourse and debate surrounding law show how Europeans and Africans understood issues and perceived interests in the major upheavals of the colonial era. Moreover, legal conflict, whether in courts or elsewhere, reveals how groups within each population responded to these upheavals, framing interpretations and arguments to mold popular and official understanding and pursuing agendas and strategies to affect immediate and distant outcomes. In this way, the focus on law enables us to see the place of culture in shaping legal responses and the role of legal conflict in turn in producing cultural change. Beyond this, studying law yields fresh insights into the lived experience of Africans during the colonial period. Work with little-used legal records, a necessary part of much legal research, generates data of unparalleled richness and detail about the daily lives of ordinary Africans, a subject about which historical data is hard to find. Such scholarship also provides us with evidence of African political and social thought, not only among the educated elite, some of whom became prominent lawyers and colonial officials, but also among Africans who were not western educated.

Colonialism changed African law—its rules, institutions, procedures, and meanings. It affected as well the way African peoples perceived and understood law. Research on law in colonial Africa thus illuminates a formative period in African legal history, one that is all the more important because it lay the foundation of modern African legal systems. Any understanding of the role of law in contemporary Africa must rest on an appreciation of the legal rules and institutions, processes and meanings created under colonialism. The history of law in colonial Africa forms an important chapter in the story of the expansion of Western law overseas. We argue throughout this introduction that the impact of African and European legal interaction was reciprocal; however, we focus primarily on the legacy of the interaction for African law. There is another important and, if anything, even less well known tale to be told about the effects of this interaction on European law. Beyond the scope of this volume, its telling awaits research by other scholars.[1]

This anthology focuses on a part of the broad history of law in colonial Africa. It looks at the engagement among and between Africans and Europeans in their mutual efforts 1) to shape and define rules and processes affecting access to resources, labor, and authority, 2) to deal with conflict stemming from divergent ideas and interests regarding resources, labor, and authority, and 3) to encode meanings of property, labor, and power relationships that emerged under co-lonialism. As we shall show, legal engagement around these issues occurred inside courts and councils and before commissions. But it is important to bear in mind that what did not come to these bodies can be as revealing as what did. We believe that investigating the intersection of law, property, labor, and authority in colonial Africa deepens our understanding of what colonialism meant to those who were empowered by it as well as to those who struggled against it. We look forward to future historical studies of other important aspects of law. The con-tributors to this volume use different sources and methods, and they employ different approaches to the study of law. The book simultaneously explores the ways that the study of law contributes to an understanding of colonialism and assesses the potential of various approaches, methods, and sources for advancing historical scholarship on law. In both regards, it charts an agenda for future research.

Studying Law in Colonial Africa

In 1963 Jack Goody bemoaned the fact that so little research had been conducted on African legal history and that what little there was neglected processes of change. And yet anthropologists, administrators, and lawyers had long found in Africa a fertile ground for their investigations.

The colonial encounter originally shaped the anthropological study of law.[2] Anthropologists first viewed law as part of an evolutionary paradigm: to Rattray ([1929] 1969) and Meek ([1937] 1949) law in African societies was reminiscent of law in an early stage of civilization. Malinowski (1926), who did not work in Africa, rejected the evolutionary paradigm. His work emphasized the positive inducements to social conformity to be found in reciprocal social relationships. For Malinowski, law comprised a broad and relatively undefined range of efforts to maintain social order. Law differed from society to society, because the maintenance of social order varied with the nature of social organization.

Neither an approach to law that stressed evolution nor one that emphasized voluntary social conformity provided much practical assistance to colonial administrators who sought to incorporate indigenous legal institutions in the operation of the colonial state. Anthropologists, some of whom were also colonial administrators or employees, turned their attention to the study of rules and procedures for resolving disputes. Schapera's handbook of Tswana law and custom (1938), based on the oral testimony of elders, catalogued legal rules largely to assist colonial administrators. Schapera's study, however, referred to rules without reference to actual adjudication. Gluckman's classic study of Barotse judicial process (1955) was based on actual disputes that he had witnessed and on information gathered from Barotse notables. What distinguished Gluckman's work was his description of the social context of disputes and his concern with how Barotse judges handled grievances put before them. The rule-oriented approach to African law well suited the practical concerns of administrators and lawyers.[3]

In colonial Africa, Europeans strove where they could to refashion indigenous societies based on Western models of good government and representations of local cultures. Law played a central role in on-going processes of cultural and political reform. As colonial officials began to see law as an instrument of social change, the evolutionary paradigm of Rattray and Meek took on new significance. Administrators expected that in the process of codifying African customary law they could modernize it and incorporate it in a pluralist colonial state or later a modern nation state. The work of Anthony Allott (1967, 1970a, 1970b, 1976) represents the marriage of the lawyer and administrator, for whom the study of African law was essentially a problem of applied science. Allott believed the task of the lawyer-administrator was to codify and systematize customary law, retaining as far as possible its specific characteristics, even as it became part of the legal codes of independent African nations. In the 1950s and 1960s, lawyers and constitution-builders throughout the continent shared his purpose.

In the postcolonial period, as anthropologists distanced themselves from the practical concerns of an earlier generation, they concentrated on the study of law as social process, focusing particularly on dispute management (Nader 1966, 1969; Nader and Todd 1978; Collier 1975). Many sought to link dispute processing to social organization, emphasizing the social correlates of different types of settlement. Others compared different kinds of societies to discover similarities and differences in mechanisms for handling disputes. John Comaroff and Simon Roberts (1981) demonstrated in their study of Botswana, that legal norms, institutions, and procedures are negotiable. They uncovered the strategies that disputants and third parties devised to deal with conflicts and advance their individual interests.

After decades of treating law ahistorically, anthropologists came in the 1980s to appreciate the need to study law in historical context. In 1978, Moore concluded a review of the analytic problems in legal anthropology by arguing that anthropologists must introduce "time" into their research on law (253–54). Legal anthropologists responded readily enough to several of Moore's other charges in the 1978 article, but with a few exceptions they ignored her call to study history. Moore redoubled her challenge in a recent book on the transformation of the legal and political practices of the Chagga. She opened the work with a plea for a "time-oriented" anthropology, which combines field and archival research and moves back and forth between investigating small-scale events and large-scale social processes (Moore 1986:1–12). The study demonstrated that Chagga "customary" law, regarded by Europeans as immutable tradition, was in fact the product of historical interaction between the Chagga people and their colonial rulers (Moore 1986:1–12). Participants in a 1985 conference on new directions in legal anthropology took up Moore's charge with an investigation of the place of history and power in the study of law. These scholars assumed that "law is a thing constructed by human agency" and that it encodes power relations (Starr and Collier 1989:3, 6–9). They went on to examine the relationship between changes in law and power in specific historical contexts.

Just as anthropologists were becoming interested in studying law historically, historians themselves were beginning to investigate the role of law in the transformation of African societies. Their work built on European social history, which had already demonstrated the value of legal records and questions for the study of changes in political economy and everyday life (D. Hay et al. 1975; E. P. Thompson 1975; Beattie 1986). Francis Snyder (1981) commenced by probing the relationship between changes in legal forms and productive relations among the Banjul of Senegal at a time of the growth of agricultural commoditization and wage labor. Contributors to the Hay and Wright (1982) anthology asked to what extent legal records provided sources for the reconstruction of African women's lives, and they explored the impact of legal changes on gender. Pursuing Ranger's (1983) concern with the invention of tradition in central Africa, Chanock (1985) examined the manufacture of customary law in colonial Malawi and Zambia by Africans and Europeans acting on their own beliefs and interests. Christelow, in his work on Algeria (1985) and Senegal (1982), treated the struggle to control Muslim courts as part of the conflict between local Muslim elites and the colonial state. While these studies raise different problems for investigation, they share a concern for long-term processes of material, institutional, and ideological change and a belief that analysis of law must be rooted in an understanding of historical context.

In the 1980s, legal anthropologists sought to bring their sub-discipline into closer conversation with social anthropology as a whole. Comaroff and Roberts (1981:3, 17–21, 216–42) rejected the treatment of law as a discrete field of inquiry and studied it instead as part of a total cultural system. Starr and Collier (1989:5–6) conceptualized legal anthropology not as an isolated sub-discipline but as a "theory-building" part of social anthropology. While the contributors to their book agreed that "anthropological understanding of legal processes needs to be based on a broader vision," they divided over the theoretical question of whether such understanding should be rooted in the investigation of social process or cultural meaning. The editors concluded, "There seems to be no way to resolve these fundamentally different stances toward how 'objective' reality is constituted" (p. 21). The theoretical debate manifested itself in different approaches to the study of law and legal systems. Some scholars adopted a cultural approach, examining discourse about laws and legal systems; while others favored an interactional approach, asking how individuals and groups use laws and legal processes for their own ends. Still other contributors advocated institutional research, which focuses on economic and political processes and treats actors as representatives of economic interests and laws as manifestations of ideological positions (pp. 21–22).

Written to promote discussion among historians and anthropologists and revised to reflect it, the essays in this volume significantly advance the historical study of law in colonial Africa. The authors represented here join the contributors to the Starr and Collier anthology in viewing law not as a body of immutable rules, institutions, and procedures but as a dynamic historical formation which at once shapes and is shaped by economic, political, and social processes. They treat law not as an impartial arbiter guided by fixed rules and procedures but as a resource that is used in struggles over property, labor, power, and authority. Whereas Starr and Collier leave us with a disjunction between social and cultural categories as the primary modes for research, several of the essays presented here seek to integrate the two. As editors, we would argue that the proper challenge of historical research is not to determine whether cultural understanding or social process is more important in constituting "objective" reality, but to discover the relationship between the two in specific historical situations. Our purpose is not to debate the primacy of actors, discourse, or institutions in legal change, but to explore the relationship among them. We share with Starr and Collier a concern that the study of legal and cultural orders be "mutually defining" (1989:12). Chapters here by Chanock, Moore, Simon Roberts, David William Cohen, and others show that Africans and Europeans in colonial Africa used law to compete for resources, labor, power, and authority in part by engaging in discourse about law and legal procedures. Contestants invoked symbols, rules, and ideas in support of particular positions, and in the process they negotiated meaning to suit particular ends. Institutional, class, and ideological forces affected debate over law and legal procedures, whether it took place in a court or elsewhere. The discourse in turn shaped the distribution of resources, labor, power, and authority in society and the content and character of local law and culture.

When Europeans conquered Africa they encountered populations with well-established indigenous and Islamic systems of law. Conquest did not destroy these systems, although it often subordinated them to metropolitan legal traditions and changed their relationship to political authority and productive relations. Indigenous law and *shari'a* law persisted alongside European civil, criminal, military, and administrative law. In addition, the colonial period gave birth to "customary" law, regarded by Europeans as indigenous law, but in fact invented by Africans and Europeans under colonialism. Most chapters in this anthology adopt the perspective not of plural legal systems—indigenous, Muslim, European, and customary — but rather of a single, interactive colonial legal system. Europeans did not impose this system fully developed. It was forged over time by Africans and Europeans pursuing interests and beliefs of their own. Participants in the process included persons of all kinds: administrators, soldiers, judges, lawyers, scholars, clerks, interpreters, missionaries, merchants, traders, farmers, and slaves, to name but a few.[4] The construction of the colonial legal system was not forged, however, by contests between Africans and Europeans alone. Europeans struggled with other Europeans and Africans with other Africans — women against men, juniors against elders, ruled against rulers — over the form, content, and meaning of law in colonial Africa.

The following section surveys the making of colonial legal systems in Africa, drawing primarily on the experiences of the French and British colonies. The discussion forms a vital chapter in African legal history. It is central as well to the economic, political, and social history of the colonial period. The mosaic of overlapping and co-existing legal rules and processes both constrained Africans and Europeans living in the colonies and created opportunities for them. The organization of courts and the jurisdiction of different bodies of law matter, because they affected who could use law, how, and to what end.

The Construction of Colonial Legal Systems

Law, Accommodation, and Commerce during the Era of the Slave Trade

Legal interaction between Africa and Europe long predated colonial rule. Trade linked the continents for centuries before conquest, and it involved Africans and Europeans in complex relationships that required them to hammer out systems of accountability and processes of dispute. These relationships centered on property and credit, the nexus of commercial interaction, but they extended outward to areas such as labor, marriage, inheritance, and kinship. Fuller understanding of the impact of precolonial contact on African and European legal rules, institutions, and procedures awaits primary research. It is clear, however, that prior to the nineteenth century, the balance of power in African and European legal interaction favored the Africans.

Early European traders in the Senegambia and on the Upper Guinea Coast looked to local rulers for protection, and they accepted the legal authority of these potentates (Rodney 1970:83–88, 117; Dorjahn and Fyfe 1962:391–97; Curtin 1975:122, 287–98). The construction of forts on the Gold Coast gave Europeans greater security and power, but even there they depended on Africans for land, labor, provisions, and ultimately for trade itself. European factors often had African wives, and they relied on these women as local patrons to mediate commercial, diplomatic, and judicial interaction with local peoples. Foreign traders on the coast accommodated African laws and customs, but with their African wives, they gave rise to racially mixed families and communities touched by western culture. With the early European traders came missionaries, who even at this time pronounced on marriage, inheritance, and other legal matters that they believed bore on the morality of their flock (Kea 1982:206–88; Priestley 1969:36–113; Yarak 1989; Searing, forthcoming).

Although the asymmetries of power in early legal interactions between Africans and Europeans favored the Africans, law was from the beginning a subject of conflict in the on-going struggle over access to trade and control of its profits. As early as the mid-sixteenth century, Portuguese traders tried to evade African laws which held that ships running aground and goods belonging to deceased Europeans and Eur-Africans became the property of local rulers. The Portuguese also attempted to minimize Africans' demands for gifts, which cut into profits from trade (Rodney 1970:91−92, 195; Brooks, forthcoming). In the late eighteenth century, British and French trading companies in the Senegambia pressed African rulers to negotiate treaties that delineated the mutual rights and obligations of the European companies and African authorities. Europeans sought the treaties in part to check the escalation of gifts and tolls. Through these agreements some African rulers finally relinquished ancient privileges such as the right to pillage wrecked ships or to inherit from foreigners who died within their domains (Curtin 1975:290). A century earlier, trading companies had begun imposing legal jurisdiction over company employees, and some extended their authority to Eur-African descendants of company employees or to Africans who had converted to Christianity (Solus 1927; Hild 1912:65 66; Moreau 1938:111).

Struggle over law, in pursuit of wealth from trade, occurred not only between Africans and Europeans but also among Africans themselves. *Afahene*, nobles who had resources necessary to trade on a large scale, dominated the external and regional trade of the Gold Coast. Until the second half of the seventeenth century, laws expressly prohibited non-afahene from trading directly with Europeans. These laws were upheld in local courts, and they underpinned the power and privilege of the nobles. Yet some commoners entered trade, accumulated resources, and joined the ranks of the afahene, indicating that a fortunate few could negotiate, manipulate, or circumvent the laws regulating trade (Kea 1982:206, 233, 295−96).

If Europeans generally accommodated African legal practices in the era of the slave trade, prolonged interaction among representatives of the cultures of the coast nonetheless profoundly affected African legal rules, institutions, and procedures. The expansion of trade created new opportunities to earn income and accumulate wealth. This altered patterns of resource use and labor mobilization, and it increased social differentiation. Both phenomena affected legal understandings of the nature and control of property and persons.

Nineteenth-Century Transformations

In the first half of the nineteenth century, the balance of power between Europeans and Africans shifted decisively in favor of the Europeans. Industrialization had widened the material and technological gap between their cultures. Europeans began to feel confident for the first time that on the African coasts, if not in the interior, they could impose their will, by force if necessary. Simultaneously, material advancement and evangelical revival strengthened the belief of most Europeans in the moral superiority of their own civilization. Westerners equated standard of morality with standard of living, and they found both wanting in Africa (Hopkins 1980:778). The British abolition of the slave trade in 1807 and its associated criminalization of slave trade commercial practices represented both the cultural framework of this new found sense of European superiority and the establishment of British maritime law in the form of courts of mixed commission. The new faith of Europeans in the moral and material superiority of their own civilization convinced them that exporting their culture would be good for Africans. Trade in agricultural commodities and conversion to Christian religion were, of course, to be the agents of change.

These fundamental shifts in the relationship between Africans and Europeans affected the character of legal interaction between them. On the coasts, Europeans became less willing to accept local practices than they had been before. Merchants, missionaries, and officials began to assume that the spread of Western legal arrangement was necessary to the growth of trade and civilization. They wanted new authorities and institutions to regulate their dealings with local people. This change was most apparent in matters touching on credit and property, but it affected other matters as well. Trade in agricultural commodities required wider networks of credit and indebtedness than had the slave trade. Up and down the coast, credit began to be secured not by the older methods of swearing oaths or forging patron-client relationships, but rather by pledging property. The pledge sometimes took the form of a written contract filed with a European authority.[5] The increased use of property pledges was part of the gradual spread of Western concepts of property, which Hopkins (1980:777—79) has shown Victorians believed was essential to establishment of a vigorous cycle of trade and development in the non-European world.

Legal changes on the Gold Coast and in the Niger Delta illustrate the shifting relationship between Africans and Europeans. Throughout the eighteenth century, the Company of Merchants Trading to Africa had exercised minimal judicial authority in its settlements on the Gold Coast. In the first half of the nineteenth century, British officers extended the reach of British law and courts, not only in the settlements but also in the surrounding territories, where they had no official jurisdiction (Priestley 1969:150—57; Kimble 1963:193—99). European powers had no formal presence in the Niger Delta, unlike on the Gold Coast. In the 1850s, however, European merchants in the area established Courts of Equity that heard cases involving commercial transactions between Europeans and Africans (Adewoye 1977a:34). These courts sat infrequently, followed no formal procedures, and administered no fixed body of law. Cases were decided by majority vote on the basis of what the merchant-judges believed the "justice" of a particular situation required. Sometimes they took local trading customs into account, but overall there was a shift toward Western understandings of property, contract, crime, and punishment. At least one of the courts ran a jail where it could incarcerate those it found guilty of offenses (Adewoye 1977a:33—35). The early nineteenth-century transformations in the balance of legal power between Africans and Europeans was not unique to Africa, but rather formed part of a world-wide process of the establishment of consular jurisdictions, through which European powers attempted to exercise control over their citizens and commercial transactions involving them.

France's Four Communes and Britain's Crown Colonies

Over the course of the nineteenth century, European powers abandoned informal commercial imperialism for formal colonial rule. The transition occurred first in France's Four Communes — St. Louis, Gorée, Dakar, and Rufisque — and in Britain's

Crown Colonies—Freetown, the Gambia, the Gold Coast, and Lagos. The legal and administrative history of these areas is in certain respects different than that of France's and Britain's later interior possessions. All had been deeply influenced by Western law prior to annexation, via trade, immigration, and, except for Lagos, company rule. Moreover, each of the coastal colonies boasted significant European and Creole populations that the ruling power believed ought to enjoy some of the benefits of metropolitan law. Finally, all of these areas experienced some form of direct colonial rule centered on newly created, Western-style bureaucracies and courts administered by European and Creole officials. In these areas the impact of European law and courts was greater than in any other part of the continent, save South Africa. Indigenous authorities and institutions played a much more restricted role in government than they would when colonialism spread to the interior, limiting the opportunity of local rulers to benefit from changes in law.

With the reoccupation of Senegal in 1817 following the Treaty of Versailles, the French fundamentally reorganized their colony and instituted a metropolitan judicial system. The tribunal of Gorée sat for the first time in 1822. In 1837, the tribunals of Gorée and Saint Louis were changed into *tribunaux de première instance*, the primary court of the French judicial system. Between 1822 and 1840, the presiding officers of these tribunals were the French commandants of the cities assisted by another senior French employee and one local notable. In 1840, provision was made for appointing professional magistrates to these tribunals and for establishing an appeals court. Under Governor Faidherbe in the 1850s, the judicial service was strengthened, but it was not until 1891 that France created the position of attorney general (*procureur général*), with administrative control over the primary and appeals courts (Hild 1912:66–67; Roberts 1990).

These courts heard both civil and criminal cases involving French citizens or those exercising French civil and legal rights. Since French policy in Senegal recognized some African inhabitants (the *originaires*) of Gorée and Saint Louis as French nationals (often referred to erroneously as citizens), they too fell under the jurisdiction of French law and brought cases before the tribunal of the first instance (see Sarr, Ch. 5 for more detailed explanation).[6] French Muslim policy, as Sarr describes, led to the establishment of a Muslim tribunal in Saint Louis in 1857, which was empowered to adjudicate civil cases involving French nationals of Muslim religious persuasion. "Councils of Reconciliation," dealing with commercial complaints between Frenchmen and African traders, were presided over by French district officers and held in major towns along the Senegal River. Unless Africans were originaires from the Four Communes, were assimilated French citizens, were involved in cases against French citizens, or had voluntarily renounced their customary civil status, they were not entitled to bring cases before the tribunal of the first instance (Buell 1928:1003; Opoku 1974:142–51). Indeed, the French colonial judicial system as it evolved in Senegal to 1903 made no formal provision for the adjudication of conflicts between Africans who were neither nationals nor assimilated citizens. Before 1903, Africans in areas controlled by France drew upon a variety of precolonial dispute management strategies, including bringing grievances before household heads, cadis, village chiefs, and occasionally before French district officers.[7] A similar division of legal jurisdiction by "nationality" prevailed in Portuguese colonies. Separate codes and separate courts applied to Portuguese nationals and *assimilados* on the one hand and the mass of Africa *indigenas* on the other (see below, 17−18; Harris 1958:6−26; Bender 1978:149−55).

The early histories of Freetown, the Gambia, the Gold Coast, and Lagos differed in significant detail, and these differences affected their legal systems (Joko-Smart 1988; Kimble 1963; Elias 1963; Adewoye 1977a). For our purposes, however, the similarities in the experiences of Britain's West African Crown Colonies are more important than the differences among them. Immediately following the annexation of Freetown, the Gold Coast, and Lagos, British officials established the first in a succession of new courts, where Europeans or Creoles assumed responsibility for hearing civil and criminal cases. At the same time, common law, equity, and statutes of general application in force in England were introduced by reception acts used throughout the British empire to impose the whole body of English law prevailing at a particular moment (Elias 1963:17−21; Seidman 1969; Joko-Smart 1988:25). Subsequently, the Crown Colony governments created bodies of statute law by passing local ordinances. The early British courts in these areas were supposed to follow English procedures and to apply English law to disputes involving Europeans and Creoles. Magistrates and judges, however, had little formal legal training and few reference books existed for their guidance. The operation of the courts was erratic, at best, and both law and procedure sometimes deviated from English practice. In the final quarter of the nineteenth century important reforms regularized the legal systems of the Crown Colonies, creating supreme courts with the same jurisdiction as the High Court of Justice in England and lower courts answerable to the supreme courts. Better-qualified judges and attorney generals were sent out, and English-trained lawyers, mostly of African descent, set up shop to advise clients and represent them in court (Joko-Smart 1988:7−14, 23−33; Adewoye 1977b:50−52ff; Edsman 1979). The professionalization of African law had begun.

African courts continued to exist in Freetown, the Gold Coast, and Lagos, and they heard most disputes between locals. On the Gold Coast, an 1883 Native Jurisdiction Ordinance defined the criminal and civil jurisdiction of the chief's courts and provided for appeal from them to the British courts (Kimble 1963: 457−64), effectively incorporating these local tribunals into the colonial legal system. In Freetown and Lagos the government did not recognize African courts, which operated outside the colonial legal system and constituted an alternative to it (Mann 1982:151−71).

In contrast to the Four Communes of Senegal, where only those with French "nationality" could turn to the French courts, indigenous peoples in British Crown Colonies sometimes took disputes to the British courts. This gave them alternative authorities to whom they could turn in disputes with one another, undermining the authority of the local rulers. When Africans appeared in British courts, magistrates and judges were supposed to apply indigenous law, so long as it was not repugnant to justice, equity, and good conscience or incompatible with local statutes. The use of British courts by Africans profoundly affected indigenous law, despite the colonial government's commitment to apply local law to local peoples. Many African practices failed the repugnancy test, in which case British officials decided cases on the basis of what they thought was right. Even when local practices were not deemed repugnant, magistrates and judges often misunderstood indigenous law, upholding in the name of custom practices that were not customary at all. The unfamiliarity of British officials with local property, labor, gender, and power relations created opportunities for litigants, in the presentation of their cases, to present local customs as they wanted them to be. In the British courts, as subsequently in the Native Courts, actors contested and reshaped local law and culture through discourse and debate. Overall, the creation of new courts and law widened the arena of conflict within the Crown Colonies.

The British courts recorded judgments, some of which were subsequently published. This created a body of precedent, turning local law into something akin to English case law (Cohn 1989:150−51; Chanock 1989:72). Precedents were invoked and debated not only in British courts, but also in indigenous ones, where actors sometimes framed their arguments against the backdrop of their understanding of how matters would be handled in colonial courts. A very different system prevailed in the Four Communes of Senegal. There the French civil code was applied to litigants excercising French civil rights. In legal proceedings in the tribunal of the first instance, the entry-level court for civil disputes, the prerogatives of the magistrate were defined by the civil code. In contrast to the British system, French magistrates applied the code; they did make case law.[8] In the tribunal of the first instance, African litigants conformed largely to metropolitan legal practices, although they also invoked Muslim oaths and called African witnesses to bolster their claims. Africans bringing grievances before the cadis of the Muslim tribunals conformed to Muslim legal practices, although increasingly, the cadis were brought under the close supervision of French judicial officials. With the establishment of native courts after 1903, Africans outside the Four Communes had access for the first time to a hierarchy of courts recognized by the colonial state. In these courts, considerable debate ensued over the meaning of custom (Beurdeley 1916:27−33).

Muslims in Freetown and Lagos petitioned the local colonial governments to have Islamic law govern their legal relationships, but with less success than their counterparts in St. Louis. The Sierra Leone administration obliged with a Muslim marriage ordinance that recognized three areas of Islamic law — marriage, divorce, and intestate succession (Joko-Smart 1988:23−37). The government of Lagos, on the other hand, denied that the legal practices of Muslims in the colony differed significantly from those of non-Muslims, and it refused to provide for the operation of shari'a law (*Lagos Weekly Record*, 28 July 1894).

Missionary Influence and Company Rule

In the final decades of the nineteenth century, European powers penetrated the African interior. In some areas missionaries preceded traders and officials, and they became deeply involved in legal affairs. These nineteenth century missionaries affected the legal order more profoundly than had their predecessors centuries earlier, owing to changes in the character of the Christian mission and in the political relationship between Europe and Africa. Chanock (1985:79) notes that in Malawi and Zambia a good deal of the time of the nineteenth and twentieth century missionaries was spent acting as judges. Missionary diaries and memoirs from Yorubaland contain numerous references to legal intervention (Phillips papers 1/1/7 1900 and 3/1−3/4 1885−1889). Chanock has shown that one of the most important consequences of missionary involvement in justice was to change

African attitudes towards legal transgression. Christian religious authorities introduced the belief that to break the law was to sin. They spread the idea that the point of judicial proceedings was to determine guilt and impose punishment. Transplanting British law, Chanock (1985:80, 128) argues, went hand-in-hand with transfusing Christian guilt. But missionaries also taught new ideas about the individual and humanist rights, and these were critically important in attracting slaves, women, and others to the alternative legal program that the missions represented.

Early missionaries also affected law in more tangible ways. Identifying religious with cultural conversion, they called on converts to embrace Western social practices as well as Christian religious beliefs. Colonial governments sometimes encoded these practices in specific legal obligations, as in the case of marriage. Throughout British Africa, colonial marriage ordinances legislated that Christian unions should be monogamous and should rest on new property and inheritance rights (Mann 1985:44ff; Phillips and Morris 1971:142–52, 176–85).

Fierce competition for spheres of influence characterized the European occupation of Africa. Reluctant to assume the burden of empire in Africa, Great Britain, France, and Germany relied on chartered companies to protect and extend their interests in large parts of the interior, without direct cost or responsibility to the metropolitan government. Many Africans first encountered European law and justice at the hands of officials of the Royal Niger Company, the British South Africa Company, the Imperial British East African Company, the French Company of Senegal, or the German East Africa Company. The founders of the British enterprises in particular won support for their projects at home by promising to spread progress and civilization as well as to uphold interests and prestige. The charters granted the British companies broad legal powers but at the same time enjoined them to pay careful regard to "the customs and laws of the class or tribe or nation...especially with regard to the holding, possession, transfer, and disposition of lands and goods, and testate or intestate succession thereto, and marriage, divorce, and legitimacy, and other rights of property and personal rights" (quoted in Allott 1976:353). Foreign Office supervision was slight, however, and boards of directors were self-interested or uninvolved. Men on the spot enjoyed great freedom to turn the administration of justice to the companies' own ends. Courts established by the Royal Niger Company along the Niger River served George Goldie-Taubman's quest for a monopoly of trade in the area (Flint 1960:9–61; Ikime 1967:62–75). Those created by the British South Africa Company in Southern and Northern Rhodesia furthered Cecil Rhodes's dream of self-governing settlements of white farmers and miners north of the Limpopo (Galbraith 1974:106–53). Chanock has argued that an unusually belligerent attitude toward justice characterized the early period of BSAC rule in Northern and Southern Rhodesia. The governments of the Rhodesias treated law as integral to the exercise of political authority and vested exclusive judicial responsibility in European officers with almost unlimited powers (Chanock 1985:71–3).

The Expansion of Empire

In the turbulent last two decades of the nineteenth century, spheres of influence ceased to satisfy European ambitions in Africa. From 1879 French soldiers defeated major resistance to carve out a vast empire in the Western Sudan and in Central Africa. British agents acquired protectorates throughout the continent by the more peaceful but nonetheless coercive tactic of extracting treaties from local rulers. Signing treaties often accompanied taking sides in local conflicts, usually with the most powerful, and was hence an intervention in local law and politics. The enlarged French and British empires differed from the Four Communes and Crown Colonies in that the inhabitants of these new territories were considered protected persons, not subject to the direct rule of European law. The French never recognized the inhabitants of their much enlarged empire as nationals, in the way that they did the originaires of the Four Communes, but regarded them instead as subjects. In principle, the concept of protectorate bound British officials to respect local customs and limited their legal jurisdiction over local peoples, but in practice officials in protectorates eventually came to assume substantially the same powers as those in the colonies (Allott 1976:348–49).

With the expansion of French territorial control under Faidherbe in the late 1850s and the 1860s and especially under Governor Brière de l'Isle in the late 1870s, the French elaborated a "native policy" that recognized the power of chiefs to dispense customary law, except when it was considered repugnant to "civilization" or when serious criminal offenses had been committed. In the immense territories conquered by France between the late 1870s and the turn of the century, a complex patchwork of overlapping legal jurisdictions developed. Until 1903, Africans seeking settlements of disputes approached village chiefs, cadis, kings, and French administrators, none of whom operated within clearly defined legal jurisdictions. Moreover, as Richard Roberts (Ch. 8) shows in his discussion of Mademba, cases sometimes proceeded within the arena of administrative law, even though sufficient evidence existed to launch civil and criminal suits.

The French colonial ministry took a first step toward reorganizing colonial administration with the establishment of the office of the governor-general of the federated colonies of French West Africa in 1895. This reform pitted a more centralized form of colonialism against the free-wheeling power of local military and civilian administrators, which had characterized the colonialism of the conquest period. Not surprisingly, one of the tasks of the newly formed government-general was to reorganize the jurisdiction of French and native law and in the process to tame administrators in the field. After several years of study, Governor-general Merlin promulgated a new legal code in 1903, which effectively created two parallel systems of justice: one for French citizens and those exercising French civil and legal rights, and the other for African subjects.

The period from the founding of the government-general to the promulgation of the reorganized legal system, 1895–1903, was of profound importance for the shape of French colonial rule (Mohkiber 1990). It is not surprising that the three chapters in this volume dealing with the French colonial legal system revolve directly or indirectly around this seven year period. Both the case against Faama Mademba Sy and the case against Kwame Kanga have their origins in this time of conflict over competing models of colonialism. Of the two, the case against Mademba represents most dramatically the tensions between the colonialism of the conquest era and the colonialism of the government-general. However, the formation of the government-general was equally critical for the outcome of the case against Kwame Kanga, because Kanga turned to the new offices of the government-general for recourse against what he considered to be injustice at the hands of a local French administrator (Groff Ch. 6). The shifting jurisdiction of Muslim tribunals in the Four Communes of Senegal, discussed by Sarr and Roberts, also had its roots in the competing models of colonialism held by magistrates, administrators, and Muslim *originaires* who held French electoral and legal rights but who also enjoyed the exceptional privilege of retaining their Muslim personal status. All three chapters discuss the politics of legal jurisdiction in colonial French West Africa and all three set legal issues against the wider context of competing colonialisms and changing political economies. Each chapter demonstrates how Africans were affected by the changes in the legal system and how they were able, in some cases, to use or resist those changes.

No analysis of the French legal system would be complete without some discussion of the *indigénat*, the system of summary administrative justice. First introduced in 1887 at the height of colonial conquest, the indigénat gave district administrators power to discipline summarily all violations of colonial regulations. The indigénat was restricted in 1888 to certain enumerated offenses, and in 1907 it was limited to 26 specific infractions. The 1903 legal code created conflicts of authority, for some offenses dealt with under the indigénat subsequently also fell within the jurisdiction of the village and provincial courts.

The indigénat was applied primarily in cases where Africans refused to pay taxes, perform corvée labor, or obey public officials. It was also used to punish those who criticized the government policy (Buell 1928:1016–1020; Asiwaju 1979; Asiwaju Ch. 10). Administrators were not obligated to hold trials before pronouncing judgments under the indigénat. They could summarily condemn an individual to a fine of up to 100 francs and imprisonment of up to two weeks. Africans could not appeal following sentencing under the indigénat, which, according to Suret-Canale, gave administrators (and briefly canton chiefs) the simultaneous powers of police, magistrate, prosecutor, and jailer (1971:335). Africans feared and despised the indigénat, because it was more arbitrary than any other form of "justice." Although progressively circumscribed, the indigénat was not abolished until the implementation of the Brazzaville agreements following World War II.

As the Portuguese expanded control over their colonies in the late nineteenth and twentieth centuries, they elaborated a colonial legal system that was based on a separation of metropolitan and native law similar to the French West African colonies. At the heart of the Portuguese colonial legal system lay the *indigenato*, which was a cultural and judirical doctrine maintaining that the mass of African subjects were not prepared to exercise Portuguese citizenship. Although some indigenas could become Portuguese citizens by adopting the "habits and customs presupposed of Portuguese common law," in reality very few ever did. As late as 1950, only 0.7 percent of the total African population had become "civilized" and thus able to exercise Portuguese civil and legal rights (Bender 1978:150–51). Conversion from one status to the other required confirmation by Portuguese colonial officials, which was often a degrading experience.[9]

The mass of Africans living in Portuguese Africa were subject to the summary administrative powers of the indigenato. Much like their French counterparts, Portuguese administrators exercised police and judicial functions, thus empowering them to accuse, arrest, try, and sentence Africans as delinquents. Portuguese district administrators were charged with economic development and labor mobilization. The indigenato and the pass book became potent means of achieving these ends. Because administrators' success and advancement often depended upon the volume of crops their region produced and the number of workers they provided, many used their powers under the indigenato to extract "stern, almost military discipline from [their] wards" (Harris 1958:9−10; see also Newitt 1981: 106−12; Isaacman 1985:17−29).

The British colonial legal system evolved differently than the French and the Portuguese. At the beginning, it made greater use of local authorities and institutions. Officials in most early protectorates started with the assumption that African legal practices were barbaric. Those that were not were nonetheless vastly inferior to Western legal practices. Rather than bypassing local systems of law and government, however, many early protectorate administrators wanted, under close British tutelage, to reform them aggressively, until they reached a civilized level. Few of these officials had any formal legal training, although a good number had public school and university educations (Gann and Duigman 1978: 175−252). Many carried in their minds a simple evolutionary scheme based on Maine's ancient law, that emphasized the development from status to contract and from torts, compensatable civil wrongs, to crimes, public wrongs punishable by the state (Chanock 1985:71−5; Allott 1976:365−68; Kuper 1988:17−35). At the same time, all protectorate governments labored under a similar constraint: the need to impose hegemony at little or no cost to the Britih taxpayer. Early administrators struggled relentlessly to contain costs, while at the same time raising revenue. Like it or not, they had no choice but to accept some type of rule through largely unreformed indigenous authorities and institutions (Berry 1988:3). Even when treaty agreements did not prohibit direct intervention, British officials retained local laws and courts much as they were, because protectorate governments had neither the power nor the resources to overhaul them.

Despite shared aspirations and constraints, no uniform policy or clear philosophy guided administrators in early protectorates. Officials on the spot developed varying systems of law and government in response to local realities and pragmatic considerations. Northern Tswana chiefs invited British protection over their territory in 1885, and they negotiated a protectorate agreement that allowed them to rule their people with minimal interference (Marks 1985:397). Prior to the reforms of the 1930s that systematized Native Administration, British officials strove to incorporate the Tswana chiefs into a system of local government only so far as was necessary to collect taxes and facilitate communication (Hailey 1957: 499−501). The chiefs retained the power to legislate and, except in murder cases, to adjudicate. Protectorate rule certainly altered the political and legal world of the northern Tswana. Simon Roberts's contribution to this volume (Ch. 7) shows Chief Seepapitso and his people involved in many new activities. But Roberts concludes that Seepapitso's legislative and judicial roles, while well-suited to the demands of protectorate government, were firmly rooted in Tswana culture. The very way the chief collected taxes—by informing, reminding, and exhorting— minimized the changes wrought by colonialism.

The story was very different in the Oil Rivers and subsequently the Niger Coast Protectorates, established in 1885 and 1893 respectively. Building on the tradition of the Courts of Equity, the Oil Rivers administration set up governing councils, composed of British officials, African chiefs, and European traders, to perform executive, legislative, and judicial functions (Adewoye 1977a:38–39). Then, in the 1890s, two aggressive British commissioners, Claude Macdonald and Ralph Moor, adopted a policy of using what they understood to be the indigenous political system for the purpose of local government, subject to the supervision of the central administration. Macdonald and Moor created native councils and minor courts, composed of chiefs who held warrants from the British commissioner, and they vested these bodies with executive and legislative as well as judicial responsibility. From the British perspective, the new system had the advantage of minimizing cost, facilitating taxation, and shoring up local authorities. In point of fact, it bore little resemblance to the indigenous political system, and it radically transformed law and government in the region. Warrants appointing chiefs rarely went to locally-recognized leaders. Moreover, the system granted the courts and chiefs powers that local authorities had never before enjoyed (Afigbo 1972: 37–112; Tamuno 1972).

The Busoga states, focus of David William Cohen's essay (Chapter 11), were subject to still a different system of colonial law and government, one first developed in the kingdom of Buganda, their more powerful neighbor. Early British officials found in the centralized, hierarchical Buganda kingdom a form of government that they could recognize and admire. The 1893 agreement with the king (the Kabaka), proclaiming the Uganda Protectorate, preserved his jurisdiction over his own people, subject to the rights of British officials to interfere in criminal cases and of his own subjects to appeal to the newly created British courts in civil cases. A famous 1900 agreement recognized the Kabaka's government as the native administration of the province of Uganda under British protection and overrule, and it upheld his council's authority to legislate on matters of local concern. Chiefs appointed by the Kabaka or a lesser authority and answerable to them administered justice, collected taxes, maintained roads, and supervised local government outside the capital (Buell 1928:537–89; Allott 1976:350–59).

Under the 1900 agreement, Buganda relinquished its claims to tributaries such as Busoga. However, Great Britain extended the colonial Buganda system of law and government to the Busoga kingdoms by dispatching educated Buganda to oversee the process of reform. Local rulers of independent Busoga kingdoms were retained at first, but later they were replaced by men without hereditary claims chosen for their ability and education. All of the county, sub-county, and village chiefs acted as judges, supervised in theory by Buganda or British officers. A series of native court ordinances introduced after 1905 reorganized and regulated the courts. Fallers concluded that the Basoga were familiar with courts of law from precolonial times and that the new legal structure introduced by the British represented for them no radical departure (Fallers 1969:48–61). A study more sensitive to history might have reached a different conclusion. Cohen's essay draws attention to the discursive strategies of "players" in the Busoga courts. It shows how these strategies themselves shaped what happened in the courts. Colonialism dramatically changed the discursive possibilities, and in this way if in no other it transformed the courts.

Indirect Rule, Native Administration, and Customary Law

Sir Frederick Lugard, appointed in 1900 to administer the British protectorate of Northern Nigeria, raised to the level of philosophical imperative policies that previously had been dictated by practical necessity. Lugard's first task was to conquer recalcitrant Emirs. Having subjugated their country, he confronted the problem of administering it. Influenced by earlier experience in India where he observed the Native States, Buganda where he served the Imperial British East African Company, and Southern Nigeria where he witnessed the policies of Goldie, Macdonald, and Moor, Lugard advocated rule through local authorities and indigenous systems of law and government. This policy of indirect rule, as Lugard labeled it, rested on the principle of incorporating African institutions into colonial law and administration. Lugard called not for "two sets of rulers — British and Native — working either separately or in co-operation," but for "a single Government in which Native Chiefs have well-defined duties and an acknowledged status equally with British officials" (Lugard 1918:298, quoted in Buell 1928:688; Perham 1937:33—60; Perham 1956, 1960; Kirk-Greene 1965:1—44).

The system of Native Administration that Lugard developed in Northern Nigeria rested on three fundamentals. First, the British recognized the Emirs as Native Authorities and used them to mediate between local peoples and the colonial state, maintaining order, adjudicating conflict, organizing labor, and collecting taxes. Second, Lugard constituted a hierarchy of Native Courts presided over by Islamic judges. These courts, examined in Christelow's essay (Ch. 9), were to apply customary and Islamic law "together with such English law as [was] embodied in rules drawn up by the Court or Chief and approved by the Governor" (Buell 1928:690). Third, Lugard established Native Treasuries, which in theory retained the ancient tribute imposed by Emirs on their subjects. English officers now assessed the tax on individual incomes, although Native Authorities collected it (Buell 1928:688—99; Perham 1937:33—60; Kirk-Green 1965:68—148).

In the face of African resistance to direct intervention and in the interest of containing administrative costs, indirect rule retreated from aggressive legal and governmental reform. European administrators still sought to civilize African institutions, but now gently and behind the scene. To rush the process was to risk losing native society's "stability, and indeed its soul. Its political and social organization [was] likely to break up, and what was before a well-ordered community, in which all the members had a definite series of obligations to one another [might] become nothing but a disorganized rabble of self-seeking individuals" (Meek [1937] 1949:326). The task of the British colonial administrator was now to reform indigenous administration from within indigenous institutions.

Indirect rule seemed to provide a neat solution to the problem of administering Britain's vast African empire. From Nigeria, amalgamated in 1914 under Lugard's leadership, a wave of administrative reforms in the interwar period spread the system of Native Administration throughout west, east, and southern Africa (Buell 1928, I; Hailey 1950—1953). Incorporating indigenous systems of law and government required identifying them and ruling through local authorities necessitated locating pliable candidates. British social anthropology was ready to tackle the former problem, and Africans could always be found to serve the British, given the rewards of office. Native Administration proved easiest to implement where well-established states existed. However, it created difficulties even there. Berry has argued that in practice indirect rule promoted instability. Although administrators failed to see it, colonial regimes imposed themselves on societies engaged in struggles over power and the terms on which it was exercised. By making traditional systems of authority the cornerstones of their strategies for governance, the British built colonial rule on conflict and change (Berry 1988:4—6).

In some places the kinds of authorities sought by the British did not exist. Where administrators could not find local rulers, they invented them, as among the Igbo of southeastern Nigeria. British officials constructed Native Administration in Igboland around Macdonald's and Moor's warrant chiefs, reaffirming their executive as well as judicial authority. Conjoining these responsibilities and vesting them in single individuals departed fundamentally from precolonial Igbo political systems (Afigbo 1972; Adewoye 1977a:40—42ff). For this reason, Native Authorities in Igboland lacked the legitimacy of their counterparts in Northern Nigeria. Charles Meek, an anthropologist sent to investigate the origins of the Aba women's war, blamed the disturbances in part of the implementation of indirect rule. According to Meek, Native Authorities were far more powerful than precolonial village-councils. Moreover, they used their judicial and executive authority to personal advantage, generating widespread hostility. When the chiefs at first supported and then began to collect new taxes, Igbo women rose in protest (Meek [1937] 1949:x; Van Allen 1972; Mba 1982:68—97).

The British were not alone in the practice of incorporating Africans and African institutions into colonial law and government. The French, Belgians, and Portuguese did so as well.[10] Just as the British administration's commitment to a particular model of indirect rule led to the Aba women's war in southeastern Nigeria, so too did the French West African government's codification of native jurisdictions and procedures spawn myriad conflicts over authority and customs. The period immediately after colonial conquest saw significant migration, urbanization, and social change (Roberts 1988:293—303). In rapidly growing urban centers and in reorganized rural communities, men and women of different ethnic groups began to enter into domestic relationships, and they began to take their grievances to native courts. In response to escalating numbers of civil conflicts over marriage, divorce, inheritance, and succession initiated by litigants professing different customs, the government-general introduced legislation specifying whose custom prevailed in different circumstances (Hild 1912:102; Beurdeley 1916:3—4, 23—31). However, finding qualified native assessors to assist both the Africans and Europeans who presided over the various tribunals was difficult. The district tribunal of Abidjan, for example, needed nine different lists of ethnic assessors. "This resulted," wrote Beurdeley, who studied the reforms on the ground, "in serious difficulties for the court, excessive expense and unreasonable slowness each time the court was in session" (Beurdeley 1916:29). As the French and other Europeans in Africa were to discover, the difficulty in administering native law was to find what was customary.[11]

Indirect rule took as a fundamental principle that customary law should be upheld among locals, unless it failed the repugnancy test or contravened local statutes. Historians and anthropologists have recently come to understand, however, that what colonial officials treated as immutable customary law was itself the product of historical struggles unfolding during the colonial period. Indigenous law, defined by Starr and Collier (1989:8—9) as "precontact native law" may have influenced customary law, but it was not the same thing. Chanock has shown in his 1985 study and his contribution to this volume (Ch. 2) that customary law was shaped by the complex interplay of European beliefs about locals and African representations of themselves. He reminds us, moreover, that European beliefs themselves often conflicted, as did African representations. Missionaries, settlers, administrators, and anthropologists all came to Africa in the nineteenth and twentieth centuries with interests and ideas of their own that colored their understanding of local culture and affected their views about native policy. These interests and ideas played themselves out in conflicts surrounding the establishment of both the laws and institutions of the colonial period (Ranger 1983; Vincent 1989). In the process of these struggles influential Europeans called into being that which they expected to find in Africa.[12]

European beliefs did not exist in a vacuum. At every point they confronted African representations of themselves. The need or commitment of colonial rulers to govern through indigenous legal and political systems created opportunities for local peoples to try to reshape their experience through the representation of custom. Discourse and debate about the way things were or should be occurred regularly in British and Native courts, as we have noted in our discussion of Crown Colonies and as Chanock, Moore, and Cohen demonstrate in their essays. They took place as well during the inquiries into land, labor, health, sanitation, and other issues that shaped policy and punctuated the history of every colony. Finally, the creation of statute law throughout the colonial period and the codification of customary law during the 1930s and 1940s created opportunities to represent and debate tradition. In each of these arenas African representations were themselves molded by indigenous ideology and local struggles over power and resources (Chanock 1985:145–216; Nader 1989:329–37).

African voices did not all carry equal weight in the discourse about custom. Inequalities in power affected the outcome of local conflicts over rules, procedures, and institutions. The fact that Native Authorities served as judges in Native courts gave them extraordinary opportunities and in some cases statutory authority to define and enforce rights, obligations, and relationships. Even in situations where the privileges of local rulers were not institutionalized, Europeans extended them great influence. When questions arose about custom, officials turned for answers to chiefs and others they regarded as repositories of local knowledge and upholders of local authority. Such persons were always men and usually elders. The reliance of officials on particular individuals or groups to define tradition gave them new advantages in the competition for resources and labor, and it augmented their power. Chanock has shown, for example, that in central Africa chiefs and elders cooperated with colonial administrators to invent customary rules regarding marriage that strengthened the control of senior men over women and junior men (Chanock 1985:145–216).

Africans in power did not find unrestricted opportunity in the emergence of customary law. Many discovered that what they could accomplish was limited by the place of customary law in the larger colonial legal system. Just as important, subordinate groups found ways to participate in the debate about custom, and they managed to shape its outcome. Slaves, women, juniors, clients, and others engaged law in courts, before officials, and during inquiries in ways that altered their lives and affected law and culture. Wright (1982:36–39, 43) and Mann (1985:113–14) have demonstrated, for example, that in the early colonial period

African women turned to magistrate's and district commissioner's courts in an effort to escape marriages with which they were unhappy. In the process they challenged the rights of men and elders in their persons. Locals also shaped the colonial legal order by ignoring or overtly resisting laws and legal procedures.

Asiwaju's contribution to this volume (Ch. 10) highlights the special complexity of borderlands in the construction of colonial legal systems and in the making of customary law. Where colonial boundaries, which were inevitably quite porous, crosscut local populations, Africans were exposed to not one but two or more sets of European-imposed laws, institutions, and procedures. Asiwaju makes clear that borderlands presented Africans with extraordinary opportunities to choose between colonial legal systems, move from one to the other, or even play them off against one another. He also reminds us, however, that borderlands confronted Africans with extraordinary intrusions, given the presence of border-specific rules and authorities.

The policy of administering their colonies through local systems of law and government became for the British and the French an ideological template for the invention of African societies that conformed to their model of colonial rule. The template linked executive and judicial authority. Native Authorities' competence to decide customary law was rooted in the very concept of indirect rule. Yet, customary law was born of the collaboration of Africans seeking to establish new forms of access to resources and labor and Europeans looking for local authorities to fill positions generated by their concepts of African societies. The following section further explores this process in the making of colonial land and labor law.

Law, Property, Labor, and Authority in Colonial Africa

The economic transformation of Africa during the colonial period created new opportunities to earn income and accumulate wealth that unleashed struggles over resources and labor between Africans and Europeans and among Africans themselves. These struggles shaped access to land, trees, water, minerals, and labor, altering local social and productive relations. They affected the structure of authority as well, because conflict over such things as land and labor was simultaneously over the authority to allocate these resources. The Aba women's war was but one of the many struggles throughout colonial Africa, some collective but most individual, over the form and meaning of authority and over access to resources and labor. European efforts to impose colonial rule with minimal cost to the folks back home had contradictory effects on this process. On the one hand, efforts to raise revenue drew Africans into ever—wider circuits of commodity production, exacerbating the conflict over resources, labor, and authority. On the other hand, concern with holding down costs led officials to try to contain the disruptive effects of rapid economic change by maintaining the stability of African societies as Europeans understood them (Berry 1988:4—8).

Law was used in struggles over resources and labor, and these struggles in turn proved central to the making of customary law itself. When conflicts emerged in African communities, colonial governments resolved to settle them by upholding local custom, in the belief that this would shore up local authorities and minimize social dislocation. Colonial rulers' emphasis on upholding custom had the unintended consequence of creating debate over the interpretation of custom itself. Europeans and Africans constructed arguments in courts and councils and before commissions about the way they wanted rights in resources and people to be, based on their beliefs and interests. They claimed that these rights were customary, or the way things had always been, to give them greater validity with Europeans and Africans (Berry 1988:7–8; Chanock, Ch. 2). Judges, administrators, and commissioners whether European or African, made customary law as they decided what to hear as well as what to find and enforce among the range of arguments presented to them. African and European contestants affected colonial legal systems as well, in selecting what to present and how to present it. What did not come before courts, councils, and commissions is sometimes as important as what did. To construct arguments about custom, actors used language, invoked symbols, and advanced ideas that were rooted in culture. In the process they negotiated cultural meaning. Rosen (1989) and Chanock (1989:69–74) have reminded us that the boundary between law and culture is fluid and permeable, and that actors bring to bear on legal discourse everyday cultural understandings. Because the relationship between law and culture is reciprocal, the discourse about custom in colonial Africa not only affected social process but also shaped cultural understanding.

Colonial Law and Property

In a masterful explication of the power of discourse about custom to shape society and culture, Chanock's contribution to this volume analyses the making of customary land law in British Africa through the interplay of state policies, African assertions, and anthropological research. Chanock shows that agricultural commercialization stimulated the development of individual land sales and land claims in many African communities. Europeans assumed that rights of private property formed the very basis of political society in civilized nations, but that such rights were foreign to primitive Africa. In the very early years of colonial rule the state encouraged individualization as a mark of evolution and progress. Attitudes changed, however, as administration spread to the interior and regimes developed systems of indirect rule. Administrators and anthropologists began elaborating models of African societies that linked the integrity of the family, community, and tribe to collective control of land. These models assumed that the authority of elders and chiefs was bound up with their right to allocate land. Fearful that uncontrolled expansion of private property rights would undermine chiefly power and produce social dislocation, colonial governments in many places began prohibiting land sales and restricting individual ownership. They promoted instead a form of land tenure founded on collective ownership and chiefly allocation, but recognizing individual use. In the name of trusteeship, colonial governments appropriated broad administrative powers over land. Chanock demonstrates that in central Africa the state pursued this policy as a means of legitimizing European land concessions on the one hand and African land reserves on the other. In West Africa, governments tried to use the doctrine of communalism to block concessions to European firms and purchases by African bourgeoisies (Meredith 1984; Martin 1988:60, 79).

Chanock stresses that Central Africans formulated their representations of customary tenure against the background of the expropriation of land by European companies and settlers. Communal ownership, which did not permit alienation, offered local peoples the best defense against further loss. He argues that, bearing this in mind, we must examine the "details of interests" (p. 72) in particular places to understand why individuals or groups represented certain things as customary when it came to land dealings. Chanock hypothesizes, however, that in general persons with little stake in the rural social order most readily defended communal ownership as customary to preserve the possibility of establishing a claim to an increasingly scarce resource. This is the reverse of what he found when he looked at labor (Chanock 1985:172−216). He goes on to qualify his generalization with a number of observations. First, assertions of rights depended on when they were made. Persons said different things at different times in their life-cycle, depending on their interests at that moment. Assertions of communal ownership and chiefly allocation solidified elders' control of land and thus their authority over juniors. Conversely, where land was becoming scarce and older generations were making claims to permanent occupation and ownership, it may have been in the interest of younger people to assert the communal package. In addition, the customary law regime did not accommodate the idea of women as landowners. Claims by women in the name of custom were seen by colonial officials as impediments to agricultural development. Put simply, Chanock views the entrenchment of the rights of senior men to allocate land as part of gender and generational struggles.

Developments on the ground sometimes pushed colonial administrators to adjust land tenure policies. In Southern Rhodesia, for example, officials in the interwar period feared social unrest in the overcrowded African reserves. A commission charged with studying agricultural land use heard testimony from white settlers and African peasants. To encourage the development of a prosperous African peasantry and act as a buffer between white lands and African reserves, where communal ownership was being imposed, the commission recommended the establishment of native purchase areas, where Africans would be allowed to acquire freehold rights in land (Palmer 1977:161−94). The freehold zones that were subsequently created were wholly inadequate to the demands of African peasants and, more interestingly for our purposes, within them disputes over inheritance plagued colonial administrators. District officers confronted seemingly intractable tension between sons and daughters claiming rights to inherit according to freehold tenure and uncles asserting as customary rights to control the disposition of estates (Cheater 1987:174−81).[13] This conflict makes abundantly clear that recognizing the rights of some involved constraining or negating those of others.

In a comparative study of the role of the colonial state in shaping conditions of access to resources in contexts of agricultural commercialization, Berry (1988: 11−19) discusses some of the local political implications of colonial land law. She notes, as does Chanock, that the manufacture of customary tenure did not stop the commercialization of land. Transactions and claims proliferated as more land was brought under cultivation to increase production for the market. The emphasis in customary land law on communal ownership and chiefly allocation did, however, give struggles over land a political dimension. Debates over ownership became linked to debates over social identity and political succession. Who belonged to lineages or communities, the boundaries and structures of which were themselves subjects of debate, became crucial, contested questions. Competition for positions of authority took on new significance and became a worthy field of investment as commercialization and scarcity of land increased. In this environment, exchanges of rights in land involved political as well as commercial transactions, as Moore's chapter in this volume (Ch. 4) so clearly demonstrates. Berry believes that in the colonial period property rights were neither transformed according to English models nor frozen in communal models but became the subject of perpetual, politicized contests.

Chanock ends his essay by arguing that the idea of communalism, and particularly of state trusteeship over land, has served the interests of post-colonial states. Immediately before independence and since then, hostility in the name of custom toward the emergence of individual rights in land combined with the development ethos to give new urgency to the assumption of the primacy of the administrative goals of the state over the rights of individuals. This has left Africans rightless against the state where land is concerned, and it has contributed to the dominance of the state over society in African nations. "A customary veil has been drawn over national confiscation of rights," Chanock concludes, "and increasing scarcity and...inequality of existing holdings [has been] disguised by the assertion of fictive rights for all" (p. 80).

Set in Lagos during a period of rapid commercial development when Britain still encouraged individualization, Mann's study of Taiwo Olowo (Ch. 3) commences where Chanock's essay leaves off: with an examination of the impact of competition for land on social relations in an African community. Mann demonstrates how a man who quite likely began life in Lagos as a slave took advantage of changes in land tenure to accumulate large and valuable land holdings. Early in his career, Taiwo used this privately owned property to secure commercial credit, which enabled him to trade on a big scale. But Taiwo's land and houses were equally valuable as places to settle dependents, particularly clients, on whom he depended for labor and political support. Indeed one of the essay's most valuable contributions is to demonstrate that Taiwo turned opportunities created by colonial legal change to the traditional end of securing loyal dependents. Living at the very beginning of the colonial period, Taiwo enjoyed rapid upward mobility of a kind that Chanock believes was made more difficult by the subsequent joint manufacture of the doctrine of communalism.

In a fitting companion to Mann's urban study, Moore's chapter investigates property transfers and chiefly interventions among an agrarian people, the Chagga of Kilimanjaro, to show the effects of changes in their political economy on the value and meaning of resources. At the end of the nineteenth century, the Chagga traded slaves and ivory and provisioned caravans passing back and forth from the coast to the interior. Many small, autonomous chiefdoms fought bitterly for control of trade routes. Following the German annexation in 1886, colonial rulers imposed peace and installed chiefs with both executive and judicial authority, fundamentally transforming the role of local rulers and basis of chiefly power. In time dozens of small chiefdoms consolidated to form a few big ones. Simultaneously, the Chagga began growing coffee for sale on the world market. Cash cropping quickly combined with population growth to produce severe land shortages. Moore examines court cases involving property transfers from patri-lineages to outsiders and discovers that in this changing context competition for control of land and cash replaced competition for control of persons and cattle as the dominant focus of transactions. She concludes that this shift in the character of conflict over resources reflected the chief's changing roles and strategies for aggrandizement and the Chagga's ever-deepening commitment to cash cropping and a money economy.

Moore's analysis of the making of land law in one African society ideally complements Chanock's general study. While Chanock emphasizes the importance of African participation, he documents most fully the role of European ideas in shaping customary tenure. Moore, on the other hand, privileges the contribution of Africans themselves. Taken together the studies detail two sides of the same process. Moreover, Moore's finding that by 1920 Chagga chiefs opposed buying and selling land for cash seems to challenge Chanock's hypothesis that the disadvantaged in African societies were most interested in defending communal tenure. It underscores his point that scholars must examine the details of interests in particular communities to understand representations of custom. During the colonial period, Chagga chiefs used their new administrative and judicial powers to assert rights to certify the legitimacy of all land transfers and land claims in return for gifts of thanks. New authority over allocation, in turn, enabled chiefs to enlarge their holdings and those of their followers. The Chagga chiefs argued, unsuccessfully, against sales because alienation made chiefly intervention less successful.

All three essays in the first section of this anthology, which deals with colonial law and property, document differentiation in African societies based on individualization and alienation of land. Our point is not to argue that this was the universal experience in colonial Africa, despite European and in some cases chiefly determination to prevent it. Lagos and Kilimanjaro were more quickly and deeply affected by incorporation into the world economy than many other parts of the continent. Even in Lagos communal tenure survived, as both Chanock and Mann recognize. In some places communal systems of access to land not only survived but also remained dominant (Grier 1987; Hart 1978). Our point is to demonstrate that studying legal questions and legal records provides an excellent and largely untried way of understanding processes of change in conditions of resource access and patterns of resource use during the colonial period. The three essays on property presented here investigate land in British Africa, but the possibilities for research are in fact much broader than this. Conflict over other resources and over labor regularly found their way into courts and before commissions and tribunals throughout colonial Africa. These conflicts were unusually well documented, and the documents in many places have been unusually well preserved, owing to the centrality of property and labor relations to colonial political economies. Research into legal questions, using legal records, will be repaid by data of rare quality and insights of exceptional force about central problems in modern African history.

Colonial Law and Labor

Colonialism set in motion struggles over labor, just as it did conflicts over property. Harnessing labor to the task of producing commodities was central to the agendas of colonial administrators and to those of African entrepreneurs seeking new forms of accumulation. From the very beginning, colonialism in Africa confronted problems of labor mobilization and control; problems which persisted throughout the colonial era. Colonial labor law and labor relations were constructed in ways similar to colonial land law and property relations, through the interplay of Africans and Europeans pursuing their particular beliefs and interests.

Anti-slavery moved to the forefront of the engagement between Europe and Africa in the mid-nineteenth century, just as slavery had occupied that position in earlier times. Embedded in anti-slavery ideology was a development model, born in Great Britain, that linked economic prosperity and free labor (Davis 1975:44–49, 346–85; 1984:154–91; Temperley 1977; Cooper 1980:24–33). Anti-slavery activists believed that abolition in the New World would end an inhumane and outmoded labor system, freeing planters to evolve into a prosperous agricultural bourgeoisie and slaves to develop into a disciplined wage-labor force. When abolitionists turned their attention to Africa, source of the slaves, they tied efforts to end the trade that had brutalized the continent to the duty to encourage the African production of agricultural commodities, for which there were growing markets in Europe. Articulating the creed in mid-century, T. F. Buxton called on reformers to extinguish the slave trade once and for all by elevating the minds of Africa's people and calling forth the capabilities of her soil (Buxton 1840:5). Popularizing it seventeen years later, David Livingstone proclaimed that Christianity could not advance in face of the slave trade. The only hope for the expansion of civilization, he argued, lay in ending the slave trade by opening an outlet for agricultural commodities to reach the sea (Monk 1968:7). Anti-slavery, and the commitment to developing agricultural commerce which accompanied it, legitimized European expansion into many parts of the continent.

No sooner had European nations acquired African territories than colonial administrators confronted tensions between the metropolitan commitment to end slavery and its desire to promote trade and stability. The very purpose of the colonies was to develop the export of agricultural commodities and minerals. Their economic viability depended on the growth of lucrative trade and prosperous African and European enterprises that could be taxed to pay for administration. Officials feared that disrupting local slavery, an important source of labor, would threaten both the production of exports and the generation of revenues. In the era of direct rule, administrators came to believe, moreover, that they could govern most economically and effectively if they maintained the local social order in the midst of rapid economic change. To this end, colonial governments incorporated local rulers, many of whom owned large numbers of slaves, and threw their weight behind indigenous systems of law and government (Berry 1988:3). In return, they received support from indigenous authorities. Freeing the slaves would have alienated local collaborative elites and disrupted the economic base of their power. For all of these reasons, many European officials felt deeply ambivalent about ending African slavery, and they proceeded with caution toward its elimination (Roberts and Miers 1988:17–24).

Racial and cultural prejudices conveniently justified a gradual approach to emancipation in Africa. European administrators, settlers, and missionaries believed that Africans were too primitive to respond on their own to new opportunities in agricultural production and wage labor. Local peoples, they thought, had to be taught not only the wisdom of cash crop production but also the value of regular work. It was too much to hope that African slaves, exposed to Europe's

civilizing influence much more recently than new world blacks, would toil duti-
fully for themselves or others once freed from their owners' control. Many
colonial officials were convinced that they took a gradual approach to emancipation for African slaves' own good, as well as to avoid economic and social
collapse (Cooper 1980:24–46). Similar prejudices underlay colonial policies designed to reshape productive relations in colonial rulers' own interests, whether
those policies coerced the production of export commodities or forced the sale of
African labor (Cooper 1981:26–39).

Intended or not, colonialism ultimately transformed precolonial economies
that rested on slavery. In some places, economic and social changes enabled
slaves to obtain access to resources and redefine their relationships with their
owners before the legal status of slavery ended (Isaacman and Rosenthal 1988:
229–34; Mann 1989). Eventually all colonial powers abolished slavery (Roberts
and Miers 1988:17–25). When they did so, local legislatures sometimes passed
proclamations intended to manage the transition to freedom. The 1874 Gold
Coast ordinances "To Provide for the Abolition of Slave Dealing" and "To
Provide for the Emancipation of Persons Holden in Slavery" abolished only the
"legal status" of slavery. In the interest of "preventing any serious social disturb-
ance resulting from a sudden mass exodus of slaves," they did not "free slaves
en bloc," although they did assure slaves who sought freedom the protection of
British courts (Dumett and Johnson 1988, 79–80). An 1897 proclamation in Zanzibar
gave slaves the right to go to court to get certificates of freedom. If they did so
their owners were entitled to compensation, but even more important from the
point of view of labor control, the former slaves themselves could subsequently
be declared vagrants unless they had a place to stay and a means of support. The
proclamation also held that former slaves had to pay their former owners rent for
the use of houses and gardens that the ex-slaves retained. When slaves applied
for certificates of freedom, courts used the opportunity to pressure them to sign
labor contracts with their owners. A decade later, on the coast of Kenya, an
ordinance gave owners the right to demand compensation when slaves left or
refused to work because the state had ceased to recognize rights over slaves
(Cooper 1980:72–176).

The anti-slavery proclamations may have strengthened beliefs that old regimes
were crumbling and given slaves new courage to challenge owners, but they did
not effectively regulate the end of slavery. Many owners and slaves reforged
relationships outside the court and independent of colonial officials. Former
slaves withheld labor from their former owners and asserted new autonomy,
while clinging to benefits that could be derived from relationships with such
important persons. Former owners continued to extract labor from former slaves
by controlling access to land, capital, and other resources and by reclassifying the
slaves as kin, wives, clients, tenants, or other subordinates (Cooper 1980:125–
232; Miers and Roberts 1988; Kopytoff 1988; Mann 1989). Courts would not
enforce owners' claims to slaves' labor. However, husbands could sue deserting
wives, patrons could summon recalcitrant clients, and landlords could prosecute
unruly tenants. When former owners brought suits against former slaves, they
often disguised claims to labor as claims to land or dwellings used by the former
slaves. Colonial law also created other mechanisms for disciplining former slaves.
Many such persons obtained credit from former owners, who sometimes went to

court and foreclosed on loans when they became dissatisfied with their former slaves' behaviour (Mann 1989).

The end of slavery, we should stress, did not abolish unfree labor. Forced labor persisted in many guises throughout colonial Africa, often recognized and enforced by law. Africans were pressed into corvée for public works, military campaigns, and mine labor, as well as for use by European planters and farmers. The Portuguese colonies used forced labor most persistently. Portugal abolished slavery in 1869 and ended obligatory apprenticeship in 1878. In 1899, however, it promulgated a new labor code that required Africans to "civilize themselves through work." In Angola and Mozambique, all "natives" who could not claim one of seven specified exemptions were liable to compulsory labor either for the colonial state or for the private sector. Failure to work in Portuguese Africa was thus a legal offense, contributing simultaneously to the criminalization of the bulk of the African population and to the emergence of myriad forms of resistance to colonialism (Harris 1958:17−25; Isaacman 1976; Newitt 1981; Henrickson 1978: 115−20).

Even where forced labor was widespread, the end of slavery occurred in the context of generalized struggles over the control of labor, as Africans and Europeans scrambled to adapt to the new opportunities and demands of colonial economies. In central Africa, for example, slavery collapsed as peasants began producing for the market and men began migrating to work in the mines of Southern Rhodesia and South Africa. In West Africa, slavery was redefined as Africans responded to new opportunities in agriculture, commerce, and to a lesser extent, government employment, especially the military (Echenberg 1990:7−24; J. M. Thompson 1989; Oroge 1973:9−10). In central Africa, the end of slavery and the migration of males reduced the supply of agricultural labor and increased the importance of household members in growing food and export crops. These developments created multiple conflicts over labor between Africans and Europeans, between settlers and states, and not least, between African men and women and elders and juniors. The dynamics and outcomes of these struggles varied from place to place. In parts of Zambia men met expanding labor needs in agriculture by increasing demands on their wives and usurping women's rights to the labor of junior males (Chanock 1985:10−16; Gregory and Mandala 1987:228−40; Muntemba 1982: 88, 96−102; Wright 1983). In southern Malawi, on the other hand, where senior women retained a say in disposing of the labor of junior men, elders of both sexes responded to growing labor needs by squeezing the existing mechanisms of youth labor recruitment. There, Mandala (1982:38) concludes, the burden of commodity production fell most heavily on boys. Everywhere conflicts over labor affected the way different Europeans and Africans represented what was customary regarding rights in people.

Just as governments tried to control the transition from slavery to freedom, so they wanted to manage the movement of Africans from peasant agriculture to European owned farms and mines and within peasant agriculture itself. In the settler colonies of southern and eastern Africa, where the settlers' way of life hinged on a regular supply of cheap, disciplined African labor, states elaborated a complex web of laws to regulate workers. Initially, regimes used legal instruments to coerce reluctant blacks into labor markets. These included such well-known measures as tax ordinances that created a demand for cash, marketing regulations that restricted the crops Africans could sell, and land acts that limited the territory peasants could cultivate (Brett 1973:186−212; Arrighi 1973:194−98; Bundy 1979:134−45). They extended to amendments to Native Authority Ordinances that empowered chiefs and headmen to recruit labor for European enterprises under the supervision of district officers (Van Zwanenberg 1975:114−23). Vagrancy laws gave teeth to other legislation by subjecting Africans who were not regularly employed to arrest and deportation.

Once Africans had been forced into wage labor, states enacted laws to enable them and employers better to control workers. These varied from Masters and Servants Ordinances and to more specific laws limiting freedom of residence, movement, and housing (Buell 1928; Marks and Rathbone 1982; Pouncey, forthcoming; Cooper 1987; Hansen 1989). The real point of the Masters and Servants Ordinances was to introduce into law a legally enforceable labor contract, supported by criminal sanctions, so that employers could more effectively hold workers who had been driven into the labor market by other measures. Helen Bradford (1987) found in her study of the Industrial and Commercial Workers Union that Masters and Servants laws were employed in rural South Africa, although "fists, whips, and guns" were even more important in controlling farm workers (pp. 52−54) Karen Hansen has shown in her study of domestic servants in Southern Rhodesia that, taken as a whole, labor legislation was designed "to break-in raw workers" by inculcating new work habits, as well as to supply and hold them (1989:50−51). Van Zwanenberg (1975:184−86) and Worger (1983, 1987:110−46) have demonstrated that the colonial state's determination to enforce labor laws, in the face of African resistance, led to widespread criminalization of workers.

Outside settler colonies, states enacted labor legislation and labor codes, shaped by debates about labor relationships. In the colonies whose economies rested predominantly on peasant agriculture, however, labor laws were neither elaborated nor enforced to the extent that they were in the settler colonies. In west Africa's peasant societies, and in the peasant sector of settler colonies, law and labor intersected in conflicts in colonial courts over relationships with implications for labor: slavery, pawnship, marriage, kinship, clientage, and tenancy. In the course of these conflicts customs were debated and decisions were taken, creating opportunities for actors to reshape labor relationships and affecting the organization and control of labor in society. Access to property and labor were interrelated in many African societies. Persons without land obtained it by entering social relationships with landowners that carried obligations for labor and support; landowners met their need for labor in part by providing land and housing to those who needed it in exchange for labor and support. Berry (1988: 22−24) has shown that African farmers who lacked the capital and/or opportunity to buy land and labor resorted to non-market methods of mobilization. Their strategies ranged from coercion to the creation of new social relations and adaptation of old ones. Mann's research (Ch. 3) documents a similar phenomenon in an urban economy. The interdependence of access to property and labor meant that legal conflict over one often had implications for the other. Only Mann among our contributors explicitly examines the opportunities that changes in land tenure and colonial law created for mobilizing and disciplining labor, but control of labor forms part of the story in many of the chapters of this anthology. Access to labor cannot be divorced from disputes over property, marriage, divorce, inheritance, and succession, all of which are addressed by our contributors.[14]

Legal struggles over conditions of access to resources and labor occurred in many different arenas: court encounters, policy inquiries, and legislative debates, to name but three of the most important. These proceedings left rich documentation in the form of transcripts and judgments from court cases, minutes and reports from policy inquiries, and memoranda and enactments from legislative debates. Careful study of these records, and of the processes that generated them, uncovers the details of interests and the character of discourse in the competition for resources and labor in colonial Africa, showing who represented what as customary and how particular individuals or groups formulated their arguments. An investigation of legal judgments and legislative enactments, as well as of more commonly studied policy decisions, uncovers the role of the state in shaping the outcome of struggles over conditions of access to resources and labor. Research of the kind we propose, examples of which are collected in this volume, clarifies the mechanisms whereby some individuals and groups in colonial societies accumulated resources and mobilized labor, while others were dispossessed. It reveals the actual processes through which older social orders were replaced by newer ones, bringing us closer to an understanding of the manner in which the expansion of capitalism and spread of colonialism reshaped African societies. But beyond illuminating who won and who lost in the competition for resources and labor, and how and why, the research enables us to comprehend better the relationship between changes in social process and cultural understanding. For it probes the role of specific historical changes in stimulating discourse about law, the place of culturally constructed arguments in forging new legal systems, and the importance of new legal systems in turn in shaping social and cultural as well as economic and political change.

Colonial Law and Authority

The contributors to this volume agree that colonial legal change provided Africans with new opportunities to enhance their authority as well as with new challenges to that authority. Several authors examine how colonial law empowered some Africans at the expense of others and how it created new asymmetries of power. They also demonstrate that although colonial law may have benefitted some individuals and groups at the expense of others, the proliferation of legal forums and introduction of new power and authority also constrained exactly those Africans who were empowered by them.

Control over law contributed to local rulers' authority and perpetuated their power in Europe as in Africa. The close links among law, power, and authority in eighteenth century England led Douglas Hay (1975:56) to conclude that the pomp and ceremony of English justice, combined with harsh punishments and frequent pardons, enabled a small ruling class to govern without a large police force or a standing army. This class's hegemony rested on its joint control over property and law.

Chanock (1985: Ch. 5) makes a similar argument with regard to the central African practices of witchcraft accusation and ordeal trials. Among the Chewa of Nyassaland, these two practices became more common during the nineteenth century than they had before, as larger numbers of slaves, and particularly of slave wives, increased social tensions. Witchcraft and ordeal became a means for Chewa headmen to shore up their authority against challenges to it. Following the Ngoni conquest of the region in the middle decades of the nineteenth century, the new rulers appropriated the ordeal and may well have increased its incidence as a way of helping to control the mass of recently conquered peoples living under them. Ordeal became "a 'state occasion,' a tool of the paramountcy." With colonial conquest, the British campaigned against ordeals as part of their effort to constrain forms of indigenous law they considered "repugnant." The colonial attack on ordeals had two consequences. First, it fundamentally influenced British thinking about the nature of African law. Ordeals, which had been common in Europe up to the thirteenth century, were believed to reflect an early and primitive phase in the evolution of law. To continue to permit ordeals even within the general orbit of customary law, argued British administrators and jurists, would be to sanction a regressive and primitive kind of law. Second, the prohibition of ordeals went to the heart of the links among power, authority, and law in central Africa. With the end of the ordeal, the ruling Ngoni headmen lost a powerful tool in their ability to govern. Chanock concludes that "conflicts were sharpened," not lessened, by the prohibition of ordeals and by related efforts to remake the traditional African legal order (Chanock 1985:85−102).

Colonial conquest and subsequent efforts to establish colonial governments transformed law and its relationship to power and authority. Some of the consequences were intended; others were not. Colonial administrators themselves often had contradictory objectives. Both British and French colonial states sought in various ways to incorporate native authority into their systems of administration, which led to the elaboration of customary law and the reinforcement of chiefly power and authority. Yet these states also limited the jurisdiction of customary law and prohibited practices deemed repugnant, which diminished the power and authority of local rulers. European administrators intervened in the exercise of the law by reviewing cases decided by African authorities and creating procedures for appeal from African to European authorities.

Three chapters in the middle section of this anthology examine the encounter between African chiefs and colonial administrators through the lens of the legal system. Simon Roberts's analysis of the experiences of Seepapitso probes the effects of British indirect rule in the Bechuanaland Protectorate, where officials indeed found "Native Authorities." Richard Roberts's discussion of Mademba and David Groff's of Kangah illuminate the encounter between Africans and the French. All three contributions show that the establishment of colonial administration simultaneously empowered and subordinated African rulers. Although French colonialism has been associated with direct administration by French officials, the French made extensive use of indigenous authorities and institutions when it suited their purposes (Crowder and Ikime 1970; Asiwaju 1970). The four essays presented here focus on the period of transition to colonial rule, providing an ideal vantage point from which to view the challenges and opportunities African rulers confronted during that formative era.

As Simon Roberts (Ch. 7) argues, Seepapitso, the Ngwaketse *kgosi* or chief, inherited in 1910 a position which had its roots in precolonial Tswana society. The Tswana kgosi were not "invented" as were, for example, the "warrant" chiefs of Igboland. Even so, the incorporation of kgosi into colonial society as "Native Authorities" transformed their precolonial roles. Roberts analyzes an extraordinary collection of documents written by Seepapitso to show that while there were continuities in the Tswana chiefs' duties and powers, colonialism changed his government in two ways. First, Seepapitso's position as an intermediary between the Ngwaketse and the British in a hierarchical colonial administration altered his authority. Concern with collecting hut tax and announcing British decrees pervades the records he kept. If the documents reflect accurately the business of government, then under colonial rule Tswana chiefs broadened their authority as they mediated between Tswana society and a supra-ordinate colonial government.

Second, our understanding of Seepapitso's power and authority and of the structure of his rule are deeply influenced by the fact that he kept written records (see also Goody 1972, 1987). Trained by European missionaries, the Tswana chief was no doubt influenced by Western models of the separation of government into executive and judicial powers. Out of what Roberts calls an "undifferentiated repertoire" of local rules and norms, Seepapitso kept separate accounts of his executive and legal activities. The British maintained Tswana kgsos in power, but the seamless web of their precolonial executive, legislative, and judicial authority had by 1910 already started to untangle as a consequence of incorporation into a larger colonial society.

Roberts portrays Seepapitso not as a "strong-man, uttering ad hoc commands in the struggle to maintain a following and pursue private aims such as the assembly of wealth and the destruction of rival potentates," but as a "constitutional figure," "the herdsman of a flock" (p. 176). This view undoubtedly reflects Seepapitso's representation of himself in the records he kept, and it is worth noting that his representation fit neatly with contemporary European understanding of cattle keeping chieftaincies. Roberts's picture of Seepapitso, however, contrasts sharply with other accounts in the literature of late-nineteenth-century Tswana chiefdoms, accounts that emphasize accumulation and differentiation leading to the growth of a prosperous peasantry on the one hand, and a landless proletariat on the other (Parsons 1973, 1977).

Mademba, king of Sinsani in the French Soudan, fared differently than Seepapitso. Crowned by the French in 1891, he could not claim authority by reference to an inherited precolonial position. Sinsani, a Muslim commercial center, had never had its own king. Richard Roberts argues that Mademba's claims to African kingship were doubly improbable because at the time of his coronation, he was an "assimilated" French citizen (see Sarr, Ch. 5; Crowder 1967). Mademba benefitted from French efforts to rule through what they imagined indigenous authorities to be. French administrators and a handful of Africans collaborated in inventing a form of Soudanese kingship, which Africans like Mademba could then fill. Mademba's lack of legitimacy did not deter him; indeed, the absence of traditional checks on his newly claimed authority empowered him. Although Mademba claimed to act as befitted an African king, he was "undone" by the maturation of the French colonial administration which introduced a form of metropolitan political and judicial accountability called *loi bureaucratique*. In 1899, the lieutenant-governor of the French Soudan heard a case against Mademba alleging administrative malfeasance. When Mademba returned to his "kingdom" in 1900, his power and authority were diminished as was his jurisdiction in legal matters, but he was still a "king." Roberts sees the case against Mademba as a conflict between two competing colonialisms: the free-wheeling colonialism of the early conquest era and the centralized, bureaucratic colonialism of the government-general period. Mademba was initially empowered by fitting into European models of African kingship. His power and authority were eventually constrained by the struggle between different colonial-isms and by the reform of the French colonial legal system.

If the maturation of French colonial law diminished Mademba's power, Kwame Kangah of the Assikasso region of the Côte d'Ivoire took advantage of it to appeal a case against him all the way to the governor-general of French West Africa in Dakar, who overturned the rulings against Kangah. Groff (Ch. 6) demonstrates how the European concept of the "rule of law" facilitated yet constrained colonial efforts to transform African societies. Colonial administrators saw in the idea of the rule of law both ideological and practical advantages. Ideologically, they used the concept to deflect criticism by anti-imperial forces in the metropole and by nascent petty bourgeoisies in Africa, who employed European political and legal rhetoric to promote their own class interests. Practically, the French believed that the rule of law would facilitate trade and commerce. As Groff describes, however, one of the unintended consequences of France's emphasis on rule of law was the new opportunities it provided aggrieved Africans to confront the arbitrariness of colonial rule itself.

In a brilliant section of his history of the ante-bellum southern United States, Genovese criticized the instrumentalist argument that law simply served the interests of the ruling class. He maintained instead that for law to have a "hegemonic" function, it must seem to apply evenly to all in society. "The judicial system...may become an instrument by which the advanced section of the ruling class imposes its view upon the class as a whole and the wider society. The law must discipline the ruling class and guide and educate the masses. To accomplish these tasks it must manifest a degree of evenhandedness sufficient to compel social conformity" (Genovese 1974:27; see also Thompson 1975). For there to be rule of law, the law must be seen to apply equally to both the rulers and the ruled. Rule of law was more often an ideology than a practice. For the ideology to be accepted by the people, however, a few celebrated examples were needed of rulers being brought to justice, as Hay (1975:32–39) has noted in his study of eighteenth-century English law.

The practice of rule of law certainly did not prevail in colonial Africa. All colonial legal systems developed forms of legal jurisdiction divided by race or "nationality." The ideology of the rule of law, however, found wide currency in colonial Africa, because of the deep ambivalence of many Europeans, particularly in West Africa, about what their "cultural mission" actually meant. This ambivalence was especially acute in French West Africa until the beginning of the twentieth century. There, the ideology of the rule of law was linked closely to both African and French representations of metropolitan society, and it could be invoked selectively by groups advocating competing models of colonialism. As Groff describes (Ch. 6), Africans sometimes called on the ideology to challenge what they considered to be arbitrary and vindictive acts by colonial administrators. In pursuit of quite different ends, French colonial magistrates used the idea in their efforts to curtail the privilege of Senegalese originaires to appear before both Muslim and French courts (Sarr and Roberts, Ch. 5). The concept of rule of law was also invoked by Mademba's prosecutor, who saw the king's abuses of power as stemming from the fact that he did not abide by the norms of administrative conduct (Roberts, Ch. 8).

Any application of the concept of the rule of law in colonial societies must be sensitive to the tensions between ideology and practice. While Kwame Kangah successfully appealed to the rule of law and had the rulings against him and the confiscation of his property reversed, he was able to do so because of the patronage networks he could manipulate. Thus, whether Kangah's case represents the actual operation of the rule of law in French West Africa or the perseverance of one man armed with accumulated political debts remains an open question. In a postscript to his study, Groff states that Kangah's victory (and by extension, the victory of the rule of law) was short-lived. After returning home, his influence enhanced by having successfully challenged the local colonial administration, Kangah was once again arrested for exceeding his administrative prerogatives. This time, Groff tells us, Kangah was at last sentenced to internal exile.

Even where the ideology of the rule of law was invoked, the actual operation of colonial legal systems remained quite arbitrary. Their arbitrariness is nowhere in this anthology presented with as much clarity as in Sarr and Roberts' discussion (Ch. 5) of the fluctuating jurisdiction of Muslim courts in colonial Senegal. In the middle of the nineteenth century, the Muslim inhabitants of the Four Communes were granted French civil and legal rights, but also the privilege of adjudicating their civil disputes before a Muslim judge (cadi). Over the course of seventy-five years, the jurisdiction of the Muslim courts was the subject of three-way conflict between colonial magistrates, who sought to extend the jurisdiction of French civil courts to all French citizens and French nationals; colonial administrators, who wanted to reward Muslims for their loyalty by granting them special privileges; and Muslim originaires, who strove to preserve both their French civil and legal rights and their rights under shari'a law. Sarr and Roberts demonstrates that far from being determined principally by concerns for judicial consistency or rule of law, the struggles over the jurisdiction of Muslim courts reflected political pressures emanating from France, from Senegal, and from the government-general of French West Africa.

The chapters by Simon Roberts, Richard Roberts, and David Groff focus on individual Africans' encounters with colonialism and colonial judicial systems. None of these authors would claim that his protagonist (Seepapitso, Faama Mademba, or Kwame Kanga) was representative; yet each chapter explores aspects of how Africans coped with changing legal systems created by the colonial encounter. Sarr and Roberts' chapter examines collective actors (magistrates, administrators, and originaires) and their various struggles to shape the boundaries of legal jurisdiction. The chapters in this middle section illustrate that colonial legal systems were constructed over time by the interaction of Africans and Europeans pursuing their own ends. In the process, new laws, institutions, and procedures were established. Subsequently, disputants adapted their grievances to fit the procedures and categories of dispute which colonial legal systems were prepared to allow. Colonialism, as we argue in the next section, changed in both dramatic and in subtle ways the terms in which conflicts were expressed.

Changes in the Terms of Conflict

Colonialism affected the pursuit and expression of conflict in African societies, just as it did the content and meaning of law and the structure and character of authority. Changes in processes of dispute varied from culture to culture and colonial power to colonial power. What these changes meant can be understood fully only through the kind of careful historical study we advocate throughout this volume. Full discussion of this issue would require more attention than we can give it here; however, we want to suggest some ways of thinking about the problem.

As part of a larger debate about the impact of the imposition of Western law on non-Western cultures, Kidder has examined local responses to the introduction of British law in India (Kidder 1978; see also Hamnett 1977; Johnson 1978; Nader and Todd 1978; Moore 1978; and Starr and Collier 1989). He observed, in an essay presented more as a model than as a construction of reality, that although the Indian colonial legal system was designed to preserve custom, the working of the colonial courts nonetheless altered processes of litigation, expressions of conflict, and strategies of litigants (see also Cohn 1959, 1989). Indians responded by viewing colonial courts as resources to be used rather than as alien institutions to be shunned.

Kidder identified several features of Indian colonial courts that altered the way litigation was handled and grievances were expressed. Two of the primary tenets of British law in the colony were that all persons should be treated equally before the law and that justice should be blind. Status differences were not to influence the outcome of legal decisions. The purpose of the colonial courts was to deal with isolated cases of conflict in which clear-cut rights and duties would be established by investigation of only those events deemed relevant to the pending case. Rules of evidence narrowly restricted the content of testimony courts would hear. Moreover, cases were always treated as involving a right and a wrong; in them judges and occasionally juries, sometimes after consultation with local assessors (or "experts") made final, enforceable decisions. Finally, the substance of the law was to be drawn from prevailing Indian custom. This required a search for a single, exhaustive definition of that custom and a careful recording of "precedent" to which judges could refer when making future decisions (Kidder 1978:159−62).

These features of colonial courts were diametrically opposed to local community practice. Equality before the law, Kidder argued, violated principles of status embedded in the caste system. The notion of isolated cases in which clear-cut rights and duties had been violated simplified the complexities of local relations, particularly those involving rights to land. Restricted rules of evidence multiplied the narrowing effect by admitting only "proximate events" into courts. Because disputes concerning land often had long histories, the admission only of evidence directly related to a dispute often distorted the nature of the conflict and fabric of local social relations. By creating an arena in which decisions awarded winners and punished losers, litigation took on a speculative air, especially for those with least to lose and most to gain.

Kidder concluded that the encounter between British law and indigenous society in colonial India had both intended and unintended consequences. The colonial courts supported the privileges of those in power, by seeking to preserve indigenous society and by drawing on Muslim clergy and Brahmin elders and scholars for statements of customary law. At the same time, the operation of the colonial courts created new opportunities for Indians of low status to challenge political authority and caste-based economic relations.

Kidder's analysis of the effects of the imposition of British law on processes of litigation and expressions of conflict in colonial India contains much of general relevance to the African experience. It provides a useful starting point for thinking about similar problems in a different cultural and colonial context. To fit Africa, however, Kidder's model needs to be revised in a number of ways. His analysis focuses primarily on the impact of the operation of colonial courts. But in Africa, the impact of colonialism on law went beyond what happened in colonial courts. Colonial states sought to eliminate certain extra-judicial means of dealing with disputes, and this profoundly affected the ways conflict was pursued and expressed. We have already discussed some of the consequences of efforts to end ordeals (pp. 32–33, above). Colonial administrators also sought to prohibit violent means of pursuing disputes, such as vengeance, feuds, and warfare. Bohannan has shown that once the Tiv could no longer fight to redress wrongs and resolve debts among members of distant lineages, they turned increasingly to the newly introduced Native courts. Deprived of older means of pursuing conflict, the Tiv made local colonial courts their own, as did other African people. Bohannan does not discuss the social consequences of outlawing violence, but he does note that "the British Administration thus brought, not merely the courts, but [also] the social system that made them necessary" (Bohannan 1968:209). Colson analyzes an incident among the decentralized, matrilineal Plateau Tonga of Northern Rhodesia, in which the operation of the colonial criminal justice system failed to satisfy an aggrieved lineage, one of whose members had been killed. The individual responsible for the killing had been arrested, tried, convicted, and imprisoned for manslaughter by colonial authorities, but neither the lineage of the victim nor that of the perpetrator rested content. Colson reports, "while they waited for the return of the body . . . so that mourning could be held, there was general uneasiness in the two communities" (Colson 1953:207).

In the precolonial period, the lineages, which were united by ties of marriage, would have prepared for armed vengeance. Husbands and wives would have returned to their kin. This did not mean that fighting would necessarily occur; representatives of the two sides would have tried to negotiate compensation. With the threat of armed vengeance gone in the colonial period and with imprisonment of the perpetrator for manslaughter seen as an unsatisfactory outcome, the aggrieved lineage dealt with the conflict in a new way. Husbands and wives did not leave their spouses and return to their kin, as they had in the past. Instead of preparing to fight, the men and women of the aggrieved lineage refused to greet the women of the perpetrator's lineage and expressed contempt for them in other public ways. The women of the perpetrator's lineage pleaded with their elders to settle the case, which the elders eventually did through negotiated compensation and ritualized apology (Colson 1953:199–211). The European prohibition of violent means of dealing with disputes did not necessarily alter the outcome of the conflict for the two lineages, but it did change the way the aggrieved lineage expressed and pursued its conflict. It induced a shift in the terms of conflict.

Turning to colonial courts, the focus of Kidder's analysis, both Fallers on the Basoga and Moore on the Chagga have remarked on the narrowing effect of the treatment of litigation by colonial courts as "cases" that involved clear-cut rights and wrongs. Fallers defined a case for the Basoga as "a proceeding to decide whether or not a particular set of 'facts' falls within the reach of one particular concept of wrong" (Fallers 1969:327). Moore said of the Chagga,

> When parties come to a Primary Court on Kilamanjaro, from the point of view of the Court, the most important thing is that their situation becomes a case, in other words, that its disposition should fit into one of the general categories from which prescribed consequences flow. A highly personal and idiosyncratic situation from the point of view of parties is easiest to deal with if it can be classified as an instance of a general category.... (Moore 1977:182–83)

That colonial courts, both European and Native, thought in terms of cases affected not only how courts themselves heard disputes, but also how Africans presented them.

In Africa another phenomenon also affected the expression of conflict in colonial courts. The state refused to recognize legal obligations inherent in certain relationships. Its courts would not enforce these obligations, and in response litigants shaped their cases to fit the kinds of obligations courts would enforce. This can be seen most clearly in disputes between owners, slaves, and their descendants, but it was true of other types of conflicts as well. As part of her anti-slavery policy, Britain did not recognize the obligations of slaves in the Crown Colonies to work for their owners, although administrators hotly debated the question of whether they should return runaway slaves from the interior to their masters (Oroge 1983; Dumett and Johnson 1988:78–86; Glover papers, files 4–6, 1870–72). In Crown Colonies, owners certainly hauled slaves into colonial courts, but when they did they had to express their conflict with the slaves in terms of obligations the courts could uphold. As we have seen, owners often presented conflict with slaves over labor as disputes over land, houses, or trees. Deprived of access to these critical resources, slaves had a difficult time denying owners their labor. Eventually, Lagos courts came to recognize the rights of slaves and their descendants to use land and houses of their owners or former owners, so long as the slaves or slaves' descendants were well-behaved. Good behavior was not interpreted by the courts as entailing regular labor. Owners and their descendants quickly learned that if they wanted to eject slaves or their descendants, for whatever reason, they had to demonstrate misconduct. Thus when Brimah Akilogun brought a suit in 1894 to eject Faliyi, the son of one of his father's slaves, from a compound in Badagry, he did not argue that the property belonged to him and he wanted Faliyi out, but rather that the slave's son had misbehaved. Specifically, Akilogun accused Faliyi of eating cats, ravishing girls, and entertaining suspicious people who were probably thieves (*Akilogun v. Faliyi*, 1894, LSCR).

The French legal code of 1903 contained no provision for disputes between owners and slaves. In his instructions to officers, the governor-general stated that no military, district, or native tribunal should hear litigation involving claims over slaves. Although the 1903 code did not abolish slavery, it limited the use owners could make of colonial courts to enforce the relationship of slavery. In 1905 the governor-general issued a decree making it an offense to deprive persons of their freedom. This decree created new opportunities for slaves to sever ties to their owners. Not all slaves, however, asserted full independence (Roberts 1988: 287–93; Klein 1988:215–17; McDougall 1988:374–84). Many maintained a relationship with their owners, but jockeyed to redefine it. As they did so, owners learned to couch their grievances against their slaves in terms that the colonial courts were prepared to accept.

The relationship between owners, slaves, and their descendants remained contested terrain for many decades; indeed it can still be contested today. Litigation in colonial courts offered an important way of altering the relationship. Parties on both sides tested the limits of what they could accomplish within the colonial legal system, by experimenting with the terms in which they expressed legal conflict. A case from the Gold Coast illustrates the point. In the early 1800s, a Cape Coast woman, Eccua Maria, purchased a female slave, Effuah Djorpah. The slave had a daughter, Abbah Kaybah, also a slave of Eccua Maria's family, who herself had two sons and a daughter by Harry Brew, a European, founding the famous Brew family of the Gold Coast. The eldest son, Samuel (Kanto) Brew acquired Brabadzi land as his "private or separate property during his lifetime" (Earnshaw 1976:16). On his death in 1823, the land became family property and devolved to his full brother, Richard Brew. The sister, Eyaapah Brew, predeceased her brother Richard, leaving no issue. Richard Brew himself died in 1849, also without issue. Justice Earnshaw, who eventually heard the case, maintained that at this point the land ought under native law and custom to have devolved to the descendants of Eccua Maria, the slaveowner, there being no one in the Brew family to inherit through the female line. But Richard Brew had written a will leaving the property to his nephew Henry Brew, son of Samuel (Kanto) Brew, perhaps intentionally to prevent the land from passing to the family of his ancestors' owners. If persons challenged the testamentary disposition, they did not do so successfully. When Henry Brew died, he too left a will bequeathing Brabadzi land to Maud Thompson, the daughter of his sister, Effuah Abroba. In 1909, Sarah Wood, head of the family that descended from the slaveowner Eccua Maria, brought a suit against Maud Thompson in the British court at Cape Coast, claiming damages for trespass on Brabadzi land. The question of trespass, as the judge noted, depended on the question of ownership. The judgment in the case, which is all we have available to us, contains no clues about why Eccua Maria's descendants initiated the litigation when they did. Perhaps they believed Maud Thompson would be less able to protect her rights to the land than the Brew men had been, whether because she was a woman or for some other reason. Or perhaps the value of the land, which was quite extensive, had recently increased sufficiently to arouse their interest in it. Whatever the reason, Sarah Wood went to court on behalf of her family in 1909, after the Brew family had possessed the land for nearly a century and lived as free persons for about as long, in an effort to secure damages for trespass, which would have demonstrated ownership of the land. Undoubtedly aware of the British policy of upholding native custom in disputes among locals, Wood argued that according to Cape Coast law, rights to land were inherited through the female line and that failing such heirs, the property of slaves passed to the families of their owners.

Wood's strategy failed. Justice Earnshaw listened to the arguments and weighed native custom, which he argued that Richard Brew's will contravened. However, he ruled that in this instance the court would not enforce custom because it was repugnant, resting as it did on an incident of slavery. The judge went on to say that if Richard Brew had died after the Emancipation Ordinance of 1874, the question would have been simple. That ordinance declared the slaves "free persons to all intents and purposes" (Earnshaw 1976:18). As the courts could not thereafter recognize the status of slavery, they would not recognize claims that rested on slavery. In point of fact administrators, magistrates, and judges rarely found disputes between owners, slaves, and their descendants simple at all, despite emancipation proclamations and other anti-slavery legislation. Africans could often effectively manage the presentation of cases. The real issues in them were not always apparent to magistrates and judges, and when they were clear, authorities did not always decide cases consistently. Many things could affect the outcome of litigation. It was not unreasonable for Sarah Wood to think that her family might obtain control of the contested land through a favorable court decision. Africans could believe that the risk of making a case in a colonial court was worthwhile, even when the consequences of doing so were far from certain. Overall, colonial legal changes undoubtedly limited the power of owners and their descendants over slaves and their descendants. However, the fact that colonial officials turned to elders and chiefs, who were often slave-owners or their descendants, for statements of custom undoubtedly helped such persons retain control of their subordinates.

The creation of colonial legal systems also helped other categories of people redefine their relationships by carefully choosing the terms in which they expressed their conflicts in court. In the early years of colonial rule, European officials regarded polygyny as repugnant and the childhood betrothal of girls as misguided. District officers, magistrates, and judges sometimes looked with sympathy on women who testified that they had been forced into marriage against their will. Women used this argument to escape from marriages that displeased them (Mann 1985:114). Later, official concern with improving the lot of benighted African women shifted to a preoccupation with curbing their loose morals, believed to have been adversely affected by colonialism, by bringing wives under the tighter control of their husbands (Chanock 1985:145−216). To cite one further example, the Marriage Ordinance introduced into Lagos in 1884 provoked public outcry because it contained a provision that permitted children over the age of twenty-one to marry without their parents' consent. Elders complained that young people would use this provision to escape parental control (Mann 1985:113).

All colonial courts in Africa had rules or traditions of procedure, and these too affected processes of litigation, expressions of conflict, and strategies of litigants. Such rules or traditions differed from French to British courts and from European to Native ones. Roberts (1990) has shown that French civil procedure followed in the tribunal de première instance in Dakar determined how cases could be pursued, and it produced written expressions of complaint, albeit formulaic and compressed ones. Procedures in British colonial courts, on the other hand, permitted more discursive, oral testimony. Courts also had rules of evidence that affected what they would take into account when making decisions and shaped what litigants said. Gluckman (1955:23−24, 163−70ff, 255−56ff) contrasted the Barotse *kuta*'s broad construal of what was relevant with English jurisprudence's narrow construal. Fallers commented regarding the operation of the Basoga courts, "All sorts of other issues may be raised in argument but only those relevant to the reach of the particular concept of wrong enter into the decision..." (Fallers 1969:327). These observations remind us that courts have distinctive rules of discourse that influence what goes on within them.[15]

Moore's analysis (1977:159–87) of a case that Elifatio, a poor Chagga peasant, brought against his brother Richard, a relatively prosperous white-collar worker, illustrates how procedures in different courts affected the presentation of a dispute. It also shows how rules of evidence affected what courts would hear. Elifatio began trying to resolve his dispute by complaining to a local community leader that his brother had uprooted saplings that he, Elifatio, had recently planted. The local community leader convened a hearing where discussion of the conflict was informal and broad-ranging. At the hearing, Richard admitted uprooting Elifatio's plants, but claimed that Elifatio had violated the boundary between plots. Community sentiment lay with Elifatio. The community leader, however, ruled in Richard's favor because, Moore concluded, legal decisions were far from disinterested and the white-collar worker was a patron worth supporting. Unsatisfied with the outcome of the community hearing, Elifatio took his case to the local primary court, presided over by a government magistrate. There procedure required the complainant to make a formal statement and then allowed the respondent to ask questions of him. The complainant's witnesses subsequently presented their statements, again followed by questions from the respondent. The magistrate could intervene at any point during the proceedings, which he did several times to rule on evidence or procedure. The community leader, who might have testified that Richard had admitted guilt at the community hearing, failed to appear in court. Of those present, only Elifatio's son had seen Richard uproot the saplings, and therefore only he was permitted to testify about the offense. But on questioning, Richard so intimidated the boy that he retracted his statement. Moreover, Richard did not admit uprooting the saplings before the magistrate. Asserting there was no hard evidence that an offense had been committed, the magistrate thus ruled against Elifatio. Moore believed the official overlooked some irregularities in the courtroom procedure that favored Richard's defense, because the two men shared the same class position.

Important though rules of procedure and evidence may have been in shaping processes of litigation and expressions of conflict, they did not dictate the way litigants presented their cases. Africans and Europeans came to colonial courts with expectations, ideas, and intentions of their own about what would go on there, and these affected the court encounter. Roberts (1990) has demonstrated that even within the limits imposed by the formulaic, written expressions of complaint required by the tribunal de première instance in Dakar, litigants found ways to mold their statements for greatest effect. Cohen's contribution to this volume (Ch. 11) examines the "remarkable distinction" between what different levels of Busoga courts saw as "appropriate, relevant, and correct facts and arguments" and what litigants and witnesses saw as "appropriate, relevant, and correct." Cohen discovers two discordant discourses in the courts: one consisting of what the litigants presented, the other of what the court heard. The litigants were driven by a need not only to make the best case, but also to evaluate the risks of bringing certain information before the courts. The court was motivated by "an economy of practice, a selectivity of hearing" born in part of a desire to get on with the business of government (pp. 241, 251–52). Cohen believes that through their voices litigants and witnesses shaped not only what went on in courts, but also the very "facts and modes" of colonial domination.

In a discussion of the construction of legal narratives in the United States,

Bennett and Feldman (1981) conclude that the prosecution and defense have different objectives in framing stories. Each side misses, or chooses to ignore, some potentially important aspect of the incident in question. Lawyers commonly create the suspicion "that key evidence in the opposition case is spurious or that it can be explained better in a different web of circumstances than the one on which the opposition has built its case" (p. 93) Cohen shows a similar process at work in the Busoga courts through an analysis of the use of indirection, allusion, and silence in the testimony of litigants and witnesses. He stresses the importance of the construction of testimony not only for the presentation of the plaintiff's and defendant's cases, but also for the control of the litigants and witnesses over the courtroom encounter itself.

In concluding this section, we return briefly to Kidder's notion that two of the primary tenets of British law in India were that all persons should be equal before the law and that justice should be blind. Important though these principles were to the ideology of rule of law in Africa, as in India, we have only to reflect on the experience of Elifatio in the community hearing and primary court or on the treatment of European officials accused of violent crimes against Africans and sent quietly home before they could be tried to remember that asymmetries of status, wealth, and power affected processes of litigation. Far from being disinterested in the pursuit of rights and punishment of wrongs, court cases were embedded in local systems of inequality. Kidder noted, as have we done, the tension in the fact that colonial courts at once supported the privileges of those in power and created opportunities for persons of lesser status to challenge established power and property relations. More important than this observation is the question of how these things were accomplished and to what end. Careful study of changes in processes of litigation and expressions of conflict yields answers to this question. It further illuminates, moreover, the relationship between changes in law, society, and culture.

Sources and Methods

The historical study of law in colonial Africa can advance only to the limit of scholars' understanding of relevant sources and methods. We therefore conclude our introduction with some discussion of these subjects. Several of the contributors to this volume open the way to fresh research by plumbing new sources for historical data about law, society, and culture. A few of the records they employ, such as Seepapitso's assembly minutes and judicial notebooks, may be unusual, if not unique. But other records exist more widely, although they have not yet been used extensively by Africanist historians and anthropologists. Such sources include the reports of legal judgments analyzed by Chanock, as well as the records of legal cases studied by Mann, Moore, Christelow, Cohen, Sarr, and Richard Roberts. The essays presented here explore the records of many kinds of colonial courts. Mann examines cases from British judges' Notebooks of Civil Cases from the Lagos Supreme Court, while Moore investigates those from Chagga chiefs' reports of disputes coming before them. Christelow, on the other hand, works with records from the Emir's court in Kano, while Cohen follows the progress of a single case through multiple levels of courts in Uganda. Sarr introduces us to the records of the court of appeals (*cour d'appel*) in Dakar, and Richard Roberts calls our attention to records of French administrative law hearings. In her study, Mann also investigates legal documents pertaining to land transactions — crown grants, conveyances, mortgages, and reconveyances.

Other contributors open new frontiers of scholarship by employing more familiar sources in innovative ways. Chanock decodes anthropological and legal texts to reveal the beliefs and interests that underlie them. Sarr discovers in administrative debates over legal reform and colonial policy the context for problems of legal practice that plagued Dakar's appeals court. Taking an imaginative bottom-up approach to international law, Asiwaju looks at the impact of border agreements and boundary commissions on local peoples, and at the effect of peoples' responses to these initiatives on international boundaries themselves. Cohen, Groff, Moore, Mann, and Richard Roberts all derive from oral data knowledge that is missing from the written record, but is essential to its interpretation.

Of the many kinds of sources used by our contributors, we believe that court records deserve special attention because of the opportunities and challenges they present for historical research. Participants in the Stanford-Emory conference on law in colonial Africa agreed that court records survive more widely than is generally appreciated, sometimes in well-ordered government archives, but usually in neglected and disorganized local record offices. Locating and organizing court records is often the scholar's first and most essential task. The essays collected here are among the first attempts to use written records of colonial courts as raw material for the study of the African past. They demonstrate that such records contain data of great richness and detail about changes in law, society, and culture, and also about the lived experience of African peoples during the colonial period. However, the essays also show that court records present serious problems of interpretation and analysis and that they must be mined with great care lest we disappoint ourselves with fool's gold.[16]

Understandings of metropolitan legal systems have influenced social science approaches to the study of law in colonial situations. French anthropologists and legal scholars working on the problem have barely used case materials, in part because in code countries such as France, cases do not make law. Rules are embodied in codes, not generated by court decisions, and it is the codes themselves that have been the focus of scholarly attention. British research on colonial law, on the other hand, has pursued a "case method" approach with great rigor, owing to the importance in common law countries of cases in generating law. Indeed, work with court cases has dominated Anglo-American study of legal anthropology. Historians interested in legal case materials have much to learn from this sub-discipline. Epstein observed that legal anthropologists have used the case method "not so much by way of illustration but as providing the raw material for analysis, the various strands in the skein of facts being teased out and dissected to reveal underlying principles and regularities" (1967:208). In his view, anthropologists extract from cases observed in the field general principles, the value of which stems directly from the nature of the case observed. The greater its importance, the larger the reach of the general explanation.

In a self-critical discussion of his *The Judicial Process among the Barotse of Northern Rhodesia*, Gluckman reflected on a problem inherent in the case method:

> I set out there to analyse the modes of thought of Barotse judges in deciding cases, and to relate those modes of thought to the economic

and general social backgrounds of Barotse life. When I had finished the book, I felt that I had made an important contribution to the problems I had tackled, but I remained dissatisfied as a sociologist. I sensed that I was on the verge of important sociological discoveries, but was not making them. It was clear to me that though I had woven my analysis out of many cases heard in court, some quoted at great length, I had in fact used each case as an isolated incident coming before the court. Yet each case was obviously but an incident in a long process of social relations, with its roots deep in the past; and often the protagonists in the case would be living together again, and their interaction would be affected by the court's decision. I had not studied that process of social life; and in my opinion here lies the next step in deepening our under-standing of law and morality—the intensive study of the process of social control in a limited area of social life viewed over a period of time (Gluckman 1967:xvi).

Gluckman reminds us in this passage that every "case" has its own history, which precedes the courtroom encounter and persists after the judges make their decision. Building on this insight, Comaroff and Roberts portray the *tsheko* (case) as a "moment in the flow of everyday life in which the intersecting biographies are crystallized and acted out and the implicit subtleties of particular relationships are laid bare" (1981:216–17). The burden of these insights is that cases can be understood only in the context of the on-going relationships of which they form a part.

Locating the courtroom encounter in this way is much more difficult for students of the distant past than it is for anthropologists and contemporary historians who have access to informants who lived at the time of the case. Court records sometimes contain information relevant to the relationship between the litigants, but most often the evidence is cursory and molded by the practices of the court itself. Litigants sometimes deliberately withheld relevant information from the view of the court, as Cohen shows in his essay. Other sources — government documents, missionary memoirs, newspaper reports, travelers' accounts, and oral histories — occasionally yield pertinent data, particularly if con-temporaries deemed the case noteworthy. Cohen emphasizes the importance of bringing information from outside court records to bear on the relationship between litigants. In an effort to place cases from the Lagos Supreme Court in the context of on-going relationships, Mann links their investigation to the study of biography. Her method involved tracing a man through court and other legal records, while at the same time researching his life in oral and other written sources. Analysis of the litigation in which he was involved could then take place against the backdrop of his life as a whole.

To Gluckman's observation about the importance of situating court cases in the context of on-going relationships, we would add the need to locate them in historical context. All of the contributors to this anthology who have worked with legal judgments or legal cases make sense of them only against the background of wider economic, political, and social change. Chanock understands judicial de-cisions regarding customary land tenure in relation to the development of British land policy. Sarr interprets problems of legal jurisdiction in Dakar's appeals court as part of administrative struggles over the nature of French colonialism. Working with documents that are quite cursory, Christelow analyzes cases of theft and homicide in Northern Nigeria by linking them to social and economic transformations that accompanied the imposition of British colonialism and expansion of agricultural commercialization. Cohen explains a prolonged Busoga headmanship case by reference to an historic pattern: territorial aggression across an indistinct political boundary between the remnants of two polities. In her work on the Chagga, Moore (1986:1–12), has made explicit the method that she and others have employed to contextualize court cases. She has emphasized the need to move back and forth between the analysis of small-scale events documented in the cases and large-scale social processes visible there and elsewhere. She has also stressed the importance of weighing evidence from court cases against that from oral and other documentary sources.

Scholars who work with case materials inevitably confront difficult problems of selection, determining which of the hundreds or thousands of cases available are worthy of analysis. Fallers believed that the Busoga courts spent most of their time adjudicating cases which sprang from "trouble spots" expressing "conflicting social demands, divergent value commitments, or 'deviant' character organization" in times of rapid change or in situations where the legal subculture differed sharply from popular culture (Fallers 1969:16).[17] More recently, Newman (1983) has used the notion of stereotypical "trouble cases" to criticize the harmony model common among legal anthropologists who see strife as aberrant and pathological (see also Nader 1989). Newman suggests that "trouble cases" are not random occurrences but stem from contradictions in social organization. "Where stereotypical kinds of disputes prevail," she argues, "there are underlying strains in the social relations of production, patterned inequalities in access to crucial resources, which are surfacing as disputes and which are addressed by prescriptive legal rules" (p. 137).

While none of the authors represented here used the idea of trouble cases, all who worked with court records assumed that in the colonial period historical change generated conflict that found expression in the courts. Contributors to this volume pulled out for close, qualitative analysis cases that exemplified pivotal historical processes. Mann, Moore, and Christelow focus on those that show the impact of economic, political, and legal changes on values and relationships. Cohen analyzes a case that reveals the power of discourse in a particular political context to shape the facts and modes of colonialism. Mann took as her principle of selection the biography of a Lagosian whose life embodied certain cultural ideals. Christelow examines cases of theft and homicide, crimes with a changing moral dimension in early colonial Kano. Interested in the consequences for the patrilineal Chagga of economic and political transformations, Moore shrewdly focused her research not on disputes over the transfer of patrimonial property among agnates but on those over its transfer to non-agnates. Moore argues that this "oblique" approach is most likely to "expose time-specific motives and conditions for allowing patrimonial property to leave the patriline" (p. 110). The important thing to note about these methods is that each provided a principle of selection, a map as it were for finding one's way through complex and voluminous records. By the same token, each left the researcher with a particular view of the historical landscape.

Participants in the Stanford–Emory conference discussed the value of sampling court records and analyzing them quantitatively. While Moore and

Mann advocated the importance of carefully reading the body of court records over time, to gain an understanding of the working of the court and the nature of the cases coming before it, none of the participants thought there was much to be gained from quantitative study of court cases. Records of individual cases are often complex texts, requiring close analysis to extract their meaning. The true significance of cases can rarely be reduced to a set of quantifiable variables.

We have already discussed how the procedures of courts and expectations and intentions of litigants and witnesses shaped legal testimony. Scholars must, of course, be sensitive to these issues as they interpret the data in court records. Here, we turn our attention to the related but different question of how the transformation of oral testimony into written text affects the historical record. This question raises a number of problems for consideration. In his discussion of the 1976 Massachusetts Mashpee Indian land claims case, Clifford cautioned, "When I report on the witnesses at the trial, the impressions are mine. Others I spoke with saw things differently. The trial record — which stenographically preserves, by a precise but not infallible technique, the meaningful, spoken words of the trial — provides a check on my impressions" (Clifford 1988:290). This anthropologist's reflection on the creation of his own legal data vividly reminds us of the fundamental point that different persons have different perceptions of what goes on in court. Most court cases present but a single perspective on the court encounter. The views of the person who created the document colored its content, whether he was a European judge, African clerk, or local ruler. So did that person's purpose in writing the document. Although sometimes difficult to determine, these things must be taken into account when working with court records.

Clifford's critique also calls to mind that court records were created by different methods and in different circumstances. Some, such as those examined by Christelow, are brief notes containing little information about what was said in court, while others are more precise, but still imperfect, transcripts. Moreover, certain court records, as in Francophone Africa, were created in preparation for cases, others were generated in court as testimony was given, and still others were written after the fact from notes or memory. The methods and circumstances of the records creation obviously affect their contents. Even the fullest transcripts, however, usually capture only words. Non-verbal forms of communication are dropped out. Clifford remarked, "[The trial record] omits gestures, hesitations, clothing, tone of voice, laughter, irony...the sometimes devastating silences" (1988:290). These omissions are particularly unfortunate because the kinds of non-verbal expressions and signs to which Clifford refers were often central to the overall effect of litigants and witnesses. At their best, court records tell only part of the story of what went on in the court, and it is wise to remember this from the onset. When possible, other accounts should be used to supplement the official record of court transactions.

Despite the limitations of court records, they can, if used carefully and critically, yield abundant exciting new data about African history. The essays presented here by no means exhaust the possibilities or challenges that these sources present. The more court records are used, the more we shall know about how to use them. However, building on the work of Chanock, Moore, Hay and Wright, and a handful of others, the essays presented here bring us a major step closer to appreciating what colonial court records can teach us about African legal, social, and cultural change. The way has been opened for fresh and imaginative research with a vast body of underused materials. We hope that scholars will take advantage of this opportunity.

As the chapters in this anthology demonstrate, students of African social change are turning for new data and fresh insights to the study of colonial legal systems and the use of colonial legal records. Law, as we have seen, played a formative role in the making of the colonial social order, and it was in turn transformed by this process in ways that have had lasting significance. Investigating the complex interplay in the legal arena between Africans and Europeans and among Africans themselves exposes the dynamics of legal, social, and cultural change, and it enables us to understand better what colonialism meant and how Africans shaped and experienced it. Court and other legal records have limitations, to be sure, but they also represent a vast and largely untapped resource, which if used carefully can yield a wealth of new data about the beliefs and interests, thoughts and actions, understanding and experience of African and European players in the colonial drama.

NOTES

1. Shula Marks, Francis Synder, David Anderson, and Richard Rathbone are examining aspects of this problem in their seminar on the dissemination of labor law in the British empire.
2. The African colonial encounter of late nineteenth century European imperialism was but the last in a three and four century history of European colonial encounters with other parts of Europe, North America, Mexico, India, Indo-China, and Algeria. These colonial encounters established important precedents for the subsequent legal and anthropological encounter with Africa.
3. Legal education in Great Britain and the United States placed great weight on the rule-centered method. This also helps account for its dominance in the field of legal anthropology.
4. Much work remains to be done on the role of judges, lawyers, clerks, and interpretors in African legal history. For a beginning see Adewoye 1977b; Edsman 1979; Joko-Smart 1988.
5. For changes in the organization of credit see, Dorjahn and Fyfe 1962:391–97; Rodney 1970:83–88, 117; Newbury 1972:81–95; Curtin 1975:122ff; Kea 1982:232ff; Mann 1987:11–13; McPhee [1926] 1970:139–40, 163–64.
6. A similar situation prevailed in the Dutch West African settlements, especially along the Gold Coast. There a handful of Afro-Dutch enjoyed the privileges of Dutch "nationality" and brought cases before Dutch colonial officials. For a suggestive use of these legal records see Yarak 1989.
7. There has been virtually no research on forms of dispute settlement among Africans in French West Africa between colonial conquest and the 1903 legal reform. In areas outside French control, precolonial forms of dispute settlement probably prevailed. In areas occupied by France, but not considered self-governing municipalities such as the Four Communes, a patchwork of legal jurisdictions prevailed. Exactly what that meant for African disputants remains to be studied.
8. Case materials survive from the tribunals of the first instance in colonial Senegal. These records are potentially rich sources for African social history, although new methods must be developed to interpret them. For a start in that direction see Roberts 1990.
9. Raul Honwana describes the case of a Mozambican who was imprisoned under the indigenato by one administrator, only to find upon further examination by another administrator, that he was no longer classified a "native" because of his many years of schooling. Disobedience was not a crime for an assimilado, and therefore the man was set free (Honwana 1988:129–30).
10. The study of customary law in Portuguese Africa and in the Belgian Congo is very thin. On Portuguese Africa see Moreira (1955), Coissoro (1984), Medeiros (1984), De Sousa Santos (1984), and Sachs (1984). On the Belgian Congo, the classic work remains that of the administrator-scholar A. Sohier (1954). Dembour (1989a, 1989b) has produced some interesting unpublished work.
11. By 1897, Governor de Trentinian of the French Soudan had already ordered his district officers to respond to a questionnaire conceived by the Berlin International Union of Law and Political Economy regarding legal customs in their districts (Roberts, Ch. 8, cites one such report). Governor Clozel sponsored another colony-wide inquiry into

customs in 1909, while Governor-general Ponty sponsored one into slavery in 1910 and another into Islamic customs in 1913. As part of a further reform of the native legal system in 1931, administrators were charged with systematically codifying custom in French West Africa. The result was a three-volume publication of the practices of the major ethnic groups in the federation (Maupoil 1939). Robinson (1988a, 1988b) traces French concern with customary law to their "Islamic" policy, which had its roots in French ethnography of the late nineteenth century.

12. We feel obliged to add a methodological note about the use of "customary law" for the study of precolonial society. Ranger (1983:212) has cautioned Africanists that traditions invented during the colonial period, whether by Europeans or Africans, distorted the past but became realities through which a great deal of the colonial encounter was expressed. Picking up on Ranger's concern with the distortion of invented tradition, Chanock asks throughout *Law, Custom, and Social Order* (1985) whether we can learn anything about precolonial indigenous law from a study of the customary law of the colonial period. He doubts that we can in Malawi and Zambia, for two reasons. First, precolonial Central Africa consisted of a mosaic of different societies that had only recently been fundamentally transformed by the Ngoni invasions. Second, missionaries, administrators, and judges imposed on African societies attributes that the Europeans carried with them rather than incorporating African realities. Customary law, argues Chanock, expressed the specificity of the early colonial encounter and can tell us nothing about precolonial traditions of law. Sally Falk Moore concludes her book on Chagga law more optimistically. She argues that it is possible to learn about precolonial indigenous law, not from customary law *per se*, but from keen European observers, in her case a German missionary of long tenure on Kilimanjaro. Moore notes, however, the potential distortions that flow from her source's concern with "normative rules" (Moore 1986:38–91).

13. As colonialism introduced new forms of accumulation, those with wealth sometimes sought new strategies to protect their property and new power to control its devolution. The introduction of a European legal instrument — the will — unleashed conflict among Africans with different interests and beliefs and between European anthropologists and administrators with competing ideas about African societies. Regarding the debate over the introduction of the will in two matrilineal societies, see Colson (1950) and Loveridge (1950).

14. Many of the court cases in Gluckman's (1955), Bohannan's ([1957] 1968), and Fallers's (1969) now-classic texts in legal anthropology revolve around disputes between husbands and wives, landowners and land users, elders and juniors, and rulers and commoners that had clear implications for labor control. The early legal anthropologists failed to explore this aspect of the conflicts because they were interested in other issues.

15. In commenting on this manuscript after it had gone into production, Richard Rathbone reminded us of the importance of understanding the cultural construction of truth when thinking about the litigants' presentation of arguments, the court's treatment of evidence, and the public's response to court decisions. For an example of such an approach, see Rathbone 1989.

16. Kristin Mann and Richard Roberts organized a series of four panels that examined these issue in more detail. These panels, "Sources and Methods for the Study of Law in Colonial Africa," took place at the African Studies Association Meeting, Atlanta, 1989.

17. Fallers concentrated his research on examples of these "trouble spot" cases, grouped into a number of dispute categories. Fallers derived the concept of "trouble spots" from Lewellyn and Hoebel's "trouble case" (Lewellyn and Hoebel 1941:29; see also Radcliffe-Brown 1933).

SOURCES

Primary

Glover Papers. Royal Commonwealth Society Library, London. Files 4–6, 1870–1872, contain correspondence relevant to the debate about fugitive slaves.

LSCR: Lagos Supreme Court Records, High Court, Lagos State, Judges' Notebook in Civil Cases, *Akinlogun v Faliyi*, 19 January 1894, pp. 113–14, 116–18.

Lagos Weekly Record, 28 July 1894.

Phillips Papers. Nigerian National Archives, Ibadan. Notes on the cases of Okoro from Modakeke, Adeosun from Akure, and David Famoreke from Ado Ewi, 1/1/7, 1900; and Diary of Charles Phillips, 3/1, 1885–1889.

Secondary

Adewoye, Omoniyi. 1977a. *The judicial system in Southern Nigeria, 1854–1954: Law and justice in a dependency*. London: Longman.

———. 1977b. *The legal profession in Nigeria*. Ikeja: Longman.

Afigbo, A. E. 1972. *The warrant chiefs: Indirect rule in Southeastern Nigeria, 1891–1929*. New York: Humanities.

Allott, Antony N. 1967. "Law in the new Africa." *African affairs* 66(262):55–63.

———, ed. 1970a. *Judicial and legal systems in Africa*. London: Butterworths.

———. 1970b. *New essays in African law*. London: Butterworths.

———. 1976. "The development of the East African legal system during the colonial period." In *History of East Africa*, vol. III, ed. D. A. Low and Alison Smith, 348–82. Oxford: Clarendon.

Arrighi, Giovanni. 1973. "Labour supplies in historical perspective: A study of the proletarianization of the African peasantry in Rhodesia." In *Essays on the political economy of Africa*, ed. Giovanni Arrighi and John Saul, 180–234. New York: Monthly Review.

Asiwaju, A. I. 1970. "The Alaketu of Ketu and the Onimeko of Meko: The changing status of two Yoruba rulers under French and British rule." In *West African chiefs: Their changing status under colonial rule and independence*, ed. Michael Crowder and O. Ikime, 134–60. Ife: University of Ife Press.

———. 1979. "Control through coercion: A study of the indigénat regime in French West African administration, 1887–1946." *Bulletin d'institut fondemental d'Afrique noire*, series B, 41(1):35–75.

Atkins, Keletso E. 1988. "'Kafir time': Pre-industrial temporal concepts and labour discipline in nineteenth century colonial Natal." *Journal of African History* 29(2):229–44.

Beattie, John M. 1986. *Crime and courts in England, 1660–1800*. Princeton: Princeton University Press.

Bender, Gerald. 1978. *Angola under the Portuguese: The myth and the reality*. Berkeley: University of California Press.

Bennett, W. Lance, and Martha S. Feldman. 1981. *Reconstructing reality in the courtroom: Justice and judgement in American culture*. New Brunswick: Rutgers University Press.

Berry, Sara. 1988. "Hegemony on a shoestring: Some unintended consequences of colonial rule for access to resources in African agriculture." Paper presented at the African Studies Association annual meeting, Chicago.

Beurdeley, E. 1916. *La justice indigène en Afrique occidentale française: Mission d'études, 1913–14*. Paris: Comité de l'Afrique française.

Bohannan, Paul. [1957] reprinted 1968. *Justice and judgment among the Tiv*. London: International African Institute.

Bradford, Helen. 1987. *A taste of freedom: The ICU in rural South Africa, 1924–1930*. New Haven: Yale University Press.

Brett, E. A. 1973. *Colonialism and underdevelopment in East Africa: The politics of economic change, 1919–1939*. London: Heinemann.

Brooks, George. Forthcoming. *African landlords and European Etrangers: A history of Western Africa to the 17th century*.

Buell, Raymond Leslie. 1928. *The native problem in Africa*, vols. I–II. New York: Macmillan.

Bundy, Colin. 1979. *The rise and fall of the South African peasantry*. Berkeley: University of California Press.

Burns, Alan. 1972. *History of Nigeria*. London: George Allen and Unwin.

Buxton, Thomas Fowell. 1840. *The African slave trade, and its remedy*. London: John Murray.

Carlen, Pat. 1976. *Magistrates' justice*. London: M. Robertson.

Chanock, Martin. 1985. *Law, custom, and social order: The colonial experience in Malawi and Zambia*. Cambridge: Cambridge University Press.

———. 1989. "Laws and contexts." *Law in Context* 7(2):68–80.

Cheater, A. P. 1987. "Fighting over property: The articulation of dominant and subordinate legal systems governing the inheritance of immoveable property among blacks in Zimbabwe." *Africa* 57(2):173–95.

Christelow Allan. 1982. "The Muslim judge and municipal politics in colonial Algeria and Senegal." *Comparative Studies in Society and History* 24(1):3–24.

———. 1985. *Muslim law courts and the colonial state in Algeria*. Princeton: Princeton University Press.

Clifford, James. 1988. *The predicament of culture: Twentieth-century ethnography, literature, and art*. Cambridge, Mass.: Harvard University Press.

Cohen, David W. 1985. "Doing social history from Pim's doorway." In *Reliving the past: The worlds of social history*, ed. Olivier Zunz, 191–235. Chapel Hill: University of North Carolina Press.

Cohn, Bernard S. 1959. "Some notes on law and change in North India." *Economic Development and Change* 8(1):79–93.

———. 1989. "Law and the colonial state in India." In *History and power in the study of law: New directions in legal anthropology*, 131–52. Ithaca: Cornell University Press. See Starr and Collier 1989a.

Coissoro, Narana. 1984. "African customary law in the former Portuguese territories, 1954–74." *Journal of African Law* 28 (1–2):72–79.

Collier, Jane. 1975. "Legal processes." *Annual Review of Anthropology* 4:121–44.

Colson, Elizabeth. 1950. "Possible repercussions of the right to make wills upon the Plateau Tonga of Northern Rhodesia." *Journal of African Administration* 2(1):24–34.

———. 1953. "Social control and vengeance in Plateau Tonga society." *Africa* 23(3):199–212.

Comaroff, Jean, and John Comaroff. 1990. "Missions, manhood, and modernity: Remaking men among the Tswana." Paper presented at the "Towards a gendered history of men in Africa" conference, University of Minnesota.

Comaroff, John, and Simon Roberts. 1981. *Rules and processes: The cultural logic of dispute in an African context*. Chicago: University of Chicago Press.

Cooper, Frederick. 1980. *From slaves to squatters: Plantation labor and agriculture in Zanzibar and coastal Kenya, 1890–1925*. New Haven: Yale University Press.

———. 1981. "Africa and the world economy." *The African Studies Review* 24(2–3):1–86.

———. 1987. *On the African waterfront: Urban disorder and the transformation of work in colonial Mombasa*. New Haven: Yale University Press.

———. 1990. "Industrial man goes to Africa." Paper presented at the "Towards a gendered history of men in Africa" conference, University of Minnesota.

Crooks, J. J. 1972. *A history of the colony of Sierra Leone Western Africa*. London: Frank Cass.

Crowder, Michael. 1967. *Senegal: A study in French assimilation policy*. London: Methuen.

Crowder, Michael, and O. Ikime, eds. 1970. *West African chiefs: Their changing status under colonial rule and independence*. Ife: University of Ife Press.

Crummey, Donald, ed. 1986. *Banditry, rebellion and social protest in Africa*. London: James Currey; Portsmouth, N.H.: Heinemann.

Curtin, Philip. 1975. *Economic change in precolonial Africa: Senegambia in the era of the slave trade*. Madison: University of Wisconsin Press.

Davis, David Brion. 1975. *The problem of slavery in the age of revolution, 1770–1823*. Ithaca: Cornell University Press.

———. 1984. *Slavery and human progress*. New York: Oxford University Press.

Dembour, Marie-Bénédicte. 1989a. "A treatise for customary law: 'Traite élémentaire de droit coutumier du Congo belge.'" Paper presented at the African Studies Association annual meeting, Atlanta.

———. 1989b. "La peine durant la colonisation Belge." Paper presented at the Société Jean Bodin, Brussels.

Dorjahn, V. R., and Christopher Fyfe. 1962. "Landlord and stranger: Change in tenancy relations in Sierra Leone." *Journal of African History* 3(3):391–97.

Dumett, Raymond, and Marion Johnson. 1988. "Britain and the suppression of slavery in the Gold Coast Colony, Ashanti, and the Northern Territories." In *The end of slavery in Africa*, 71–116. See Miers and Roberts 1988.

Earnshaw, Justice. 1976. *Judgements delivered at Cape Coast Castle, Gold Coast, by Mr. Justice Earnshaw, 1900–1910, with introduction*. Accra-Tema: Council for Law Reporting.

Echenberg, Myron. 1991. *Colonial conscripts: The tirailleurs sénégalais in French West Africa, 1857–1960*. Portsmouth, N.H.: Heinemann.

Edsman, Björn M. 1979. *Lawyers in Gold Coast politics, c. 1900–1945: From Mensah Sarbah to J.B. Danquah*. Uppsala: Almquist and Wiksell International.

Elias, T. Olawale. 1963. *The Nigerian legal system*. London: Routledge and Kegan Paul.

Epstein, A. L. 1967. "The case method in the field of law." In *The craft of social anthropology,* ed. A. L. Epstein, 205–30. London: Tavistock.

Fallers, Lloyd. 1969. *Law without precedent: Legal ideas in action in the courts of colonial Busoga*. Chicago: University of Chicago Press.

Flint, John. 1960. *Sir George Goldie and the making of Nigeria*. London: Oxford University Press.

Fyfe, Christopher. 1962. *A history of Sierra Leone*. London: Oxford University Press.

Galbraith, John S. 1974. *Crown and charter: The early years of the British South Africa Company*. Berkeley: University of California Press.

Gann, Louis, and Peter Duignan. 1978. *The rulers of British Empire, 1870–1914*. Stanford: Stanford University Press.

Genovese, Eugene. 1974. *Roll, Jordan, Roll: The world the slaves made*. New York: Vintage.

Gluckman, Max. 1955. *The judicial process among the Barotse of Northern Rhodesia*. Manchester: Manchester University Press.

———. 1965. "Reasonableness and responsibility in the law of segmentary societies." In *African law: Adaptation and development*, ed. Hilda Kuper and Leo Kuper, 120–46. Berkeley: University of California Press.

——. 1967. "Introduction." In *The craft of social anthropology*, ed. A. L. Epstein, xi–xx. London: Tavistock.

Gocking, Roger. 1989. "The changing attitude towards inheritance in the British courts of the Gold Coast, 1870–1935." Paper presented at the African Studies Association annual meeting, Atlanta.

Goody, Jack. 1963. "Feudalism in Africa." *Journal of African History* 4(1):1–18.

——. 1972. *The myth of the Bagre*. Oxford: Clarendon.

——. 1987. *The interface between the written and the oral*. Cambridge: Cambridge University Press.

Gray, J. M. 1940. *The history of Gambia*. Cambridge: Cambridge University Press.

Gregory, Joel W., and Elias Mandala. 1987. "Dimensions of conflict: Emigrant labor from colonial Malawi and Zambia, 1900–1945." In *African population and capitalism: Historical perspectives*, ed. Dennis Cordell and Joel W. Gregory, 221–39. Boulder: Westview.

Grier, Beverly. 1987. "Contradiction, crisis, and class conflict: The state and capitalist development in Ghana prior to 1948." In *Studies in power and class in Africa*, ed. Irving Leonard Markovitz, 27–49. New York: Oxford University Press.

Hailey, Lord. 1950–1953. *Native administration in the British African territories*. Parts I–V. London: Her Majesty's Stationery Office.

Hailey, Lord. 1957. *An African survey: A study of problems arising in Africa south of the Sahara*. Oxford: Oxford University Press.

Hamnett, Ian, ed. 1977. *Social anthropology and law*. London: Academic Press.

Hansen, Karen Tranberg. 1989. *Distant companions: Servants and employers in Zambia, 1900–1985*. Ithaca: Cornell University Press.

Harris, Marvin. 1958. *Portugal's African "wards:" A first-hand report on labor and education in Mocambique*. New York: American Committee on Africa.

Hart, Keith. 1978. *The political economy of West African agriculture*. New York: Oxford University Press.

Hay, Douglas. 1975. "Property, authority and criminal law." In *Albion's fatal tree: Crime and society in eighteenth century England*, 17–63. New York: Pantheon. See Hay et al. 1975.

Hay, Douglas et al. [Peter Linebaugh, John C. Rule, E. P. Thompson, and Cal Winslow.] 1975. *Albion's fatal tree: Crime and society in eighteenth century England*. New York: Pantheon.

Hay, Margaret Jean, and Marcia Wright, eds. 1982. *African women and the law: Historical perspectives*. Boston: Boston University.

Henriksen, Thomas. 1978. *Mozambique: A history*. London: Rex Collings.

Hild, Eugène. 1912. *L'organisation judiciaire en Afrique occidentale française*. Paris: Emile Larose.

Hinderer, Anna. 1877. *Seventeen years in the Yoruba country*. London: Religious Tract Society.

Hogendorn, J. S., and Paul E. Lovejoy. 1988. "The reform of slavery in early colonial Northern Nigeria." In *The end of slavery in Africa*, 391–414. See Miers and Roberts 1988.

Honwana, Raúl. 1988. *The life history of Raul Honwana: An inside view of Mozambique from colonialism to independence, 1905–1975*, ed. Allen F. Isaacman. Boulder: Lynne Rienner.

Hopkins, Anthony G. 1973. *An economic history of West Africa*. London: Longman.

——. 1980. "Property rights and empire building: Britain's annexation of Lagos, 1861." *Journal of Economic History* 40(4):777–98.

Ikime, Obaro. 1967. *Niger delta rivalry*. London: Longman.

——. 1968. *Merchant prince of the Niger Delta: The rise and fall of Nana Olomu, last governor of the Benin River*. London: Heinemann.

——. 1977. *The fall of Nigeria: The British conquest*. London: Heinemann.

Isaacman, Allen. 1976. *The tradition of resistance in Mozambique: Anti-colonial activity in the Zambesi Valley, 1850–1921*. Berkeley: University of California Press.

——. 1985. "Chiefs, rural differentiation, and peasant protest: The Mozambican forced cotton regime, 1938–1961." *African Economic History* 14:15–56.

Isaacman, Allen, and Anton Rosenthal. 1988. "Slaves, soldiers, and police: Power and dependency among the Chikunda of Mozambique, ca. 1825–1920." In *The end of slavery in Africa*, 220–53. See Miers and Roberts 1988.

Johnson, Harry M., ed. 1978. *Social system and legal process.* San Francisco: Jossey-Bass.

Joko-Smart, H. M. 1988. "The judicial and legal system of Sierra Leone." Paper presented at the Stanford-Emory Conference on Law in Colonial Africa, Stanford University.

Kea, Ray A. 1982. *Settlements, trade, and politics in the seventeenth-century Gold Coast.* Baltimore: Johns Hopkins University Press.

Kidder, Robert L. 1978. "Western law in India: External law and local response." In *Social system and legal process*, ed. Harry M. Johnson, 155–80. San Francisco: Jossey-Bass.

Kimble, David. 1963. *A political history of Ghana: The rise of Gold Coast nationalism, 1850–1928.* London: Clarendon.

Kirk-Greene, Anthony H. M. 1965. *The principles of native administration in Nigeria: Selected documents, 1900–1947.* London: Oxford University Press.

Klein, Martin. 1988. "Slave resistance and slave emancipation in coastal Guinea." In *The end of slavery in Africa*, 203–19. See Miers and Roberts, 1988.

Kopytoff, Igor. 1988. "The cultural context of African abolition." In *The end of slavery in Africa*, 485–503. See Miers and Roberts 1988.

Kuper, Adam. 1988. *The invention of primitive society: Transformations of an illusion.* London: Routledge and Keegan Paul.

Lewellyn, K. N., and E. A. Hoebel. 1941. *The Cheyenne way.* Norman: University of Oklahoma Press.

Loveridge, A. J. 1950. "Wills and the customary law in the Gold Coast." *Journal of African Administration* 2(4):24–28.

Low, D. A. 1973. *Lion rampant: Essays in the Study of British imperialism.* London: Frank Cass.

Lugard, Frederick. 1918. "Revisions of instructions to political officers on subjects chiefly political and administrative." In *The principles of native administration in Nigeria: Selected documents, 1900–1947*, ed. Anthony H. M. Kirk-Greene, 68–148. London: Oxford University Press.

Malinowski, Bronislaw. 1926. *Crime and custom in a savage society.* London: Kegan Paul.

Mandala, Elias. 1982. "Peasant cotton agriculture, gender, and intergenerational relationships: The Lower Tshiri (Shire) Valley of Malawi, 1906–1940." *African Studies Review* 25(2–3):27–44.

Mann, Kristin. 1982. "Women's rights in law and practice: Marriage and dispute settlement in colonial Lagos." In *African women and the law: Historical perspectives*, 151–71. See Hay and Wright 1982.

——. 1985. *Marrying well: marriage, status, and social change among the educated elite in colonial Lagos.* Cambridge: Cambridge University Press.

——. 1989. "Redefining servitude: From slavery to tenancy-clientage in late nineteenth century Lagos." Paper presented at the African Studies Association annual meeting, Atlanta.

Marks, Shula. 1985. "Southern Africa, 1867–1886." In *The Cambridge History of Africa*, vol. 6, ed. Roland Oliver and G. N. Sanderson, 359–421. Cambridge: Cambridge U P.

——. 1986. *The ambiguities of dependence in South Africa: Class, nationalism and the state in twentieth century Natal.* Baltimore: Johns Hopkins University Press.

Marks, Shula, and Richard Rathbone, eds. 1982. *Industrialisation and social change in South Africa: African class formation, culture, and consciousness.* London: Longman.

Martin, Phyllis. 1987. "Leisure and sport in colonial Africa." Paper presented at a conference, New perspectives on colonial Africa, University of Illinois.

Martin, Susan M. 1988. *Palm oil and protest: An economic history of the Ngwa region, Southern-Eastern Nigeria, 1800–1980.* Cambridge: Cambridge University Press.

Massell, Gregory J. 1968. "Law as an instrument of revolutionary change in a traditional milieu: The case of Soviet Central Asia." *Law and Society Review* 2(2):179–228.

Maupoil, Bernard. 1939. *Coutumiers juridiques de l'Afrique occidentale française*. Paris: Publications du Comité d'études historiques et scientifiques de l'Afrique occidentale française.

Mba, Nina Emma. 1982. *Nigerian women mobilized: Women's political activity in southern Nigeria, 1900–1965*. Berkeley: Institute of International Studies.

McDougall, Ann. 1988. "A topsy-turvy world: Slaves and freed slaves in the Mauritanian Adrar, 1910–1950." In *The end of slavery in Africa*, 362–88. See Miers and Roberts 1988.

McPhee, Allan. [1926] reprinted 1970. *The economic revolution in British West Africa*. New York: Negro Universities Press.

Medeiros, Carlos. 1984. "Kwandu law: The evolution of a juridicial system among an Herero people of South-western Angola." *Journal of African Law* 28(1–2):80–89.

Meek, Charles Kingsley [1937] reprinted 1949. *Law and authority in a Nigerian tribe: A study in indirect rule*. London: Oxford University Press.

Meredith, David. 1984. "Government and the decline of the Nigerian oil-palm export industry, 1919–1939." *Journal of African History* 25(3):311–29.

Miers, Suzanne, and Richard Roberts, eds. 1988. *The end of slavery in Africa*. Madison: University of Wisconsin Press.

Mohkiber, James. 1990. "Forms of authority and the ordering of empire: The native justice system in colonial Senegal, 1903–1912." Unpublished B.A. honors thesis, Department of History, Stanford University.

Monk, William, ed. 1968. *Dr. Livingstone's Cambridge lectures*. Farnborough, Hants: Gregg International.

Moore, Sally Falk. 1977. "Individual interests and organizational structures: Dispute settlements as 'events of articulation.'" In *Social Anthropology and Law*, 159–88. See Hamnett 1977.

———. 1978. *Law as process: An anthropological approach*. London: Routledge and Kegan Paul.

———. 1986. *Social facts and fabrications: "Customary" law on Kilimanjaro, 1880–1980*. New York: Cambridge University Press.

Moreau, Paul. 1938. *Les indigènes d'A.O.F.: Leur condition politique et économique*. Paris: Editions Doman-Montchristien.

Moreira, Adriano. 1955. *Administração de justiça ãos indígenas*. Lisbon: Agéncia Geral do Ultramar.

Muntemba, Maud Shimwaayi. 1982. "Women and agricultural change in the railway region of Zambia: Dispossession and counterstrategies, 1930–70." In *Women and work in Africa*, ed. Edna G. Bay, 83–103. Boulder: Westview.

Nader, Laura. 1966. *To make the balance*. Berkeley: University of California Extension.

———. ed. 1969. *Law, culture and society*. Chicago: Aldine Press.

———. 1989. "The crown, the colonists, and the course of Zapotec village law." In *History and power in the study of law: New directions in legal anthropology*, 320–44. See Starr and Collier 1989a.

Nader, Laura, and Harry F. Todd, eds. 1978. *The disputing process: Law in ten societies*. New York: Columbia University Press.

Newbury, C. W. 1972. "Credit in early nineteenth century West African trade." *Journal of African History* 8(1):81–95.

Newitt, Malyn. 1981. *Portugal in Africa: The last hundred years*. London: C. Hurst.

Newman, Katherine S. 1983. *Law and economic organization: A comparative study of preindustrial societies*. Cambridge: Cambridge University Press.

O'Barr, William M., and John M. Conley. 1985. "Litigant satisfaction versus legal adequacy in small claims court narratives." *Law and Society Review* 19(4):661–701.

Opoku, K. 1974. "Traditional law under French colonial rule." *Verfassung und Recht in Ubersee*, 7:139–53.

Oroge, E. Adeniyi. 1973. "The fugitive slave question in Anglo-Yoruba relations, 1861–1886." Paper presented at the Historical Society of Nigeria annual meeting, Zaria.

Palmer, Robin. 1977. "The agricultural history of Rhodesia." In *The roots of rural poverty in central and southern Africa*, ed. Robin Palmer and Neil Parsons, 221–54. Berkeley: University of California Press.

Parsons, Q. Neil. 1973. "Khama III, the Bamangwato and the British, with special reference to 1895–1923." Ph.D. dissertation, University of Edinburgh.

———. 1977. "The economic history of Khama's country in Botswana, 1844–1930." In *The roots of rural poverty in Central and Southern Africa*, 113–43. See Palmer 1977.

Perham, Margery. 1937. *Native administration in Nigeria*. London: Oxford University Press.

———. 1956 and 1960. *Lugard*. 2 vols. London: Collins.

Peterson, John. 1969. *Province of freedom: A history of Sierra Leone, 1787–1870*. London: Faber and Faber.

Phillips, Arthur, and Henry Francis Morris. 1971. *Marriage laws in Africa*. London: Oxford University Press.

Pouncey, Hillard. Forthcoming. *Politics of colonial policy making: Labor law implementation in British West Africa, 1820–1940*. Lewiston, N.Y.: E. Mellon Press.

Priestley, Margaret. 1969. *West African trade and coast society: A family study*. London: Oxford University Press.

Radcliffe-Brown, A. R. 1933. Primitive law. In *The encyclopedia of the social sciences*, vol. IX: 202–206. New York: Macmillan.

Ranger, Terence. 1983. "The invention of tradition in colonial Africa." In *The invention of tradition*, ed. Eric Hobsbawm and Terence Ranger, 211–62. Cambridge: Cambridge University Press.

Rattray, R. S. [1929] reprinted 1969. *Ashanti law and constitution*. Oxford: Clarendon.

Rathbone, Richard. 1989. "A murder in the colonial Gold Coast: Law and politics in the 1940s." *Journal of African History* 30(3):445–461.

Roberts, Richard. 1988. The end of slavery in the French Soudan, 1905–1914. In *The end of slavery in Africa*, 282–307. See Miers and Roberts 1988.

———. 1990. "Text and testimony in the *tribunal de première instance*, Dakar, during the early twentieth century." *Journal of African History*, 31(3):447–63.

Roberts, Richard, and Suzanne Miers. 1988. "The end of slavery in Africa." In *The end of slavery in Africa*, 3–68. See Miers and Roberts 1988.

Robinson, David. 1988a. "Ethnography and customary law in Senegal." Paper presented at the Stanford–Emory Conference on Law in Colonial Africa, Stanford University.

———. 1988b. "French 'Islamic' policy and practice in late nineteenth-century Senegal." *Journal of African History* 29(3):415–35.

Rodney, Walter. 1970. *A history of the Upper Guinea Coast, 1545–1800*. London: Oxford University Press.

Rolland, Louis. 1940. *Précis de législation colonial (colonies, Algérie, protectorats, pays sous mandat)*. Paris: Librairie Dalloz.

Rosen, Lawrence. 1989. "Islamic 'case law' and the logic of consequences." In *History and power in the study of law: New directions in legal anthropology*, 302–19. See Starr and Collier 1989a.

Sachs, Albie. 1984. "Changing the terms of the debate: A visit to a popular tribunal in Mozambique." *Journal of African Law* 28(1–2):99–108.

Salacuse, Jeswald. 1969. *An introduction to law in French-speaking Africa*. Charlottesville, VA: Michie Company.

Sarr, Dominique. 1974. "Le chambre spéciale d'homologation de la cour d'appel de l'AOF et les coutumes pénales de 1903–1920." *Annales Africaines* 1:101–16.

———. 1975. "Jurisprudence des tribunaux indigènes du Sénégal: Les causes de rupture du lien matrimonial de 1872 à 1946." *Annales Africaines* 2:143–78.

Schapera, Isaac. 1938. *A handbook of Tswana law and custom*. London: Oxford University Press.

Searing, James. Forthcoming. *Door of no return: Atlantic commerce, slavery, and colonialism in the lower Senegal, 1700–1865.*

Seidman, Robert B. 1969. "A note on the construction of the Gold Coast reception statute." *Journal of African Law* 13(1):45–51.

Snyder, Francis. 1981. *Capitalism and legal change: An African transformation.* New York: Academic.

Sohier, Antoine. 1954. *Traite élémentaire de droit coutumier du Congo belge.* Brussels: Maison F. Larcier.

Solus, Henry. 1927. *Traité de la condition des indigènes en droit privé; Colonies et pays de protectorate (non compris l'Afrique du Nord) et pays sous mandat.* Paris: Recueil Sirey.

Sousa Santos, Bonaventura de. 1984. "From customary law to popular justice." *Journal of African Law* 28(1–2):90–98.

Starr, June, and Jane F. Collier, eds. 1989a. *History and power in the study of law: New directions in legal anthropology.* Ithaca: Cornell University Press.

———. 1989b. "Introduction: Dialogues in legal anthropology." In *History and power in the study of law*, 1–28. See Starr and Collier 1989a.

Suret-Canale, Jean. 1971. *French colonialism in tropical Africa, 1900–1945*, trans. Till Gottheiner. London: C. Hurst.

Tamuno, T. N. 1972. *The evolution of the Nigerian state: The southern phase, 1898–1914.* London: Longman.

Temperley, Howard. 1977. "Capitalism, slavery, and ideology." *Past and Present* 75(1):94–118.

Thompson, E. P. 1975. *Whigs and hunters: The origin of the Black act.* New York: Pantheon.

Thompson, J. Malcolm. 1989. "In dubious service: The recruitment and stabilization of West African maritime labor by the French colonial military, 1659–1904." Ph.D. dissertation, University of Minnesota.

Unger, Roberto M. 1986. *The critical legal studies movement.* Cambridge, Mass: Harvard University Press.

Van Allen, Judith. 1972. "Sitting on a man: Colonialism and the lost political institutions of Igbo women." *Canadian Journal of African Studies* 6(1):168–81.

Van Zwanenberg, R. 1975. *Colonial capitalism and labour in Kenya, 1919–1939.* Nairobi: East Africa Publishing.

Vincent, Joan. 1989. "Contours of change: Agrarian law in colonial Uganda, 1895–1962." In *History and power in the study of law*, 153–67. See Starr and Collier 1989a.

Worger, William. 1983. "Workers as criminals: The rule of law in early Kimberley, 1870–1885." In *Struggle for the city: Migrant labor, capital, and the state in urban Africa*, ed. Frederick Cooper, 51–90. Beverly Hills: Sage.

———. 1987. *South Africa's city of diamonds: Mine workers and monopoly capitalism in Kimberley, 1867–1895.* New Haven: Yale University Press.

———. 1988. "Industrialization and incarceration: Punishment and society in South Africa." Paper presented at the Stanford–Emory Conference on Law in Colonial Africa, Stanford University.

Wright, Marcia. 1982. "Justice, women, and the social order in Abercorn, Northeastern Rhodesia, 1897–1903." In *African women and the law: Historical perspectives*, 33–50. See Hay and Wright 1982.

———. 1983. "Technology, marriage, and women's work in the history of maize-growers in Mazabuka, Zambia: A reconnaissance." *Journal of Southern African Studies* 10(1):71–85.

Yarak, Larry. 1989. "West African coastal slavery in the nineteenth century: The case of the Afro-European slaveowners of Elmina." *Ethnohistory* 36(1):44–60.

PART II

PROPERTY AND THE ACCUMULATION OF WEALTH

2

Paradigms, Policies and Property: A Review of the Customary Law of Land Tenure

MARTIN CHANOCK

The brotherhood of the larger group may still cohere, but the brethren of some family are always wishing to have their shares separately...

Henry Sumner Maine

The land question was crucial to the politics of the colonial period and vital in many parts of Africa to the development and success of anticolonial movements. Pressure on and confiscation of land was a fundamental feature of colonialism, especially in East and Central Africa. In this context, as Meek observed, "rights over land are more jealously treasured than any other form of rights." This has not, of course, been forgotten by historians and social scientists, as there is a huge literature on the politics of land, on land use, on agriculture, on the development of peasantries, and so on, a literature that recognizes the centrality of land in African social formations. But it is a literature that has, I think, often forgotten the question of *rights* on the level about which Meek was thinking. Writing after the Second World War, Meek thought that "It would be impossible to exaggerate the importance of the subject of land tenure in the colonies" (Meek [1946] 1968:5). These matters have been generally canvassed in an excellent article by Elisabeth Colson (Colson 1971). My intention in this essay is to try to revive the sense of importance that Meek attached to these issues.

In my writing about the history of customary law, I have emphasized its making during the colonial period in the process of a dialogue between the colonial state and its African subjects (Chanock 1985). I have suggested that the economic transformation of Africa during the colonial period had its impact first on those laws which define the nature of control over dependents and their labor. The development of a customary law legitimizing the control of persons in new ways was followed by the emergence of a customary law of property in general, and land in particular. I shall attempt in this paper to outline this development and to show how our picture of customary tenure is the product of colonial economic transformations, and the interplay between state policies, African assertions, and the products of social science. My focus is a general one, based on the methodological view that general studies must precede particular ones, not follow them. I have looked at colonial Africa as a whole, particularly because my main purpose is to analyze the legal, anthropological, and policy discourses about land rights, and how these were generally conceived. But where I have discussed particular conflicts over land, the locus of my account is East and Central Africa, in particular Zambia, Malawi, and Tanzania. The core of my argument is that the models of the customary law of land tenure were, to a significant extent, instruments of colonial land policies. They were produced in the circumstances of initial dispossession and confinement, and served both the colonial governments as a justification for these, and African communities as an apparent defense against further land loss. The effects of the dominance of these discourses, and the policies which they both produced and reflected, have continued into the postcolonial period in which the inhabitants of East and Central Africa find that, while their land has been screened from market forces, they are effectively rightless against the state. The customary land law, the imagery of which celebrates the entitlement of all as members of the community, has become a component of the dominance of state over society in Africa.

Property, Civilization, and Savages

As my focus is on the power of discourses to shape reality, I think that to understand the development of policies with regard to land tenure, we must begin with the broad context of social, legal, and economic philosophy with which the British approached Africa. The notion of a right to property as a natural human right, necessary to human nature, a just reward for labor, and the very basis of a proper political society was deeply embedded in nineteenth-century British political theory. (Macpherson 1978). Across the spectrum of political and legal thought, property had increasingly come to be seen as meaning private property, and liberals and conservatives were agreed that, in Henry Maine's terms, several property was the basis of civilized society. Furthermore as Jeremy Bentham put it, "Property and law are born together and die together" (Macpherson 1978:51–52), while in contrast, the possession enjoyed by savages was "miserable and precarious." The importance of these views is the *contrast* between the rights enjoyed in civilized and savage societies, which created the basis for a perception of and prescription of fundamental differences. This set the stage for the nature of the rights which would be recognized in Africa. The colonial state, as I have shown (Chanock 1985), refused to recognize certain rights over people while endorsing others, and was to recognize rights over labor only if secured by contracts of a particular sort. It would also engage with the question as to what rights over land would secure legal protection. While the colonial period closed with a general atmosphere of suspicion of individual land rights, as I shall show, it opened with the dominance of ideas about the evolutionary superiority of Western concepts of individual property rights. Yet communal rights to land, ideologically judged to be primitive, were eventually accorded a recognition denied to various forms of bonded labor.

We also need to think about the overall view of economic behavior in primitive and African societies. This is not the place to review the development of economic anthropology and its influence, but it is a part of the land tenure story. Early administrators approached Africa with certain basics in mind. These were the broad evolution of human societies from status to contract; the contrast between individualism and communalism; and, even among the anthropologically minded, a contrast between rational and irrational economic behavior. An essential part of this picture was the model of land tenure, the basic features of which were that land was held in some form of communal tenure and could not be sold by individuals, and that all had a more or less equal right to land. As the twentieth century progressed, the view that there was one kind of proper economic behavior was diluted by the demonstration that what was economically rational depended on the society in which it happened. This enabled colonial rulers to hold to the basic principle that there was, really, one kind of economic rationality towards which all societies were ultimately moving, and towards which colonial policy should aim, while at the same time conceding that there were forms of African economic behavior, in the long run irrational, but explicable in terms of African societies. African economic behavior and institutions could therefore be accommodated as customary. This was compounded by the tendency over the colonial period to look with increasing favor on Africans being "customary." African urbanization was seen as unnatural, townsmen as abnormal, as "growing up polluted" (White 1983:183–84; Iliffe 1983). Likewise, African success in the new rural economy, being predicated on non-customary behavior, was wrong for Africans at their perceived stage of development, even if at the same time it was right in terms of overall human evolution (White 1983). Iliffe remarks that rural capitalism was seen "not only as socially and politically dangerous, but somehow improper for Africans like guitars or three piece suits" (Iliffe 1983:137). The framework of suspicion and of tight control over rural entrepreneurs meant condemning their desire to increase their landholdings as unnatural and greedy, in a sense economically right, but not customary and therefore not legitimate. Gradually a picture of a customary economic world was built up according to which institutions in the realm of custom, like landholding, were judged. Even customary institutions that did not fit this picture were judged illegitimate. (Thus, for example, the colonial government of Tanganyika, acting within the ambit of the view that there could be no landed and landless in customary society, refused to recognize the legitimacy of customary share-cropping tenancies [Young and Fosbrooke 1960:64–69]). Ideas about social development in the broadest sense must be understood first, as they interact with the growing prerogatives of economic development, the necessities and limitations in governing each colonial society, and with the resistances and political and economic ambitions of Africans in the production of a customary law of land tenure.

Shaping the Imperial Legal Regime

Still considering general conceptions of African society, we must think about the importance of overall conceptions of the nature of African political institutions, because these, like general conceptions of African economic behavior, were a fundamental ingredient in the making of land law. It has become a commonplace that over large parts of colonial Africa the European governments created chiefs, and that, even where strong indigenous institutions of political leadership existed prior to colonial rule, the indigenous rulers were endowed by the colonial states with a set of powers quite different from those they had had before (Chanock 1985). There is a profound connection between the use of the chieftaincy as an institution of colonial government and the development of the customary law of land tenure. The development of the concept of a leading customary role for chiefs with regard to the ownership and allocation of land was fundamental to the evolution of the paradigm of customary tenure. Administrators and analysts celebrated a model of tenure characterized by the often-quoted African saying that "Land belongs to a vast family of which many are dead, few are living and countless numbers are still unborn" (e.g. Meek [1946] 1968: facing title page.) But in the broad approach to the institutions of primitive government the chiefs were seen as the holders of land with rights of administration and allocation. Rights in land were seen as flowing downward. Whatever they were, they were derived from the political authority, rather than residing in the peasantry. This essentially feudal model not only fitted British ways of thinking about state and society, but was necessary if there was to be any linkage between British land law and African. Exactly what the rights of the chiefs were was a constant matter of dispute, resolved in varying ways in different territories and often left unclear. But it was a field into which African rulers at all levels could fruitfully insert their own definitions of their "customary" powers. Broadly speaking, British policy aimed at limiting the legal recognition of chiefs as owners in the sense of English law. But it conceded that they had political rights, as trustees for the community as a whole, and as allocators. The consequence of this was the conception that rights to land were acquired only through political allegiance. This concept of land tenure was part of a delicate political balance. As Meek explains, as the right to use land was dependent on allegiance to a chief, the authority of the chiefs, sub-chiefs, and heads of clan and family was bound up with the land. "The grant, therefore, to individuals of absolute rights of ownership would tend to disrupt the native polity, and so, too, would the indiscriminate sale of private lands by chiefs. The control of alienation of land has been in consequence one of the main planks of the British system of 'Indirect Rule'" (Meek [1946] 1968:10). The authority of the chiefs was maintained by their role as allocators of land, and so was the dependence of their subjects. Exploitation was to be curbed by not allowing the chiefs the right to sell land, and, by the same means, curbs were to be put on the freedom of the subjects, by preventing them from buying land.

This general paradigm was given legal endorsement by the Privy Council in cases worth rehearsing because they provided the legal framework and touchstone within which land policies were evolved in British Africa. In the Southern Rhodesian land case the Privy Council rejected the notion that the Ndebele could have had individual rights in land. It is important to understand the political context in which the ruling was made. The British South Africa Company, which had conquered, and then ruled, Rhodesia claimed that it owned the lands on the basis of cession by Lobengula, the ruler of the Ndebele. The Aborigines Protection Society intervened on behalf of the Africans of Southern Rhodesia, claiming that Africans had rights, which had not been ceded. The Crown contested both these claims (Chanock 1977a; *In re Southern Rhodesia 1919 A.C.*, 215–16, 233–34). It was important to ascertain whether the rights held by Africans were the kind of individual rights of ownership recognized in English law, because if they were, they would not, according to established international law, be affected by a change in sovereignty. If they were lesser rights, the land became the Crown's on conquest. The Privy Council approached the question in terms of social evolution. It found that Southern Rhodesian Africans had no individual rights in land. The legal authority with which it fortified itself was South African. Innes C.J. (Chief Justice) was credited with having found that for the Ndebele, "the notion of separate ownership in land or of alienation of land by a chief was foreign to their ideas" (*Hermansburg Missionary Society v. Commissioner for Native Affairs 1906 T.S., 135 at 142*). Between the English and the Ndebele, said the Privy Council, "there was in all juridical conceptions, a great gulf fixed, which it would, perhaps, be only fanciful to try to span." Some tribes were so low in the scale of social organization that it would be "idle to impute to [them] some shadow of rights known to our law and then to transmute it into the substance of transferable rights as we know them."

This view received endorsement and elaboration by the Privy Council two years later (*Amodu Tijani v. Southern Nigeria (Secretary) 1921 A.C.*, 399.) Lord Haldane, who briefly canvassed Indian and Canadian Indian community titles, quoted with approval the 1898 Report on Land Tenure in West Africa which declared that "individual ownership of land is quite foreign to native ideas. Land belongs to the community, the village and the family, never to the individual." All members of the community had "an equal right" but "in every case" land was controlled or allocated by the chief or headman. In Southern Nigeria, said Haldane, "a full usufructuary title rests in a chief on behalf of the community of which he is the head." These rights had been recognized "as the outcome of deliberate policy." Even where machinery had been established for defining the rights of individuals, it had not been directed to the modification of the usufructuary rights. And, even where individuals in Lagos held land as individuals under Crown grant, it reverted to the customary regime on their death (404–05).

This sweeping endorsement of the rights of the polity over the individual was generalized empire-wide by the Privy Council five years later (*Sobhuza II v. Miller and others 1926 A.C., 518 at 525*). Lord Haldane said that for "the true character of native title to land throughout the Empire including South and West Africa with local variations the principle is a uniform one....The notion of individual ownership is foreign to native ideas. Land belongs to the community not to the individual." But this title was not itself absolute. "The title of the native community generally takes the form of a usufructuary right....Obviously such a usufructuary right, however difficult to get rid of by ordinary means of conveyancing, may be extinguished by the action of a paramount power which assumes possession of the entire control of the land." The rationalized legal regime, therefore, recognized neither individual nor community ownership; all was subject to a hierarchy of powers of allocation, at the pinnacle of which was the Crown. Two further points might be made. The first is the very narrow empirical base on which these sweeping views rested: in essence they were derived from the basic philosophical models I have outlined earlier. The second is their empire-wide application and relevance. While "law in action" derives its meaning from local situations and conflicts, we must not lose sight of the general overarching legal framework as a major ingredient of each situation.

Communalism, Individualism, and Administration

Against this background of notions of African economic behavior, and the powers of chiefs, the colonial legal system etched its version of the customary land law, a version essentially necessitated by the need to validate early land alienations. The summoning into existence of the customary regime was hugely convenient, for to treat indigenous rights as if they were the equivalent of rights recognized in English law would have created a plethora of embarrassing problems. And to treat Africans as people who had not "evolved" the institution of private property in land not only gave vastly greater scope to the state, but it also functioned as a powerful ideological criticism of African societies. Individual title could be thought of as a distant goal of policy, while in the meantime the colonial regimes would handle land in the best interests of the population. Attempts to assert individual rights could gain no recognition because they were by definition not legal. Furthermore administrative and anthropological research appeared to confirm the lawyers' paradigm. Cheater has pointed out that "anthropologists concerned with property law in colonial Africa tended to take for granted its existence at a particular point in time," and that they emphasized "the institutional duality of colonial and indigenous assumptions and procedures concerning property," failing to take into account how the law was generated in particular contexts (Cheater 1987:173). I think it is fair to say that, taken as a whole, the anthropological writing about tenure did not come to grips with analysis of the circumstances in which the picture of the customary world was being produced. But the subjects of their research were acutely aware of contexts. The pictures they produced of the customary world, both the dominant "communal" one, and one which sometimes legitimated individualism, were pointedly political. They knew, to borrow Kandawire's words "how subordinate the system of customary land was and how futile it is to discuss it outside the all embracing colonial situation" (Kandawire 1980:136).

Colonial research into, and discussion of land tenure, took place in a highly politicised context. Corporate and settler ambitions to limit African landholding and secure that of Europeans were met with the immense resentment and anxiety of peoples already displaced and of people fearing further loss of their most essential resource. In the politics of the colonial situation discussion of land rights had, realistically, to be in terms of groups. The land, as Africans emphasized over and over again was *ours*, not yours. Communalism, to Africans who asserted it, was a way of certifying African control of occupation, use, and allocation of land, rather than a description of rights exercised. Individualism was a code word for sale to Europeans. All enquiries about land during the colonial period were dominated by fears of land loss, and by subsidiary anxieties. As C. M. White observed, when investigating traditional systems of landholding in colonial Northern Rhodesia, assertions by the community of allodial ownership might be "motivated by such considerations as land shortage or fear of it. . . ." And there were other possibilities in a rapidly changing world such as "jealousy of more enterprising and successful agriculturalists" (quoted in Mvunga 1982:32). In colonies with settler communities like Northern and Southern Rhodesia and Kenya, all matters related to land and agriculture were dominated, from the African point of view, by the fears of further land loss. In Northern Rhodesia the powerful nationalist campaigns against agricultural improvement schemes were fuelled by the fear that the point of making Africans produce more from the land was to justify making less available for them (Dixon-Fyle 1977). Meek found that the fear that land might be used as a basis for taxation "may preclude close investigations into native systems of tenure or attempts to alter them" (Meek [1946] 1968:10). As liberal anthropologists built their versions of customary systems of tenure in this context, they too emphasized those features which would defend African land holdings—the rights of the group and the inalienability of rights. While the lawyers had erected their models to fit early land confiscations, Crown control and political powers, the anthropological rationales that reinforced the legal models were quite different, and were defensive of the post-confiscation status quo.

As British anthropological scholarship developed, it departed from the notion of universals in human economic behavior and institutions, and embraced a world of cultural specificity. Western terminology to describe African land systems was rejected; even analogies were considered dangerous, though, like the lawyers, some anthropologists found it hard to resist dabbling in feudalism. The problem was how to categorize African landholding without falling into what was now seen as the initial error of contrasting Western individualism with the "communism" of primitive societies. It had become perfectly and increasingly plain as experience of the societies under colonial rule accumulated that Africans were asserting individual claims and that they used land in individual ways. But nonetheless anthropologists sought ways to accommodate this with the original general picture of a communal regime. A 1966 conference on African customary law specifically rejected the notion that the individual rights exercised by Africans were much like the rights exercised in Europe (Gluckman 1969a:56–57). Schemes such as Gluckman's idea of a hierarchy of what he called estates of administration, which provided a framework in which to accommodate concurrent claims by superiors and subordinates, seemed to meet the conceptual needs (Introduction). As Sheddick felt able to write in 1954, the communal v. individual rights controversy had passed out of anthropological usage. The prevailing view was that there was no joint ownership except "within a strictly limited body of actual kindred." But this discovery of how people had been behaving during the colonial era did not lead to a concession that individual rights were legitimate in customary tenure. The polity replaced the community as the ultimate respository of rights. Individual rights, as Sheddick said, were subordinate to "tribal" ones; the "diadic approach finally crystallised into the concept of society holding as the basis of collective or public control, a superior tenure within which there exists a multiplicity of private rights and interests." The right to use land, he urged, depended on political allegiances. There were thus two aspects to a study of land rights: the right to use, and the right to administer. *"In this way ownership resolves itself into administration,* that is the trusteeship, apportionment and regulation of the use of the land" (Sheddick [1954] 1970; my italics). This was perhaps the ultimate statement of the colonial state's view, a total rejection of rights existing beyond administration.

Ideas like these and the lawyers' paradigm of "estates of benefit and estates of control" are evidence of the desire to systematize, to treat the competing rights and interests which had developed in the colonial economy as if they represented the logic of a system, when they really were evidence of the opposite of a system, of a struggle between different interests to position claims as legitimate in the eyes of the colonial government. In analysis representative of the lawyers' view, Allott set out the main features of African land tenure late in the colonial period. The basic point was the dominant role of groups and communities in tenure, with the rights of individuals being limited to the use of family property and dependent on membership of the political community. This system went together with shifting cultivation, subsistence agriculture, lack of fertilization or improvement of land, and a relative abundance of it. Titles were impermanent and boundaries undefined. Most important there were no commercial transactions in land, there being no need and no demand (Allott 1970). But, he noted, while this system remained "in full or partial operation," land tenure was "a most explosive subject" and inter-tribal and inter-racial feeling were at their highest when land was involved. For this reason and because of the pressures of the commercialization of agriculture, development of the land tenure system was essential. Population pressue, land scarcity, and the growth of cash cropping were strengthening the position of the individual against both family and political authorities. Titles were becoming more certain and more static, and commercial dealing in land was growing.

The question of how to respond to the growing assertion of individual rights, and especially to the sale of land, became the crucial terrain of conflict over customary tenure. For it seemed fairly plain that this was not customary behavior, and therefore not legitimate for Africans to engage in. It appeared to offend against both the legal and the sociopolitical regimes of colonialism and against the view of African social institutions sanctioned by both conservative administrators and liberal anthropologists. When Meek wrote that in many parts of Africa "the holders of usufructuary rights in land are now endeavouring to convert them into indefeasible titles and are arming themselves with bogus deeds often obtained from bogus lawyers at considerable expense" (Meek [1946] 1968:235), it is clear that to him it was more than the deeds that were bogus, it was the whole process and the motivations of the actors. This process of assertion of individual rights has also generally been reproved in retrospect by historians. Typical is Boahen's summation: "the commercialisation of land...led to the illegal sale of communal land by unscrupulous family heads" (Boahen 1985:794). As we will see below, few supported Allott's call for a swift legal accommodation to these developments. Meek thought that the "confusion" reigning in African systems of tenure was not traceable to the customary systems in which ideas were neither vague nor ill defined, but were due to new economic conditions and legal conceptions "to which the indigenous systems have not yet had the time to make the necessary accommodation" (Meek [1946] 1968:235).

Individualizing Rights in Land

We must now look more closely at the question of the connection between the colonial regime of customary law, and the idea that individualization and commercial dealing in land were essentially non-African. "Among the Barotse and the Tswana," wrote Gluckman, "land could not be sold traditionally, *and could not under the colonial regimes because of policies establishing African reserves*" (Gluckman 1969b:56; my italics). In precolonial times there had been no market, but in the colonial period it was government prohibition that stood in the way of sales. Prohibitions of this sort were introduced early and widely in British colonial Africa because people did not behave traditionally. What could be done under customary law in land dealings became subject to close and detailed control and definition by colonial government. In the first place we must realize that any kind of rights in *land* were really a product of the new colonial state. As Gluckman pointed out, in Lozi society the law of property was "intricately intertwined" with that of status, and a man's relationships "run through his chattels as well as his land" (Gluckman 1969b:261−62). Or, in Bohannan's terms, people had "traditionally seen land and kinship in a single set of images," thinking in terms of a social map, rather than a geographical one (Bohannan 1964:139, 146). Rights in specific pieces of land were of brief duration during cultivation, but people always had rights in the "genealogical map" of their lineage. The important rights were, therefore, interpersonal; through them access to land was reached and proved. The Tiv, he wrote, had great difficulty with emerging notions of property in the new agricultural economy, "for they believe that to attach people to a piece of land is tantamount to disavowing his [sic] rights in social groups. Hence any notion of landed property is resisted. Not incorrectly, Tiv view 'property' in land as the ultimate disavowal of their social values" (Bohannan 1963: 109−10). But the colonial state transformed the nature of rights. It, rather than the lineages, became the source and guarantor of whatever rights it deemed to be customary.

There are other ways too in which the basis of the old system was being undermined. The idea of the *pax Britannica*, of which much was made during the colonial period, has justly become unfashionable. But whatever new parameters of violence with regard to dispossession of land and forms of forced labor were created by colonialism, a new form of security led to great changes in patterns of land use and residence. In many parts of Africa people spread from fortified villages and hilltop settlements to cultivate lands they had been unable to use safely before. Colonial governments had to resort to compulsory villagization to concentrate populations for administrative purposes. New lands were opened up by people no longer dependent on immediate kin for security. These conditions led the colonial regimes to fall back on an emphasis on the chiefs' political control over lands in order to maintain a system of local political control. But the circumstances also meant that the users of land could assert new rights. We can see not a sudden abandonment of the "social map" but distinct changes in it, as well as a readiness to make it subject to new economic opportunities.

Among the first questions to emerge were those of permanence of occupation, and of inheritance. Relative permanence in the right to use, and the right to bequeath land, were both conceded, or recognized, by colonial governments, as being part of a customary regime far more readily than other rights. Colonial

administrative policies made village sites more permanent; new agricultural techniques, such as the use of ploughs and the introduction of new crops, all created
the conditions for the recognition of rights of occupation different from those
within the customary system. Gradually the idea that African cultivators held
secure rights as individuals gained acceptability, though the rights recognized
were still characterized as usufructuary. The establishing of permanent rights
itself depended on the state, for otherwise, as Lambert remarked with a nice note
of realism, "perpetuity is a function of the memory of the local residents" (Lambert
[1947] 1970:379).

The developing customary law then had to devise an answer to the question
of whether these rights could be bequeathed, and by whom to whom. This issue
became a part of the broader struggle over the reshaping of the social map. I have
described elsewhere the issues raised in the process of the narrowing of circles of
economic obligation (Chanock 1991) and it is within this bitterly contested arena
that the customary law of inheritance of property in land is created. The tension
between the ideology of the larger group, and the economic ambitions of many of
its members, is reflected in the tensions between the official version of customary
rights in land, and the rights for which many were actually striving. In the
process of the "narrowing of kinship circles," as Lambert wrote, "one of the
fastest losers is undoubtedly community in land" (Lambert [1947] 1970:383).
Demands for the partition of land came frequently to both customary and colonial
courts, particularly once cash crops were introduced. This should not be seen as
something that occurs gradually, towards the end of the colonial period as the
result of a long evolution. In West Africa the Northern Nigerian Lands Committee
noted in 1908 that "group conceptions are being eroded by individual claims," as
soon, that is, as these claims could be made (Macdowell 1969:269). In areas where
cocoa was introduced, Meek pointed out, "lands begun to be freely partitioned
towards the end of the last century." In 1912 the Planters Union stated that an
inheritor's share became "his, absolutely, to do what he likes with" (Meek
1957:298).

But there was also spirited opposition to individuation within African societies. And it is here that we get to the heart of the problem of how to
characterize customary land tenure. We must step back from systemization, and
distance ourselves from those ideologies of traditional communalism espoused
by policy makers, anthropologists, and Africans. Our questions must be instead
about specific conflicts of interest about land during the colonial period. Just who
was pressing for a greater individualization of rights? What sort of new rights (if
any) did they have in mind? Who was resisting this pressure and why? As Meek
noted, there were "two distinct tendencies" at work. "On the one hand, there is a
widespread tendency towards the partitioning or individualisation of lineage
lands." On the other hand, "A lineage will usually postpone a legal partition of
its lands as long as possible since it is realised that ownership in common of
undivided land is the most powerful means of preserving the unity and strength
of the lineage." Furthermore, "there is a tendency for lineage claims to land to
become consolidated — to become proprietary instead of usufructuary" (Meek
1957:299, 297). The complex development of the West African law of family
property by the colonial courts must be understood in this context. The new
customary law evolved by the courts was more sympathetic to family claims than

to individual ones, and complex analogies with corporate rights in property in English law were employed to give respectability to the policy-oriented law which was generated. In the different contexts of East and Central Africa this kind of litigation was not a feature of the development of land law in the colonial period, and there the dominant input remained that of the administration rather than the courts.

Even more difficult to deal with than conflicts over partition at death were the developments in the areas of leasing, mortgage, and sale (though the use of these words suggests a specificity of ideas and practices that did not reflect reality). Here too we must pose our questions in terms of conflicts of interest rather than customary v. non-customary behavior. We have noted the fundamental concerns of the colonial governments about these matters: a fear of social dislocation, often cast in a protective framework of concern over the creation of an indebted peasantry and a landless class. These forebodings began early in the colonial period and were fuelled by the experiences on the broader scale in the Indian empire, and in the African context, of Zanzibar in the 1930s. Writing after the Second World War, Meek worried about the "new disparity in the division of land. Wealthy natives have been buying up large areas, and planting them.... These new capitalists, if unchecked, may acquire, as their own, land which is now in the public domain." He foreshadowed debt, landlessness, and "all the other evils which accompany the freedom to traffic in land." Colonial governments were giving consideration to "the desirability of legislation to control the sale and mortgage of land, prohibit its acquisition by absentees, to limit the maximum and minimum acreage of native holdings" (Meek [1946] 1968:96). Extensive legal intervention by the state was consistently proved to be necessary to maintain the customary regime. Native authorities and district officers were given wide powers to check dispositions of interests in land.

Rights, Interests, Gender, and Life-cycle

The general interests of the colonial regime in withholding from Africans the right to deal with land commercially seem well established. The legal fiction of maintaining a customary regime was a part of the policy of creating, controlling, and subsidizing a particular type of peasantry (Bohannan 1964:140). But how can we approach the question of sale in the customary law from the African side? One of our problems is how to find what law "is" (or "was"). We need to qualify a picture in which courts, or commissions, or panels, objectively "discover" what law is, or what rights exist "out there." A fundamental part of this discovery is the political situation in which they operate, and the interplay between the interests of governments, courts, commissions, informants, and the interests of those being adjudicated on or enquired into. To these we must add the overall ideological positions according to which these expressions of interests are rendered into coherence. Neither the reports of commissions, nor those of courts, nor the "raw material" of informants' statements and opinions, are a discovery of law. Common law jurisprudence has been comfortable with this position for a long time. It no longer pretends that common law courts simply "find" law. It knows that they "make" it by choosing among a range of possibilities what to "find."

We must apply this same analysis of process to the commissions of enquiry into land law, to the findings of scholars, and to the assertions of those whose law it was.

Assertions about the nature of what could legitimately be done with land could only be made by Africans during the colonial period if presented in terms of what had been sanctioned by custom. Only in this way could the assertion be heard as valid by the colonial rulers, and in this way too it could summon up reserves of ideological support in African communities. With this in mind, what can be done with the overall picture that land belonged to the community, and the powerful claim that it could not be sold, bearing in mind that as soon as it was possible to do so large numbers of people readily thought that other ways of dealing with land were legitimate? Each situation has really to be examined in its own terms if the details of the interests being expressed are to be understood, but here some generalities can be attempted. One might note first that there is not necessarily a correlation between the developments of cash cropping, a peasantry eager to acquire more land, and the discarding of the whole of the "customary" societal package. When I looked at the development of the "customary" law of persons in terms of the need to control household labor in the cash economy, it appeared to be the case that those who were doing economically well within the limits imposed by the colonial regime were those who had the most interest in promoting a "customary" view of control of persons, a view, that is, that could be presented and validated in custmary terms (Chanock 1985). But the same people would not necessarily adhere to a completely customary package with regard to land. I have also pointed to the widespread rejection of the customary law of marriage especially by those who had little stake in the rural social order. But with regard to land, these seem to be the people who would most readily defend the customary view, to preserve the possibility of establishing a claim to an increasingly scarce resource. Then we might consider the position of the large numbers who migrated between the urban and rural worlds. A customary view of the law of persons protected their "home" marriages, but was ignored by them in towns. A customary land law was vital to preserving their inalienable claim as a member of the community to land at home but, where the migrants were financially successful, stood in the way of their acquisition of more and better land. Class is better used not as an indicator of who would and who would not endorse a customary world view, but as a guide to which features of the customary package would appear essential. But, broadly speaking, it appears to be a starting point to see a customary law of persons being endorsed by those at the top of the social and economic order in colonial African societies and rejected by those beneath, while the position with regard to a customary land law would be reversed.

Many qualifications would need to be made. One would be to take our focus back from the wider perspective of class to the world of family and life-cycle. The assertions about rights in land would seem to depend on when they are being made. In particular the definition of rights on death, when an inheritance is in dispute and complex questions of expectations and family solidarity and emotions are involved, might be quite different from the rights proclaimed in response either to new economic opportunities, or outside challenge from settlers, or government-inspired development and reallocation schemes. A cultivator might say "mine" when title was challenged, or if it was advantageous to sell or mortgage, may think in terms of "ours" — in terms of nuclear family — when asserting a right of inheritance against a larger group of kin, or "ours" — in terms of a lineage — if the claimant was outside the lineage (as a spouse might be). Ideas about entitlement to family property are not really legal descriptions in any culture. There are also different generational influences on the claims of rights. If it became accepted that land belonged to the user and that the rights in it automatically devolved on death, elders would lose an important part of their control over the acquisition of rights by the next generation. This control was ensured if the property could be represented as "family property", reverting to the "family," however defined, for redistribution. Conversely, where land is becoming scarce, and there are increasing claims to permanent occupation and ownership made by the established generations, the young would need to assert "customary" communal rights to preserve their chances of acquiring and holding land.

Also of vital importance for the framing of "customary" definitions was the question of gender. We must think about the effects on womens' rights in land of over half a century of defining customary law. The ambivalence of the colonial regime towards the recognition of male rights in land was not a problem when it came to women: the customary law regime of the colonial states did not accommodate at all the idea of women as landowners. As development and improvement came to be a focus of colonial policy this became very clear. Claims by women, in the name of custom, were viewed with impatience as an impediment to the development process. At first colonial governments gave the question little thought: it was, as Meek put it in 1946, "a subject to which little attention has been paid." In a recent survey on the Gold Coast, he recounted, the government had been "surprised" to find that nearly 40 percent of the independent cocoa farmers were women (Meek [1946] 1968:8). This grew from an irritation produced by surprises to something of an obsession. In matrilineal areas the rights exercised by women were seen as an obstacle in the way of the creation of a proper system of land tenure. "The men are a floating population," wrote Lambert Stokes, "and it is the women who are tied to the land. Family life is unstable and there is no solid ground to build a modern form of land tenure" (quoted in Pachai 1973:697). The matrilineal system, as I have pointed out, was seen as part and parcel of backwardness, as a man had no incentive to improve land "over which he had tenuous and transitory tenure and no prospect of handing it on to his son" (R. W. Kettlewell, quoted in Chanock 1977b:404).

To pursue this question we must go back to the connections between land rights and status. Rights to use land were connected with marriage. In some places a woman acquired rights to use lands in her husband's place of residence through marriage — rights that were forfeited if the marriage dissolved. In other places it was the husband's rights which were so acquired and extinguished. Under the colonial system it was far more likely that male rights of use could become hardened into permanence regardless of the continuation of the marriage than womens' rights. Men found it easier to establish their rights to retain land when marriage ended than women did, especially where colonial regimes recognized a customary right established by clearing the land. While husbands retained rights in land they had cleared, they also began to assert ownership of land cleared by women on the grounds that it had been done as part of the performance of the duties of a wife (Mvunga 1982:42−43, 45). As land became a scarce resource, the capacity of married women to acquire their own lands was "severely curtailed" by the growing reluctance of husbands to acknowledge that wives had their own fields. If women returned to their parents' villages at the end of marriage they would, in any case, have to leave their fields behind, and, even where distances were not great, might be refused the right to cultivate by the headman on the grounds that they were no longer resident.

Customary Law and the Colonial Context: Central Africa

It is clear that the story of the formation of the customary land law during the colonial period must take into account the developing gender struggle over land, just as it must consider conflict between generations. The entrenchment of the idea of the right to allocate land is a part of these struggles. But perhaps a greater emphasis should be placed on the colonial context in which these conflicts took place. The "rightlessness" of women that results from the development of the colonial land regime is but a part of the overall story of the interweaving individualization, protective and communal ideologies, the development ethos, and the facts created by the early colonial land grab. By focusing a little more closely on Central Africa, it might be possible for me to bring out some of these themes with greater clarity.

Two features dominate the context in which customary tenure was approached and defined. The first was the question of the validity of the original land concessions, and the second the creation of a segregated system of landholding, with African land holding confined to or "protected in" Native Reserves, trust lands, or other legally segregated areas. The early legal enquiries into the nature of indigenous tenure took place because of the need to determine the validity or otherwise of "concessions" and grants of land made by chiefs in the early years of colonial contact. The focus was on what rights could be derived from grants of land made by chiefs, and the answer was, as we have seen, to endorse a view of the customary regime that would support the validity of those grants. Where ultimate control of the land had been considered to rest on conquest, as in Southern Rhodesia, we have seen that the Privy Council took the view that the Ndebele had no adequate concept of ownership. But where, as for example in Nyasaland, the rights of the Crown and settlers depended on the validity of the grants from the chiefs, the Nyasaland High Court held that the chiefs and people were sufficiently civilized to understand the concept of ownership of land and to transfer good title, for to hold otherwise "would at once raise up the ghosts of long decided legal question involving title" (Nunan J. in *Supervisor of Native Affairs v. Blantyre and East Africa Ltd.* [Nyasaland, 1903]; Mvunga 1982:10). The image of the system was repeatedly etched in official documents. The chief secretary of the Northern Rhodesian government told the North Charterland Enquiry in 1932 that African land was "vested in the chief, to be allotted by him in accordance with the needs of the tribesmen..." and that, while it was individually used, it reverted to the chief when abandoned (quoted in Mvunga 1982:15). The observable facts of individual use could not be converted into individual rights without undermining the whole basis of the validity of the concessions. Thus the two apparently contradictory features of individual use and "communal" ownership were put together as if they were mutually supportive parts of an indigenous system. A Northern Rhodesian government Select Committee in 1945 put the pieces together: "native land tenure...can be described as communal ownership by the tribe vested in the Chief, coupled with an intensely individual system of land usage. Every individual member of the tribe has the right to as much arable land as he needs for himself and his family, and as long as he is making use of this land he enjoys absolute legal security of tenure.... The European conception of individual ownership of land has no part in the traditional system of land tenure" (Mvunga 1982:17). If we are to understand the need to imagine this odd system with its mixture of chiefly powers, communalism, individual use and security, but no ownership, we must remember again that African landholding was effectively confined to areas designated for African occupation. To imagine individual rights inside reserves creates the possibility of conceiving of such rights having existed outside them, and also the potential for Africans to demand legitimately and to establish such rights in European areas. Only if the indigenous system were different from the British one could the validity of a segregated property regime be maintained. The reserves had, therefore, in terms of property law, to be reserves of the rightless, legally dependent on chiefs and communalism, in spite of observed patterns of usage. That this was fundamentally in the interests of the existing African polities hardly needs emphasizing.

Those who investigated the land systems had no difficulty in determining how land was used. Writing in 1945, Gluckman refuted the ruling paradigm. He identified two fundamental errors: the first was that land rights were communal and that all members of a community had equal rights to land use; the second was that chiefs were allocating overlords. The working of the land and the appropriation of its products were "highly individualistic." Every type of African land tenure was reducible to the ownership of specific rights by individuals, "securely held" (Gluckman 1945:8, 10−11). Gluckman drew his support from local studies of land tenure by Godfrey Wilson and Lucy Mair. There was no division in the anthropological observation on these points. White's investigations in the 1950s confirmed that rights over arable land "are essentially individual − acquired by the individual, enjoyed by him, and disposed of by him" (White [1958] 1970:257). Not only was the "tribe" an inappropriate group to conceive of as a holder of rights, but so too was the family, unless reference was meant to the "natural family" of man, wife and children. "The sum total of rights which make up the features of African land tenure in Northern Rhodesia can only be regarded as equivalent to individual tenure" (White, quoted in Mvunga 1982:17).

But this observed pattern of individual usage and rights was not acknowledged to be "ownership" in law, nor allowed to develop into it. Gluckman combined his discovery of individual rights with an insistence that they depended on membership of the political community, and the importance of the connection he saw between being the subject of a chief and having the right to use land was honed into his concept of a "hierarchy of estates," which I have discussed above. White, on the other hand, found no hierarchies of authority to allocate, even among those with a strong history of political centralization (Mvunga 1982:20). But it was

Gluckman who was most in accord not only with colonial imagery, but with colonial policy. The concentration of villages, the statutory elevation of chiefs and headmen, the growing strength of ethnic identities — all gave a concreteness to the administrative model of customary law. Native Authority orders in Northern Rhodesia after the Second World War laid down that

> No person may start a garden without permission of the Headman and no headman may distribute gardens unless he has been allotted land for gardens by the Native Authority...(quoted in Allan 1948:93).

The hierarchy of estates did exist, perhaps not in precolonial societes in the way set out by Gluckman, but in the colonial administrative rules. Access to land was to be totally controlled administratively. Membership of the political community was now closely controlled. Transfer from one chief to another could only be achieved by written permission of the chiefs involved and had to be recorded by the district commissioner. A powerful allocatory regime had been summoned out of the disorderly and individualist assertion of rights in the real world. These developments must also be related to the context of the allocation of land to whites, and the creation of reserves. Africans could not now afford to admit that no one had rights over vacant lands until individuals asserted them by using it. Responses to queries about the nature of rights in land in the Reserves that was not being used were governed by the same consideration that fuelled the hostility to agricultural improvement schemes, the fear that more land would be taken for white use. Communal rights were therefore asserted, and were closely connected to ethnic identity and belonging to a particular polity as, in the conditions of increasing overcrowding (or fear of scarcity), the previously porous boundaries between villages and chieftaincies were vigorously enforced and transgression penalized.

Thus the experience of, and growing fears about, land shortage produced apparently contradictory images of the customary law: an emphasis on the security of individual title and a strengthening of claims to communal, lineage, and reversionary titles. Rights of all kinds over whatever lands possible were asserted to secure them against outside intrusion. Both the emphasis on individual rights and the assertion of communal ones were logical responses to the same situation. This logic is reinforced when we consider the assertion of another basic element of the customary law, the impossibility of sale. In many parts of Africa people readily extended their individual rights of use into an assertion of a right to buy land, once the political and economic conditions for a market in land had appeared. I have already said that sale was regarded with suspicion by colonial governments for much of the colonial period. Motivated partly by protective instincts, they refused to recognize the "illegal" sales entered into by their untraditional subjects. These were generally protective instincts, and the point must be made that land was usually sold by the economically distressed, not by the entrepreneurial in a developing market. In areas where there was substantial development of commercial farming, the interests of the successful clashed with the administrative image of customary law, and the emergence of negotiable family title in West Africa may be seen to be a way of reconciling different images of what was legitimate in customary terms. But in Central Africa it was, as noted above, fear of loss of land permanently to whites which dominated the production of the customary land law. Thus, in spite of individual acquisition and use of land, it was vigorously asserted that sale was impossible in customary law. This view became immensely significant ideologically. All over Zambia, Mvunga writes, "it is insisted, and there is thorough unanimity in this, that land cannot be, and is not sold" (Mvunga 1982:37). But the disputes that did arise over the legality of sales do indicate a difference of interests rather than a fundamental principle. Colson records a 1955 case in which the kinsmen of the seller contested his right to sell and remarks also that men were under pressure from potential heirs to prevent them from alienating land. On death the heirs claimed the right to revoke any dispositions. "This is due to land hunger rather than to any belief that land is sacrosanct..." (Colson 1960:304). The circumstances which created the assertion of the illegitimacy of sale weakened the potential for individual use to harden into a recognition of ownership. This added to the influence of the assertion of communal rights over vacant land, which, as Colson remarks "inhibited the development of individual rights in waste land because it was deemed that such rights encroached upon the ancient right of some community, lineage or 'tribal' polity" (Colson 1971:196).

Survey, Registration, and Definition

There is another aspect to understanding the entrenchment of the idea of customary land tenure, and this concerns the overall failure of the colonial states in Africa to survey land and introduce land registries (Simpson 1976). Because of the lack of accomplishment, this is a largely untold story, yet it is important to the assessment of the abilities of the colonial state that it left Africans essentially without creating the basis for the kind of legal land regime that at the outset had been believed to be both desirable and inevitable. Had this ambition been achieved, the creation of conditions for individual holding with legal security might well have had an influence on the development of ideas about legitimacy in landholding. It is impossible to assess what might have been the impact of a non-occurrence, but it is instructive nonetheless to think about the possibilities. If the colonial state had had not only the political desire, but more importantly, the administrative capacity and resources, to survey land and register titles, would a different kind of peasantry have emerged from the colonial period, one that would have confronted the development ambitions of the successor states from a different position? It had been initially envisaged that land would be surveyed and a Torrens-type land registry (that is, one in which the registration provided a legally indisputable title) introduced. Extensive efforts at survey were made, for example in Uganda, and on the Kenya coast, but, on the whole, the effort was simply too costly. Even where it was relatively advanced, ambitions soon retreated. The goal of a Torrens system retreated in favor of giving a possessory title, i.e. a title that could be challenged in court (Meek [1946] 1968:92−95). As the colonial period drew to a close, lawyers began to notice with some anxiety that little had been achieved. There were renewed calls for a registration of title based on the Torrens system (Bensti-Enchill in Cotran and Rubin 1970:261; Allott in Iliffe 1971:8). But what sort of rights could be registered?

Allott called for "a system of registration of title which would use predominantly English terms to describe customary interests in land and which should...enable land to be dealt with in ways such as lease or mortgage which derive from English law" and for a definition of ownership in predominantly English terms (Allott in Iliffe 1971; Allott 1970:265). But a land registry, registered titles, and a definition of ownership raised a specter of legality that ran quite contrary to the reign of colonial administration. Colonial government had been predominantly extra-legal; administrative "discretion," and not the promotion of legal rights had been its *modus operandi*. A published response to Allott's call sums up adequately. "For over 60 years," wrote S. R. Simpson, "Settlement Officers in the Sudan have been successfully determining ownership *without the help of any definition*, and in Kenya during the last five years, ownership of over a million plots has been decided by Committees. Even in West Africa...ownership has been determined in over 3000 cases in Lagos, and ownership is not defined." Allott's response was very much to the point. "Why should it be left," he asked "to the discretion of administrative officers what they place and do not place on the register?" (Allot 1970:267, 270; my italics).

Development and Land Tenure

As the colonial era began to move towards a close, the institutional, ideological, and political pressures for a legal recognition of "ownership" were weaker than those that favored the customary regime as it emerged to cope with a multitude of new pressures. The assumption of the primacy of the administrative goals of the state over the rights of the inhabitants, which had characterized colonial government, gained new edge and urgency as the development ethos became predominant. A sense of impatience with the idea of proprietal rights developed as they were subordinated to the goals of development. While at the beginning of the colonial era Africans were found wanting for not having a sufficiently developed sense of private property, at its end, they were judged for being too individualistic and fecklessly selfish. W. M. Macmillan, for example, prescribed a progam of far-reaching changes to address the problems of the "typical Africa" which was "neither South Africa nor Uganda, nor the economic whirlpools of the West Coast, but those almost amorphous communities whose people still use and enjoy the poor fruit of the land without any need to think about rules of tenure." "Less is now heard," he wrote, "of the need to solve African land problems on lines consonant with the law and custom of a time when the land alone had to provide a meagre subsistence for all." The future stability of Africa required more than an understanding of the old order; it needed "a clear appreciation of the new calls that are being made upon it [which] Governments should actively control and direct." Conservation, afforestation, fertilizing—all required a communal effort. But the image of a traditional community celebrated in the customary law was insufficient to meet his requirements.

> Africa is far from being a ready made community....Left to themselves, the younger school, already ardent for freehold, would saddle Africa with the worst abuses of African land systems; the older, jealous of their privileges, would allow the old forms to harden and fossilise. Africans in

general have a clear enough sense of *meum* and *tuum* but are weak in appreciation of truly common interests.

How the wheel had turned! In the new environment, in which the "object and test of sound land tenure must be more intensive use of the land," the problem was defined as reconciling "the reasonable rights of individuals with the continuance of a public control that will be more broadly based than the old family system" (Macmillan 1949:81−83).

I have quoted this at length because it so accurately embodies the tone of the final colonial years, and encapsulates the views that came to dominate the state's approach to land issues. The issue was no longer what rights peasants could be said to have in their land, but the urgent requirements of public control and government direction of a too-individualist and not sufficiently comunally-minded peasantry. The various strands that contributed to the hostility towards individual rights in land were now interwoven with the development ethos. Policies had to deal with overcoming the "diseases of land tenure" − fragmentation and multiple ownership. (Simpson 1976:239). Concepts, rights, and priorities on the ground were seen as an impediment to the primacy of the state's goals, a state of mind that was among the legacies of the colonial to the postcolonial state. There were different emphases within the common theme. Meek observed with protective regret that land was becoming "commercialised" and the basis of tenure individualized, and that "many peasants are becoming labourers on land which was once their own." The need was for "far more positive policies in the planning of land use; for the preservation and if possible the extension of community rights; for greater control over sale and mortgage...for the general building up of a tradition of good husbandry which will prevent the present occupiers from attempting to exploit their trust." There had to be more settled systems of holding land, a huge increase in acreages of crops grown, reduction of fallow periods − a new farming which would mean "extensive alterations in the methods of holding land" (Meek [1946] 1968:2, 5).

The strong sense of a coming crisis − of over-population, food production, agricultural methods, conservation, and class division in the African peasantry − was common to all the colonial analysts. But there was disagreement on strategy. Some continued to espouse freehold tenure as the key to increasing production (Chanock 1977b; Gertzel 1984). But there were important and overriding reservations. The most important was, as Meek put it, that freehold rights "tie the hand of government in all schemes of agricultural advance. Ignorant peasants armed with freehold rights may soon destroy the country's capital." On the other hand, "effective" state ownership assured the "maintenance of the fertility of the soil" (Meek [1946] 1968:6−8). This preoccupation dominated in Zambia. As White wrote, "unless the basic problem of introducing improved agriculture is tackled, no amount of innovations in land tenure will arrest the degradation of the soil" (White 1958:254). And so the idea grew that the legal nature of tenure was not a "real" problem, but a superficial preoccupation, which should give way to the serious issue of agricultural production, and that the rights according to which land was held should be contingent upon the priorities of development. This perception was also to carry over into the postcolonial development era. And then there was the question of stability. Freehold would not necessarily stabilize because it led to the growth of a landless class of laborers, and a difficult one of tenants. Peasant cultivators, with rights subject to the state, would seem to be the best subjects for development, and the most politically docile. In view of these considerations, it is not surprising that in most cases the colonial governments, already under severe political challenge from nationalist movements fuelled by anxiety over access to land, did not encourage the transition from the individual rights of use to a legal recognition of ownership.

The Image of Tenure and the Postcolonial States

The usefulness of the image of the customary law of land tenure was not lost on the rulers of the postcolonial states. Indeed the postcolonial period is important to an understanding of the firming of customary imagery. The ideologies, policies, and ambitions of the new states and governments have had a fundamental effect on the creation of knowledge about customary land tenure. The jurisprudence of the customary regime which developed closely followed the image that governments made necessary. Researchers, lawyers, and academics have often, in modern Africa, not worked in an effectively free, critical, and plural environment, and perhaps, even if they did, one should no more expect a scholarship separate from state ambitions to develop in the postcolonial than in the colonial periods. The new governments have commonly asserted a total control over the lands in the name of protection of African customs. A customary veil has been drawn over national confiscation of rights, and increasing scarcity and the inequality of existing holdings disguised by the assertion of fictive rights for all. Development has been seen very much as a state initiative and state control of land was therefore considered to be fundamental. This process has been commented on in relation to Senegal by Xavier Blanc-Jouvan (1972:223–25; 235–37). "It is this essential idea," he writes, "that allows today's Senegalese leaders to claim that they are returning to the old 'communalist principle' which is 'the ethical foundation of the nation' and which constitutes 'one of the components of negritude.'" The problem of restricting individual rights in land in the public interest was more easily solved where the rights were seen to be "only rights of usage and enjoyment granted by the group to the individual." The "demands of a planned and directed economy are perfectly consistent with the old communal concepts of customary law." In an intellectual atmosphere in which individual rights were "criticised and disparaged" in both France and Africa, the idea that the inevitable triumph of modern law was a necessary prelude to economic development gave way to an acceptance of a customary communalism.

The communal imagery of the customary regime was crucial to the enunciation of the development policies of Tanzania and Zambia. Julius Nyerere wrote in his essays on African socialism, "To us in Africa, land was always recognised as belonging to the community....The African's right to land was simply the right to use it; he had no other right to it, nor did it occur to him to try to claim one." Kenneth Kaunda's *Humanism in Zambia* proclaimed specifically: "Land, obviously, must remain the property of the State today. This in no way departs from heritage. Land was never bought. It came to belong to individuals through usage and the passing of time. Even then the chiefs and elders had overall control although...this was done of behalf of all the people" (quoted in Mvunga 1982:86–87). Both Zambia and Tanzania faced on independence the question of how to deal with legal regimes in which different racial groups held land under different tenurial systems. Both chose to continue the colonial policies which limited the legal rights Africans could exercise over land. James has written that the Tanzanian government was "unduly cautious," as in the traditional sector, the "ancient principles" had "by the time of independence given way to changes based on the private ownership concept in the face of (i) land scarcity, (ii) recent settlements because of population migration, and (iii) the introduction of permanent crops. Likewise landlord and tenant relationships had developed over the years..." (James 1971:21–22). Whatever the usefulness of the image of the customary regime, real customary law failed the government. In 1963 90 percent of the district councils in the country agreed to draft customary law rules which purported to secure to every Tanzanian over the age of 18 years the right to not less than ten acres of land, which was, as James points out, "inconsistent with the policy of socialisation of land tenure." And the widespread "illegal" dealings in land under the customary regimes demonstrated that "The traditional land controlling machinery is obviously unsatisfactory for implementing the government's land policies for fostering land use, preventing land accumulation, fragmentation and exploitation, and generally limiting the commodity aspect of land" (pp. 66–67).

In Zambia the beginnings of the postcolonial period were marked by a more defensive reaction to white pressures on land. There was considerable disquiet about the possibility that a new regime of tenure would, by encouraging purchase and sale, deprive Zambians of land in the interests of a white-dominated commercial agricultural sector. This contributed powerful support to the government's rhetorical endorsement of customary communalism, and an overall political power exercised by chiefs, now succeeded to by the state. But, as Mvunga writes, customary land tenure in Zambia could not justify the generalization that an individual's rights were derived from customary political authorities. "The only available argument consistent with 'heritage' relates to the prohibition of land sales. There is evidence that customary law does not recognize that land...is a saleable commodity for a cash consideration. The tenor of this proposition, of course, can only stand on the premise that customary law, in this respect alone, is not amenable to the pressures exerted by a cash economy" (Mvunga 1982:76, 86–88).

In Malawi too, the new land regime, though the product of a state with a different political and developmental philosophy, did not grant individual title to the land users. An allocatory regime, reflecting an image of custom, put power over landholding into the hands of state bureaucrats on local Land Boards, and family heads, who divided the shares of land allocated to families (Pachai 1973:696). Family members, in the customary regime, supposedly had a right to a share of family property, but there was, of course, no way in which they could secure their claims. What was referred to as "unallocated garden land" (Customary Land Development Act 1967, s 20) remained under a "customary" regime in that it could not be individually owned. But in relation to any land which came to be part of a development scheme, the customary powers of the *mwini dziko* or "owner of the land" were specifically abolished by statute. Furthermore any customary rights could be altered or terminated if deemed by the minister to be "uneconomic or inconvenient...or inconsistent with the development scheme"

(Adjudication of Title Act S9 [1] and 13[1]c). As in Zambia, the shadow of a customary regime usefully existed side by side with a large estate sector; rights in that sector were not subject to the same administrative fiat.

An indigenous *system* of land tenure did not exist under colonial conditions, but its shadow was summoned into existence by both colonial and postcolonial states, essentially to retard the establishment of freehold rights for Africans, in an economy which was otherwise becoming increasingly capitalist. The sharpest point of legalist dispute concerned the question of sale and purchase. Purchase did not normally provide an extra means of access to land for those without: essentially it was a means of adding to the holdings of the already successful, while sale was essentially forced by economic distress. On the one hand, the mythology that insisted that sale and purchase were not legitimate because they were not customary was a benign mythology. Yet, while my purpose is not to lament the cause of the lost Kulaks, I think it worth reflecting about the effects of the relegation of African populations to a form of legal rightlessness in land. The special African genius for communal rather than individual dealing with land can usefully be seen throughout the twentieth century as the state's myth, only marginally relevant to the rights and securities people have tried to establish. The insistence that African landholding remain within a customary legal regime has been as much a relegation as a protection. Not only have people been deprived of full land rights in terms of the dominant, imported legal system, the dominant system has distorted the rights recognizable and assertable in the customary one. The lack of security in landholding and occupancy is even more pointed in urban areas than in rural ones. "Illegal" dealings in land among the rightless squatters in the cities of East and Central Africa demonstrate the importance of the problem. The urban question should help to lend emphasis to my final aim, which is to draw attention to the political aspects of the land rights question. Legal rights in land need to be thought about in a context different from the one in which they have normally been placed — a sort of superstructural side-issue of development policy. We can think about them instead as central to the nature of the modern African polity, and the role of, and "rule of" law in African states. For these important economic, and ultimately political, rights, remain subordinate to an administrative regime, which offers landholders no rights as against the state. One need not espouse romantic ideas about rights, or the rule of law, to see that this has consequences for the political society.

SOURCES

Allan, William, et al. 1948. *Land holding and land usage among the Plateau Tonga of Mazabuka District*. Cape Town: Rhodes-Livingstone Institute/Oxford University Press.

Allott, Anthony. 1970. "Modern changes in African land tenure." In *Readings in African law*, See Cotran and Rubin 1970. 236–49. London: Frank Cass.

Bentsi-Enchill, K. 1965. "Do African systems of land tenure require a special terminology?" *Journal of African Law* 9:114–21.

Blanc-Jouvan, Xavier. 1972. "Problems of harmonisation of traditional and modern concepts in the land law of French-speaking Africa and Madagascar." In *Integration of customary and modern legal systems in Africa*, 216–38. New York: Africana.

Boahen A. Adu. 1985. "Colonialism in Africa: Its impact and significance." In *Africa under colonial domination 1880–1935*, ed. Adu Boahen, 782–809. Unesco General History of Africa, vol. 7. London: Heinemann.

Bohannan, Paul. 1963. "Land 'tenure' and land tenure." In *African Agrarian Systems*, ed. Daniel Biebuyck, 101–15. London: Oxford University Press.

———. 1964. "Land use, land tenure and land reform." In *Economic transition in Africa*, ed. Melville Herskovits and Mitchell Harwitz, 133–49. Evanston: Northwestern University Press.

Chanock, Martin. 1977a. "Agricultural change and continuity in Malawi." In *The roots of rural poverty in southern Africa*, ed. Robin Palmer and Neil Parsons, 369–409. London: Heinemann.

———. 1977b. *Unconsummated union: Britain, Rhodesia, and South Africa 1900–1945*. Manchester: Manchester University Press.

———. 1985. *Law, custom, and social order*: the colonial experience in Malawi and Zambia. Cambridge: Cambridge University Press.

———. 1991. "A peculiar sharpness: an essay on property in the history of customary law in colonial Africa." *Journal of African History* 32 (1):65–88.

Cheater, A. P. 1987. "Fighting over property: The articulation of dominant and subordinate legal systems governing the inheritance of immovable property among blacks in Zimbabwe." *Africa* 57(2):173–96.

———. 1990. "The ideology of 'Communal Land Tenure' in Zimbabwe: Mythogenesis Enacted?" *Africa* 60, 188–206.

Colson, Elizabeth. 1960. *The social organisation of the Gwembwe Tonga*. Manchester: Manchester University Press.

———. 1971. "The impact of the colonial period on the definition of land rights." In *Colonialism in Africa*, ed. Victor Turner, 193–215. Cambridge: Cambridge University Press.

Cotran, Eugene, and Neville Rubin, eds. 1970. *Readings in African law*. London: Frank Cass.

Dixon-Fyle, Maxwell. 1977. "Agricultural improvement and political parties on the Tonga Plateau, Northern Rhodesia." *Journal of African History* 14 (4):579–96.

Gertzel, Cherry. 1984. "East and Central Africa." In the *Cambridge history of Africa 8*, ed. Michael Crowder, 383–457. Cambridge: Cambridge University Press.

Gluckman, Max. 1945. "African land tenure." *Human Problems in British Central Africa* 3:1–12.

————, ed. 1969a. *Ideas and procedures in African customary law*. London: Oxford University Press.

————. 1969b. "Property rights and status in traditional African law." In *Ideas and procedures in African customary law*, ed. Max Gluckman, 252–65. London: Oxford University Press.

Iliffe, John. 1971. *The integration of customary and modern legal systems in Africa*. New York: Africana.

————. 1983. *The emergence of African capitalism*. Minneapolis: University of Minnesota Press.

James, Roden William. 1971. *Land tenure and policy in Tanzania*. Toronto: University of Toronto Press.

Kandawire, J. A. K. 1980. "Village segmentation and class formation in Southern Malawi." *Africa* 50(2):125–45.

Kettlewell R. W. 1965. "Agricultural change in Nyasaland." *Food Research Institute Studies* 5: (3):229–85.

Lambert, H. E. [1947] reprinted 1970. "Land tenure among the Akamba." In *Readings in African law*. See Cotran and Rubin 1970.

Macdowell, C. M. 1969. "The breakdown of traditional land tenure in Northern Nigeria." In *Ideas and procedures in African customary law*, 266–78. See Gluckman 1969a.

Macmillan, William Miller. 1949. *Africa emergent*. Harmondsworth: Penguin.

Macgaffey, Wyatt. 1970. *Custom, law and government in the lower Congo*. Berkeley: University of California Press.

Macpherson, Crawford Brough, ed. 1978. *Property: Mainstream and critical positions*. Oxford: Blackwell.

Maine, Henry Sumner. 1861. *Ancient law*. London: John Murray.

————. 1871. *Village communities in the East and West*. London: John Murray.

Meek, Charles Kingsley. [1946] reprinted 1968. *Land law and custom in the colonies*. London: Frank Cass.

————. 1957. "Land tenure and land administration in Nigeria and the Cameroons." In *Readings in African law*, 293–302. See Cotran and Rubin 1970.

Mvunga, Mphanza P. 1982. *Land law and policy in Africa*. Lusaka: Mambo Press.

Pachai, Bridglal. 1973. "Land policies in Malawi: An examination of the colonial legacy." *Journal of African History* 14(4):681–98.

Sheddick, V. [1954] 1970. "Land tenure in Basutoland." In *Readings in African law*, 258–59. See Cotran and Rubin 1970.

Simpson, S. Rowton. 1970. "Towards a definition of absolute ownership, II." In *Readings in African law*, 258–59. See Cotran and Rubin 1970.

————. 1976. *Land law and registration*. Cambridge: Cambridge University Press.

White, C. M. [1958] 1970. "Terminological confusion in African land tenure." In *Readings in African law*, 254–58. See Cotran and Rubin 1970.

White, Luise. 1983. "A colonial state and an African petty bourgeoisie: Prostitution, property, and class struggle in Nairobi, 1936–1940." In *Struggle for the city: Migrant labour, capital, and the state in urban Africa*, ed. Frederick Cooper. Beverly Hills: Sage.

Young, Roland, and Henry Fosbrooke. 1960. *Land and politics among the Liguru of Tanganyika*. London: Routledge and Kegan Paul.

The Rise of Taiwo Olowo: Law, Accumulation, and Mobility in Early Colonial Lagos

Kristin Mann

In the nineteenth century, Lagos underwent rapid and far-reaching change, which set the stage for the development of the twentieth-century city and laid its social as well as physical foundation. In 1800 the community was a small fishing, trading, and farming village, belatedly emerging as a center of the trans-Atlantic slave trade, although it had had earlier, limited contact with international trade (Newbury 1961:17–32; Law 1983; Adefuye 1987:39–43). A heterogeneous population of several thousand was ruled by a king, four classes of chiefs, and other appointed officials whose power and authority were highly fluid (Aderibigbe 1975:1–9; Smith 1979:2–17; Agiri and Barnes 1987:18–32). By 1900 Lagos had developed into an important port and a major commercial and colonial capital that linked European and African producers and consumers. A more cosmopolitan population of about 50,000 lived primarily by trade, although some fishing, farming, and craft manufacturing still occurred and wage labor was beginning to develop (Newbury 1961:49–61, 123–73; Hopkins 1964; Mann 1985:11–34). Great Britain bombarded Lagos in 1851, replacing a hostile king with a more compliant claimant. A decade later, Her Majesty's government annexed the town and surrounding territory and imposed direct colonial rule (Ajayi 1961:96–105; Smith 1979:18–33, 111–27).

Many forces fueled and shaped the transformation of Lagos's economy and society. The king, selected chiefs, and a few favored commoners and slaves dominated, if not monopolized, the slave trade, which augmented their wealth and power and increased economic and political differentiation within the town

(Hopkins 1980:782–83; Law 1983:343–48; Adefuye 1987:39–43). At the same time, the rise of the slave trade provoked conflict among local big men over the distribution of political power and commercial profits. This exacerbated rivalry within the royal lineage among claimants to the throne that erupted periodically into brutal civil war (Aderibigbe 1975:10–16; Oroge 1971:171–74; Smith 1979: 14–17; Law 1978:35–59). Equally important, the slave trade increased the size of Lagos's slave population. By 1850, greater than half of all Lagosians may have been of slave origin (Interviews: Iṣola Bajulaiye 1984; S. B. A. Oluwa 1985; A. L. A. Ojora 1984 and 1985; and A. W. A. Akibayo 1985).

As the growth of capitalism transformed Britain throughout the course of the eighteenth century, capitalists strove to adapt modes of organizing labor to the principles and demands of the capitalist economy. By the end of the century an increasingly influential sector of Britain's ruling class had come to view slavery as wrong and archaic and to advocate the economic and moral superiority of wage labor. In the early nineteenth century, Great Britain abolished her own slave trade and began pressuring other nations to end theirs (Davis 1975:349–460; Craton 1974:239–84; Temperley 1977:94–118; Cooper 1980:24–46). Reformers believed that abolishing the slave trade in Africa required creating new opportunities for local peoples to sell agricultural products to Europe (Buxton 1840). British officials cited the abolition of the slave trade and development of legitimate commerce as reasons for the annexation of Lagos (Smith 1979:120, 140; Cell 1970:274–83). By the middle of the nineteenth century, the trade in human beings along the Western Slave Coast was giving way slowly and fitfully to trade in palm produce — first palm oil and later palm kernels — for which there were growing markets in industrial Europe (Newbury 1961:34–76; Hopkins 1968:584–92; Manning 1982:9–17, 27–36, 50–6). Lagos's king and chiefs found the new trade in agricultural products less profitable than the old trade in slaves. To complicate their problems, legitimate commerce was more democratic than the slave trade. With relatively few barriers to entry, persons could begin selling palm produce on a small scale and, if diligent and shrewd, become highly successful. The new trade created opportunities for commoners and slaves independent of the king and chiefs, and it gave rise to new men and women of wealth and influence. It undermined the local rulers' economic base and control of slaves and other subordinates at precisely the moment when the bombardment and annexation had undercut their political authority (Hopkins 1980:782–83; Mann 1985:15–17; Mann forthcoming).

The introduction first of British consular authority and then of colonial rule stimulated the development of the new international trade and attracted to Lagos Brazilian and Sierra Leonean repatriated slaves and European merchants and missionaries (Kopytoff 1965:3–60; Verger 1968:753–630; Newbury 1961:77–96; Hopkins 1964:20–96; Ajayi 1965). Immigrants from the interior began to arrive in increasing numbers after mid-century, pulled by economic opportunity and pushed by wars in the hinterland. Population growth and commercial development combined to increase greatly the demand for land on which to build residences and storehouses. Immigrants from the interior obtained use rights to land from chiefly and other local families that owned it communally. Some Brazilians, Sierra Leoneans, and Europeans turned to the king for grants to land, which it is doubtful that he had the right to make. The repatriated slaves had become familiar with private property rights in Brazil and Sierra Leone. From the beginning they and the Europeans treated land grants from the king as giving them individual rights of absolute ownership, although local land tenure recognized no such rights. Soon after their arrival, repatriated slaves began buying and selling land. A market for real estate developed and land prices started to escalate. For the first time land began to be alienated and individually owned, and it started to have commercial value. The alienation, privatization, and commoditization of land were well underway. The new land rights did not supplant communal tenure, but rather coexisted with it. However, the original landowning families lost control of much of the most valuable property in the town before they realized its value (Mann 1987).

The new international trade was based almost entirely on credit, owing to a shortage of capital throughout the economy. European and African merchants extended credit to traders, who in turn offered it to other traders. In Yorubaland a great chain of credit linked all of the participants in the new international trade, from the local producers and consumers to the European, Sierra Leonean, and Brazilian exporters and importers (McPhee 1970:100; Newbury 1972:81−95; Mann 1987). From the beginning, merchants and traders had difficulty collecting debts. In the 1850s, they looked unsuccessfully to the king and chiefs to bring defaulters to terms. Later Sierra Leonean and Brazilian repatriated slaves established a short-lived and ineffective court to settle disputes involving debts (Newbury 1961:60−61; Smith 1979:36, 79; Adewoye 1977:46−47). To provide themselves a modicum of protection, merchants began demanding that traders pledge property as security for loans, and land quickly became the preferred form of collateral. Soon many traders themselves adopted this precaution. By the 1860s the practice of mortgaging land to get commercial credit had become widespread.[1] The more land persons could offer as security, the more credit they could get and the bigger their trading operations could grow. The link between land ownership and trading opportunities was close and real, and it provided a great incentive to acquire privately owned land.[2]

In the 1870s merchants and traders began charging interest on loans, and by the 1880s interest had become a common feature of the credit system. The interest on short-term (six to twelve month) loans varied in the early 1870s from 5 to 10 percent annually, but by the 1880s and 1890s it had jumped to a whopping 30 to 60 percent annually (mortgages, Lagos Land Registry). The practice of charging interest on commercial credit demonstrates that by the late nineteenth century commercial capitalism in Lagos had developed to the point that money itself had been commoditized. Interest on loans became an important source of income for those who had capital.

After the annexation, the colonial government set a high priority on furthering the development of the new international trade. Administrators believed this required creating a climate in which merchants and traders could feel secure about debts and property rights. The colonial government recognized grants of land from the king as conveying individual rights of absolute ownership, which European officials identified with progress and civilization and saw as essential to the growth of trade (Hopkins 1980:788−90). Within months of the annexation, the acting governor began granting land in the name of the crown, and by 1880 about 3,200 grants had been made. Later the government introduced compulsory registration of conveyances, mortgages, and other legal instruments pertaining to land (Elias 1962:316–18; Coker 1958:189–90; Simpson 1957:36–38). Slowly and cautiously Great Britain constructed a bureaucracy that assumed responsibility for most aspects of government (Smith 1979:126–27; Newbury 1961:79–95). More boldly, colonial officials extended English law to Lagos and introduced colonial courts with authority to settle disputes involving debt, property, and other civil as well as criminal matters (Elias 1963:17, 40–57; Adewoye 1977:31–136).

The king and chiefs survived alongside the new colonial government. The treaty of cession explicitly left the king authority "to decide disputes between natives of Lagos with their consent, subject to appeal to British laws" (Burns 1969:319). The Supreme Court Ordinance of 1876, which systematized the colony's judicial administration, held that nothing in it should deprive "natives" of the benefit of local law, providing it was not "repugnant to natural justice, equity and good conscience" or incompatible with colonial legislation and providing that the parties to disputes had not entered into any transaction on the basis of English law (Ordinance No. 4, 1876, in Richards 1894). The king and chiefs retained prestige and authority in the eyes of many Lagosians, and they continued to perform important political, judicial, and religious functions. However, there could be little doubt that ultimate political power and legal authority had now passed to the British.

As Lagos grew into an ever-larger and more important commercial and colonial capital, a market for rental property developed and this increased the value of land as an economic resource. Those who owned desirable property in choice locations found that they could realize sizable incomes from renting land and buildings. In addition, land values appreciated during the second half of the nineteenth century, making real estate a good speculative investment. When Lagos entered a long trade depression in the 1880s, renting property and buying land supplanted commerce as the most lucrative economic activities in the town, with the possible exception of lending money. By the end of the nineteenth century, owning land and controlling capital had become major forms of wealth and bases of inequality. Moreover, these two forms of wealth were closely related, owing to the organization and importance of the new credit system (Mann 1987).

Trade required the control of people as well as capital (Coquery-Vidrovitch and Lovejoy 1985). The volume of a merchant's or trader's turnover, and thus in part the amount of his profit, depended on the effectiveness with which he could organize distribution. Some wage labor existed in Lagos, particularly with the colonial government, missionary societies, European firms, and educated Africans, but labor was slower than land and money to commoditize. In commerce, the dominant economic activity, means other than wage labor existed for organizing distribution. Many African merchants and traders owned slaves who bought and sold goods for them, although after the annexation the owner-slave relationship became the focus of intense conflict and some slaves managed to redefine their status.[3] Merchants and traders also gave goods on credit to wives or other dependents who traded on their behalf in return for a share of the profits. Using slaves, wives, and dependents to move goods had the advantage that social relations underpinned and helped regulate the commercial relationship. A small amount of business was conducted on a cash basis, using either currency of bills of exchange. Many sales were to independent traders who bought goods on credit and then sold them, often also on credit, in Lagos and interior markets. Traders frequently could not repay their loans plus interest and retain sufficient capital to trade. Such persons needed to extend their credit regularly if they were to remain in business, and many became caught in a downward spiral of perpetual indebtedness. When this happened, traders lost their autonomy. They could not easily switch suppliers to obtain better prices, cheaper credit, or more attractive goods, but rather they were tied commercially to their creditors. Moreover, these traders sometimes found that creditors expected them to become loyal clients. Refusal could result in foreclosure. This would mean loss of landed property if the loan was secured and possible imprisonment if it was not.[4] The credit system itself gave those who commanded capital a means of mobilizing and controlling labor.

The penetration of Islam, which preceded 1850, and of Christianity, which followed it, introduced new religious and cultural values into Lagos (Gbadamoṣi 1978: Ajayi 1965; Ayandele 1966). Just how profoundly these two world religions altered the beliefs, understanding and behavior of the masses of converts remains an open question. However, each transformed the lives of some of its adherents. With Christianity came Western education, which brought new skills as well as new ideas. Literacy gave a few men the opportunity for more advanced education, which in turn offered the prospect of relatively secure and lucrative employment in the colonial service or one of the professions — law, medicine, or the ministry. But perhaps more important, advanced education ensured persons influence and opportunity in the growing colonial society, where both whites and blacks relied on educated Africans to perform vital services (Mann 1985:25−34; Ayandele 1974).

By the end of the nineteenth century Lagos was a different and more complex community than it had been at the beginning. New actors had burst on to the historical scene. New opportunities existed in trade, money-lending, and agriculture to earn income and accumulate wealth. New forms of land tenure had emerged and new mechanisms of credit mobilization had been forged, which altered the value and meaning of land and capital as economic resources. The redefinition of the owner-slave relationship and the arrival of large numbers of immigrants stimulated the development of new means of organizing labor and support. To complicate matters, the British had imposed new structures of political and legal authority, and some Africans found ways of working within them to pursue individual or communal ambitions. Finally, Islam and Christianity had introduced new religious beliefs and cultural values. A number of Lagos men and a smaller number of Lagos women were able to take advantage of the new opportunities to amass wealth and power and to redefine their position in Lagos society (Mann forthcoming). The remainder of this essay examines the life of one such man, Taiwo Olowo, to see how he achieved upward social mobility.

Taiwo was not a typical Lagosian, but he was archetypal. During the course of his life he rose from humble status to become one of the most powerful Africans in the community. Taiwo accumulated great wealth and used it to build a huge personal following of wives, children, slaves, clients, and other subordinates. He translated his wealth and following into influence with Europeans and control over other Africans. Manifesting what Karin Barber (1981:40) has called the Yoruba's "competitive ambitious ethos" and "dynamic impulse to self-aggrandizement," Taiwo personified one of the highest ideals of Yoruba culture: the self-made man. His experiences cannot be generalized. Few shared his precise circumstances, much less enjoyed his spectacular successes. Taiwo warrants investigation because of his historical significance and because he represents certain Yoruba ideals. An examination of his life, moreover, illuminates the mechanisms of accumulation in late nineteenth-century Lagos. It shows how a rising big man used his wealth and power, uncovering his values and aspirations as well as his strategies for mobility. The essay also probes the way legal changes in colonial Lagos affected Taiwo's life. It demonstrates the advantage he took of new property rights, contractual agreements, bureaucratic structures, and judicial proceedings in his quest of self-advancement.

Data about Taiwo's life come from government dispatches, missionary records, private correspondence, and newspapers, standard sources for colonial African history. More significantly from the point of view of this volume, they also come from the wealth of little-used legal records that exist for Lagos and some other parts of colonial Africa. These records include the Judges' Notebooks of Civil and Criminal Cases from the Lagos Supreme Court, which date from the 1870s and contain extensive notes in English on the testimony of litigants and witnesses in all cases heard by the court.[5] Lagos's legal records also include instruments pertaining to land: Crown grants, conveyances, and deeds of gift.[6]

Colonial legal records have limitations, as do all historical sources. Crown grants and conveyances contain too little information about both the persons and property involved in transactions to be very useful on their own. Moreover, conveyances and mortgages are incomplete. Many parties to land deals either did not execute written documents or failed to record them at the land office. The judges' notebooks are more complex than the land records, and they present at once more difficult and more interesting problems of analysis. Records of court cases are more relevant to certain kinds of research than to others. The bulk of the civil cases, for example, deal with debt and property, although a wide range of other matters came less commonly before the court. Debt and property cases themselves illuminate a host of related issues: trade, credit, inheritance, slavery, gender, kinship, and magic to name but a few. The civil court records are biased towards persons of wealth and education, however, much less so than I had expected. Slaves, paupers, women, and others who were socially disadvantaged came before the supreme court; indeed, its records constitute one of the few sources of detailed information about the historical experiences of such groups. Generated through the process of dispute, court records could leave the researcher with an exaggerated picture of conflict. They reveal little about the many Lagosians who avoided the problems that drove litigants to court or who resolved such problems without recourse to legal action. Moreover, the supreme court records might easily create a misleading impression of the process of dispute itself. Illiterate Lagosians took grievances to the courts of the elders, chiefs, and *Oba* or king, far more often than they did to the colonial courts. Some litigants in the supreme court had earlier aired grievances in a Yoruba tribunal, and the judges' notes often contain information about what happened before the indigenous authority. Thus the records illuminate the workings of the Yoruba courts that existed unofficially alongside the colonial courts. Read uncritically, however, the documents would give a mistaken impression of the relative importance in local culture of Yoruba and colonial forums for dispute settlement.

Court records also present other subtler problems. Testimony was usually given in Yoruba and then translated into English by a court interpreter for the judge, who took notes on the case. The words that come down to us are at best one and often two removes from the person who spoke them. They represent one European account of what went on in the court room. If we had accounts by African participants, they might read very differently. To interpret the disputes one must weigh conflicting and sometimes contradictory testimony of litigants and witnesses without the benefit of intonation, look, gesture, and other behaviour that helped contemporaries make sense of it. The mere fact of appearing in the supreme court affected what persons said and how they said it. Rules of evidence and procedure shaped the presentation of legal arguments, as did the presence of judges, clerks, and lawyers.

Granting these limitations, legal records constitute, if used carefully, an exceptionally rich source for the study of colonial African history. The documents yield unparalleled data about changes in the organization of trade, production, and labor that accompanied the penetration of European capital. They illuminate the struggle over resources and labor among and between Africans and Europeans that lay at the heart of the shaping of the colonial political economy, showing who won and who lost, how and why. The testimony of litigants and witnesses in court cases casts in bold relief both the lines of conflict—who was making what claims—and the terms of debate—how particular groups were framing their arguments. Analysis of the discourse in court cases lays bare what Chanock (1985) and Berry (1988) have called the struggle over the interpretation of custom in colonial Africa. In so doing it illuminates the historical construction of African law, meaning, and culture itself. Finally, court records throw light on the inner worlds of the colonizers and the colonized, opening to scrutiny discourse, ideology, and consciousness.

This essay is designed in part to explore a particular method of using legal records. I have traced Taiwo over the course of his life through land and court records and then combined the data from these sources with information from other records to reconstruct his biography. This method had a number of advantages. It rendered useful Crown grants and conveyances, documents that contain insufficient information to be of much value on their own. Moreover, it enabled me to weigh the data from the legal records against that from other sources and to construct from the fragments a mosaic that is richer than the sum of its parts. This was particularly valuable when interpreting the court cases in which Taiwo appeared. Gluckman pointed out that litigation is but a moment in an on-going relationship among individuals and that it must be understood in the context of what precedes and follows the court encounter (Gluckman 1967:xvi). Yet taken in isolation, court records often contain little information about long-term relationships. Coupling an analysis of court cases with the study of biography enabled me to read the records of what went on in the courtroom against the background of what happened before and after the case. It permitted me to understand the disputes in the context of Taiwo's overall life and character.

In recent years Africanists have used life histories very productively to elucidate aggregate processes of economic, social, and political change. Scholars have found in this method a way to capture the experiences of groups who for a

variety of reasons do not appear in traditional sources and to bring the richness
and immediacy of individual experience to bear on the study of structural
transformation. The data in life history research comes from personal narratives
told to the researcher or to earlier listeners who wrote the stories down (Wright
1975; Alpers 1983; Beinart 1987; Isaacman 1988; Berry 1985; and Geiger 1987).
Conjoining the study of biography and legal records extends certain advantages
of life history research to individuals whose narratives do not survive. The
method provides a rare internal view into the social history of Lagos and the
colonial legal system. It enables us to see the late-nineteenth-century world from
Taiwo's perspective, and to discover how he responded to and made sense of the
rapid economic, political, and legal changes unleashed by agricultural commerce
and British colonialism. The focus on law and biography breaks down the
boundaries in traditional legal studies between analysis of the state, institutions,
and law, on the one hand, and persons, thoughts, and actions on the other,
treating these subjects as a single field of investigation (Chanock 1989:69). This
essay deals with a prominent man about whom a wealth of information exists.
However, the introduction of legal records into the repertoire of historical sources
creates possibilities for research into the experiences of more obscure individuals
as well. The technique can be broadened, moreover, to reconstruct collective as
well as individual biography, illuminating the shared experiences and aggregate
behavior of groups of actors (Stone 1971:46-79).

Taiwo's origins are obscure, and the data about them are conflicting. Tradition
holds that he was born in the early nineteenth century into the royal family of
Iṣeri, an Awori town on the Ogun River about fifteen miles north of Lagos. Taiwo
is supposed to have visited Lagos with his father as a child and moved permanently to the growing coastal town after his father died. Ọba Oṣilokun, who
reigned between about 1820 and 1829, purportedly placed the boy in the household of Ogunmade, where he began making baskets (Loṣi 1914:82; Law 1968:
46-54). Taiwo's obituary states, on the other hand, that he first came to Lagos in
1848, as a man in his mid-thirties, for the purpose of trade and on the recom-
mendation of his great friend Jacob Ogunbiyi (LWR, 23 February 1901; LS, 27
February 1901). In the 1860s, Taiwo himself signed a letter in which the co-
authors referred to themselves as former slaves (PP, Natives...to Col. Ord, 1864).
These divergent accounts of Taiwo's origins may contain errors of fact. Lagos's
slave population increased exponentially in the first half of the nineteenth century,
and Taiwo may indeed have been Oṣilokun's or Ogunmade's slave, something
that both tradition and obituaries would likely omit. However, the evidence in
the letter is not conclusive. The document was written to defend slavery and
persuade the colonial government not to abolish it. The authors argued that
slavery was not an oppressive institution and that slaves could rise to positions
of prominence in local society, citing themselves as examples. If a slave in Lagos at
some time in his life, Taiwo must have been freeborn in Iṣeri. He eventually
became Ọlọfin, or king, of the town, and while it is possible that a former slave
could have been chosen to fill the office, it is not likely. Many free persons
migrated to Lagos and attached themselves voluntarily to the king or a local big
man. Taiwo could first have come to Lagos in this way. An alternative explanation
reconciles the apparent contradictions in the three fragmentary accounts of the
great man's origins and may be closest to the truth. Taiwo could have been

captured as a boy and brought to Lagos as a slave. He might then have escaped or been freed and returned the short distance home, only to migrate to Lagos in search of trade as an adult. Whatever the truth of Taiwo's origins and early life, he was not born into a Lagos family of wealth and privilege.

In the 1840s, Taiwo became a follower of Osilokun's son, Kosoko, Oba from 1845 to 1851 and leader of the most powerful faction in a deeply divided town. Taiwo quickly became one of Kosoko's favorites, and through association with the Oba he obtained access to opportunities and resources that helped him get a start in Lagos. Kosoko had good relations with European and Brazilian merchants, and soon Taiwo began trading with them, possibly in slaves but probably in other commodities (Smith 1979:11−40; interview: Olofin of Iseri, 1974). Asogbon, a war chief, helped Taiwo obtain from Faji, one of Lagos's wealthiest women, land near the center of the island on which to build a house (Losi, 1914:82−83). Taiwo needed a residence of his own if he were to begin to build a family and personal following. It is unclear whether Taiwo fled with Kosoko to Epe when the British bombarded Lagos and deposed the king in 1851. If so, he probably did not stay there long. Almost immediately, Kosoko's people began drifting back to Lagos (Smith 1979:26−33, 40−43, 49−58). Taiwo was not yet so powerful that his return would have caused a stir. Most tellingly, he retained his land, which the new king's supporters probably would have seized if it had sat vacant for long. During the 1850s, Taiwo married, fathered his first child, and began to acquire male and female slaves (interviews: Olofin of Iseri, 1974; Kofo Pratt, 1984). But not until after the annexation, as the entered his sixth decade, did Taiwo emerge as one of the leading men of his generation.

When Governor Freeman invited Kosoko to return to Lagos in 1862, a close and mutually beneficial relationship began between Taiwo and successive British representatives. Taiwo performed many services for his new friends, and they gave him information and assistance that enabled him to increase trade, attract followers, and consolidate power (LWR, 23 February 1901; LS, 27 February 1901; PP, Rowe to Derby, 1883). Taiwo lost no time in using the new colonial bureaucracy and legal system to further his own ends. At the end of the decade, he became a Christian, either to improve his standing with the Europeans or because he experienced a genuine religious conversion. Whatever the reasons, Taiwo worshipped daily at Holy Trinity Church, took the Christian name Daniel Conrad, and contributed generously to Christian causes (LWR, 23 February 1901; LS, 27 February 1901; Kopytoff 1965:365, n. 87). However, he steadfastly resisted two outward signs of Christianity, monogamy and church marriage (interviews: Olofin of Iseri, 1974; Kofo Pratt, 1984; Mann 1985).

In 1863, Lieutenant-Governor Glover introduced Taiwo to the agent of G. L. Gaiser, a leading German firm, who advanced him goods or money on credit for the purpose of buying palm oil (Losi, 1914:83). Taiwo sent slaves and other dependents to trade at Ikorodu, Epe, Ejinrin, and other lagoon-side markets, as well as at Badagry, Porto Novo, and Abeokuta. In addition, he gave goods and money on credit to traders from Lagos and the interior (PP, Natives...to Col. Ord, 1864). Taiwo regularly settled his account with Gaiser by supplying the firm with palm oil for export.

Also in 1863, Taiwo obtained a Crown grant to one of the best plots of land along the Marina, where he erected a building for trade (Losi 1914:83). Taiwo's was the nineteenth grant to be issued by the colonial land office, showing the speed with which he seized new opportunities created by the British annexation. By 1871, Taiwo had obtained thirteen additional Crown grants; ten to plots at Oko Faji and one each to plots at Igboṣere Road, Victoria Road, and Oke Popo, among the most desirable locations in the growing commercial and colonial capital (LLR, Crown grants). By taking out Crown grants, Taiwo redefined his rights and secured his title to the land he had been allocated by Chief Faji, and he laid claim to other property as well. During the 1860s, Taiwo also bought at least six plots of land at Oko Faji and two at the Marina (LLR, conveyances). These Crown grants and early purchases laid the foundation for a sizable urban land holding, and it is instructive to look at how Taiwo used the property. At Oko Faji, along the street that came to bear his name, Taiwo built a large compound where he himself lived surrounded by wives, children, slaves, and clients (interviews: Ọlọfin of Iṣeri 1974; Kofo Pratt 1984). Taiwo rented one property to Robert Campbell, a liberated slave from Jamaica, for an annual rent of £18 (LLR, lease, Taiwo to Campbell, 1868). He used the other properties as stores and warehouses or as residences for additional slaves and clients. During these years, Taiwo also acquired rural land on which slaves and tenants developed successful farms (interview: Kofo Pratt, 1984; PP, Natives...to Col. Ord, 1864). For men such as Taiwo, the accumulation of land, people, wealth, and power went hand-in-hand. Owners had an obligation to house the slaves whose labor they controlled. Big men needed to be able to house clients and other dependents if they were to command their services and support. Without land, Taiwo could not have acquired slaves and built a big personal following. Without slaves and followers, he could not have accumulated wealth and exercised power. On Taiwo's farms, slaves and tenants produced palm oil for export and grew food crops for sale in local markets or consumption by Taiwo's household (interview: Ọlọfin of Iṣeri).

    If G. L. Gaiser required that Taiwo pledge property to secure credit, the firm's agent did not register the agreement at the colonial land office. Gaiser may have given Taiwo credit on trust, thanks to Lieutenant-Governor Glover's introduction. In 1866 Taiwo traded for a short time with the Hamburg firm William O'Swald, which asked him to mortgage a property at the Marina in return for "money and goods lent from time-to-time" (LLR, mortgage, Taiwo to Phillippi, 1866). In 1867, the agent for Regis Aîné, a French firm, lent Taiwo goods and money sufficient to buy 40,000 gallons of palm oil, and Taiwo guaranteed this large loan by mortgaging seventeen properties. Regis Aîné renewed the loan three times within the next three years (LLR, mortgages, Taiwo to Bounard (?), 1867; Taiwo to Rowland, 1867; and Taiwo to agents of Regis Aîné, 1868 and 1870). Taiwo appears as vendor in no subsequent recorded mortgages, perhaps because by the 1870s his reputation was sufficiently well-established that his creditors no longer required them. In the 1860s, Taiwo had amassed wealth and established a far-flung commercial organization by trading in palm oil. He also had made money selling arms to the Egba during the Ijaye war (PP, Bashorun to Glover, 1863). At about this time, Lagosians gave him the praise name Olowo, which means literally "man of money," in recognition of his great riches. Taiwo's large land holdings undoubtedly bolstered his creditworthiness, even when they were not formally pledged as security for loans.

    Taiwo used his economic resources to acquire influence in Lagos and its environs. He did so by performing wide-ranging services for both rulers and commoners. These included such things as making introductions to important Africans and Europeans and providing information about new opportunities and regulations. The services also included offering assistance collecting debts, settling disputes, and raising money for bridewealth, funerals, and celebrations (interview: Ọlọfin of Iṣeri, 1974; LWR, 23 February 1901; LS, 27 February 1901). In return for such favors, Taiwo could expect the recipients to support him in his undertakings. Taiwo's access to the ọba and governor made him an effective intermediary in Lagos for interior towns. Soon he became the official *baba isale*, or Lagos representative, of Iṣeri, Ikorodu, and other nearby towns. This position gave him privileged access to their markets and trade routes and special influence in their affairs (Cole 1975:25, 31–38; Biobaku 1957:88).

The following story illustrates how Taiwo turned such influence to personal advantage. In the late 1860s, a group of Egba traders who owed Taiwo money stopped coming to Lagos when they could not repay their debts. Taiwo pressed the Egba authorities at Akeokuta to help him collect his money, but he received no satisfaction. Taiwo then took steps to coerce repayment by persuading the village of Iṣeri to close an important Egba trade route that it controlled. Governor Sir Arthur Kennedy insisted that Taiwo order the blockade lifted, but in return arranged with the Egba authorities for Taiwo to collect his money, precipitating an Egba blockade named for Taiwo Olowo (Loṣi 1914:83; Payne 1893:18).

Oshodi Tapa, Kosọkọ's second in command, died in 1868. When Kosọkọ himself died four years later, Taiwo was the most powerful of the former ọba's many followers and assumed the leadership of his mighty faction. This greatly increase Taiwo's power in the region (Cole 1975:28; Baker 1974:25).

Taiwo conducted much of his own business on credit. Indeed, one informant said that his oriki was *olowo ele*, meaning "man of money made from credit" (Asiwaju, per. comm). Social ties bound him to many of his debtors, and these were often as effective as mortgages in guaranteeing repayment of loans. But by the mid-1860s, Taiwo himself had begun accepting title to landed property as security for loans and registering the agreements at the colonial land office. In December 1866, one Abobaccari asked Taiwo to advance him goods or cowries for the purpose of trade. Abobaccari proposed to secure the loan by mortgaging land and buildings at Shoulu Street (LLR, mortgage, Abobaccari to Taiwo, 1866). In August 1868, a trader named Latiri owed Taiwo £58.9.0 and could not pay his debt. Taiwo insisted that Latiri secure the loan by mortgaging a house and land at Oko Faji (LLR, mortgage, Latiri to Taiwo, 1868). Over the course of the next twenty-two years, Taiwo registered eighty additional mortgages at the colonial land office (LLR, mortgages). These recorded agreements probably represent the tip of the iceberg. Some traders made oral agreements with Taiwo which were neither written down nor recorded. Others simply gave Taiwo their Crown grants or conveyances, on the understanding that he would return them if they repaid their debts and that the property would become his if they did not (*Robbin v. Taiwo*, 1894, LSCR).

For Taiwo and other local merchants and traders, the meaning of mortgages was more complex than it might first appear. Mortgages were economic agreements which secured debts and protected merchants against loss. Taiwo may have required mortgages of some traders and not others because he regarded them as poor or uncertain credit risks. However, mortgages were also a means of tying traders to merchants and of turning debtors into subordinates. Twenty-one of Taiwo's eighty-two recorded loans were repaid, and the properties that secured them were reconveyed. Fifteen of the debtors defaulted, and Taiwo sold their land. The records contain no information about the outcome of the remaining forty-six loans.[7] Land and court records reveal that Taiwo often lent more than the value of the property pledged to secure loans and that the proceeds from the sale of property frequently did not cover debts.[8] These records also show that Taiwo often carried debts well beyond the date agreed upon for default and long after the trader had stopped doing business with him. In February 1881, for example, a farmer named Momodu asked Taiwo to advance his son Seidu money and goods for the purpose of trade. Momodu mortgaged to Taiwo the house in Ṣapara Street where he and his family lived. Seidu traded with Taiwo for ten years and then stopped, leaving a debt of £53. In December 1896, one Ajaratu sued Seidu to recover a different debt and the court ordered the Ṣapara Street house sold. Taiwo entered an interpleader, asserting that the house belonged to Momodu and that he, Taiwo, had prior claim to the property under the mortgage of February 1881 (*Ajaratu v. Seidu*, 1896; *Taiwo v. Oduntan*, 1896, LSCR).[9] Taiwo probably tolerated a measure of indebtedness in many of the forty-six documented mortgages that did not end decisively in either reconveyance or foreclosure. He and other big men may sometimes have hesitated to foreclose for fear of alienating public opinion and losing followers. In the case at hand, it is possible to construe Taiwo's motive as charitable. By 1896 Momodu was old and blind. The sale of his Ṣapara Street house would have left him and his family homeless. Whatever Taiwo's reasons for failing to foreclose in this instance, he and others often used indebtedness to bind traders to them and create dependents. Chronic, revolving indebtedness robbed traders of their independence, kept them coming back for more goods or money, and turned them into faithful servants. When the trading relationship ended, the debt created a life-long subordinate. If a debtor incurred his creditor's displeasure, then the creditor could insist on immediate repayment of the loan and sell the debtor's property if the money was not forthcoming (interviews: A. W. Animaṣaun, 1974; S. B. Affini, 1974; I. L. Apatira, 1973; and D. O. Oshodi 1974). Indebtedness in general and mortgages in particular gave Taiwo great power over people.

The establishment of the colonial legal system reinforced the new property relations that were emerging in the early colonial period and consolidated the control of big men such as Taiwo over land, capital, and people. The introduction of new laws and courts gave creditors mechanisms in addition to mortgages for managing credit relations and enforcing debt repayment. Creditors could sue debtors in the colonial courts if no land had been mortgaged to secure the loan or if the value of the land mortgaged was not sufficient to cover the debt. In such cases, the court could order the debtor's real and/or personal property sold to pay off the loan. Persons whose assets did not cover their liabilities could be sentenced to prison. When this happened, relatives, patrons, or friends often agreed to repay or secure the loan so that the debtor might be released from prison. The new laws and courts also provided land owners powerful means to uphold their title to property. Taiwo used the supreme court both to collect debts and to recover possession of land from persons who encroached on it or from slaves, clients, and tenants whom he wished to eject (*Taiwo v. Cole*, 1887; *Taiwo v. Aluyo*, 1894; *Taiwo v. Wright*, 1887; *Taiwo v. Supiao*, 1889, LSCR). In many of these cases Taiwo seems to have been as interested in disciplining people as he was in recovering land and capital. Sometimes the mere threat of legal action was enough to bring subordinates into line. Often no threat was needed: locals knew where power lay. If slaves, debtors, wives, or other subordinates challenged Taiwo, they ran the risk of being hauled into court, as the following cases show.

In the 1860s, an Egba man named Oduntan traded with Taiwo. He then retired from business, still indebted by Taiwo's account. In the 1890s, the same man started bringing palm oil and palm kernels to Taiwo for sale to Witt and Bush. On one occasion, Taiwo refused to give Oduntan the money realized from the sale of the produce. Oduntan sued Taiwo for the amount in the supreme court, but evidently thought better of the idea, because he did not show up at the trial and the judge dismissed the case. Taiwo had tolerated Oduntan's debt for thirty years without making much effort to recover it. However, the moment Oduntan challenged him, Taiwo pressed the Egba authorities at Abeokuta to collect the money owed him. An Egba tribunal reviewed the case and ordered Oduntan to pay Taiwo £368. Still not satisfied, Taiwo asked the supreme court to issue a warrant for Oduntan's arrest on the grounds of indebtedness. During the subsequent trial, Taiwo claimed that Oduntan owed him £486.8.0, the balance for goods sold and delivered (*Taiwo v. Oduntan*, 1896, LSCR).

In the 1880s, a woman Okilu and her brother Ayiekoroju approached Taiwo through an intermediary. The pair said that they were having trouble with people at their hometown, Ikorodu, where Taiwo had considerable influence, and they asked for help. The nature of the trouble is unclear, but Okilu subsequently claimed that the Ikorodu people would not let her have the man she wanted. Soon after, Taiwo sent some cloth to Ikorodu, and Okilu, her brother Babatunde, her mother Ekonu, and her "servant" Ramatu came to live in Taiwo's compound. Later Ekonu gave £10 to Odunsi, one of Taiwo's "boys."[10] After a number of years, Okilu left Taiwo's household and began living with a man named Ajayi. She and her mother subsequently asked for the return of the £10, which they maintained had been given to Odunsi for safekeeping. First Odunsi and then Taiwo refused to return the money. Taiwo claimed that he was entitled to it as partial payment for the cloth that he had sent to Ikorodu in the 1880s on Okilu's behalf. Okilu quarreled with Taiwo over the money, and immediately thereafter he began pressing her for an additional £25, which he said she still owed him for the cloth. A few months later Taiwo sued Okilu, Ayiekoroju, and Ekonu for the amount in the supreme court. At the trial Okilu maintained that when she had first asked Taiwo for help, he had encouraged her to become his wife. She denied asking Taiwo to supply her the cloth on credit and implied it was bridewealth sent to Ikorodu. For his part, Taiwo denied that Okilu had been his wife and, by implication, that the cloth was bridewealth. Had Taiwo wanted to ask for return of bridewealth, he probably would have included Ajayi, Okilu's new mate, among the defendants. In the cases Taiwo clearly presented himself as an aggrieved creditor, not as a wronged husband (*Taiwo v. Ekonu . . .*, 1896, LSCR).

What interests me about these cases is that Taiwo initiated legal action to recover alleged debts immediately following altercations with the defendants. In the first case, Oduntan had summoned him before the supreme court. In the second, Okilu had left his compound to live with another man and then had quarreled publicly with him over money. Taiwo brought these suits not so much because he was worried about collecting money owed him as because he wanted (1) to reassert his control over the defendants, (2) to punish them for challenging his authority, and (3) to send a message to foes and followers alike that they could not mess with him with impunity. In the second case, it is not at all clear that Okilu owed Taiwo money. The fact that Taiwo used a charge of indebtedness as the mechanism to discipline the woman underscores both his understanding of indebtedness as a means of creating and maintaining subordinates and his belief that it was a legal obligation that the British courts would recognize and uphold. In the cases discussed here debt was the mechanism of subordination. In other instances land ownership played a similar role. If slaves or other subordinates who occupied land at Taiwo's pleasure failed to serve him or to show proper deference, he could order them to vacate. If they refused, he could take them to the colonial court and, assuming he could prove title to the land, expect that the British authorities would eject them.

Taiwo lost his suits against both Oduntan and Okilu, demonstrating that he did not always get what he wanted by going to the supreme court. In the first case, the judge ruled that Taiwo had made his own decision to take the matter before a Yoruba tribunal at Abeokuta and that the colonial court could not now interfere with the ruling of the local authorities. Somewhat contradictorily, the judge then stated that Taiwo's claim was very old, his books were very badly kept, and his eyewitnesses were all illiterate. On the basis of the facts, the court could not sustain Taiwo's claim for £486.8.0 (*Taiwo v. Oduntan*, 1896, LSCR). If Taiwo was to collect any money from Oduntan, he would have to rely on the Egba authorities at Abeokuta. In the second case, the judge simply found for the defendants, without giving reasons. In general, the court was sympathetic to women who argued that they had been coerced into marriage. The fact that Taiwo lost these two cases does not mean that his strategy of using litigation in the supreme court to help discipline and control subordinates was necessarily a failure. In other instances the court found for Taiwo (*Taiwo v. Aṣode*, 1895; *Taiwo v. Aluyo*, 1894, LSCR). Even when it did not, the emotional, psychological, and financial cost of a court case to his subordinates was much greater than it was to him. Taiwo was not intimidated by the colonial legal system. He could afford to hire the best lawyers, and he knew that in any quarrel he would have thousands of supporters.[11] Few of his opponents could draw on comparable resources, and many found the colonial legal system mysterious and off-putting, if not threatening. Whether or not Taiwo won a case, he succeeded in subjecting the defendant to an unpleasant ordeal and in communicating to others that he would retaliate against those who thwarted him.

Taiwo lost favor with the British temporarily in the 1870s, when Sir John Pope-Hennessy, governor of Britain's West African settlements, arrived in Lagos determined to reserve certain of the local administrator's policies (Cole 1975:32; Biobaku 1957:90–95). At about the same time, Taiwo became embroiled in a bitter conflict with Ajasa, head of Lagos's *Ogboni* cult and a rising power in the local community. The two men fought over control of trade, markets, and people in Lagos and its hinterland, as well as over influence with the ọba and colonial administrators. Each used all of the means at his disposal—economic, political, legal, and magical—to increase his own wealth and power and to bring down his opponent. Taiwo and Ajasa both commanded large and loyal followings that harassed one another continually, until British observers believed that the community teetered on the brink of civil war (Cole 1975:29–44; PRO, Evans to Stanhope, 1886). Records of supreme court cases show that both sides used litigation in the colonial court to try to protect their members and discredit their enemies. A brief discussion of two cases captures something of the character of the Taiwo-Ajasa conflict and reveals the tactics employed to pursue it.

In 1884, Ogubote, a follower of Ajasa, brought suit in the supreme court against Taiwo and one of his henchmen, Adu. Earlier in the year, Ogubote and several other Ajasa supporters had asked Taiwo to intervene in some trouble at their village, Ebute Iga. Taiwo sent a messenger to look into the matter. Ogubote used this as a pretext to charge Taiwo in the colonial court with driving him from home and selling his wives and children into slavery. Ajasa must have known that few things would threatened Taiwo's reputation with the British more than an accusation of selling free women and children into slavery. Ogubote also claimed that Taiwo had demanded sixty bags of cowries and four sheep when begged to stop the harassment. Taiwo succeeded in convincing the court that the charges were false and part of a conspiracy to discredit him politically (*Ogubote v. Adu*, 1884, LSCR). Taiwo himself could be guilty of provocation. In the early 1880s, he ordered his people to seize the goods of some of Ajasa's supporters and prevent them from trading at Iro market. When several of the victims sued for damages in the supreme court, Albert Owolabi Taiwo, eldest son of Taiwo Olowo put a curse on one of them. In this instance the court found Taiwo guilty, and the judge sternly warned him not to engage in any more illegal activities. The Crown subsequently convicted A. O. Taiwo of administering poison or a "noxious thing" (PRO, Evans to Stanhope, 1886).

Despite Taiwo's temporary loss of favor with the British and long, costly feud with Ajasa, he continued to accumulate wealth and power. In the 1880s, a decade of deepening economic depression, he managed to make money exporting palm produce and importing textiles. He also continued to sell arms, now to Ibadan, one of the protagonists in the Kiriji war (Akintoye 1971:130, 170; PP, Young to Derby, 1885, and Kings...to Deputy Governor, 1884). During the 1880s, Taiwo accumulated additional wives, children, and slaves, and he also attracted ever more clients, often at the expense of other local big men. In 1885, Chief Aṣogbon brought suit in the supreme court to recover possession of land and houses inhabited by dependents who had deserted him to serve Taiwo, once a client of Aṣogbon's predecessor (*Aṣogbon v. Jinadu Ṣomade*, 1885; *Aṣogbon v. Yesufu Okin*, 1885, LSCR). By the 1880s, Taiwo had thrown off allegiance to all patrons. The British government removed a great thorn in his side in 1884, when it deported Ajasa, his single rival. With Ajasa gone, Taiwo was second to no man, save perhaps the ọba and British administrator. His influence stretched from Porto Novo to Kano, and he exercised great power in Lagos and its hinterland (LWR, 23 February 1901; LS, 27 February 1901; *Macaulay v. Taiwo*, 1884, LSCR). When delegations visited the colony from Ibadan and Ijebu, Taiwo alone enjoyed the privilege of presenting them to the British authorities (Cole 1975:63, 170, 199).

At some point Taiwo became the ọlọfin, or king, of his hometown, Iṣeri. This office brought with it wives, slaves, and followers, as well as farm land, palm trees, and trading canoes. All further increased the great man's wealth (*Taiwo v. Odunsi Sarumi*, 1913, NLR; interview: Olofin of Iseri, 1974). Taiwo never took a title in Lagos, although mechanisms existed for incorporating outsiders into the traditional elite. Perhaps Taiwo eschewed Lagos titles because he believed joining the town's traditional political hierarchy would compromise his standing with British officials. Or perhaps he found Christianity incompatible with the responsibilities of titled officials, although if this was the case it is difficult to understand why he would have agreed to become olofin of Iseri. Most likely, the *oba*, who ratified all chieftaincy appointments, blocked Taiwo's way, believing that he was already too powerful.

During the closing years of the nineteenth century, Taiwo continued to invest his wealth in land. Between 1870 and 1892, the date of his last documented purchase, Taiwo bought at least twenty-one pieces of real estate and acquired three more when debtors defaulted on loans, bringing to forty-six the total number of his documented acquisitions in the city of Lagos alone (LLR, conveyances and mortgages). Taiwo almost certainly acquired additional plots for which he had neither Crown grants nor conveyances. The property acquired in the 1870s and 1880s lay at Oko Faji, Victoria Road, and Tinubu Square, the same choice locations as his earlier acquisitions. At this time, Taiwo also obtained houses at Badagry and other nearby towns (LLR, conveyance, Taiwo to Mogaji, 1899; interview: Kofo Pratt, 1894).

Between 1870 and 1899, Taiwo sold sixteen plots of land in Lagos, and from the sales he realized profits that varied considerably (LLR, conveyances). A precise rate of return on urban real estate is usually impossible to calculate, because there is no way of knowing if land was divided or if buildings deteriorated or were improved between purchase and sale. Taiwo may have sold the land to generate cash. Plots disposed of in 1884 and 1888 realized £520 and £1000, respectively (LLR, conveyances, Taiwo to Williams 1884; Taiwo to Campbell, 1888). Alternatively, he may have sold the land because he no longer wanted it or had a client or friend who wished to purchase it.

In 1877, Taiwo leased land and buildings on the Marina to Regis Ainé for a period of ten years, at an annual rent of £72 (LLR, lease, Taiwo to Regis Ainé, 1877). In 1900, he leased a different plot on the Marina to the Manchester firm Pickering and Berthoud for twenty-five years, at an annual rent of £175 for the first ten years and £250 for the subsequent fifteen. Pickering and Berthoud erected a factory on the site at a cost of £3442, which was to be repaid from the rent at the rate of £50 per year. When the amount had been repaid, the building was to become Taiwo's (LLR, lease, Taiwo at Pickering and Berthould, 1900). These leases demonstrate that at the very end of the nineteenth century Taiwo joined the ranks of Lagos's growing *rentier* class. However, rents were not as important to him as they were to some of his contemporaries, or as they would become to subsequent generations of Lagos's propertied class. Taiwo's wealth derived from trade and farming, both of which used slave labor, and from the surplus he extracted from dependents in his capacity as a big man. Control of land was essential to each of these activities, but it alone does not explain Taiwo's wealth and power.

Shortly before Taiwo died, he gave two properties on the Marina to his eldest son, Alfred Owolabi, in consideration for "natural love and affection"

(LLR, deed of gift, Taiwo to Taiwo, 1898). The remainder of his Lagos land devolved to his heirs as family property, while the land at Iṣeri that he held as ọlọfin passed to his successor (*Taiwo v. Sarumi*, 1913, NLR). One of Taiwo's descendants remarked, as a measure of her ancestor's greatness, that in the fourth generation the family is still deriving considerable income from the land that he acquired (interview: Kofo Pratt, 1984).

Taiwo died on the twentieth of February, 1901. Bishop James Johnson conducted his funeral, assisted by Lagos's Anglican clergymen of African descent (LWR, 23 February 1901; LS 27 February 1901). Thousands attended the subsequent Yoruba rituals, which lasted for three days, many coming from hundreds of miles away. Two years after Taiwo's death, he was honored by the performance of the Adamorisa play, reserved for persons of the very highest status (Loṣi 1914:85; LS, 12 August 1903). No greater tributes could have been paid this powerful Lagosian. At the time of Taiwo's death a local newspaper lamented:

> The death of Chief Taiwo removes from the stage...a man of great prominence and one who unquestionably wielded a greater influence than any other individual member of the community....Chief Taiwo was a true type of African "big man." With him money became wealth in the fullest sense of the term, for he...utilized it...as to make it so, and the result was that his name was a household word in all the surrounding country, while he was respected and revered far and wide...[T]he native population at large will realize that on his death one of the great lives of the Yoruba country has been closed.
>
> (LWR, 23 February 1901).

Taiwo's remains rest still in an elaborate tomb which stands on the lone undeveloped plot along Broad Street, in the heart of downtown Lagos. That his bones kept developers at bay during the real estate boom of the 1970s and 1980s bespeaks his lasting importance in Lagos's history.

Reconstructed from legal records and a wide range of other sources, Taiwo's biography shows that the rise of legitimate commerce and imposition of colonial rule created new opportunities in trade and politics that enabled some Africans of humble origins to amass wealth and power and to redefine their position in Lagos society. Taiwo first obtained access to trade and land through personal relations with African patrons. After the annexation he parlayed contacts with the British administrator into greater opportunities in trade. Credit extended by German, British, and French firms enabled him to overcome a lack of capital and participate in the new palm produce trade on a big scale. When the colonial government began issuing Crown grants and Lagosians started buying and selling land, Taiwo wasted no time redefining rights to land that he already occupied and obtaining much additional privately owned land. No sooner was the colonial land office opened than Taiwo used it to record and secure debts and to assert and protect rights to land. Taiwo's large landholdings and his good relationship with Europeans helped him secure continued access to credit. Control of land and capital enabled the rising Lagosian to acquire wives, slaves, clients, and other dependents, and once under his sway, to ensure that they remained loyal subordinates. Taiwo invested his growing wealth not only in trade and land but also in people; the ability to mobilize labor and support was essential to both his commercial success and political power.

At the same time that Taiwo was consolidating his base in Lagos, he began extending his influence into its hinterland. He became the official baba isale of some towns and took the title of ọlọfin at Iṣeri, his birthplace. However, Taiwo's influence reached even where he occupied no official position in the local political hierarchy. The extension of influence consumed valuable resources, since it often required performing tangible services. But it also proved an excellent investment. Taiwo employed his close contacts and considerable influence with Africans and Europeans to increase trade, collect debts, protect property, and control subordinates, as well as to pursue his personal vendetta against Ajasa, his greatest rival and archenemy. The colonial legal system recognized and encouraged the development of new property relations created by the penetration of commercial capitalism. Taiwo turned to the supreme court to enforce payment of debts and uphold title to land, as well as to harass enemies and discipline subordinates. Few Lagosians responded more quickly or shrewdly than Taiwo to the new legal opportunities created by colonialism. Changes in Lagos's law and courts were fundamental to the process through which Taiwo accumulated wealth and power.

As Taiwo's wealth increased, he invested in more of those things that had made him rich and powerful to begin with — trade, land, and people. While some of his wealth took new forms and had been accumulated through new means, his aspirations remained quite traditional: to establish himself, in the words of his obituary, as "a true type of African big man." Taiwo accomplished his spectacular rise to preeminence in the decades immediately following the British annexation by accommodating Yoruba hopes and dreams to the new economic, political, and legal environment of the early colonial age. Recognizing the genius with which Taiwo turned new opportunities to old ends, a newspaper article published following his death remarked that the great Lagosian represented "the strongest link that bound the present life with the traditions of the past" (LWR, 23 February 1901).

NOTES

1. Mortgages at the Lagos Land Registry establish this point.
2. In the largest single land deal in the nineteenth century, J. P. L. Davies mortgaged fourteen parcels of real estate to Child Mills and Company in return for £60,000 annual credit. For a copy of the mortgage, dated 18 March 1872, see vol. 15, p. 141, Lagos Land Registry. In 1919 P. J. C. Thomas mortgaged the bulk of his real property in return for £150,000 credit (Hopkins 1978:309–10).
3. Interviews: D. O. Oshodi, 1974; A. L. A. Ojora 1984 and 1985; and Iṣola Bajulaiye 1984. Supreme court records capture the conflict between owners and slaves.
4. The Judges' Notebooks of Civil Cases, The Lagos Supreme Court, contain detailed information about the organization of trade. Interviews: T. A. Doherty 1974; A. W. Animaṣaun 1974; and S. A. Braimah Igbo Forrest, 1974 and 1985.
5. Earlier courts existed, but I have been unable to find their records. Nor have I found the records of the Police Magistrate's Court that existed along side the supreme court after 1876. The Judges' Notebooks of Civil and Criminal Cases, the Lagos Supreme Court, are kept in the tower of the High Court, Lagos State, and may be examined by permission of the registrar of the court. Records of the District Commissioner's Courts at Badagry (1865–1913) and Epẹ (1889–1909) survive in the Nigerian National Archives, Ibadan, but I have not used them extensively.
6. Land records are kept in the strong room of the Lagos Land Registry and may be examined upon application to the director of that office.
7. I derived these data by identifying all mortgages in Taiwo's name and then tracing the properties mentioned in them through conveyances and reconveyances in Taiwo's name.
8. I arrived at this conclusion by comparing the amount of the loan plus interest for which landed property was pledged as security with the amount realized from the sale of the land in cases of foreclosure. When the supreme court ordered property sold to repay a loan, it usually specified the amount of the loan plus interest and the sum realized from the sale of the property. Data from court records corroborate the conclusion reached from a study of land records.
9. Additional evidence comes from comparing information in mortgages about the dates when loans were due with information in conveyances about the dates that land pledged as security for loans was sold or reconveyed.
10. "Boy" was probably the English translation of the Yoruba word ọmọ, used to refer to many different relationships of subordination. It is sometimes impossible to tell exactly what type of relationship the word implies.
11. Lawyers Charles Forsythe, C. A. Ṣapara Williams, Joseph Egerton Shyngle, and George Ernest Moss all represented Taiwo at different times.

SOURCES

Oral

Sufianu Brimah Affini, July 1974, 21 Şopono Street.
Alhaji Abdul Wuhabi Animaşaun, 20 February 1974, 45 Martin Street.
Chief Işola Bajulaiye, *Eletu Odibo* of Lagos, 15 November 1984, *Iga Eletu Odibo*.
Işmaila Lawal Apatira, December 1973, Apatira Street.
T. A. Doherty, April and May 1974, 23 Odunlami Street.
S. A. Braimah Igbo Forrest, January 1974 and February 1985, 7 Palm Church Street.
Prince Abdul Lasisi Ajayi Ojora, 15 October 1984 and 32 January 1985, 14 Chapel Street.
Olofin of Işeri, March 1974, Işeri.
Chief S. B. Ajasa Oluwa, 30 January 1985, 2/4 Oluwa Court.
Chief Durojaiye Olajuwon Oshodi, January 1974, Oshodi palace.
Mrs. Kofo Pratt, 18 September 1984, 33 Ademola Street.
Professor A. I. Asiwaju, Dept. of History, Univ. of Lagos, April 1988.

Archival

PRO: Public Record Office, London
    Colonial Office Dispatches, Lagos Colony, 147/56, Evans to Stanhope, 6 August 1886.
PP: Parliamentary Papers
    xxxvii, 1865, Ord Report, Appendix E, Natives of Lagos to Col. Ord, 27 December 1864.
    xxxvii, 1865, Papers Relating to the Wars among the Native Tribes, Enclosure 1 in no. 6, Bashorun and Chiefs of Abeokuta to Glover, 3 October 1863.
    lx, 1887, Correspondence Respecting the War between Native Tribes in the Interior, no. 10, Rowe to Derby, 30 May 1883; Enclosure 5 in no. 13, Young to Derby, 9 January 1885; and Enclosure 6 in no. 13, Kings of Ekitiparapo to Deputy Governor, 9 June 1884.

Legal Records

LLR: Lagos Land Registry, Lagos
    Crown grants to Taiwo
    Conveyances citing Taiwo as vendor or vendee, especially:
      Taiwo to Williams, 30 September 1884, vol. 9, p. 14.
      Taiwo to Campbell, 2 June 1888, vol. 12, p. 417.
      Taiwo to Mogaji, 11 November 1899, vol. 36, p. 142.
    Mortgages citing Taiwo as vendor or vendee, especially:
      Taiwo to John B. Bounard (?), 20 February 1864, vol. 4, p. 247
      Taiwo to Henri Rowland, 29 October 1867, vol. 5, p. 139
      Taiwo to Robert Phillippi, 25 December 1866, vol. 4, p. 189.
      Taiwo to agent of Regis Ainé, 16 October 1868, vol. 7, p. 5.

Abobaccari to Taiwo, 10 December 1866, vol. 4, p. 176.
Latiri to Taiwo, 13 August 1868, vol. 6, p. 232.
Leases from Taiwo, especially:
  Taiwo to Robert Campbell, 21 April 1868, vol. 8, p. 99.
  Taiwo to Regis Ainé, 1 March 1877, vol. 25, p. 327.
  Taiwo to Pickering and Berthold, 21 April 1900, vol. 44, p. 139.
Deeds of gift from Taiwo, especially:
  Taiwo to Taiwo, 13 April 1898, vol. 31, p. 314 and vol. 32, p. 404.
LSCR: Lagos Supreme Court Records, High Court, Lagos State. Judges' Notebooks in Civil
  Cases, especially:
  D. C. Taiwo v. Yesufu Ajigbolafe, 11 December 1879, vol. 2, p. 229.
  David Macaulay v. D. C. Taiwo, 5 June 1884, vol. 5, p. 316.
  Ogubote v. Adu and D. C. Taiwo, 2 September 1884, vol. 5, p. 385.
  Aṣogbon v. Jinadu Ṣomade, 9 November 1885, vol. 6, p. 127.
  Aṣogbon v. Yesufu Okin, 16 November 1885, vol. 6, p. 136.
  D. C. Taiwo v. S. J. M. Wright, 31 March 1887, vol. 7, p. 28.
  D. C. Taiwo v. Francis Cole, 13 September and 29 December 1887, vol. 7, pp. 242
    and 352.
  D. C. Taiwo v. A. Supiao, 13 February 1887, vol. 9, p. 48.
  Oṣeni Robbin v. D. C. Taiwo, 4 April 1894, pp. 283–86.
  D. C. Taiwo v. Sumonu Aluyo, 23 July 1894, p. 108.
  D. C. Taiwo v. Aṣode, 22 July 1895 and 21–22 October 1895, pp. 168 and 264–65.
  D. C. Taiwo v. Ekonu, Ayiekoroju, and Okilu, 6 September 1896, pp. 329–34.
  D. C. Taiwo v. Oduntan, 17 December 1896, vol. 18, pp. 309, 325–28, 330–34,
    335–40, 342–45.
  Ajaratu v. Seidu, 22 December 1896, vol. 18, p. 315.
NLR: *Nigerian Law Reports*
  R. L. Taiwo v. Odunsi Sarumi, 30 April 1913, vol. 2, pp. 106–7.

Newspapers

LWR: *Lagos Weekly Record*, 23 February 1901.
LS: *Lagos Standard*, 27 February 1901 and 12 August 1903.

Books, Dissertations, and Articles

Adefuye, Ade. 1987. "Ọba Akinṣemoyin and the emergence of modern Lagos." In *History of
  the peoples of Lagos State*, ed. A. Adefuye, B. Agiri, and J. Osuntokun, 39–43. Lagos:
  Lantern Books.
Aderibigbe, A. B. 1975. "Early history of Lagos to about 1850." In *Lagos: The development of
  an African city*, ed. A. B. Aderibigbe, 1–26. Ikeja: Longman.
Adewoye, Omoniyi. 1977. *The judicial system in southern Nigeria, 1854–1954: Law and justice
  in a dependency*. Atlantic Highlands, New Jersey: Humanities.
Agiri, B. A., and Sandra Barnes. 1987. "Lagos before 1603." In *History of the peoples of Lagos
  State*, ed. A. Adefuye, B. Agiri, and J. Osuntokun, 18–32. Lagos: Lantern Books.
Ajayi, J. F. Ade. 1961. "The British occupation of Lagos, 1851–1861." *Nigeria* 69:96–105.
———. 1965. *Christian missions in Nigeria, 1841–1891: The making of a new elite*. Harlow:
  Longman.
Akintoye, S. A. 1971. *Revolution and power politics in Yorubaland, 1840–1893: Ibadan
  expansion and the rise of Ekitiparapo*. New York: Humanities.
Alpers, Edward A. 1983. "The story of Swema: Female vulnerability in nineteenth-century
  East Africa." In *Women and slavery in Africa*, ed. Claire C. Robertson and Martin A.
  Klein, 185–200. Madison: University of Wisconsin Press.

Ayandele, E. A. 1966. *The missionary impact on modern Nigeria, 1842–1914*. London: Longman.

———. 1974. *The educated elite in Nigerian society*. Ibadan: Ibadan University Press.

Baker, Pauline H. 1974. *Urbanization and political change: The politics of Lagos, 1917–1967*. Berkeley: University of California Press.

Barber, Karin. 1981. "Documenting social and ideological change through Yoruba *oriki*: A stylistic analysis." *Journal of the Historical Society of Nigeria* 10:39–52.

Beinart, William. 1987. "Worker consciousness, ethnic particularism and nationalism: The experiences of a South African migrant." In *The politics of race, class and nationalism in twentieth century South Africa*, ed. Shula Marks and Stanley Trapido, 286–309. London Longman.

Berry, Sara. 1985. *Fathers work for their sons: Accumulation, mobility and class formation in an extended Yoruba community*. Berkeley: University of California Press.

———. 1988. "Hegemony on a shoestring: Some unintended consequences of colonial rule for access to resources in African agriculture." Paper presented at the African Studies Association Annual Meeting, Chicago.

Biobaku, Saburi O. 1957. *The Egba and their neighbors, 1842–1872*. Oxford: Clarendon Press.

Burns, Alan. 1969. *History of Nigeria*. London: George Allen and Unwin.

Buxton, Thomas Fowell. 1840. *The African slave trade, and its remedy*. London: John Murray.

Cell, John W. 1970. *British colonial administration in the mid-nineteenth century: The treaty-making process*. New Haven: Yale University Press.

Chanock, Martin. 1985. *Law, custom, and social order: The colonial experience in Malawi and Zambia*. Cambridge: Cambridge University Press.

———. 1989. Laws and Contexts. *Law in Context* 7:68–80.

Coker, G. B. A. 1958. *Family property among the Yorubas*. London: Sweet and Maxwell.

Cole, Patrick. 1975. *Modern and traditional elites in the politics of Lagos*. Cambridge: Cambridge University Press.

Cooper, Frederick. 1980. *From slaves to squatters: Plantation labor and agriculture in Zanzibar and coastal Kenya, 1890–1925*. New Haven: Yale University Press.

Coquery-Vidrovitch, Catherine, and Paul E. Lovejoy. 1985. *The workers of African trade*. Beverly Hills: Sage.

Craton, Michael. 1974. *Sinews of empire: A short history of British slavery*. Garden City: Doubleday.

Davis, David Brian. 1975. *The problem of slavery in the age of Revolution, 1770–1823*. Ithaca: Cornell University Press.

Elias, T. Olawole. 1962. *Nigerian land law and custom*. London: Routledge and Kegan Paul.

———. 1963. *The Nigerian legal system*. London: Routledge and Kegan Paul.

Gbadamosi, T. G. O. 1978. *The growth of Islam among the Yoruba, 1841–1908*. London: Longman.

Geiger, Susan. 1987. Women in nationalist struggle: TANU activists in Dar es Salaam. *International Journal of African Historical Studies* 20:1–26.

Gluckman, Max. 1967. "Introduction." In *The craft of social anthropology*, ed. A. L. Epstein, xi–xx. London: Tavistock.

Hopkins, A. G. 1964. "An economic history of Lagos." Ph.D. dissertation, University of London.

———. 1968. "Economic imperialism in West Africa: Lagos, 1880–1892." *Economic History Review* 21:584–92.

———. 1973. *An economic history of West Africa*. London: Longman.

———. 1978. "Peter Thomas un commerciant nigérian à l'épreuve d'une économic coloniale en crises." In *Les Africains*, vol. 9, ed. Charles-André Julien, 309–29. Paris: Editions J. A.

———. 1980. "Property rights and empire building: Britain's annexation of Lagos, 1861." *The Journal of Economic History* 40:777–98.

Isaacman, Allen F. ed. 1988. *The life history of Raúl Honwana: An inside view of Mozambique from colonialism to independence*. Boulder: Lynne Rienner.

Kopytoff, Jean Herskovits. 1965. *A preface to modern Nigeria: The "Sierra Leonians" in Yoruba, 1830–1890*. Madison: University of Wisconsin Press.

Law, Robin. 1968. "The dynastic chronology of Lagos." *Lagos Notes and Records* 2:46–54.

———. 1978. "The career of Adele at Lagos and Badagry, c. 1807–1837." *Journal of the Historical Society of Nigeria* 9:35–59.

———. 1983. "Trade and politics behind the slave coast: The lagoon traffic and the rise of Lagos, 1500–1800." *Journal of African History* 24:321–48.

Loṣi, John B. 1941. *History of Lagos*. Lagos: Tika Tore Press.

McPhee, Alan. 1970. *The economic revolution in British West Africa*. New York: Negro Universities Press.

Mann, Kristin. 1985. *Marrying well: Marriage, status, and social change among the educated elite in colonial Lagos*. Cambridge: Cambridge University Press.

———. 1987. "Trade, credit, and the commoditization of land in colonial Lagos." Paper presented at a conference, New perspectives on colonial Africa. African Studies Center, University of Illinois.

———. Forthcoming. "Women, landed property, and the accumulation of wealth in early colonial Lagos." *Signs*.

Manning, Patrick. 1982. *Slavery, colonialism and economic growth in Dahoney, 1640–1960*. Cambridge: Cambridge University Press.

Newbury, Colin W. 1961. *The western slave coast and its rulers*. Oxford: Clarendon Press.

———. 1972. Credit in early nineteenth century West African trade. *Journal of African History* 13:81–95.

Nicolson, Ian F. 1969. *The administration of Nigeria, 1900–1960*. Oxford: Clarendon Press.

Oroge, E. Adeniyi. 1971. "The institution of slavery in Yorubaland with particular reference to the nineteenth century." Ph.D. dissertation, University of Birmingham.

Park, A. E. W. 1963. *The sources of Nigerian law*. London: Sweet and Maxwell.

Payne, John Augustus Otonba. 1893. *Table of principal events in Yoruba history*. Lagos: Andrew H. Thomas.

Richards, Edward Harrison. 1894. *Ordinances, orders and rules in force in the colony of Lagos, 1893*. London: Stevens and Sons.

Simpson, S. Rowtan. 1957. *A report on the registration of title to land in the federal territory of Lagos*. Lagos: Federal Government Printer.

Smith, Mary. 1965. *Baba of Karo: A woman of the Muslim Hausa*. London: Faber and Faber.

Smith, Robert S. 1969. *Kingdoms of the Yoruba*. London: Methuen.

———. 1979. *The Lagos consulate, 1851–1861*. Berkeley: University of California Press.

Stone, Lawrence. 1971. Prosopography. *Daedalus* 100:46–79.

Tamuno, T. N. 1972. *The evolution of the Nigerian state: The southern phase, 1898–1914*. London: Longman.

Temperley, Howard. 1977. "Capitalism, slavery and ideology." *Past and Present* 75:94–118.

Verger, Pierre. 1968. *Flux et reflux de la traite de Nègres entre le Golfe de Benin et Bahia de Todos os Santos du dix-septième au dix-neuvième siècle*. Paris: Mouton.

Wood, J. Buckley. 1933. *Historical notices of Lagos, West Africa*. Lagos: Church Missionary Society Bookshop.

Wright, Marcia. 1975. "Women in peril: A commentary upon the life stories of captives in nineteenth-century east-central Africa." *African Social Research* 20:800–819.

4

From Giving and Lending to Selling: Property Transactions Reflecting Historical Changes on Kilimanjaro

SALLY FALK MOORE

Methodological Prolegomenon

Reconstructing history from the statements of the living has its perils. "On Kilimanjaro land is the most important thing. Land goes from fathers to sons. That is the way it is here. That is our custom from long ago," a senior Chagga man instructs the anthropologist in 1974. They sit in front of his rectangular, tin-roofed, mud-walled house. "And did you inherit this very *kihamba* (banana garden) from your father? And did he receive it from his father?" Old Selemani answers as if the localized Chagga patrilineages now in place had always been there, located precisely where they are as he speaks. It is as if every son had always acquired his land from his father.

Such indigenous narratives about the permanent norms of "traditional" culture are problematic for a time-conscious anthropology. They are equally troublesome for an anthropologically aware history. Past changes are well known to hide inside the framework of "traditional" institutions. History can be inconveniently masked where the invocation of "custom" is a form of present legitimation.

Hard evidence of the realities of land acquisition among the Chagga of Kilimanjaro exists. It can be found in the records of law cases, the reports of the provincial commissioners and other government officials, and in the oral history of particular plots of land. And those realities are (and have been) much more complex and varied than old Selemani's words suggest. He was right that sons often inherit from their fathers. There is agnatic inheritance that tends to be lineal. But there are also (and were in the past) other ways to acquire plots both from within and from outside of the lineage. In 1900 there was plenty of unoccupied bush land for the taking. Any man could pioneer and "develop" a new plot. By 1950 there was no bush land available, though for the well-off there were still some plots to be had for cash. Thus changing forms of external acquisition (i.e. from *outside* the patriline) exist and have existed alongside of the chains of inheritance from fathers to sons. And even the agnatic arrangement varied. Land might be had from a grandfather or an uncle, or from another agnatic kinsman who happened to die without sons. Circumstances differed because of the variable configuration of families and their fortunes. The size of holdings varied, as did the accidents of fate: who died first, how many sons there were in any lineage branch, and the like. Even inside the lineage there often was much more to the story than might be suggested by Selemani's statement about a simple succession from father to son.

Other misconceptions could result from projecting into an earlier time Selemani's emphasis on the centrality of land. To be sure, the Chagga have been cultivators as far back as anything is known of them, and in the sense that land has provided basic sustenance, it has always been deeply important. But a century ago there was an abundance of land and there was no cash cropping. If there was a shortage of anything, it was of other resources, of which two were particularly marked — a shortage of persons (both as labor and as political and economic clients) and a shortage of cattle (for consumption and for various forms of exchange). Today on Kilimanjaro, cash cropping, land scarcity, and overpopulation have given a new twist to the priorities. Current urgencies have also reshaped the way the past is remembered. A corrective insight into the circumstances of the colonial period in the words of those who were living through it can be found in the records of thousands of law cases heard in the local courts on Kilimanjaro.

I have recently published a book on a century of Kilimanjaro's history through the analysis of its so-called "customary law" (Moore 1986). At its most general, the thesis of that work was that what passed for "customary law" in the colonial period was a profoundly transformed version of earlier arrangements, in many respects an artifact of the colonial period. Local practices continued to change, as they do to this day, while being steadfastly certified as "customary" both by local people and by central governments. This paper should be read as a first postscript on the methods and conclusions of that larger work. But the intention of this paper is to do more than to place a few more unpublished cases on the record. The legal disputes I have chosen to describe here give some new glimpses of the consequences for the Chagga of the major economic and political changes that occurred in the region during the colonial period: the end of interchiefdom wars, the advent of cash cropping, the enormous increase in population, the progressive worsening of the land shortage, and the step-by-step transformation of the role of chiefs. The cases show that there were basic shifts in the interchangeability of different resources as the colonial period progressed, and concomitant shifts of practice. But perhaps even more interesting to the historical project from a theoretical point of view, the cases chosen also demonstrate the results of a methodological experiment. In selecting which of several thousand cases might illustrate certain economic changes most clearly, I employed an unusual criterion: I looked for cases which showed transactions between persons who were not agnatic kin, cases which also concerned the alienation to "outsiders" of patrimonial interests in persons and property.

The rationale was this: if, among the Chagga cases, one were to confine one's attention to controversies over agnatic inheritance, these would be bound to give rich testimony to the way patrilineages reproduced themselves locally from generation to generation. Like Selemani's statements, correct in themselves, but incomplete, this would leave an overwhelming sense of the persistence of cultural form. But if transactions are at issue in which the transfer is of patrimonial property to non-agnates, those being "non-routine" are far more likely to expose time-specific motives and conditions for allowing that patrimonial property to leave the patriline.

This method has been productive for the reconstruction of Chagga history. It could easily be applied to other settings in Africa and elsewhere. Attention to non-agnatic transactions serves to modulate the bias toward continuity and "reproduction" that would otherwise be built into a kin-focused approach. The logic of inheritance from father to son does not necessarily demand explications of the contemporaneous context. But the time-specific reasons why patrimonial property found its way to persons outside the patrilineage or from the public domain into private hands does require attention to the changing political and economic milieu. Imbedded in the strategies of what Habermas calls the "life world" are refractions of larger-scale circumstances (Habermas 1987:118, 151).

The legal transactions and contestations between non-agnates selected for presentation here concern material interests in persons, in cattle, in land, and in cash. The ways in which (and the times at which) persons, cattle, land, and cash were or become interchangeable are obvious indicators of transformations in the political economy of the region. But because the legal cases and transactions urgently concern individuals, they also give insight into the human and cultural meanings of these systemic changes.

The Historical Background, a Brief Sketch

For the Chagga the colonial period could be said to have begun in 1886 when Kilimanjaro was incorporated into German East Africa (Stahl 1964:177). Thirty years later, in 1916, the British defeated the Germans and thus began their administration of the area. British rule continued until independence was achieved in 1961. The formal political sequence gives no indication of the fundamental changes in African life that colonial rule effected.

In the precolonial century the peoples of Kilimanjaro had been involved in the slave and ivory trades. They also had had a significant role in the provisioning of caravans. Hundreds of men plied their way from the coast to the interior and back again each year. They needed places to rest and to restock their supplies. Chagga chiefdoms welcomed this provisioning trade. In the same period, the several dozen politically autonomous chiefdoms on Kilimanjaro were chronically at war with one another. The inter-chiefdom fighting was probably closely related to competition over trade routes. Periodically one chiefdom would dominate others for a time, sometimes by forming a set of alliances. Eventually the leading alliance would collapse, the dominant chiefdom would be defeated and another would be ascendant for a time. A several-century history of these rivalries, rises and falls is known in outline (Stahl 1964).

There is no doubt of the openness of Chagga chiefdoms to contacts with the coast and the interior in the nineteenth century. By 1848 there were Swahili speakers permanently lodged in the entourage of the chiefs. They may have been there much earlier. By the 1880s the Chagga chiefdoms in the long-distance trade had acquired more than imported cloth and trade beads. They had rifles. There is even evidence that the cash economy had begun to penetrate. When Sir Harry Johnston spent some months on the mountain in the early 1880s, he rented a plot of land for himself and his servants and paid the chief in rupees (Johnston 1886:191–93). Johnston offered Mandara twelve rupees a month. Mandara demanded 100 and said he would not allow explorer Johnston to collect any more specimens of plants and butterflies until he paid the higher rent. As an insulting joke, Mandara sent Sir Harry a basket of vegetable refuse to "add to your collection" and demanded to be paid a few ells of cloth in return for the garbage. The Chagga still controlled their beloved Kilimanjaro and were not intimidated by Europeans. They were soon to lose their political autonomy, but in the meanwhile they continued to bargain for whatever they could extract from their European visitors.

The German colonial peace put a stop to the fighting, hanged some chiefs, deposed others, and made the installed chiefs answerable to their colonial rulers. The old long-distance and provisioning trades ended. Over time the political arena was completely reorganized. What had been dozens of chiefdoms were consolidated into fewer and fewer, first by the Germans, later by the British. This conveniently reduced the number of entities with which the colonial governments had to deal. The basis of chiefly power was transformed, as was the role itself.

In both the German and the British periods, each chiefdom had a law court presided over by the chief. Since there was no separation between executive and judicial powers until nearly the end of the colonial period, the judicial role was an extension of chiefly administrative authority. It served as an arm of the colonial government in matters such as prosecuting the failure to pay taxes. And, as we shall see, it sometimes served the personal interests of the chiefs. The courts were much more than instruments for the perpetuation of "customary" law.

From the violent upheavals of the beginning of the colonial era, through the more peaceful decades that followed, and until the present, most Chagga have lived in localized clusters of patrilineally related households. Each household is situated in the midst of its own separate garden compound, the boundary of which is clearly marked by a living fence of dracaena. The gardens produce subsistence crops of bananas, millet, and vegetables, and the Chagga also keep a few cows, sheep and goats. Those were the very foods supplied to the caravans in the old days. Today they are largely cultivated and kept for domestic consumption. And today there is one more important cultivar growing in the gardens: coffee bushes. Just as the nineteenth century traffic in the long-distance trade ended, a substitute form of commerce emerged. The Europeans introduced coffee-growing in the 1890s and the practice gradually spread over the whole mountain. Coffee became a major source of cash as each household added coffee seedlings to its gardens. For a while Arabica coffee made the Chagga relatively prosperous.

Fortunate in the climate and soil of their mountain, fortunate in the continuous availability of water, fortunate in having had a remarkably benign district officer assigned to them at the beginning of the British period who helped them reorganize their coffee production and fought for their interests, the Chagga adapted to their changing circumstances with a will. Most of them became Christians. Many were educated at mission schools, some at government schools (Shann 1956). As a people, they became addicts of education and came to share many of the ideas of progress held by their colonial rulers.

However population growth eventually denied them the continuing prosperity associated with their once-burgeoning coffee economy. Today the household gardens are too small to satisfy ever-increasing cash needs. The only families which remain prosperous are those with members who have salaried jobs or paying businesses in addition to coffee gardens. The Chagga are suffering from a severe land shortage. From a population estimated at 100,000 in 1900, the Chagga multiplied to 600,000 by 1978 (1978 Population Census). Land shortage was already perceptible in the late 1920s. At that time there was anxiety on the part of chiefs that the buying and selling of land for cash was about to begin. Up to that point the customary payment for transferred land had been "a cow and a goat." The chiefs wanted to forbid entirely the commerce in buying and selling of land for cash (Griffiths 1930:63, 88). They had no success in making such a rule law, no doubt because their colonial masters thought a market in land would be a sign of evolutionary progress. Moreover, the provincial commissioners must have been entirely aware that in their regulation of land matters the chiefs were not disinterested parties.

During the colonial period chiefs used their administrative powers gradually to appropriate increasing control over the allocation of unused land. For the service of assigning a plot of land to a new holder, they received valuable "gifts of thanks" from beneficiaries. It is no wonder then that in their judicial and administrative capacities, chiefs who had once confined themselves to approving the allocation of uncultivated wilderness became more and more involved in the business of certifying the legitimacy of all land transfers and land claims. As a consequence they were increasingly able to use their positions to enlarge their own landholdings and those of their kinsmen and other favorites. Probably in the late 1920s when they were arguing against land sales for cash, their fear was that a cash market in land would render chiefly interventions less profitable, perhaps ever superfluous. This is one of the many bits of evidence that converge to suggest that early in the century competition for control over persons and cattle was the dominant focus of transactions, while by 1930, control over land and the pursuit of cash were beginning to become central. Almost from the inception of the colonial period transactions in all four—persons, coffee, land and cash—existed contemporaneously, so the periodization of the pre-1930 and the post-1930 economies is to be understood as a matter of emphasis, not as a contrast between absolutely different circumstances. What was involved was a long-term cumulative shift, a directional transformation, in demography, in production and exchange, and in cultural and political ideas.

The Cases

The three sets of cases that follow have in common the transfer of agnatic property to a non-agnate. They differ from one another in almost every other respect. *The first set of cases* shows an economic preoccupation with property in cattle in the first half of the colonial period. These cases also expose Chagga attitudes toward controlled human beings and differentiate sharply between male and female. In the first case a biological daughter is treated as a "pawn," and offered as a pledge for a cattle debt. In the second, an unrelated, captured male child comes to be treated legally as a son and is preferred as an heir to a biological daughter. The dispute between them is over the inheritance of cattle. *The second set of cases* concerns the attempts of men to give land to their sons-in-law and the historical change in attitude toward such transfers. Such gifts become less acceptable as land shortage becomes more acute. The assertion of patrilineal interest becomes stronger, not weaker over time. This is one of many indications that the characteristics of "the patrilineage" are historically specific and not necessarily "the same" from one period to another, even though the entity called "the patrilineage" persists. *The third set of cases* concerns three types of situation affected by increasing land shortage: the attempts by land lenders to reclaim their land and terminate tenancies at will, the attempts to classify unoccupied land as "abandoned" in order to install new holders, and instances in which loans of cash are secured by land used as collateral. The last type of case shows how the use of land as collateral created a new mode through which land became vulnerable to transfer out of patrimonial control. Together the three sets of cases clearly reflect the implications of an ever-deepening commitment to cash cropping and a money economy. Incidentally they also bring to light the shifting role of chiefship, as chiefs strategized to serve their own interests in a changing economic milieu.

Transactions such as are reported in these three sets of cases, many of them involving loans and collateral, have a special use for the historian. Such transactions expose changing Chagga ideas of economic equivalence at particular moments in their past. A time series of relevant law cases can demonstrate the changing connections between different categories of exchangeable resources. The cases chosen for discussion here show substantial shifts in the kinds of debts that Chagga men could incur and in the kind of collateral they could offer when borrowing. Indirectly the cases illuminate the strategies that individuals could use to advance their own interests, the kinds of choices that were available. At the beginning of this century human beings could be offered as collateral in cattle transactions. Many later cases show that subsequently animals were regularly traded for land. After several more decades land itself could be offered as collateral for large loans of cash.

Radical changes also took place in the modes of official intervention. In the early cases the chief appears on stage rapaciously using every occasion to acquire personal rights over persons and cattle. However, at that time a chief's consent was not necessary to transfer land (see Gutmann [1926]:305; HRAF:273, on the German period when the chief's consent was not needed). Later chiefs were more constrained in matters of persons and beasts and instead concentrated on increasing their income through patronage and land acquisition. At that point they actively interposed themselves in all land allocations and transactions (Hailey 1938:848 cites a Chagga Native Authority regulation legitimating the transfer of land only *if made with the authority of the chief).* Thus in the middle colonial period the chiefs' "traditional" dual capacities as allocators of unoccupied fields and as presiders over litigated controversies expanded and came to have entirely new significance. For everyone, the shift to coffee cultivation and the increase in population produced a reinterpretation of the value of land as against cattle and cash and concomitantly the revision of many land-related practices. Throughout, the chiefs and other dispute hearers were presumed to be invoking and applying "customary law" rules. That was what their colonial governors both expected and required. To the extent that the Chagga did actually use the "traditional" rules, this apparent reiteration of the past was done in rapidly altering circumstances. The significance changed. The cases give clear evidence of this historical sequence.

Case Set I

a.   Pledging a child in exchange for a cow:
a human being as collateral in the early 1900s

A case in which a child was used as collateral for a cattle loan arose in the first decade or two of this century. The controversy was heard before Salema, the chief of Moshi, who ruled from 1900 to 1917. We owe the description of the situation to the missionary, Bruno Gutmann, who was on Kilimanjaro when the case was litigated (Gutmann [1926]:128–29; HRAF:111–12; cited and discussed in Moore 1986:106–107). The case involved one of Chief Selema's subjects who had borrowed a cow to pay a cattle debt and who had failed to repay the beast.

Some years before the hearing, the borrower, Mavin Ovenja, had obtained an animal from his wife's sister's husband to satisfy a cattle creditor who was pressing him. The wife's sister's husband lived some distance away in another chiefdom. By way of collateral, Mavin gave one of his daughters to the lender. The idea was that when that daughter was old enough to marry, if the debt had not been paid, the lender could either betroth the girl to his own son without paying bridewealth or could let her marry someone else and collect the bridewealth from the marriage. (In the meanwhile he had the use of her labor.) In time the borrower's daughter was duly betrothed to the lender's son. All would have been well except that the young woman refused to marry the son and ran away, back to her parent's house.

The chief resolved the case by paying his subject's cattle debt himself. This was not simply an act of generosity. By doing so the chief acquired the right to the debtor's daughter's bridewealth. He stood in the place of the original creditor. The chief, acting as judge, both settled the debt and inserted himself as successor to the legal rights of one of the parties before him. The case neatly demonstrates the way the chief could use his role in the early colonial period as lender of capital, as a person directly involved in the transactions of his people when he chose to be, and possibly also as a strategizing patron who had his own material interests at heart when he moved to intervene. (It is not clear from the case whether the chief took the girl into his own household. The frequent use of female child labor by the chiefs in their households at the time was deplored by Gutmann who called it a form of slavery ([1926]:388–89; HRAF:348–49)).

Thus a daughter and/or her future bridewealth appears to have been one of the best forms of security a man without beasts could offer against a "borrowed" animal. Animals that were borrowed to be disposed of (as opposed to animals borrowed for "keeping") were used to pay bridewealth, were slaughtered in ritual, or were used to pay debts. Lending a cow to be thus consumed or given away involved a high risk. The lender was taking a considerable chance if, as was frequently the case, the borrower had uncertain prospects of acquiring a beast with which he might later make a repayment. The creditor who pressed for repayment had recourse to the other major scarce resource: labor. A defaulting cattle-debtor either had to supply a child as a debt-slave, or had to work off the debt through his own labor (Gutmann [1926]:231−32, 472, 477−79; HRAF:204−05, 424, 429−30). Bananas and other produce form the debtor's garden were sometimes due to the creditor for a time, but there is no talk of the creditor acquiring a right to the land itself (Gutmann [1926]:231−32, 474−86; HRAF:204−05, 426−37).

There was another, entirely different form of cattle "borrowing" in which the borrowed cow was not to be disposed of, but rather placed for "keeping" to be fed and bred. The borrower got the milk and manure and had certain rights to meat at slaughter time. Such a cow could be demanded back at will by the lender. That kind of cattle placement was often (usually?) made with non-kinsmen to conceal assets from relatives who might demand that a beast be "loaned" to them (see Moore 1986:67−70). Since the return of the cow so placed could always be demanded by the owner, and the possessor had no right of alienation or disposal, there was less need for any form of collateral. However, taking children as security may have reduced the likelihood that the possessor of the animal would pretend the beast had died while in fact transferring it to someone else. Thus the practice of child placement as collateral may not have been unusual just before the turn of the century when it appears to have been commonplace for the inhabitants of Moshi and Marangu to place their cattle with men in Rombo. In return, and by way of security, the Rombo cattle keepers gave their children as collateral/hostages to the cattle lenders. Early in the colonial period the Germans ended this practice and the debt-pledge children were returned (Gutmann [1926]:479; HRAF:430).

Despite the colonial prohibition, the use of female children as collateral seems to have continued long after German times in some places on the mountain. Case number 7 Mwika 1930 (in volume labelled Kitabu cha Shauri 1927) mentions another female child given in lieu of the debt of a cow. When she reached adulthood the young woman ran away and returned to her father. The man who had supplied the cow sued the father of the girl in 1929, and the girl's father was then ordered by the court to pay three cows. The father then fell ill and died. The subsequent 1930 case was brought by the court against the man to whom the cows were to have been paid because he had appropriated one of the cows of the son of his debtor by force instead of bringing the matter to the chief. For using self-help rather than coming to the chief, the man was fined 20 shillings. In this case there was no question of the chief taking on the debt of his subject. Instead there was a strong assertion of the power of the court and its monopoly on enforcement.

There is always much less certainty about founding an argument on the absence of evidence than on its presence, but as far as one can tell, early in the century the Chagga never offered *land* as collateral against the borrowing of cattle.[1] It seems entirely logical, economically and socially, that land would not have been a desirable form of collateral at that time. First of all, land was not a particularly scarce resource. Bush land was plentiful. The colonial imposition of peace, and the mandatory end of the interchiefdom wars took the danger out of living at the outskirts of existing settlements. Bush land was thus not only available but had stopped being undesirable. Since every man had had enough land to fill the subsistence needs of his household, and could get more by cultivating bush, even had it been possible, the opportunity to acquire an extra kihamba plot from a debtor probably would not have been particularly attractive. Moreover, landholding in the banana belt was closely associated with membership in a lineage and local community. For creditors to appropriate a piece of land in the heart of the debtor's kinship area would not have had much attraction. The creditor or his kinsman would likely have been unwelcome outsiders. Thus any garden plot, even if it was economically equivalent to another, was not socially interchangeable with other pieces of land of the same size and productivity. Hence the availability of land and the social correlates of landholding made land an unsuitable form of collateral for cattle debts.

That was the situation in the early years of this century when the practice of coffee cultivation was at its inception. At that time most arable land was still used exclusively for food crops, most of which were consumed locally. In that pre-1916 period there was no cash market in land. There was a kind of individual property in particular plots for married adult males, with associated, but conditional, rights of disposition. Coffee was first introduced in the Kilema mission in 1895 (Shann 1956:29–30). The subsequent German imposition of taxes probably provided a spur to coffee cultivation and certainly hastened the generalization of the cash economy. Taxes were first imposed in 1897, but it was possible to work off the obligation by doing labor on public projects. By 1905 free labor in lieu of taxes was abolished and paid work was substituted (Iliffe, 1979:160). But for the Chagga coffee provided a way of obtaining cash without working for the colonial government or for the settlers.

For those early years of the century there seems good reason why I can find no mention of land offered as security for a cattle debt, or any other debt. The cases confirm what other indications suggest. In that period the highest value seems to have been put on human labor and on cattle.

b. An "adopted" war captive and his right to inherit cattle: human beings as prizes of battle in 1930

In some of the late nineteenth-century accounts of Kilimanjaro, there is substantial mention of the slave trade (Johnston 1886:97, 180, 184). Slaves were certainly part of the caravan traffic to the coast that passed through the Kilimanjaro area. There is no convincing evidence that the Chagga themselves kept slaves as such, though they incorporated women and children who were war captives into their households (Johnston, 1886:165 and case in this section). There is good reason to believe that adult male Chagga war captives were sold into the trade. Sir Harry Johnston said that when he reproached the Chagga chief, Mandara, for slaving, Mandara replied to the following effect, "What am I to do? To kill captives would be wrong. To return them to my enemies would mean that they would just attack me later. If I keep them in my own land, my people would say, 'if strangers are to occupy the soil, where is the room for our children to cultivate?' Then what can I do but sell them to the Arabs" (paraphrase of Johnston 1886:181). Mandara's allusion to the slaves as enemy warriors implies that his reference was to male captives.

The legal status of "adopted" young captives was raised in 1930 in litigation over an estate. A man who had been a captive child, one Kilegho of Kirueni village, sued his stepsister, Rebeka, of Mrimbo village, for eight cows and six goats, which he alleged was his proper share of his stepfather's estate (21 Mwika 1930 in Kitabu cha Shauri Mwika 1927). Rebeka was the biological child of Kilegho's stepfather. It is of interest that there was no controversy over the land of his stepfather to which he seems to have succeeded. His undisputed succession to the land implies that his stepfather's agnates had sufficient land not to contest his right. It also speaks to the legal incapacity of women to share in agnatically transmitted lands, though they could in some circumstances inherit cattle.

Kilegho's testimony says, "Many years ago my father brought me as a captive from the war. I was very young—I had only four teeth, two on the upper jaw and two on the lower. When I arrived Rebeka was suckling and I shared the same mother with her. My status in the family was like that of any other child. My father had no other son. Then father died and left me with mother Matemu. I stayed with her until she died and I inherited the property of my father.

"By this time Rebeka had married in Keni Mriti [in Rombo where she lived with her husband]. Before father died he gave Rebeka one cow. He also gave Kinangaro and Kiloka, the sons of his younger brother, one cow each. Some weeks after the death of my father the relatives of my mother came to claim *mahari* [bridewealth]. I gave Sifueli [sister of mother] one cow, the remaining part of the bridewealth which my father had not paid." Among the Chagga bridewealth obligations were usually not paid in full at the time of marriage but paid gradually over time. There often were payments still due when the woman died. The argument being made in the court was that an adoptive son who undertook to honor the bridewealth obligations of his deceased stepfather was behaving like a real son to his cost, hence should be deemed by the court to be a son. "Later Sifueli came to me and told me that Rebeka and Kinangaro wanted to steal my cows. She then advised me to give her my cows to keep for me because she did not want me to be robbed. I agreed and she went away. The next day she came with Daniel. I took them and showed them two cows, one of which was being looked after by Kikwani and the other by Katore. Daniel wrote down the signs of the cows. I also told them about other people who had my cows and I asked them to go there and take them or put down their signs.

"After all of this, Sifueli went to see Rebeka and they plotted to appropriate my cows. I would not have realized what the situation was had it not been for the subsequent action they took. They slaughtered one of my cows without informing me. When I got the news I asked Sifueli why they slaughtered my cow without my consent. She told me to bring the case before the Chief. I did. The case was heard and Sifueli said that she had possession of my cows on orders from Rebeka. Then I decided to bring a case against Rebeka before the court."

Rebeka the defendant said, "My mother Matemu died and left the cows to me. Now in the court I have been asked whether I gave Sifueli permission to hold Kilegho's cows. The cows do not belong to Kilegho. In the previous case the elders sentenced me and ordered me to pay Kilegho five cows. The three remaining cows were to be left for me. I disagreed with the decision. Kilegho and I have been in conflict for a very long time. However, I was forced to pay him the five cows and the court promised that it would reconcile me with Kilegho. I refused to be reconciled with Kilegho but agreed to pay him five cows. Of the six goats he is claiming, five of them have died and the last one will die soon since it is very ill."

Judgment: "Rebeka has no right to the inheritance although the property belonged to her mother. According to custom, such inheritance is only for males, for sons. Although Kilegho was not born of Rebeka's mother nor was he the son of her father, the parents had accepted the captive boy as their son because they had no other son. Thus the court judges that Kilegho is entitled to five cows and Rebeka to three cows. The reason is that though Rebeka is the real child of the parents, she is a female. With regard to the goats, Kilegho is to investigate whether they are alive or dead and must inform the court." The court also said, "There are many people who have inherited as Kilegho has done, and it is not a new thing in the village." Rebeka lost her fee of 12 shillings 50. Those present were Chief Solomoni II and nine elders.

This case is not only evidence of the adoption of male captives in the upheavals of the late nineteenth century, but also shows clearly that such adopted male captives had greater rights of inheritance than female biological children. The case gives some sense of the considerable number of animals a household might have had at the time, and that the practice of placing them in the households of others continued. Here, given the circumstances, the court found reason to treat a non-agnate as if he were an agnate.

Case Set II

Two attempts to transfer inherited land to a son-in-law, one successful, one unsuccessful

The two instances that I shall describe here occurred over what must roughly have been a fifty-year period. Both involved the question of the consent of kinsmen to the alienation of land to an outsider, a man who was not a member of the lineage. In both cases a father of daughters sought to bestow land on a son-in-law. In Chagga law the father needed the agreement (tacit or explicit) of his agnates to make such a transfer of patrimonial property (Gutmann [1926]:306; HRAF:275). What is interesting is that in the earlier transfer (which occurred between 1910 and 1920) there proved to be no problem about allocating land to sons-in-law. In the later case (1959) the donor was thwarted by his kinsmen who withheld their consent. These cases show that the use of the agnatic consent rule was intensified as the colonial period progressed and land became scarce, even though other patrilineal ties were gradually attenuated. Thus the public political place of patrilineages weakened over the course of the century, and the existence of the missions and the spread of formal education diminished the hold of patrilineages over ritual matters. Nevertheless, patrilineal kinship became ever more important as an avenue to land, and patrilineal ties remain of major significance to this day.

The earlier of the two cases of land transfer to sons-in-law concerns Kinyala, a member of the M—lineage. Kinyala saw his three daughters married between

1910 and 1920. Having no sons, he gave each son-in-law a plot of land close to his own within the territory controlled by the M—lineage, but along its outside border (data from mapping and genealogical inquiry during fieldwork).

The oral report that Kinyala's kinsmen agreed to the transfer at the time seems entirely reliable. He was in the grandparental generation of senior men whom I knew. Not only did his descendants report that such consent was given, but they acted accordingly. When the original grantees died, no members of the M—lineage tried to reclaim the land on any ground, least of all that consent had been withheld, and the present generation would surely have made such claims had there been a shred of evidence to go on. When asked about this in the 1970s, one of the men in the lineage asserted that he and his kinsmen were barred from reclaiming the land because of the promises made by their ancestors. Today, the descendants of Kinyala's sons-in-law hold those plots with undisputed authority (see Moore 1986:228, situating Kinyala in the genealogical chart of his patrilineage). Their lands have simply dropped out of the M—'s lineage territory and form part of the heritable land of families from other lineages. This is an instance in which there is every reason to believe that the legal rules about alienation with consent described by Gutmann were in fact observed (Gutmann [1926]:302–9; HRAF:270–6).

A contrasting instance of an attempt to transfer land to a son-in-law occurred in 1959 (field material collected in the 1970s). Siara, a respected senior man, tried to give his son-in-law a plot of land from his own patrimony, but his kinsmen refused to agree to this. Subsequently Siara appealed to the chief to overrule their decision, but the chief upheld the kinsmen. Siara's was an odd case. Siara did have two sons, but one was a Catholic priest, hence would never marry and have children, and the other had been disinherited because of a quarrel between father and son. The disinherited son no longer lived on Kilimanjaro. What is more, that son's only surviving offspring were female. Siara argued that he had the right to alienate to a son-in-law since he "had no sons" in any social sense. His biological sons would never establish a line of descendants for him.

The chief decreed that Siara could not give away the land of his lineage in that way. Siara was, however, allowed to *sell* his land, take the proceeds, and give the money to his son-in-law to buy another plot. Thus the chief was not conserving the land for Siara's sons. I assume (but unfortunately did not ask) that Siara sold the land to one of his agnates, since by that time (1959) the consent rule had turned into a rule of first refusal. (A man who wished to sell was said to be obliged to offer his plot to his agnates before selling to any outsider.) What distinguishes this case is that Siara had not wanted to sell, but rather to *give* the land to his son-in-law. He wanted his daughter and grandchildren to live nearby. The same rule applied. The rule of first refusal was used as if a gift to a non-agnate were equivalent to an offer to sell.

The two "son-in-law transactions" suggest a certain historical continuity. Each involves the same stated legal norm: that the alienation of patrimonial land to a non-kinsman requires the consent of agnates. One might be tempted to say, then, that the legal rule was the same from 1910 into the 1950s. But to say no more would be a distortion, an overemphasis of form over content, since it omits crucial changes in the context. Over the century, coffee cultivation, population increase, and land shortage had made men more jealous of their agnates' land,

and ever less likely to agree to its alienation especially if they could afford to buy it themselves. The rule of "first refusal" constituted a substantial transformation of the agnatic consent rule. In its practice, the localized patrilineage of the 1950s was was an artifact of the conditions of the 1950s. The patrilineage was not simply an atemporal entity perpetuating a "tradition." The new historical circumstances in which an old legal rule was used had become part of the new meaning of that rule.

Case Set III

a. Loaned land, coffee planting, and the payment of animals for land in the 1920s and 1930s

Unlike loaned beasts, loaned land cannot be consumed by a borrower or made to disappear. Thus lending land was less risky than lending cattle and was often done. Among the Chagga loaned land could always be retaken by the donor, provided that it was possible to prove that all rights had not been transferred to the borrower, and that compensation was paid for improvements. A 1929 case shows the mounting tensions that arose over loaned land once coffee growing became an issue (26 Mwika 1929). The lawsuit was brought by a commoner named Joshua, of Kondeny village, against Naomi, the daughter of the then chief of Mwika, Mangi Solomoni of the Orio lineage. Joshua was unrelated to the Orios. The chief did not preside at the hearing since it involved a member of his immediate family (his daughter), but it seems likely that the village headmen and elders who heard the case were not uninfluenced by the chief's interest in the outcome. This formal judicial standing-back from a case because the judge is an interested party contrasts strikingly with the earlier case of the pledge child, in which the chief involved himself directly in the affairs of the disputants before him, and so-to-speak made himself a party to their transactions by interposing himself personally and financially in the resolution of their dispute. This change was probably of colonial provenance.

In 1921 (date not mentioned directly but inferred from internal evidence in the case text) one Joshua had asked Ngapanyi Orio (a relative of Chief Solomoni) for a piece of land on which to live. Ngapanyi provided him with an undeveloped piece of land and Joshua built a house on it and planted a banana grove. Three years later (probably in 1924) the case says that the government ordered everyone to plant coffee.[2] Joshua told Ngapanyi Orio that he wanted to plant coffee on the plot. Ngapanyi refused him permission to do so, asserting his right as an owner to refuse such an improvement. Had Ngapanyi allowed Joshua to plant the coffee, and had he later wanted to reclaim the land (as loaned land), he would have been obliged to pay compensation for the coffee bushes. That would have been expensive.

According to Joshua's testimony, Ngapanyi not only refused Joshua permission to plant coffee, but also forced him to transfer the land, house, and banana grove to Naomi, Chief Solomoni's daughter. It was understood that she would have to compensate Joshua for his improvements on the land, namely the house and the banana grove. Naomi was originally to pay two goats for the house. Naomi did not pay the two goats but instead gave Joshua a young heifer for the house and promised to pay him an additional goat later on for the banana grove.

Five years passed. Then in 1929 Ngapanyi Orio claimed his kihamba from Joshua, I suppose on the theory that Joshua was still the basic loanee, though Naomi was the resident occupant of the land. (Since the full "redemption price" had not been paid to Joshua, Ngapanyi could not yet claim the land as his own.) This reclaim demand was discussed by the elders (i.e., it did not go formally to the court) and Ngapanyi was ordered to pay Joshua two goats for the banana grove which Joshua had planted. Joshua then told Naomi to leave the kihamba which belonged to Ngapanyi Orio. She refused because she had bought the house and had paid a heifer for it and wanted to be compensated for giving it up. Joshua then took Naomi to court in the present case.

Naomi testified that she had returned to Mwika chiefdom from Mamba when her husband died. At that time she had gone to her father, Chief Solomoni, to ask him to help her to find a place to live. Joshua then agreed (under duress?) to "sell" her the house and the banana grove (not the land, but the improvements) for three goats. She did not manage to get the three goats, but paid a heifer (the equivalent of two goats) instead. Five years elapsed, and then Joshua brought her to court in this case to get the kihamba back so that he could return it to Ngapanyi Orio. Naomi said, "If Joshua wants me to move, let him bring my cow, the same cow and not another, whether it is alive or dead."

The decision in the case was as follows: Joshua was to return Naomi's cow as it was alive and now fully grown. Naomi was to turn over the kihamba to Ngapanyi Orio. Ngapanyi Orio was to pay Joshua two goats for the banana grove.

Joshua seems to have ended up with very little, and was also out of pocket for the two shilling court fee. What is apparent from the case is that little value was set on the kihamba until coffee growing was quite general and local land shortages were beginning to be felt. Land loans were treated as tenancies-at-will (as they had been even in German times and continued to be until legislatively abolished after independence). A reclaiming lender had always had to pay compensation for improvements in order to repossess his land, but that was the only constraint on ousting the loanee at any time. However, until land became the vehicle for a cash crop and became scarce and valuable, there was seldom reason to reclaim it. Land loans were heritable. The position of lender and borrower were inherited by the sons or other successors of the original parties and the relationship might go on forever, marked by the annual giving of ritual gifts to reassert the loan before witnesses.

This case, though jumbled in the record, is interesting on many scores. First, it shows that a widowed daughter of a chief could come home to her father and expect to be given a piece of land to live on in the patrilineal domain. Second, it suggests that the chief regarded it appropriate to require his kinsman to oust the unrelated holder of loaned land for such a purpose. There is a sense here of the power of the chief to impose his will on his agnates. Third, despite her highborn connections, the daughter seems not to have been able to muster the full payment of three goats. Was that a matter of poverty or disdain for the debt shown by a chief's daughter? It must have been clear from the beginning that all that was being transferred to Naomi was the right to occupy since no woman could acquire a disposable right in land. Thus the basic legal issue in the case was whether Joshua, the original loanee, still had an interest in the land as against his own lender, Ngapanyi Orio, because full compensation had neither been paid by Naomi, nor by Ngapanyi. Fourth, it shows that at that time and place lineage land was easily transferrable to non-kin provided it was merely loaned. Fifth, the case also suggests the standard of value equivalence: three goats for a house and banana grove, or a heifer and a goat. Improvements were what determined the price of reclaim, not some other notion of the value of the land itself. The emphasis on land loaning and redemption and the use of beasts in exchange, suggest a very different economy from that which prevailed later on.

How early in the century did cash transactions for land take place? As mentioned, earlier in 1927 the chiefs vehemently opposed the buying and selling of land and said it should be prohibited (Griffiths 1930:63, 88). Yet by the 1930s the case records give indications of some full transfers of land for debts. In one instance a man appropriated land his debtor had temporarily abandoned. (The nature of the debt is unspecified.) The court allowed the creditor to keep the land because (1) the debtor had not made a timely objection, and (2) had also obtained a substitute plot from the chief, i.e. had abandoned the land his creditor had appropriated (10 Mamba 1930). Another Mamba case shows that a debt of animals was directly applied to the purchase price of a piece of land (32 Mamba 1931). In that case the defendant had sold the plaintiff a plot of land for three goats and a cow. The defendant had owed the plaintiff three goats, a debt which his father had incurred and he had inherited. In payment for the land, the debt was to be written off, and the plaintiff-buyer-creditor was also to pay one cow in addition, as well as to pay cash compensation for an improvement—i.e., for some coffee trees that had been planted on the land.[3]

The reason the defendant-debtor-seller gave in court for urgently wanting to transfer ownership to the plaintiff was not only to erase the debt of the goats and to acquire a cow and some cash, but because he feared that since he had moved to another chiefdom and the land was not occupied, he would lose all rights to it. He states in the case record that he had heard that there was a move on by the *mchilis* (headmen) and the *mangi* (chief) to appropriate all unoccupied land. His fears were well founded (see Griffiths Land Tenure Report 1930:63, 88). To salvage what he could, he decided to dispose of the abandoned kihamba and sell it to the plaintiff for the cow, the erasure of the debt and the payment of coffee-bush-compensation.

In another case (26 Mamba 1932) two men claimed the same kihamba that had earlier been an object of controversy between their fathers. The defendant was in occupancy. The plaintiff wanted the kihamba back. At one point in their various quarrels, the defendant offered to pay the plaintiff a cow for the kihamba in which he was a resident. The court held that the offer to buy the land for a cow was tantamount to an admission by the defendant that he did not own the land. The court thus ruled that the plaintiff was the rightful owner of the plot, and could recover it, but should permit the defendant to use the bananas growing on it for a period of two years to give the defendant time to obtain and develop another kihamba. These cases all speak of sales, but the land is being "sold" largely for beasts, rather than for cash (see also 25 Mamba 1932).

These cases are not only of interest because they suggest the form of transaction in which land was obtained from the chiefs or purchased from others in the early 1930s but also because of what they indicate about geographical mobility and the continued existence of some vacant plots. In the first (10 Mamba 1930) both the plaintiff and the defendant had moved from Mamba to Marangu (two neighboring chiefdoms) and had obtained land from the mangi (chief) of Marangu. This suggests that there was still no absolute land shortage everywhere at the time, since plots in some areas could still be had on request. The second case (32 Mamba 1931), involved a man (the occupier) who moved to Mwika from Mamba, as well as one who moved from Marangu to Mamba. Other Mamba cases in the same period also mention persons who moved.[4] The many instances in which the original owner had for one reason or another ceased to occupy his land and then wanted to sell it or reoccupy it seemed to be particularly problematic and particularly indicative of historical change. In the days of land plenty an absentee could always expect to obtain land on his return and in theory, at least, had a preferential right to his original plot. In precolonial days, when the rule had its origins, the absence of a man was most often either to fight in distant wars or to be involved in the long-distance trade. What seems to have crept into the law during the colonial period as land shortage made itself felt was that land was deemed to be permanently abandoned the moment the holder settled elsewhere. Land shortage and the chief's potential reversionary right probably lies in the background of what seems to have been an increasingly precipitous assertion of abandonment (Gutmann [1926]:62, 302–09; HRAF:50. 270–76).

It was always in the chief's interest to appropriate or reallocate abandoned plots. He received a "gift of thanks" and a grateful subject every time he allocated any land (see for example 46 Mamba 1933). In Mamba the chief's interest seems to have become enlarged over time to the point where the Native Authority (i.e., the chief) claimed that it had a continuing interest in land even after it was allocated. In 56 Mamba 1940 a man was prosecuted for selling a kihamba without the consent of the Native Authority. The kihamba was one of two that had been allocated to the defendant's father and which he, the defendant, had duly and properly inherited. Nevertheless, he was fined ten shillings for selling a kihamba which "belonged to the Native Authority." He was ordered to pay within ten days or be imprisoned for twenty. Chiefs were increasingly in competition with their subjects for the control of land and control over transactions in land. The cases from the 1930s give clear evidence that this tension existed even at a time before the money economy had created a cash market in land.

b. Land as collateral for a loan of cash in 1957

Twenty years later, the picture was quite different. In Mwika in 1957 a case was brought that illustrates the profound change in the economy and in relative values that had taken place since the 1930s (44 Mwika 1957). In 1954 plaintiff and defendant made an agreement that plaintiff would lend defendant 1320 shillings. Defendant was to repay the money within two years plus a "profit" of 5 percent. If the defendant failed to repay the cash, the plaintiff had the right to appropriate the defendant's kihamba on payment of an additional 1880 shillings—in other words, the defendant's kihamba was the collateral for the original loan. Plaintiff and defendant were not kinsmen. The court ruled that the plaintiff could pay the additional 1880 shillings and take the kihamba.

Here land and cash are fully interchangeable. The relative value of beasts has gone down. In 1954 a standard official value was put on a cow of 200 shillings. All other animals were declared to be worth 50 shillings. A notice to this effect was sent to all the courts by the paramount chief (Keni Mriti Mengwe File in courthouse, labelled Kazi za Baraza 1951– , Document 38, Notice to All Primary Courts). The contrast with the price of a piece of land is dramatic. Even though one does not know the size or quality of the kihamba sold for 3200 shillings, the magnitude of the difference in price is so great that the time was clearly over when the old conventional "price" for a kihamba, a cow and a goat, had been acceptable.

Conclusion

To review a small group of legal transactions and disputes that occurred over a fifty-year period in one small corner of Africa is not to establish the basis for sweeping historical generalization. But the cases suggest lines of analysis that could be mined further. The present inquiry deepens the level of detail in the history of one locality and simultaneously illustrates some general methodological strategies.

The conceptual innovation introduced here was to approach economic and social change obliquely. The rationale is that change in social systems that are (or were) strongly kin-oriented can be profitably explored through a sequence of property transactions between persons who are not kin. Among the Chagga legal disputes that involve patrimonial property (or rights) acquired by non-agnates have proved to be very revealing. The rationale is that transfers of property that do not directly reproduce the kinship structure are likely to be the repositories of important clues about changes in the operation of the total system of allocation and exchange. The pattern of transfers within the lineage through inheritance and conventional allocation is by definition culturally conceived as reiterative. But the parallel existence of property transfers in which, from the point of view of the acquirer, the property is of extra-lineal provenance puts lineage affairs in a larger context. The Chagga transfers noted here concerned persons, cattle, land and cash.[5]

It is clear that among the Chagga a non-agnatic transactional world existed alongside the descent-based one long before the cash economy worked its major transformations. Some patrimonial property leaked into those transactions. Some historical changes are more visible in that non-agnatic domain than in the kin-based nexus, which had to legitimate itself in the courts during the colonial period by claiming to be traditional, customary, and ruled by norms. The non-agnatic transactions appear very much more directly as contract-like arrangements, or, in the case of appropriations and allocations, as discretionary acts. This is not to say that contract-like arrangements do not exist *within* lineages, or that lineage members do not exercise discretion in their allocations. On the contrary the negotiation and renegotiation of agnatic relationships is one of the basic facts of Chagga lineage life. But the rhetoric that surrounds lineage affairs often redefines the negotiated and discretionary as pragmatic exceptions made within the general practice of normative kinship "custom." The choice made here to concentrate on certain transfers of property to (or from) non-agnates tries to escape from the ideology of descent to inspect occasions for other rationales of action.

The cases described illustrate a series of transformations in human relationships, in political roles, and in economic values. These change the content of law. Thus what was once a generalized right to reclaim land that one had once occupied after a period of absence was subtly changed by a broadened concept of "abandonment." Greed for land in time of shortage led to a preference for interpreting the legal status of unoccupied plots as "abandoned," in order to install new holders. Also, as land came to be bought and sold the requirement that agnates consent to the transfer of patrimonial land to make such a transfer valid gradually became translated into a right to first refusal in case of sale. There are substantial contrasts between the cases in the pre-1916 period, those around 1930, and those in the 1950s. Some of these are an exercise in changing equivalences, for example, the case series that proceeds from a time when children were offered as collateral for cattle debts, through a period when beasts were exchanged for land, to a later point where land was offered as collateral for borrowed cash. The cases also give clues about changes in the chiefly role from a time when chiefs might interpose themselves personally in the affairs of those who brought their cases to him, through a time when the chief withdrew from a case in which he had an interest, to a point where chiefs intruded in every sale or assignment of land by requiring that their consent be obtained for a valid transfer to exist. Some of these changes seem to have taken place because of the intentional and direct intervention of the colonial government (such as the attempt to terminate the use of pledge-children, the pressure on chiefs not to be judges in their own causes, and the order to plant coffee). Other changes seem much more the product of non-legislated transformations in the economy. The shift from a preoccupation with the value of beasts to a preoccupation with the value of land and the increasing use of cash surely reflect the deep economic consequences of cash cropping, demographic increase, and land shortage.

Some of these cases clarify the particular manner in which at various times the patrimonial property of one man could find its way out of his patrimonial stream into the heritable hoard of another man who was not agnatically related. Others show some of the ways that property could be acquired from a chief, or by a chief, and suggest how important the acquisition of land and its allocation must have been to the formation of the chiefly role during the colonial period.

The instances reviewed here are few. There are many more cases to similar effect in the files. Even the ones noted here suffice to show that law cases can be used to extract telling details about a sequence of changing local circumstances over a historical period. Local law cases reflect the local history of African peoples rather than the history of the Europeans who ruled them. Methodologically, if certain types of property transfer are treated as "diagnostic events," that treatment not only sharpens the focus of analysis, and provides a basis for case selection, but the cases become a running commentary on the changing economy and surrounding relationships (Moore 1987). In a society in which ideas about kinship inform the legal frameworks that surround many claims to major items of property, there is no more telling confirmation of deep changes inside the kin-based property system than to examine shifts at its periphery.

NOTES

1. See tables showing the changing subject-matter of cases in various chiefdoms during the British colonial period in Moore 1986:174–79.
2. That may well have been the way the matter was understood and communicated in Mwika. Major (later Sir) Charles Dundas, who was the officer in charge of the district from 1919 to 1924, relentlessly pressed coffee cultivation on the Chagga, thinking that would emancipate them in many different ways. One of his methods was to lend money to the chiefs to buy coffee seedlings for planting in their chiefdoms (Rogers 1972: 236–39).
3. There were complicating circumstances. The defendant's own right to the land was not unencumbered. The kihamba in question was one that the defendant had allowed a third party to use for a time—i.e., the land was "loaned." The third party had planted the coffee bushes on the land, but there was no question that he was only a borrower and not an owner. The plaintiff, the new owner, had agreed to pay compensation for the coffee trees. Normally that would have been the obligation of the defendant, the original owner and lender of the land. As indicated earlier, under Chagga law, a land lender who wants to reclaim his land must pay the land borrower compensation for any improvements before he can reappropriate it. However, in this case, the compensation for the coffee trees was never paid by either the defendant or the plaintiff, since the borrower abandoned the land, moved to Mwika (another chiefdom), and died there without having been compensated.
4. In 32 Mamba 1930, the defendant's father had moved from Mamba to Marangu; in 49 Mamba 1931, the father of the two parties had moved to Rombo, where he had bought a kihamba; in 59 Mamba 1933 the defendant had moved from Marangu to Mamba in 1917 and had been allocated a kihamba by the chief. The plaintiff claimed that the allocation was invalid because that very kihamba was his heritable property. The court found that it might once have been his heritable property, but because he had abandoned it and had accepted another kihamba from the chief in lieu of the original one, and had lived in the substitute kihamba for many years, he was not in a position to receive any rights he might once have had. In 45 Mamba 1933, a man explained that he had abandoned his kihamba in Mamba to settle in Moshi. He brought the 1933 case when he returned many years later. His suit demanded that the chief evict the occupier and reinstall him. The occupant said the kihamba was his and had been inherited from his father. Not only had the then occupant been born in that kihamba, but the occupant's father had died there and the plaintiff had made no claim to the land after the death. The court refused to evict the occupier on several grounds. It said that had the land really belonged to the plaintiff he would have made an earlier claim. The case record also makes it plain that this was an old issue. When the plaintiff had returned to Mamba the first time, he had made his first request of the chief (to reinstall him) and the chief had refused at that time and allocated a substitute kihamba to him to live in.
5. Transactions between non-kin in non-patrimonial goods and services constitute an important but quite different topic which has not been addressed here.

SOURCES

Gutmann, Bruno. [1926] reprinted 1961. *Das Recht der Dschagga*, trans. by A. M. Nagler, Human Relations Area Files. New Haven: Yale University Press. (Cited here as HRAF).

Habermas, Jurgen. 1987. "Lifeworld and system: a critique of functionalist reason." In *The theory of communicative action*, trans. Thomas McCarthy, vol. 2. Boston: Beacon Press.

Hailey, Lord. 1938. *An African survey*. Oxford: Oxford University Press.

Iliffe, John. 1979. *A modern history of Tanganyika*. Cambridge: Cambridge University Press.

Johnston, H. H. 1886. *The Kilimanjaro expedition*. London: Kegan, Paul, and Trench.

Moore, Sally Falk. 1986. *Social facts and fabrications: "Customary" law on Kilimanjaro, 1880–1980*. Cambridge: Cambridge University Press.

———. 1987. "Explaining the present: Theoretical dilemmas in processual ethnography." *American Ethnologist* 14(4):727–36.

Rogers, Susan Geiger. 1972. "The search for political focus on Kilimanjaro." Ph.D. dissertation, University of Dar es Salaam.

Shann, G. N. 1956. "The early development of education among the Chagga." *Tanganyika Notes and Records* 45:21–32.

Stahl, Kathleen M. 1964. *The history of the Chagga people of Kilimanjaro*. Mouton: The Hague.

Unpublished Sources

Griffiths, A. W. M. Land tenure report Moshi District. Copy in possession of Professor P. H. Gulliver, and in the Manuscript Collections of Africana in Rhodes House Library, Oxford, MSS Afr. s. 1001, 1930, pp. 63, 88.

Case reports from courts of Mwika, Mamba, Marangu, Kilema, Keni-Mriti Mengwe, and Moshi Town, 1927–1961. Once located in local courthouse buildings on Kilimanjaro, later in the faculty library of the Law School of the University of Dar es Salaam. All case records are handwritten in Swahili.

Government Publications

1978 Population Census, Vol. IV. A summary of selected statistics. Bureau of Statistics, Ministry of Planning and Economic Affairs, Dar es Salaam, Tanzania, 1978.

PART III

LAW, POWER, AND AUTHORITY

5

The Jurisdiction of
Muslim Tribunals in
Colonial Senegal,
1857–1932

Dominique Sarr and Richard Roberts[1]

In the spring of 1889, leading Muslim notables of Saint Louis presented Governor Clément-Thomas of Senegal a petition signed by 1,250 inhabitants concerning the recently enacted restrictions on the jurisdiction of the *cadi* (or Muslim judge) in matters pertaining to the Muslim law of inheritance and the cadi's control over the disposition of orphans. In response, the governor convened a commission to study the 1857 decree, which had established Muslim tribunals in Senegal. The events of 1889 were part of an on-going three-way struggle between the inhabitants (also called the *originaires*) of the four communes of Senegal, who sought to protect their special legal status; the officials of the colonial judiciary, who sought to reconcile the jurisdiction of courts in the colony to metropolitan traditions and under whose pressure restrictions on the cadi's were imposed; and the colonial administration, which wanted to avoid internal controversies as it sought to extend and to consolidate its recent territorial conquests.

This chapter is concerned with the peculiar political and legal tensions found only in the four communes of Senegal—Saint Louis, Gorée, Rufisque, and Dakar—where a handful of Senegalese Muslims exercised the legal and electoral rights of French citizens. By itself, however, the grant of legal and electoral rights was not problematic. What caused conflict between these three sets of actors was that the administration's "Islamic" policy permitted Muslim citizens of Senegal (in contrast to Muslim citizens of Algeria) the privilege of using Muslim courts to adjudicate cases involving Muslim personal status.[2] Colonial magistrates, many of whom were professional jurists committed to upholding the integrity of the law, found the persistence of Muslim personal status under the umbrella of the French civil code to be a troubling anomaly. From 1889 to 1932 they sought to restrain progressively the jurisdiction of Muslim courts. This chapter examines the pressures to preserve and to limit the jurisdictional reach of Muslim courts from 1857, when Governor Faidherbe established the Muslim Tribunal of Saint Louis, to 1932, when the minister of colonies re-established the limited jurisdiction of Muslim law.

Over the seventy-five years examined here, these three groups of actors did not pursue consistent goals. On the contrary, magistrates generally supported the administration's policies until 1889, when they started to pursue the goal of judicial consistency in matters of jurisdiction more independently. Not all administrators in Senegal were equally committed to an "Islamic" policy, which involved protecting the special legal status of loyal Muslim originaires. Nor was the community of originaires unified in their efforts to preserve their special legal status. Although it is beyond the scope of this chapter, divisions among the originaires in terms of the defense of their special status sharpened around 1913, as they petitioned the minister of colonies for the abrogation of the reform of the judicial system promulgated the year before.[3]

The Making of the Colonial Legal System in Senegal, 1798–1903

French merchants began regular trade along the Senegambia coast in the early seventeenth century. By the 1670s, French trade had become the privilege of a series of royal chartered companies. The pace of trade, especially in slaves, increased dramatically in the late seventeenth century, peaked in the early eighteenth, and declined after mid-century. Throughout the eighteenth century, however, French merchants in Saint Louis and Gorée traded in slaves, but increasingly, their commerce revolved around the trade in gum arabic. Between 1740 and 1840, gum dominated Senegal's commerce only to be replaced by peanuts. Peanuts continue to dominate Senegal's export trade (Curtin 1969: Ch. 6; Curtin 1975).

Senegal was a colony primarily of commerce, not of settlement. The success of French commerce depended upon political and economic alliances with Africans and Afro-Europeans and mutually beneficial relationships involving credit, prices, and assortment of goods. Saint Louis and Gorée were increasingly populated by French, African, and mulatto merchants engaged in wholesale and retail commerce (Curtin 1975; Brooks 1976).

As did so many towns and villages throughout France in 1789, a committee of French inhabitants of Saint Louis drafted a *cahier de doléances* (a formal list of grievances), which they forwarded to the Constituent Assembly in Paris. The cahier addressed the concerns of the townspeople about the monopolistic trading privileges of the chartered Senegal Company and petitioned for its abolition in favor of freer trade. Preoccupied with metropolitan issues, the National Assembly finally turned to colonial issues in 1794. The Assembly abolished slavery in French colonies and decreed that all men living in the colonies would henceforth enjoy the rights of French citizens (Johnson, 1971:40, 79). By 1802, however, rebellion had broken out in Saint Domingue, Europe was at war, and Britain had occupied Gorée. In 1809, Britain occupied Saint Louis. As part of Napoleon's political and military strategies, he re-established slavery in the French empire and suspended the 1794 decree granting citizenship. Under the Treaty of Paris in 1814, however, France regained its African possessions.

France returned to Senegal in 1817 with ambitious plans for colonial development. Governor Roger sponsored experiments with different crops and loosened restrictions on the commerce in gum, which had become essential to the commercial life of the colony with the decline in slave exports. Efforts to induce European settlement and crop diversification were disappointing. The economy of the small colony continued to revolve around commerce (Hardy 1921; McLance 1986; Webb 1985). Successful commerce depended upon sustained relations between French, African, and Afro-European traders and the adjudication of their conflicts.

In 1822, a tribunal was established in Gorée, which heard cases involving French citizens of metropolitan origin. In 1830, a local decree "received" the French civil code in effect in France and expanded the rights of citizenship, which Napoleon had suspended in 1794 (Salacuse 1969:21–23). According to the principles of the 1830 decree, all "persons born free and living in Senegal or its dependencies will have the rights of a French citizen as guaranteed by the Civil Code" (Guèye 1955:30, quoted in Johnson 1971:79).[4]

Extending the French civil code to the free inhabitants of Saint Louis and Gorée confronted the fact that the majority of the Senegalese were Muslim. For them, marriage and the organization of the family were founded in religion and in religiously sanctioned law. Muslim law, which had its source in the Koran, was inseparable from faith. As such, Muslim law lay outside the purview of the civil legislator, whose jurisdiction was defined by the legal separation of church and state.[5] At its very foundation, then, Muslim law was incompatible with the French civil law tradition.

The Muslim inhabitants of these two towns welcomed French legal and political rights, but they did not welcome changes in their personal status that negated their rights to have conflicts over family and related civil issues heard by Muslim judges. Instead, all cases under the civil code were heard by French administrators, who were assisted by local notables. In 1840, provision was made to employ professional magistrates to preside over the courts of the first instance, which lay at the base of the French judicial system. Cadis, if they participated at all in these courts, did so as assessors or advisors to the French magistrates.

Bowing to the sustained pressures of the Muslim inhabitants, Governor Baudin convened a consultative committee composed of Muslim notables in December 1847, which was charged with advising the French tribunal on issues of Muslim law submitted to the courts. The minister of the marine and navy, the metropolitan minister in charge of colonial affairs, replaced this consultative committee with a Muslim tribunal following the decree of 22 April 1848 (Ndiaye 1984). This decree, however, was never enacted. It was overtaken by the revolutionary events of 1848, which led to the fall of the Orleanist monarchy and the rise of the Second Republic. The Second Republic reiterated its commitment to the extension of political and legal rights of citizenship to all free inhabitants of Senegal. Over the next half-century, these rights were also extended to the African inhabitants of Rufisque and Dakar.

In 1852, however, Louis Napoleon rescinded the electoral rights of the inhabitants of Saint Louis and Gorée. But he did not undo the extension of legal rights. Ambiguities of the jurisdiction of French and Muslim law remained unresolved until the forceful governorship of Louis Faidherbe in 1854. Faidherbe was a military engineer, who came to Senegal with considerable Algerian experience. Part of his strategy for the expansion and consolidation of French control in Senegal lay in building the core of an army around African recruits and in encouraging Muslim collaboration. Encouraging Muslim collaboration involved including prominent Muslims in his political affairs bureau, building mosques, sponsoring Arabic education for interpreters, subsidizing the pilgrimage of loyal Muslim notables, and in recognizing Muslim legal jurisdiction (Schnapper 1961; Cruise O'Brien 1967; Robinson 1988). In 1854, Faidherbe re-established the consultative committee on Muslim law and in 1857 he strengthened the jurisdiction of Muslim courts by establishing a Muslim tribunal in Saint Louis. The 1857 decree recognized the jurisdiction of Muslim tribunals in matters of family law, inheritance, and related civil matters (Quellien 1910:224–25).

The Muslim tribunal of Saint Louis was part of Faidherbe's "Islamic" policy, which fostered the loyalty of many Senegalese Muslims to France at a time of militant Islamic revolution in West Africa (Robinson 1985, 1988; Klein 1968). It had the unintended consequence of creating ambiguities concerning legal jurisdictions. It thus established fertile ground for the continued tensions between judicial officials, colonial officials, and the Muslim originaires in Senegal.

The Second Republic's 1848 legislation had made clear its commitment to the principle that liberty, equality, and fraternity had to govern all the inhabitants of the colonies without distinction of race or civilization. Assimilation of the citizens of Senegal accorded them full French nationality and the privileges of electoral rights and civil status. French law, thus, had to apply equally to all citizens.

Yet to grant the Muslim inhabitants of Saint Louis and Gorée all the civil and political rights held by Frenchmen of metropolitan origin ignored significant differences in civilization. Convinced of the superiority of their civilization and sharing a fear and disdain of Islam, which spread widely through colonial circles following Muslim resistance to French colonial expansion in Algeria, colonial magistrates considered any refusal to apply French legislation to Africans contrary to both natural law and the colonial policy of assimilation (see for example Carrère and Holle 1855). Certainly not all magistrates in Senegal were so inclined, but enough were to put pressure on the administration through their legal decisions and in their work on the 1903 colonial legal code to question the legal bases behind granting Muslim originaires exemption from the civil code. To what extent, then, did a politically motivated administrative act—like that of 1857 establishing the Muslim tribunal—pose inherent contradictions to the organization and to the integrity of the French judicial system in colonial Senegal? Was it possible to allow these African "citizens" to submit to the principles of French public law on the one hand and to principles of religiously inspired private law on the other?

The net result of the tensions between judicial officials and colonial administrators was competing efforts to preserve and to restrict the jurisdiction of Muslim law. When the administrators prevailed, the legal order of metropolitan origin coexisted with the legal order based upon Muslim institutions. Such coexistence was not founded in legal guarantees, but instead was the result of administrative decisions to ignore the implications of the separation of French civil status and religious law (Schnapper 1961:110–27). In contrast, when the magistrates prevailed, Muslim law was restricted and cadis were reduced to advising French tribunals of Muslim legal traditions.

The African inhabitants of Saint Louis and Gorée were not passive victims of debates raging between two branches of the colonial administration. On the contrary, they shared in the right to participate in municipal self-government, granted by French President Thiers in 1872, following the establishment of the Third Republic. Moreover, the 1872 decree reinstated the rights of Senegalese originaires to be represented in the National Assembly by their own deputy. In the hands of a vocal constituency, the municipal governments and the deputy could bring considerable pressure on the colonial government (Johnson 1971:38–62).[6]

Despite their political prerogatives, the special legal status of the inhabitants of the four communes was not unchallenged by judicial authorities. Those judicial officials and magistrates involved in drafting the 1903 legal code and those officials at the Appeals Court in Dakar acted to restrict the jurisdiction of Muslim courts.

The Magistrates' Challenge and the 1903 Legal Code

As part of its efforts to reorganize colonial government, the government-general of French West Africa began the process of revising the colonial legal code. The new legal code, promulgated on 10 November 1903 followed the principles that

> it was absolutely necessary to unify the administration of justice, formerly submitted to different systems in each colony of the federation. Moreover, it was absolutely necessary to assure our nationals and all those who are assimilated, of the benefits of the French legal jurisdiction and legislation, regardless of the location of their residence. But it is also necessary to guarantee to the natives under our control, in everything that is not contrary to our essential principles of humanity and civilization, the maintenance of their customs, based on private law appropriate to their mentality and their social state (Quellien 1910:227).

In one swift blow, the magistrates and judicial authorities who drafted the 1903 code abolished the special legal status of the inhabitants of the four communes. Consistent with the concepts of assimilation, all French citizens were to benefit from French civil law in both its private and public forms. All cases involving French citizens were henceforth to be heard before Courts of the First Instance.

Drafters of the code also established a parallel but separate native legal system with its own hierarchy of courts (Mohkiber 1990). The 1903 legal code recognized but did not favor Muslim law. Article 49 established a tribunal at the provincial or canton level, composed of the chief of the canton (or province), assisted by two notables appointed by the lieutenant-governor in consultation with the attorney-general. If the canton contained Muslims, then one of the two notables was to be a cadi. Article 56 established the next layer, the tribunal at the district level. This tribunal was composed of a district officer and two notables, nominated each year by the lieutenant-governor of the colony. As in the tribunal at the canton level, if the district contained Muslims, then a cadi—or, in his absence, a Muslim notable—would be one of the two native members. Article 75 set guidelines for the operation of the native tribunals, which formed the base of the customary legal system. In his instructions to district officers, Governor-general Roume noted that "native justice applies to all local native customs.... These tribunals will judge, following customs widely accepted....These customs may be more or less modified by practice and by Muslim law, or they may be untouched by Muslim influence. They deal mostly with civil affairs relating to contracts, property, obligations, kinship, marriage, inheritance, guardianship, and succession." Roume exhorted his subordinates to pay scrupulous attention to divergent practices, in efforts to reach general principles, which would at some later date form the basis of *coutumier général*. Such codification would become the rule (règle) of native tribunals in civil matters.[7] And finally, the decree established an appeals court in Dakar. The code also specified that a cadi or, in his absence, a leading Muslim notable act as an assessor to the tribunal of the first instance in all cases involving Muslims.

Although the 1903 legal code restricted the jurisdiction of the Muslim tribunals, it nonetheless recognized the special place of the cadi—and by extension of Muslim law—in the proceedings of the newly established tribunals. Colonial magistrates in Senegal could not do otherwise, since Muslims constituted the majority of many districts and because of the long-established "Islamic" policy. But they did not have to recognize the special jurisdiction of Muslim courts. Indeed, Muslim law in the 1903 legal code had become merely the first among many customary laws.

The judicial officials who drafted the 1903 legal code operated within the idiom of judicial assimilation, which had already become apparent in their 1889 challenge to Faidherbe's Muslim tribunal. Already in 1889 the magistrates aspired to "the restriction of Islam and to the penetration of French ideas" (Commission 1889, ANRS M 15). In the debates of the 1889 commission, the magistrates recommended a return to the 1847 system of a consultative committee to advise French tribunals on questions submitted by Muslim litigants. All cases would be deferred to French civil law tribunals, where, as needed, officials could turn to the assistance of Muslim assessors. Although the magistrates in the 1889 debates were prepared to accept the cadi's direct role in litigation involving marriages, divorces, and the settlement of inheritances valued under five hundred francs, the net effect of the commission's recommendations was to restrict the jurisdiction of Muslim law and to reduce Muslim legal authority to an advisory role.

In their arguments, the magistrates emphasized that neither the decrees of 1830 or 1833 promulgating the Senegalese civil code made any distinction between Africans born free within the colonial territory and Europeans. It was only Faidherbe's 1857 decree that constituted a generous exception and allowed a considerable extension of Muslim legal jurisdiction in Saint Louis.

In response to the 1889 commission's recommendations, the administration reiterated its long-standing support for the special status of the inhabitants of the four communes and called for the scrupulous respect of Islam. The administration argued that Muslim justice was a particular form of justice that required special magistrates. The administration was especially concerned to maintain the loyalty of Muslims at a time of considerable political disorder and religiously inspired rebellions against French territorial conquest. The continued maintenance of the magistrates' position of legal assimilation of all French citizens in the 1903 legal code was thus a further blow to the administration's Islamic policy (Mokhiber 1990). Yet, the administration fought back. On 22 May 1905, the administration decreed the re-establishment of the Muslim tribunal in Saint Louis and the struggles for control over legal jurisdiction thus entered another phase.[8]

Administrators, Magistrates, and Originaires: The Jurisdiction of Muslim Courts

Rather than clarifying the jurisdiction of French civil law, Muslim law, and customary law, the 1903 legal code created further ambiguities. Africans living in the jurisdiction of the Saint Louis and Dakar inferior courts, and of the Kayes Court of the Justice of the Peace of Extended Competence were under the jurisdiction of French civil code tribunals.[9] Outside of these three towns, all African litigants were forced to turn to native tribunals. How did this affect the Senegalese originaires?

The special confirmation session of the Appeals Court of Dakar, when the highest court in the colony reviewed lower court decisions, used the imprecision of the 1903 legal code to grant jurisdiction over the originaires to the French courts. In its decision of 22 May 1906 the court reiterated the magistrates' position that "Senegalese born in the four communes of Senegal are under the jurisdiction of the French courts" (cited in *Affaire Mamadou Sacko et al.* 1910, ANRS M 79). The court based its decision on the following points: did the originaires not possess the same political rights as those of French origin? Did not Governor-general Roume say that the 1903 legal code tended "to assure our nationals and all those who can be assimilated to them the benefits of French jurisdiction and legislation, whatever their place of residence" (Roume, n.d., ANRS M 79)? This decision of the confirmation session effectively shielded the originaires from the jurisdiction of native tribunals (Guyon 1911, ANRS M 83).

The competing arguments on legal jurisdiction presented by the colonial administration, which favored the continued retention of the originaires' special personal status — and thus access to Muslim courts — and by the magistrates, who were in favor of judicial assimilation, made their way up the administrative ladder to the Ministry of Colonies in Paris. The Ministry of Colonies in turn put pressure on the government-general of French West Africa to resolve the problem by placing all Africans under customary law, which would have the consequence of respecting their separate personal statuses and permitting litigants recourse to their own ethnic customary law. As part of the general reorganization of the native judicial system of 1912, Article 2 placed the originaires under the jurisdiction of native tribunals. The 1912 decree thus sought to alleviate the legal anomaly of the originaires. On the one hand, the decree upheld their electoral rights, but on the other, it excluded them from the jurisdiction of French courts, because they, like other Africans, were assumed to want to maintain their personal status. Although the intent of the decree was conciliatory, the originaires were not pleased with the diminution of their special judicial status. On 1 August 1913, they sent the Ministry of Colonies a petition demanding the repeal, or at least the modification, of the decree of 1912. In support for their grievances, the originaires invoked the oft-repeated remonstrations of their loyalty and fidelity. They cited the long-standing legal underpinnings of their special status by citing the 1830 and 1833 decrees granting them rights of citizenship. They concluded that the decree of 1912 constituted, for the "sons of Saint-Louis, the loyal agents of the peaceful expansion of France into all its African colonies," a denial of justice and equity (Petition 1913, ANRS M 87). The General Council of the colony joined in the protests. At its meeting of 12 October 1913, councilors Georges Crespin and Galandou Diouf jointly sponsored a motion calling for the repeal of Article 2 of the 1912 decree (Lieutenant-governor 1913, ANRS M 87).

The protests by the originaires and the Council General led the goverment-general in Dakar and the Ministry of Colonies in Paris to recant. To satisfy the aspirations of the originaires, "who had served the French work in Africa and whose devotion had never ceased," the Minister of Colonies, in conjunction with the Minister of Justice, withdrew the offending article.[10]

Their victory over the 1912 decree was a Pyrrhic one, however, because the originaires were again placed under the principles of judicial assimilation, which they had fought against since 1889. Although they were now firmly under the jurisdiction of the French courts in their home districts and in the major towns of the other colonies of French West Africa, the originaires were answerable to native jurisdiction in other areas or when they were not carrying the proof of their birth. In a colony where registries of civil status had not yet been firmly organized, such proof was not always available (Joucla 1917:1–20).

Although for the moment the principles of judicial assimilation won out, enough ambiguities remained for the Appeals Court of Dakar to impose its own interpretations on the legislation concerning the jurisdiction of Muslim law for the originaires.

Restricting the Jurisdiction of Muslim Courts: The Jurisprudence of the Dakar Appeals Court

The Appeals Court, in general, was committed to the principles of judicial assimilation and it considered that grant of French political and legal rights was incompatible with Africans' efforts to maintain their personal status.[11] But, para-doxically, the magistrates of the Appeals Court eventually granted Muslim orig-inaires the power to choose the venue for their litigation on a case-by-case basis even as they progressively restricted the scope of the jurisdiction of Muslim law. Within the scope of the Court of Appeal decisions discussed here, the court simultaneously upheld and restricted the jurisdiction of Muslim courts and the originaires special legal status.

In 1925, Moussa Ndiaye summoned his wife Fatou Ly before the cadi of Rufisque to compel her to return to the conjugal domicile. Neither Ndiaye nor his wife were originaires, but since they lived within one of the four communes, they assumed that they had the right to bring their case before the Muslim court. Following Muslim law, the cadi ordered her return. If she refused, her kin were obliged to return the bridewealth provided by her husband's kin. In her case before the Appeals Court, the appellant raised the demurrer of the jurisdiction of the Muslim court. She and her husband, having neither French citizenship nor assimilated European status, were only answerable to the native jurisdiction.

In its ruling of 8 January 1926, the Court accepted this argument, which, while not addressed to the peculiar issue of the originaires, nonetheless had the consequence of restricting the jurisdiction of Muslim courts. In so doing, the Court argued in terms of the 22 March 1924 decree, which limited the jurisdiction of the French courts in favor of native tribunals. Native tribunals with Muslim assessors were to have jurisdiction over African litigants (*Affaire Fatou Ly*, Cour d'Appel, 1926).

The Court concluded that the originaires of the four communes, and those who had been naturalized, were, in principle, the only Africans under the jurisdiction of the French courts. In the spirit of restraining the formal jurisdiction of Muslim law, it argued that "Muslim tribunals do not have competence except where it had been expressly taken from the French tribunals and not included in the jurisdiction of the native tribunals." In its ruling, then, the Court limited the jurisdiction of Muslim courts without clarifying the jurisdictional issues surrounding the originaires' personal status.[12]

In another ruling on 1 April 1926, the Appeals Court tested the limits of judicial assimilation. The Court argued that neither the decrees of 5 November 1830 nor that of 24 April 1833 had the effect of imposing European status on Senegalese living in Gorée and Saint Louis. Nor was their Muslim personal status withdrawn by the law of 29 September 1916, which reiterated the full extension of citizenship to the originaires and their descendants, including the obligation of military service, and did not modify their personal status. The magistrates ruled that French tribunals were thus not competent to handle cases relative to their personal status. The Court concluded that cases involving their personal status were thus exclusively answerable to Muslim law and well within the competence of the Muslim courts that applied it.

In a 1929 case (*Affaire Pathé Ndoye contre Dithié Timbane*, Cour d'Appel, Rec. 1929.2.182), the Court heard arguments concerning the competence of Muslim courts in cases involving originaires. At issue was whether, and under what conditions, originaires could by-pass Muslim courts in cases involving Muslim personal status. The Court decided that French courts could occasionally decide issues of Muslim personal status. To support this jurisprudence the Court elaborated two arguments. First, Senegalese Muslims *could* bring their legal disputes before the French courts. This argument drew on the decision of the Appeals Court of 17 June 1898 (Cour d'Appel, Rec. 1899.2.45) that stipulated (based on Articles 2 and 4 of the 1857 decree) that Muslims were free to bring their disputes before a French court. When Muslims so chose, they submitted themselves to the rules of competence and procedures of French law for that case only. In other cases, they remained under Muslim law.

The second argument was that a Muslim summoned before the French court must invoke its incompetence at the beginning of the proceedings. Nothing, the Court argued, prohibited an originaire, who had conserved Muslim status through faith, from renouncing the benefits of French personal status in a particular judicial case. The decree of 1857, which created the Muslim justice system in Senegal, and those of 1903, 1905, and 1910, which defined its jurisdiction and determined the rules of its competence, did not fix forever the personal status of the originaire. To the contrary, according to Article 4 of the 1857 decree and Article 31 of the decree of 16 November 1924, Muslims could bring their disputes before French courts. In its decision, the Appeals Court returned to the argument that granting of citizenship to the originaires was a "favor," and not an obligation imposed on them.

In its decision, the Court thus recognized the tenuous coexistence of French and Muslim legal jurisdictions, and it further blurred the boundaries between them by permitting originaires to choose the jurisdiction of their case on a case-by-case basis. Although this decision was the logical necessity flowing from ambiguous legislation, the president of the Appeals Court underlined the magistrates' general dislike of coexistence. "It is by exception, and by tolerance, that native French subjects remain under Muslim law in certain instances; to place them under French law is to return them to the rule" (cited in Bonnichon 1931:88−89).

The 1926 and 1929 decisions of the Appeals Court regarding the jurisdiction of Muslim law for originaires was clearly a victory for the Senegalese Muslims. But the Court was not prepared to give cadis unquestioned power to adjudicate all civil matters. In the course of their further deliberations, the magistrates delimited the power of the cadis in matters central to the jurisdiction of Muslim law.

In terms of inheritance, the Court recognized in principle the cadi's competence to decide disputes relative to the inheritance rights of the Senegalese of the four communes. For example, the Appeals Court and subsequent colonial legislation defined more precisely the conditions under which the cadi had competence to deal with the restitution of objects seized by another Muslim at the opening of probate. Although the Appeals Court did not question the cadi's role in inheritance, it did, however, limit the cadi's competence to deal with civil litigation which might have criminal components.[13]

The Appeals Court also tinkered with the cadi's competence in marriage. Under Muslim law, bridewealth is one of the essential elements and constituents of matrimonial ties. For the Appeals Court, however, bridewealth was not always constitutive of marriage. Thus, cases regarding the restitution of bridewealth could not be considered relevant to a case regarding marriage. The court also determined that French courts were the only ones cognizant in cases involving the restitution of dowry, that is goods or wealth brought by the wife to the conjugal unit and only French courts could hear cases brought by a Muslim widow against her matrimonial guardian. Furthermore, the Appeals Court also restricted the competence of the cadi in cases of conflicts over goods between spouses and it eventually impinged upon the cadi's authority regarding the disposition of minors.[14]

Although the Appeals Court in Dakar acknowledged the special legal status of the originaires, its judicial decisions progressively limited the jurisdiction of Muslim tribunals. If it could not apply the concepts of judicial assimilation, then it pursued the goal of limiting Muslim law to a simple reserved domain and empowered French courts to apply Muslim laws.

Conclusion

After seventy-five years, the ambiguities of the legal jurisdiction of Muslim courts was finally ended with the promulgation of the decree of 20 November

1932, which reinstated the competence of Muslim tribunals. According to Article 5 of this decree, Muslim tribunals had exclusive cognizance over civil affairs between Muslim originaires or their descendants regarding marriages, questions of inheritance, donations, and testaments. They were to judge "in conformity with Muslim law, except in areas where local custom prevailed." In contrast, non-Muslim originaires brought their disputes before the French tribunals, which were obligated to include an assessor belonging to the custom of the parties to the dispute. The 1932 decree, building on the relative competence provision of the Appeals Court, effectively created two coexisting legal systems for Muslim originaires and their descendants. Muslim law thus applied in certain cases, particularly when the option to apply French law was not exercised. French law, however, prevailed in all other cases unless limited at the outset of the proceedings.

Article 3 of this decree, however, gave the governor-general the task of creating and suppressing the Muslim tribunals according to the needs of the changing colonial situation. Thus, in 1933, the governor-general maintained the Muslim tribunals of Saint Louis, Dakar, Rufisque; created a new one in Kaolack; and suppressed the one in Kayes (Moreau 1938:158−60).

The 1932 decree was the culmination of the struggles by the originaires to preserve their special legal status. Faced with the impossibility of the complete assimilation of the Senegalese originaires, magistrates and administrators alike were forced to recognize their peculiar legal status. In contrast to colonial Algeria, where French citizenship extended to native Algerians conferred with it the jurisdiction of the French civil code, in Senegal, the French citizens of Muslim persuasion retained the rights to turn to Muslim courts for adjudication in cases concerning the Muslim personal status.

As this chapter has shown, the study of the forces shaping the jurisdiction of Muslim law in colonial Senegal must be situated within the larger context of political and social history.

NOTES

1. To our great sadness, Dominique Sarr died suddenly before he had the opportunity to revise this conference paper. Although he had received the editors' suggestions for revisions — and had agreed in principle to them — he did not have the opportunity to make the changes we suggested. Richard Roberts has thus rewritten Sarr's paper in light of the editors' suggestions. Although he has been able to draw upon secondary materials, Roberts has not been able to check the original archival sources. The source material cited in this chapter, then, should be considered suggestive rather than definitive.
2. There was a politically significant imprecision between the granting of "citizenship" and the granting of legal and electoral rights of citizenship. While unambiguous "citizenship" was offered Africans who passed the qualifications for "assimilation," naturalized French citizens did not have the privileges of retaining Muslim personal status. See Buell 1928:I, 646−53; Opoku 1974; Johnson 1971.
3. Roberts would like to thank Martin Klein and David Robinson for their very helpful comments on his revisions. Roberts could not, however, satisfy all their concerns.
4. The decree of 24 April 1833 further confirmed the principles of the 1830 decree by declaring that "every free person possesses, in the French colonies, civil rights and political rights under the conditions prescribed by law."
5. By far the best discussion surrounding the politics of legal jurisdiction of the Muslim tribunals is Schnapper (1961). Schnapper argues that the debates on the jurisdiction of Muslim tribunals in Senegal date from 1832, fully twenty-five years before a Muslim tribunal was enacted in 1857. Cruise O'Brien (1967) discusses how the anticlericism of the French military and administrators in Senegal contributed to a pro-Muslim orientation, especially toward those Senegalese willing to collaborate with the French.
6. These municipalities were called *communes de plein exercise*. They had municipal councils elected by eligible citizens, and a mayor elected by the council, governed matters relating to the police, public health, utilities, streets, and collected municipal taxes. In addition, Senegalese towns had a long tradition of advisory councils, which were constituted to advise the governor on local affairs. In 1879, the councils in Saint Louis and Gorée became elected bodies, although they still had advisory status. They could, and they often did, debate a wide range of issues including changes in legal jurisdiction.
7. Bull. officiel 1903:943−63; Roume 1905, cited in Quellien 1910:226−31. Indeed, the codification envisioned by Roume eventually resulted in a three-volume series entitled *Coutumiers juridiques de l'Afrique Occidentale française* (Paris: Publications du Comité d'Etudes historiques et scientifiques de l'Afrique Occidentale française, 1939). Whether these studies were used by the native tribunals is unclear.
8. Muslim tribunals were re-established in Saint Louis, Dakar, and Kayes in 1905 and extended to Rufisque in 1907. In 1911, Ponty decreed that all decisions in Muslim courts must henceforth be recorded in French. His stated concerns were that this would ensure impartiality on the part of Muslim cadis and assessors, but it also opened the door to more effective control over Muslim tribunals (Moreau 1938:156; Hilde 1912:103).
9. The Kayes Court appears to be an anomaly, but since Kayes was the headquarters of the government of Haut-Sénégal-Niger, the court may have had to serve a number of functions.

10. The decree of 9 March 1914. See also Lebrun n.d., ANRS M87.
11. According to Moreau's study of native policy in French West Africa, the "tendency of jurisprudence was to restrain as afar as possible" the 1857 decree creating the Muslim tribunal in Saint Louis and the 1905 re-establishment of Muslim courts (Moreau 1938:157).
12. In so doing the Court followed its argument of 2 June 1911, when it argued that the Muslim tribunals had "exceptional" jurisdiction only and that Muslims who were not originaires could not bring cases before it (Moreau 1938:155–58).
13. The court's arguments drew on the following legislation, 12 July 1946, 20 June 1902, 3 April 1920, 23 January 1925, 12 May 1927, 5 August 1932.
14. The Court based itself upon the decrees of 2 February 1906 and 20 January 1905, among others.

SOURCES

Archival

Archives Nationales, République de Sénégal (ANRS) Commission 1889, Procès verbal de la Commission, 24 April 1889, file 35–103, ANRS M 15

Roume, n.d., Instructions aux Administrateurs sur l'applications du décret du 10 Novembre 1903, file 7, ANRS M 79.

Guyon 1911, Proposition de l'administrateur en chef, au Conseil du gouvernement, June 1911, file 41, ANRS M 83

Petition 1913, Délégués de la ville de Saint Louis à Ministre des Colonies, 23 April 1913, Saint Louis, file 74, ANRS M 87.

Lieutenant-governor 1913, letter to governor-general, 13 December 1913, ANRS M 87.

Court Cases

Affaire Mamadou Sacko et al., Jurisprudence de la Chambre d'Homologation, 1910, ANRS M 79

Affaire Fatou Ly contre Moussa Ndiaye, Cour d'Appel, Rec. 1926.

Affaire Pathé Ndoye contre Dithié Timbane, Cour d'Appel, Rec. 1929.2.182

Cour d'Appel, Rec. 1899.2.45

Secondary

Bonnichon, A. 1931. *La conversion au Christianisme de l'indigène musulman algérien, et ses effets jurisidiques*. Paris: Librairie du Recueil Sirey.

Brooks, George. 1976. "The *signares* of Saint-Louis and Gorée: Women entrepreneurs in eighteenth century Senegal." In Nancy Hafkin and Edna Bay, eds., *Women in Africa: Studies in Social and Economic Change*, 19–44. Stanford: Stanford University Press.

Buell, R. L. 1928. *The native problem in Africa*, 2 vols. New York: Macmillan.

Carrère, Frédéric, and Paul Holle. 1855. *De la Sénégambie français*. Paris: Firmin Didot Frères.

Coutumiers juridiques de l'Afrique Occidentale française. 1939. Paris: Publications du Comité d'Etudes historiques et scientifiques de l'Afrique Occidentale française.

Cruise O'Brien, Donal. 1967. "Towards an 'Islamic policy' in French West Africa, 1854–1914." *Journal of African History* 8 (2):303–16.

Curtin, Philip. 1969. *The Atlantic slave trade: A census*. Madison: The University of Wisconsin Press.

———. 1975. *Economic change in precolonial Africa: Senegambia in the era of the slave trade*. Madison: The University of Wisconsin Press.

Guèye, Lamine. 1955. *Etapes et perspectives de l'Union française*. Paris: Editions de l'Union française.

Hardy, Georges. 1921. *La mise en valeur du Sénégal de 1817 à 1854*. Paris: Emile Larose.

Hild, Eugène. 1912. *L'organisation judiciaire en Afrique Occidentale française.* Paris: Emile Larose.

Johnson, G. Wesley. 1971. *The Emergence of Black Politics in Senegal: The struggle for power in the Four Communes, 1900–1920.* Stanford: Stanford University Press.

Joucla, Edmond. 1917. "Organisation de l'Etat-civil en Afrique Occidentale français." *Recueil génerale de jurisprudence, de doctrine et de législation coloniale et maritime,* 1–20. Paris: La Tribune des Colonies et des Protectorats.

Klein, Martin. 1968. *Islam and imperialism in Senegal: Sine-Saloum, 1847–1914.* Stanford: Stanford University Press.

McLance, Margaret. 1986. "Commercial rivalries and French policy on the Senegal River, 1831–1858." *African Economic History* 15:39–68.

Mokhiber, James. 1990. "Forms of authority and the ordering of empire: The native justice system in colonial Senegal, 1903–1912." BA honors thesis, Department of History, Stanford University.

Moreau, Paul. 1938. *Les indigènes d'A.O.F.: Leur condition politique et économique.* Paris: Editions Doman-Montchrestien.

Ndiaye, Seck. 1984. "Les tribunaux musulmans du Sénégal de 1857 à 1914." Unpublished mémoire, University of Dakar.

Opoku, K. 1974. "Traditional law under French colonial rule." *Verfassung und Recht in Ubersee* 7:139–53.

Quellien, Alain. 1910. *La politique musulmane dans l'Afrique Occidentale française.* Paris: Emile Larose.

Robinson, David. 1985. *The holy war of Umar-Tal: The Western Sudan in the mid-nineteenth century.* Oxford: Clarendon Press.

———. 1988."French 'Islamic' policy and practice in late nineteenth-century Senegal." *Journal of African History* 29(3):415–436.

Salacuse, Jeswald. 1969. *An introduction to law in French-speaking Africa.* Charlottesville, VA: The Michie Company.

Schnapper, Bernard. 1961. "Les tribunaux musulmans et la politique coloniale au Sénégal (1830–1914)." *Revue historique de droit français et étranger.* 39:90–128.

Webb, James. 1985. "The Trade in gum arabic: Prelude to French conquest in Senegal." *Journal of African History* 26(2–3):149–68.

6

The Dynamics of Collaboration and the Rule of Law in French West Africa: The Case of Kwame Kangah of Assikasso (Côte d'Ivoire), 1898–1922[1]

DAVID GROFF

In December 1914, Joseph Mas, *chef de poste* of Assikasso acting on the orders of Louis Clerc, the *commandant* of the *cercle* of Indénié in the southeastern Ivory Coast, sequestered the possessions of Kwame Kangah, an Anyi-Juablin notable and long-time French collaborator in the region. The stated reason for this action was Kangah's absence without permission from his duties as linguist in the court of Nana Ehua Kouao, the local Anyi paramount or *famien*.

What makes this otherwise unexceptional episode interesting historically is that Kangah, unlike many other African subjects at the time, did not yield to his apparent fate but rather chose to fight the local colonial administration by legal and political means. What is most interesting of all is that he eventually won his battle and gained the restoration of his possessions. By examining how this case arose in the first place and how Kangah managed to win it, we can learn a good deal about the opportunities colonial conquest and especially the establishment of colonial administrative and legal systems provided individual Africans for accumulating wealth and expressing power. Such an examination also can tell us something about the status of the rule of law in the formative period of French colonial rule in West Africa. What the case suggests is that, under certain circumstances, determined individual Africans could advance their own personal interests by exploiting both the clientelistic relationships inherent in the colonial situation and the colonizers' own need to uphold some semblance of the rule of law as a means of establishing the legitimacy of their imperial enterprise. Yet it also reveals the precariousness of such individual African successes in the face of the colonizers' overriding imperative to maintain their domination.

The contradictory nature of the colonial situation in Africa is perhaps nowhere so apparent as in the colonizers' attempts to institute Western-style rule of law while maintaining and institutionalizing their political and economic domination. For the British and French, in particular, the establishment of some reasonable facsimile to the rule of law was both an ideological and practical imperative. Ideologically, the rule of law was necessary both because of the positive dictates of the two countries' liberal traditions and the need to defend the colonial enterprise against the rhetorical attacks of domestic critics and vociferous members of the nascent African petty bourgeoisie. What a noted Indian historian recently wrote concerning the Raj applies equally well to British and French colonial regimes in sub-Saharan Africa:

> The colonial state was established by force and force remained its ultimate sanction — the mailed fist beneath the glove — and was often used....But it was not based just on force. It was also based on the creation of a certain amount of civil liberties, and a certain toleration of and civil behavior toward its opponents. Even while suppressing, it observed certain rules of law and codes of administration (Chandra 1985:2).

From a more immediately practical standpoint, some form of rule of law was also needed in order to facilitate colonial commerce and promote the establishment of capitalist productive relations. Such practical considerations notwithstanding, however, it is clear that the idea of the rule of law in a colonial context served primarily as a means of external legitimation.

Whatever its general functions may have been, the ideal of the rule of law with its emphasis on formal egalitarianism and impersonal procedural guarantees of fairness could not easily square with the practical exigencies of colonial rule, especially those arising out of the problems inherent in the establishment and maintenance of viable collaborative mechanisms at the local level (Robinson 1972:120–24; Weiskel 1980: 142–71). By their very nature such mechanisms required the colonizers to accommodate the interests and ambitions of local elites, often at the expense of would-be counterelites and the general population. As Martin Chanock has argued, accommodation in the legal sphere involved a joint effort by the colonizers and local traditional elites to create laws and procedures that buttressed the political and economic hegemony of the former while protecting the latter against the full consequences of the kind of social change unleashed by colonialism (Chanock 1985:4, 237; 1982:53–67; Snyder 1982: 90–121). The legal systems that emerged were not simple amalgams of preexisting European and African law, as has sometimes been suggested, but rather wholly new creations growing out of the dialectics of the colonial situation. In the process of their creation, as well as in their day-to-day operation, such systems frequently involved degrees of arbitrariness and levels of coerciveness inconsistent with the ideal of the rule of law. Yet by their very nature, they also opened up opportunities for Africans willing to collaborate in the colonial project.

Both the arbitrariness and the opportunity were especially marked in the early years of colonial rule, as the colonizers sought to reduce African resistance and to create workable collaborative mechanisms throughout their newly won empires. The opposition had to be crushed by whatever means necessary, but *interlocuteurs valables* had also to be found and drawn into reliable working relationships. In the process the colonizers opened up new opportunities for personal advancement to certain ambitious Africans. The relationships established between such Africans and the colonial administrators with whom they worked were of a clientelistic nature. That is, they were personal relationships based on inegalitarian patterns of exchange marked in their day-to-day operation more by reciprocity than clear-cut domination (Fatton 1987:93; Lemarchand 1977:100–123). In the early years especially, such clientelistic ties between individual African collaborators and European colonial administrators formed the basis of viable administrative and legal systems at the local level. In effect, the colonizers could not rule effectively without their African collaborators, a situation that obviously opened up opportunities for the latter while imposing constraints on the former. The case of Kwame Kangah represents an object lesson in both the opportunities and constraints created by the operation of a colonial collaborative mechanism.

The Origins of *l'Affaire Kanga*

What the French referred to as *"l'affaire Kanga"* arose within the context of an effort to forge a durable collaborative mechanism in Assikasso and institutionalize a legal system compatible with the larger goals of French colonialism. This affair had its origins in the interplay between the dynamics of the Anyi-Juablin social system and the requirements of local colonial administration. At least some of the impetus for the administration's action against Kanga came from Nana Ehua. Both men had gained their positions in 1898 in the aftermath of the crushing of a Juablin revolt and the execution of its leader, Ehua's predecessor, Nana Yaw Fum (Groff 1980:202–70; 1989:2–24). Both Ehua and Kangah had willingly collaborated with the French in the creation of an administrative infrastructure in Assikasso. However, their relationship had never been an easy one, primarily because Kangah had for some time been Nana Ehua's main political challenger.

The rivalry between these two men grew out of the long-term effort by Kangah, the son of royal slaves, to establish himself as an autonomous power in Juablin society.[2] The rise of Kwame Kangah illustrates the suppleness of the Anyi social system. As a youth he had won the confidence of his master, Nana Agnini Bile, the Juablin ruler during the 1880s and early 1890s. As a reward, he was placed in charge of royal trading expeditions operating between Cape Coast and the Muslim entrepots in the north (interview: Kangah Malan, 6 July 1975). This involvement enabled him to accumulate a slave entourage and create his own extended residential group or *aulo*.[3] In a society in which a man's wealth was based largely on the size of his personal following, Kangah seems to have been well on his way to establishing himself as a "big man," an able *rassembleur d'hommes*,[4] prior to the arrival of the French in the mid-1890s.

According to Kangah's descendants, his growing prominence had caused resentment among members of the royal family and led to tensions between him and Nana Yaw Fum, Agnini Bile's successor as Juablin *famien*. Exactly how these tensions manifested themselves prior to the arrival of the French is not clear from the available evidence. However, given Kangah's betrayal of Yaw Fum during the 1898 revolt, it seems reasonable to suggest that Kangah harbored a sense of grievance against the royal *aulo*. By surreptitiously providing food and water to the French during Yaw Fum's siege of their post at Assikasso, he had gained favor with the victorious colonizers, among them François-Joseph Clozel, who, nineteen years later, as governor general of French West Africa, would play a major part in resolving Kangah's case. Kangah's reward for his support of the French cause was an appointment to the position of linguist, the chief spokesperson for the Juablin paramount (ANCI, Cheruy 1911). From this position, which he held on and off for fourteen years, he exercised considerable local personal power and accumulated a good deal of wealth. Indeed, in the view of some French officials, he came to exercise greater power than Nana Ehua, the legitimate Juablin ruler. As the *chef de poste* of Assikasso put it in 1908: "[Ehua] no longer has any authority. The village is in fact commanded by a son of slaves named Kanga" (ANCI Post of Assikasso, June 1908). Given such French perceptions, it is hardly surprising that Nana Ehua welcomed an opportunity to assert himself against his rival.

Traditionally, an Akan linguist served as the spokesperson for a chief, faithfully communicating the latter's thoughts and wishes to his followers. Appointed by the chief and serving at his pleasure, a linguist was expected to be one of the chief's most loyal supporters. Under French rule, however, the linguist, like the chief, became a line officer of the colonial administration.[5] As such he had to gain the approval of the French as well as that of his chief. As a colonial subaltern, he spent much of his time executing the policies of the administration. For Kangah this meant that he had to help collect taxes, recruit forced labor, and control smuggling along the border with the Gold Coast. Prior to the organization of the local colonial court system in 1903, it also meant that he played a large role in resolving civil disputes throughout the Assikasso region.

Such a position was obviously a difficult one involving substantial personal risks for the individual occupying it. But it also could be a most lucrative one, providing numerous opportunities for personal accumulation. So it was for Kangah. In his capacity as linguist[6] and in the related role of assessor on the local colonial court, a position he assumed after 1903, he won recognition by the French as the de facto chief of Assikasso and amassed considerable wealth, mainly, it appears, through corruption. At the same time, he became embroiled in numerous disputes and earned a reputation for unscrupulousness both among this fellow Anyi and the French.[7] At times his actions overstepped the bounds of colonial propriety and brought down disciplinary penalties upon him.[8]

Yet prior to 1913 Kangah always managed to overcome his difficulties and reemerge as a force to be reckoned with in local politics. This resilience seems to have been mainly the result of his personal dynamism, as manifested in his tireless efforts on behalf of the administration and in his equally energetic activities as a producer and trader of rubber. For all their complaints about his character, the French continued to rely on him in their efforts to maintain and extend their control over Assikasso. His dynamism and intelligence represented a marked contrast to what the French perceived as Nana Ehua's lassitude and general lack of leadership. As Cheruy, commandant de cercle in Indénié, noted in 1911:

> There is not a chief worthy of the name in Indénié. The hereditary provincial chiefs are worthless: Bile in Béttié is an unhappy drunk, without will, without prestige; Boa Qwassi in Indénié is insignificant and of doubtful honesty; *Eihua in Assikasso, is without fortune and dependent on Conga, the former political agent who served us during the troubles in Assikasso (1898) and whose wealth dates from that time* (ANCI, Cheruy 1911:61, my emphasis).

This French perception of Ehua's weakness and Kangah's contrasting power and wealth no doubt accounts in large part for the tendency found in some of the official French documents on l'affaire Kanga to identify Kangah as an Anyi "chief."[9] It is also evident in the portrayal of him in a colonial post card dating from the first decade of the century. In this portrait we encounter a jauntily self-confident old man dressed in a sumptuous Kente cloth, seated on an Akan stool under a ceremonial umbrella, attended by five young boys holding goldleaf-covered swords of office. The caption reads "Kouame Kanga, chef des agnis."

Kangah, for his part, did little to discourage the notion that he was the true chief of the Juablin. In his petition to Governor-General Clozel written in January 1917, at the height of the dispute, he referred to himself as "I, whom you appointed chief and honored with your confidence..." (ANCI, Kangah to Clozel, January, 1917). His sense of self-importance is also evident in the sobriquet he gave himself: "Androua," which means "he who would compare himself with me will lose" (interview: Kangah Ahua, 23 May 1975).

Whatever their regard for Kangah's personal abilities, local French administrators like Cheruy nevertheless felt apprehensive about his long-term impact on the stability of the collaborative mechanism they were trying to institutionalize in Assikasso. For these men knew only too well that Kangah was not the true "chef des agnis," and that his position possessed little legitimacy in Assikasso. Notwithstanding their notorious general tendency to disregard traditional indigenous concepts of legitimacy when establishing their rule in Africa, the French in Assikasso seem to have been most anxious to insure that their collaborative mechanism possessed at least some modicum of traditional authority. It was this anxiety that may help account for the local administration's willingness to side with Ehua in his dispute with Kangah.

The local administration's concern about Kangah's limitations as a collaborator might have remained in the realm of vague anxiety but for the effects of an economic crisis. In 1912 world market prices for natural rubber, the main export of southeastern Ivory Coast, plummeted.[10] By mid-1913 they had collapsed entirely. The resulting fall in African cash incomes greatly increased the burden of the annual head tax and reduced the consumption of imported goods. The French response was to push ahead with a campaign of forced cocoa cultivation in the hope of creating an alternative source of export revenue.[11] This campaign, which reached its highest intensity during 1913, caused much local dislocation and called forth considerable African resistance. Coupled with the hardships caused by the collapse of rubber prices and the burdens created by the head tax, forced labor, and military recruitment, the campaign led many Africans to emigrate to the neighboring Gold Coast, where British rule appeared less onerous (Asiwaju 1976:577–94). Amid such tensions and dislocations, it became imperative for the colonizers to do everything in their power to strengthen the local collaborative mechanism, if they were to maintain their domination.

The Development of "l'Affaire"

It was against this background that in August 1913, Kwame Kangah crossed the border into the Gold Coast accompanied by two of his wives and three boys from his aulo. Before departing, he had obtained from Clerc an official leave from his functions as linguist. His professed reason for making the trip, as he later explained in a letter to the governor-general sent during the height of the dispute, was to collect on a debt owed him by an Asante living in Kumasi (ANCI, Kangah to Clozel, January 1917). When Kangah's stay exceeded the time allotted under his leave, Clerc concluded that he had absconded, a plausible supposition under the conditions prevailing at the time.

Fearing that Kangah would remove his wealth from the colony, Clerc made an agreement with Kangah's eldest son, M'Bea, formally recognizing the latter's right to control his father's considerable fortune, subject to the surveillance of the chef de poste in Agnibilekrou. As Pailles, the chef de poste, wrote in his report on the episode, this attempt to freeze Kangah's assets reflected the standard French policy toward the families of Africans who had allegedly fled from the colony (ANCI, Pailles, 22 November 1913).

The agreement held for just over a year. Then on 17 December 1914, Clerc and Mas, Pailles's successor as chef de poste, seized Kangah's house and other assets, charging that M'Bea had violated the terms of the arrangement by surreptitiously transferring gold and English currency to his father in the Gold Coast. Since a new inventory of Kangah's holdings showed that five large gold nuggets and a quantity of shillings valued at 450 francs had in fact disappeared and could not be accounted for, Clerc's charge appeared well founded (ANCI, Clerc to Angoulvant, 10 January 1915). Given the administration's general anxieties over the effects of the on-going economic crisis and the war that had broken out the previous August, it is not surprising that Clerc acted in so punitive a manner.

If matters had ended there, the episode would merely represent one more instance of colonial repression and not a particularly interesting one at that. But matters did not end there and what happened next neatly illustrates the difficulties inherent in the colonialists' attempt to create a legal order that at once solidified their domination and provided a workable means of resolving disputes among Africans.

From the point of view of the local administration, Kangah was not only guilty of absconding from the Ivory Coast but also of deserting his post as linguist. Thus on one level, Clerc and Mas's action of 17 December amounted to the formal removal of Kangah from his official administrative duties. But a linguist was not merely a low-level official in the colonial bureaucracy; he was also a Juablin traditional office-holder. As such he had to be dealt with, at least to some extent, on the basis of Juablin "customary law." Otherwise the action of punishing him could not be made to appear as legitimate either locally among the Juablin or at the upper levels of a colonial administration ever anxious to avoid local disorder, especially during wartime.

Thus, the problem for the local administration was to find a way of dealing with Kangah that was workable and yet consistent with both Anyi and French legal norms. After much consultation with Nana Ehua and his entourage, Clerc and Mas decided that the best solution was to treat Kangah as a deceased person and transfer his wealth to his legal heir (ANCI, Clerc to Angoulvant, 10 January 1915). On the advice of the queen mother and several other knowledgeable persons from the royal aulo, Clerc designated Koffi Yeboua, a member of Ehua's entourage, as Kangah's "heir" and, in May 1915, turned over to him Kangah's estate.[12]

As reported by Clerc in a letter to Lieutenant-governor Angoulvant, Kangah's fortune consisted of a large two-story house, a sum of English shillings equivalent to about 14,460 francs, gold dust worth 600 francs, 58 gold nuggets of undisclosed value and various goldleaf-covered *attributs de chef* (ANCI, Clerc to Angoulvant, 10 January 1915). Initially, Clerc had proposed to divide this fortune, turning over the coins and gold to Yeboua and the chiefly regalia to Ehua. His express purpose in making this division was to "render [Ehua]...the authority he needs so badly" (ANCI, Clerc to Angoulvant, 10 January 1915). Angoulvant, however, vetoed this plan on the grounds that:

> among the Agnis, wealth being most often only an attribute of authority, it would be contrary to custom to deprive the heir of so consequential a fortune of the chiefly emblems that, so to speak, justify it. In this matter you must conform as much as possible to the practices to which the Agni populations are so attached (Angoulvant to Clerc, 11 February 1915).

Here we see an indication of the tensions and uncertainties surrounding any attempt by the administration to make its practices conform with its conception of "customary law." Both Clerc and Angoulvant sought to base what was, in effect, a politically motivated decision on Anyi legal norms, as they understood them. Clerc, given his interest in buttressing Ehua, read these norms in such a way as to justify a division of Kangah's fortune. Angoulvant, though also no doubt sensitive to the need to support Ehua, felt compelled to stick to what he assumed to be a stricter interpretation of Anyi law provided by earlier ethnographic research, most notably that presented in the cercle monograph of 1911. As it turned out, neither man was on especially firm ground. Yet in the event, Angoulvant, in his role as lieutenant-governor, simply imposed his view of Anyi legality on Clerc. Accordingly, the centerpiece of the final resolution was the transfer of Kangah's entire fortune to Yeboua.

In retrospect, it is apparent that this resolution was not in any meaningful sense based on either Anyi legal custom or French colonial law. As Fardet, Clerc's successor as commandant de cercle later pointed out, the decision to transfer Kangah's possessions to his supposed heir, Yeboua, was based on the notion of "civil death," a concept wholly foreign to both colonial law and Anyi inheritance customs.[13] Although Clerc and Angoulvant seem to have acted in good faith, their action was not, in fact, based on a synthesis of French and Anyi law, as they claimed, but rather represented a precedent-setting, ad hoc resolution of an immediate political problem worked out in close collaboration with the Juablin royal aulo, whose members could hardly be expected to act in a disinterested manner with regard to their old antagonist, Kangah.

The ad hoc, political nature of Clerc's action against Kangah should not surprise us. For what we have here is an example of an attempt at what Chanock has aptly called "the making of customary law," a cooperative effort on the part of colonial administrators and African traditional authorities to transform fluid customary practices into firm legal principles supportive of their own immediate political interests (Chanock 1985:8–10). Such a process with quintessentially political and ad hoc, since it involved on-going negotiated adjustments between European and African legal concepts and practices. As Chanock emphasizes in his study of Northern Rhodesia and Nyasaland, such adjustments occurred within the context of conflicts between interested parties. Moreover, in his view, the colonial officials and indigenous elites who cooperated in resolving such conflicts were themselves invariably interested parties to them. The "customary law" that evolved out of this process of mutual adjustments reflected primarily, though certainly not exclusively, the special needs and interests of these two groups, each of which desired above all else to maintain its control over the mass of Africans.

In the case at hand, the local administration and the Juablin royal aulo responded to Kangah's apparent defection by cobbling together a mutually beneficial arrangement and presenting it as a happy marriage between French and Anyi legal concepts. Under its terms Nana Ehua was able to rid himself of his chief rival and to enrich a supporter, while the French were able to make Kangah an example of the consequences of disloyalty.

Had Clerc, Mas, and Nana Ehua succeeded in pulling it off, their resolution of l'affaire Kanga would have been a bold exercise in the making of customary law. But they were not to succeed. What they did not count on was the determination and tenacity and ingenuity of Kwame Kangah, the strength of old patronage ties, and the need on the part of the upper levels of the French colonial administration to uphold a certain conception of the rule of law.

Kangah Fights Back

The decision to bestow Kangah's legacy on Koffi Yeboua created a furor in Agnibilekrou. The town quickly divided into two camps as the various constituent residential kin groups lined up behind either Nana Ehua or Kangah. How far Kangah's support extended beyond his own large aulo cannot be determined from the available evidence. It is clear, however, that his support was substantial enough to worry Nana Ehua and Koffi Yeboua. In July 1915, in a letter to Clerc, Mas observed:

> You know the internecine quarrels that divide Agnibilekrou into two camps: on the one hand, the party of the deserter Kanga; on the other, the party of Eihua. It is this second party that is rejoicing at present over its possession of Kanga's fortune which I, myself, seized. This party

nevertheless does not consider its victory complete as long as Kanga's son, Béa, continues to reside in the village and its ardent desire is that I do everything possible to get Béa driven out. With Kangah still alive, the heir Coffi Yeboua and his worthy master, Eihua, are not at all reassured and, in spite of your recent pronouncements in Agnibilekrou regarding Kanga, they are extremely fearful of being dispossessed (ANCI, Mas to Clerc 7 July 1915).

Mas refused to expel M'Bea for fear of exacerbating an increasingly tense situation. His refusal, however, only served to anger Nana Ehua and Yeboua who added a new dimension to the controversy by accusing Mas of extorting 1500 francs from Yeboua as a bribe for having selected him as Kangah's heir. Mas's response to this charge was to humiliate Nana Ehua by publicly slapping him and threatening him with prison under the *indigénat*, the French system of administrative law empowering local administrators to take summary action against individual "natives" perceived to threaten public order (ANCI, Mas to Clerc, 7 July 1915).[14]

Amid these tensions, Kwame Kangah began making overtures to the administration requesting permission to return to Agnibilekrou. His initial request to Mas was rejected on orders from Clerc, but he persisted in his efforts, eventually enlisting the commandant of the neighboring cercle of Bondoukou to mediate on his behalf (ANCI, the Administrator of Bondoukou to the Administrator of Indénié, 18 October 1915). By May 1916 Clerc had relented for reasons that are not altogether clear from the archival record.[15] Perhaps he hoped to defuse the controversy by letting Kangah come back and argue his case before the *tribunal de province* in Agnibilekrou, the court with jurisdiction over civil disputes. This hope was no doubt fueled by the death of Nana Ehua in March of 1916. Whatever his general objective, however, it is clear that his immediate intention was to make a conciliatory gesture to Kangah. Accordingly, Clerc issued an order permitting the latter to return to Agnibilekrou and encouraging him to think that he might be restored to his past functions (ANCI, Fardet to Lapalud, 24 May 1917).

If Clerc had hoped to mollify Kangah by allowing him to return home, he quickly suffered disappointment. For Kangah no sooner arrived home than he began agitating for the restoration of his fortune. What is more, he refused to take his case to either the tribunal de province in Agnibilekrou or the *tribunal de cercle* in Zaranou, the courts set up handle civil cases.[16] His refusal is hardly surprising given the composition of these courts. Each consisted of the principal colonial administrators and indigenous chiefs and notables from the region over which it claimed jurisdiction in civil cases. Thus, if Kangah took his case to the tribunal de province in Agnibilekrou, he faced judgment by a court dominated by Mas and supporters of the late Ehua. If he went directly to the higher tribunal de cercle, as was permitted under colonial law in extraordinary circumstances, he had to present his case before a group presided over by Clerc. Since Kangah staunchly maintained that he was a victim of a conspiracy by Clerc, Mas, and the Juablin royal aulo, one could hardly expect him to place much trust in either of these courts. Moreover, having served for many years as an assessor on this court, Kangah knew only too well both its strengths and limitations as a vehicle for dispensing justice.

Instead of taking his case to the local tribunals, he chose to appeal directly to the upper reaches of the administration. First he petitioned the lieutenant-governor of the Ivory Coast, requesting him to intervene on his behalf. When the lieutenant-governor proved unreceptive, rejecting his petition out of hand, he enlisted a recently retired French customs inspector as an adviser and advocate. Then, on this man's advice, he boarded a ship in Grand Bassam and traveled to Dakar to take his case directly to Clozel, the governor-general of French West Africa. For an old African who spoke little French, such a novel course of action showed considerable courage and not a little daring.

Although the French colonial administration did all it could to discourage its African subjects from seeking the legal counsel of European lawyers or other advocates, it could not always prevent them from doing so.[17] Back in 1913 Nana Ehua had hired a French lawyer named Ostench to help him resolve several disputes between him and Pailles, the chef de poste (ANCI, Fardet to Lapalud, 24 May 1917). Kangah's action was thus not unprecedented even in Assikasso. To be sure, the colonial administration sought to prevent Africans from obtaining legal counsel and reviled any European who tried to serve as an advocate for African interests. Thus there were obviously severe constraints upon what such people could hope to achieve.

Under such circumstances it is difficult to assess just how much assistance Lambert, the man engaged by Kangah, was able to provide him. To be sure, members of the Ivory Coast administration tended to regard Lambert as the instigator of Kangah's audacious and, from their point of view, embarrassing initiative. According to Lieutenant-governor Lapalud, for example, it was Lambert who persuaded Kangah to undertake the voyage to Dakar. This may have been so, but it also seems likely that Kangah did not need much persuasion, just a little encouragement. He had known Clozel personally since the late 1890s, when the latter served as the first commandant de cercle in Indénié. According to Kangah's family, he had helped Clozel during the siege of Assikasso, providing food to the Frenchman after he was seriously wounded trying to break the siege of the post (interview: Kangah Assemien, 21 July 1975). For a man like Kangah whose career had been largely based on the establishment of clientelistic ties with French administrators, it seems probable that a trip to Dakar loomed as an opportunity to appeal to an old patron. Moreover, given Kangah's political energy and pugnaciousness, it is not inconceivable that he himself came up with the idea for the trip.

Yet whatever Lambert's role in Kangah's decision to go to Dakar, there can be little doubt that he helped the old man with the logistical arrangements for the trip. Nor can there be much doubt about his importance in helping Kangah formulate and write his petition to Clozel. In this petition, Kangah presents his case with a mixture of measured obsequiousness and brash self-assertion:

> Having been the victim of a great injustice, I have come here before you, the great chief of the blacks and whites, to recount this affair and appeal to your strong sense of fairness. All the blacks of the Ivory Coast remember your never-failing benevolence and I, whom you appointed chief and honored with your confidence, have not forgotten it (ANCI, Kangah to Clozel, January 1917).

After this opening appeal, he proceeded to provide a detailed refutation of the charges against him. No, he had not absconded, but had only gone to the Gold Coast to settle a family matter; his long delay in returning was simply a function of the time-consuming nature of African palavers. If his intention had been to abscond, why did he leave most of his family and wealth behind in Agnibilekrou? Moreover, why should he want to abscond? He had no reason to do so. Finally, on what grounds could the administration justify its confiscation of his personal property? It belonged to him and not to the local chieftaincy stool. All in all, Kangah concluded, he had been the innocent victim of an arbitrary attack by the local administration, an attack whose ill effects had been compounded by the insensitivity with which the lieutenant-governor had greeted his demands for justice:

> I vainly petitioned the administration of the Ivory Coast which has not followed up my initiatives. I am old now. I have worked hard. I have always been devoted to the cause of the French. I come asking you to make them give me back my possessions because I have committed no crime. As soon as I completed my business in Kumasi, I returned to the country where I was born in order to end my days there (ANCI, Kangah to Clozel, January 1917).

Clozel gave Kangah a personal audience and received his petition sympathetically. Impressed by the old man's courage in travelling all the way to Dakar to put his case, the governor-general demanded a full explanation from Lieutenant-governor Lapalud. When the latter replied by simply reiterating Clerc's account of the affair, the governor-general wrote back upbraiding him for not having insisted on a judicial resolution and for having simply assumed the lawfulness of Clerc's seizure of Kangah's assets. In Clozel's view Lapalud and Clerc had shown insufficient understanding of the issues at stake in the case:

> the question is not that of replacing Kouame Kanga in his functions as village chief. That could have been justified by his prolonged absence and regulated according to local traditions. Instead, what we have here is a man who is complaining that his personal possessions have been confiscated without due process in the name of the administrative authority and handed over to an individual who appears to have no right to them.
>
> It is not for me to pronounce on the correctness of Kouame Kanga's assertions, but you should recall that it is also not for the administrative authority of Abengourou to decide if the possessions claimed by this native were his personal property or an attribute of his function as village chief (ANCI, Clozel to Lapalud, 24 February 1917).

For Clozel, then, the local administration's action against Kangah, whatever its motives or larger justifications, had violated basic procedural fairness. In other words, it had contravened the ideal of the rule of law in whose name France presumed to rule its colonies. The only proper solution was to submit Kangah's case to an established court. But such a solution was problematic insofar as it involved the tribunal de province in Agnibilekrou or the tribunal de cercle in Abengourou. Recognizing that these courts, given their composition, could not provide an impartial hearing of the case, Clozel ordered Lapalud to submit the matter to a tribunal in a neighboring region where similar "customary law" prevailed.

In terms of its rhetoric, Clozel's letter to Lapalud would appear to confirm the governor-general's support for the principle of the rule of law. Certainly, in the letter he was at pains to emphasize that the colonial administration was not above the law and could not deprive a French subject of his possessions without due process. But can we be certain that such apparent high-mindedness provides a sufficient explanation of Clozel's behavior? Although there is no direct evidence for any other explanation, it seems highly unlikely that Clozel acted out of so simple a motivation. Given his previous association with Kangah in Assikasso, it is plausible to suspect that patronage had something to do with the governor-general's response to Kangah's petition. It also seems likely that Clozel feared the possibility of scandal should Kangah's grievances be ignored. Indeed, it is clear from Clozel's letter to Lapalud that one of the aspects of the case that troubled him most was its potential usefulness to critics of the French *mission civilisatrice*. How else are we to construe the following comment made toward the end of the letter:

> Whatever else it may be, this affair deserves to be studied with the utmost care. It is absolutely necessary that it be carefully regulated in order to avoid anything that might have the appearance of a denial of justice or of simple negligence on the part of the local authorities (ANCI, Clozel to Lapalud, 24 February 1917).

Subsequent events were to justify the governor-general's concern.

Whatever the vagaries of Clozel's motivation, his response greatly encouraged Kangah, who returned to the Ivory Coast more determined than ever to gain restitution of his possessions. With the assistance of Lambert, he set about the task of pressing his case in Abengourou, the *chef lieu* of the cercle of Indénié. To the consternation and anger of the local administration, he succeeded in obtaining certain confidential documents on his case and used them to buttress his charge that Clerc, Mas, and Nana Ehua has conspired against him (ANCI Fardet to Lapalud, 24 May 1917).[18]

At the same time, acting no doubt on the advice of Lambert, he sought to intensify the pressure on the local administration by petitioning the French Chamber of Deputies via Gratien Candace, a deputy from Guadaloupe (ANCI, Présidence de la Chambre de Députés, 1 June 1917). This move suggests that Kangah, or in any case Lambert, recognized and was prepared to exploit a major vulnerability of the French colonial state: its ultimate subordination to the semi-democratic workings of the metropolitan political system and its corresponding need to justify and legitimize its actions to potentially critical parliamentary investigators.

Kangah's effort paid off. In a memorandum to the minister of colonies dated 1 June 1917, a parliamentary commission on colonial affairs commented:

> The Commission does not find in the materials contained in the dossier evidence permitting it to reach an opinion on this affair. If the reported account is correct, it well understands that a chief who abandons his post can be revoked, but even if Koami Kanga had wanted to emigrate, it doesn't see any legal basis for punishing him by confiscating his property. Moreover, natives who are French subjects are neither slaves nor serfs and if they are not satisfied with the regime to which they are subject, we do not arrogate to ourselves the right to maintain their attachment to the colony. The Commission asks that the minister of colonies see to it that a serious investigation be undertaken of this affair (ANCI, Présidence de la Chambre de Députés, 1 June 1917).

It is difficult to assess with any certainty the precise role played by this parliamentary intervention in the subsequent resolution of the case. The minister did not formally respond to the Commission until 7 August, well after the local administration had resolved the affair by returning Kangah's assets to him. Nevertheless, it seems very likely that the Ivory Coast authorities became aware of Kangah's petition to parliament fairly early on and that such awareness enhanced their desire to settle with Kangah.

In any case, settle they did, but not through the regular judicial procedures of the tribunal de province. By May 1917 the whole affair had become an enormous source of embarrassment for the Ivory Coast administration from the lieutenant-governor down to the commandant of Indénié. It had brought an unwanted intervention by the governor-general in the internal affairs of the colony. And to make matters worse, the inquiry precipitated by this intervention had disclosed that Mas had indeed extorted 1500 francs from Koffi Yeboua shortly after seizing Kangah's assets and had, in all probability, also embezzled the money he had accused M'Bea of sending to Kangah in the Gold Coast.[19] Disturbed by these disclosures and discomfited by Kangah's increasingly bitter public denunciations of the administration, Lapalud and Fardet, the newly appointed commandant de cercle in Indénié, moved to resolve the matter as expeditiously as possible.

Falling back on a 1906 decree by the government-general recognizing the right of individual African subjects to resolve civil disputes through mutually agreed upon conventions,[20] they pressured Yeboua to reach an agreement with Kangah, restoring to the latter his confiscated wealth. They themselves agreed to reimburse Kangah out of government funds for the money Mas had apparently embezzled.[21]

Conclusion

Kangah had won, but what are we to make of his victory? Can it be said to have constituted a victory for the principle of the rule of law? The answer to this latter question is a highly qualified "yes." The resolution process had been a messy one in which the regular court system had played no significant part. If anything, the system had shown itself incapable, in this instance at least, of rendering justice impartially. In view of his own long service in the local tribunals, Kangah's lack of confidence in these courts underscores their lack of legitimacy as vehicles for administering justice. Moreover, the local administration's decision to resolve the affair out of court rather than follow the governor-general's advice to take it to a tribunal in a neighboring cercle hardly stands as a ringing endorsement of the court system.

Nevertheless, the governor-general had acted to insure that Kangah received such legal protections as were enshrined in French colonial law. Of course, this action no doubt had much to do with Clozel's personal ties to Kangah and his fear of providing ammunition for critics of the mission civilisatrice. Yet the fact remains that he acted and justice was finally carried out. In this respect, the case shows that the rule of law operated, at least to a limited extent, in French West Africa.

Unfortunately, there is a postscript to the case that removes some of the glitter from the French achievement and suggests the degree to which the rule of law was constrained by the colonial situation and the imperatives of the collaborative mechanism. The local administration had rendered justice to Kangah but not with any great enthusiasm. Predictably, its representatives worried about the impact the case would have on their rule in Assikasso. Moreover, Kangah did nothing to allay their fears. In October 1917, Fardet reported:

> The only fact of some importance to note for the third trimester is the reinstallation at Agnibilekrou of Kangah, ex-deserter who has regained his fortune. Convinced that he has been persecuted by the local administration, he seems to have the intention to avenge himself by creating for it, by his counsel and pernicious example, as many difficulties as possible.... His hateful and mendacious speeches easily find a receptive audience among the population, which admires him for having re-established his fortune (ANCI, Fardet, Report on the Political Situation, 1917).

The commandant went on to complain that Kangah had boasted of being "above the law" and refused to create cocoa plantations. Worst of all, from Fardet's point of view, Kangah supported his rebellious declarations by citing "an official document" stating that "if native French subjects are not satisfied with the regime to which they are submitted, we do not arrogate to ourselves any right to maintain their attachment to the colony." Obviously, Kangah had received a copy of the parliamentary memorandum and was trying to make the most of it.

Such behavior by a "native" was intolerable from the local administration's point of view and had to be stopped. In a context defined by wartime hardships and anxieties concerning the success of the cocoa campaign, the administration was not about to allow someone like Kangah to spread further discord in Assikasso. Thus it is not surprising that Kangah's every action came in for scrutiny by the local colonial authorities. Early in 1918 he was arrested and imprisoned for fifteen days under the indigénat for having "made fetish" and administered *le bois rouge*, an Anyi judicial ordeal. Later in the year he was again arrested and accused of usurping the role of native magistrate by participating in a village tribunal. This time his case went before the tribunal de cercle and Fardet, its presiding officer, imposed a four-year prison sentence and ten-year *interdiction de séjour*.[22] The administrative records contain little information on the actual execution of this sentence, but a member of the Kangah family reported to me in 1975 that Kangah spent several years in exile in the northern Ivorian cercle of Korhogo (Interview: Kangah Assemien, 31 July 1975).[23]

It is noteworthy that all the charges made against Kangah in 1918 had to do with his alleged usurpation of judicial prerogatives. Ironically, these were precisely the kinds of activities that Kangah had performed during his years as linguist and court assessor. Whatever the validity of the charges, they clearly arose out of the administration's anxiety over the threat posed by Kangah to the continued operation of the local collaborative mechanism. The fate of this obstreperous old Anyi suggests that while the French colonizers felt compelled to defend the legitimacy of the mission civilisatrice by invoking the rule of law and sometimes even upholding it, their overriding concern remained the maintenance of their local collaborative mechanisms. Kangah had accumulated wealth and gained a certain measure of personal power by exploiting this concern. His career illustrates what individual Africans could achieve by seizing the opportunities thrown up by the colonial situation. Yet his downfall reminds us once again of the powerful constraints on African achievement inherent in that situation.

NOTES

1. I conducted the study resulting in this article in the Ivory Coast in 1974–75 under a fellowship from the Foreign Area Fellowship Program. I presented an early version at the American Historical Association's annual meeting in New York in December 1985, and made revisions while participating in a seminar at Duke University sponsored by the National Endowment for the Humanities. I have benefitted greatly from the incisive comments of Kristin Mann, Richard Roberts, John Cell, and the participants in the Stanford-Emory Conference on Law and Colonialism in Africa. The conclusions, opinions and other statements in this paper, of course, represent my own views and not necessarily those of either the funding agencies or my colleagues.

2. My main source on Kangah's early life is the oral testimony of Assemien Kangah, one of the elders of Kangah aulo during the time of my field work in Assikasso. As a young man, Nana Assemien was very close to Kwame Kangah, serving as his chief body servant. When Kangah traveled to Dakar in 1917, Nana Assemien went along as his sole companion. Other important oral sources were Kangah Malan, the head of Kangah aulo and Kangah Ahua, one of Kangah's sons. Kangah's early ties with the royal family and his slave origins are also described in Clerc's report to the lieutenant-governor dated 20 October 1916, which may be found in ANCI VI-23/6, MM 69.

3. An aulo consisted of several kin or fictive kin-related domestic groups united under the authority of a male elder called an *aulo kpagne*. Because the Juablin, like other Akan peoples, combine matrilineal descent with patrilocal residence, aulo membership could be based on either maternal or paternal ties. The core of every aulo consisted of an aulo kpagne and several of his matrilineal kinsmen including his uterine brothers, his unmarried, widowed, or divorced uterine sisters, and the latters' infant children. It also sometimes included his nephews by uterine sisters living in other residential units. To this core group were added the wives of the aulo kpagne and his brothers, their unmarried daughters, their sons who had not yet received an inheritance elsewhere, their son's wives and dependents, and their own slaves and pawns. This corporate group was bound together not only by common residence and allegiance to an aulo kpagne, but also by common ritual observance and participation in certain collective economic activities, notably gold mining, rubber processing, and long-distance trade. How large these units were in the late nineteenth and early twentieth centuries is impossible to say with precision. But on the basis of what my informants told me, I would estimate that they varied in size between two dozen and a hundred or more members.

4. The phrase comes from Claude Hélène Perrot (1976:173–87).

5. For descriptions of the duties of the linguist or porte-canne, see: Post of Assikasso, monthly report for September 1909, ANCI 1EE 45(2).

6. Kangah is listed as an assessor in the tribunal de province of Assikasso for 1905, 1906, 1908, 1909, 1911, 1912, and 1913 in the *Journaux Officiels* for those years. In his monthly report for September 1906, the chef de poste for Assikasso briefly commented on the abilities of the assessors in the tribunal de province. He characterized Kangah as "very smart, competent." ANCI 1EE 44(2).

7. See, for example: Benquey to the chef de poste for Assikasso, 8 March 1900, ANCI XIV–8–21; Administrator of the cercle of Bondoukou to the chef de poste of Assikasso, 13 August 1904, ANCI NN 55, XIV–8–20; and chef de poste for Bondoukou to the chef de poste for Assikasso, 3 June 1905, ANCI VI–12–58.

8. The post report for January 1902 mentions that Kangah had recently spent eight days in jail for illegally imposing a fine. In March 1905, the chef de poste reported to the commandant that Kangah had been recently reintegrated as linguist following a period of exclusion brought on by some undisclosed misdeed. The former document may be found in ANCI 1EE 43(2), the latter in ANCI VI–12–58.

9. In his letter to Governor-general Clozel dated 6 December 1917, Lieutenant-governor Lapalud apologized for having incorrectly referred to Kangah as a chief in his earlier communications, but partially excused himself on these grounds: "C'était à la verité un porte-canne tres remuant et qui annihilait à peu prés son chef." This letter may be found in ANS-AOF 5 G 73.

10. For information on the fall of rubber prices, see: the administrator of Indénié to the lieutenant-governor, 1 December 1913; and Graphique des prix du terme de caoutchouc de plantations à Anvers, comparés aux cours du Para à Londres pendant l'année 1913. Both of these documents are in ANCI XI–11–84.

11. Information on this campaign may be found in "Le Développement de la culture du cacaoyer," J.O.C.I., 15 March 1916; Post of Assikasso, agricultural report for the fourth trimester, 1914; cercle of Indénié, Agriculture Service, General Report, 1917, 31 December 1917. See also Groff 1987:401–16.

12. Administrator of Indénié to the lieutenant-governor, 10 January 1915. See also: the Administrator of Indénié to the lieutenant-governor, 20 October 1916, also in ANCI VI–23/6, MM69.

13. Fardet, administrator of Indénié, to the lieutenant-governor, 24 May 1917, ANCI VI–23/6, MM69. The legal doctrine of "civil death" held that persons convicted of serious crimes involving substantial jail sentences also relinquished their legal personality and hence all their rights, including that of either receiving an inheritance or passing one on. However, "civil death" had been abolished in France in 1854. See Breton 1982:51–52.

14. For good descriptions of the indigénat system of summary administrative "disciplinary penalties," see Buell 1928:1016–20 and Asiwaju 1979:35–71.

15. Corruption may have played some part in this decision. In his letter to the lieutenant-governor, dated 24 May 1917, Fardet, Clerc's successor as commandant, reported that Mas had extracted a bribe from Kangah in return for negotiating the latter's return to Agnibilekrou. ANCI VI–23/6, MM69.

16. For detailed descriptions of the French colonial justice system, see: Buell 1928:1002–1020 and Michellet and Clement 1906:135–58.

17. On 22 April 1917, Lieutenant-governor Lapalud sent a telegram to Fardet declaring: "Vous prie faire connaitre à Lambert conseil de Kanga qu'il n'existe en justice indigen d'autre forme procédure que celle résultant coutumes locales (stop). Or ces coutumes n'ont jamais prévu réprésentation par un Blanc devant Tribunal (stop)." ANCI VI–23/6, MM69.

18. In this letter Fardet speculates that the source of the leak was a certain auxiliary clerk named Ahécoro whom he characterizes as: "Dahoméen prétentieux et d'esprit anti-administratif, propagandiste de la Ligue des Droits de l'Homme...."

19. Fardet to the lieutenant-governor, 24 May 1917. See also: Government General of French West Africa, rapport du conseil administratif, Session of 16 August 1917, ANCI VI–23/6, MM69.

20. Lapalud blamed the failure to resolve the dispute through the courts on the influence of Lambert: "Si l'affaire Kanga n'a pas reçu une solution judiciaire c'est...parce que le sieur Lambert lui a fait retirer la plainte qu'il avait formulé devant tribunal de subdivision." Lapalud to the governor-general, 6 December 1917, ANS AOF 5 G 73.

21. Lieutenant-governor Lapalud to the Administrator of Indénié, 8 June 1917. Conventions entre indigenes dans les conditions du décret du 2 mai, 1906, 6 June 1917, ANCI VI−23/6, MM69.
22. These incidents are reported by M'Bea Kangah in a letter to the lieutenant-governor dated 14 April 1918. ANCI VI−23/6, MM69.
23. Some confirmation for this report comes from the cercle report for the third trimester of 1924 in which Ernest Gerette, the commandant, comments on Kangah's docile behavior since his return to Agnibilekrou. This document may be found in ANCI 1EE 59(1/4).

SOURCES

Oral

Assemien Kangah, 31 July 1975, Agnibilekrou.
Kangah Malan, 6 July 1975, Agnibilekrou.
Kangah Ahua, 23 May 1975, Koguinan.

Archival

ANCI: Archives Nationales de la Côte d'Ivoire, Abidjan.
Administrator of the cercle of Bondoukou to the chef de poste of Assikasso, 13 August 1904, NN 55, XIV−8−20.
Administrator of the cercle of Bondoukou to the administrator of Indénié, 18 October 1915, VI−23/6.
Administrator of Indénié to the lieutenant-governor, 1 December 1913, XI−11−84.
Administrator of the cercle of Indénié to the lieutenant-governor, 10 January 1915, VI−23/6, MM69.
Administrator of Indénié to the lieutenant-governor, 20 October 1916, VI−23/6, MM69.
Angoulvant to Clerc, 11 February 1915, VI−23/6 MM69.
Benquey, administrator of the cercle of Bondoukou to the chef de poste of Assikasso, 8 March 1900, XIV−8−24.
Cercle de l'Indénié, Poste d' Assikasso, extrait du registre de Conventions entre indigenes, 22 November 1913, VI−23/6, MM69.
Cercle de l'Indénié, Agriculture Service, General Report, 1917, 31 December 1917, XI−43−426.
Chef de poste of Bondoukou to the chef de poste of Assikasso, 3 June 1905, VI−12−58.
Chef de poste of Bondoukou to the chef de poste of Assikasso, 4 June 1905, VI−12−58.
Clerc, Louis, rapport au lieutenant-gouverneur, 20 October 1916, VI−23/6, MM69.
Cheruy, Monographie du cercle de l'Indénié, 18 July 1911, p. 61. 3 Mai, No. 1.
"Le Développement de la culture du cacaoyer," *Journal Officiel de la Côte d'Ivoire*, I, 15 March 1916.
Fardet, administrator of Indénié, to the lieutenant-governor, 24 May 1917, VI−23/6, MM69.
Fardet, cercle de l'Indénié, rapport sur la situation politique et tournées, Third Trimester of 1917, VI−23/6, MM69.
Gerette, Ernest, commandant du cercle de l'Indénie, rapport du troisième trimester, 1924, 1EE 59(1/4).
Governor-general of French West Africa to the lieutenant-governor of the Ivory Coast, 24 February 1917, VI−23/6 MM69.
Government General of French West Africa, rapport du conseil administratif, session of 16 August 1917, VI−23/6, MM69.
Graphique des prix du terme de caoutchouc de plantations à Anvers, comparés aux cours du Para à Londres pendant l'année 1913, XI−11−84.

Kanga, Kwame, ex-chef du village d'Agnibilekrou, Côte d'Ivoire à Monsieur le Gouverneur-Général de l'AOF, January 1917, VI–23/6, MM69.
Lapalud to Fardet, telegram, 22 April 1917, VI–23/6, MM69.
Lapalud to the administrator of Indénié, 8 June 1917. Conventions entre indigenes dans les conditions du décret du 2 mai, 1906, 6 June 1917, VI–23/6, MM69.
Mas to Clerc, 7 July 1915, VI–23/6, MM69.
Kangah, M'Bea, to the lieutenant-governor, 14 April 1918, VI–23/6, MM69.
Poste d'Assikasso, rapport mensuel, January 1902, 1EE 43(2).
Poste d'Assikasso, rapport mensuel, March 1905, VI–12–58.
Poste d'Assikasso, rapport mensuel, September 1906, 1EE 44(2).
Poste d'Assikasso, rapport mensuel, June 1908, 1EE 45(1).
Poste d'Assikasso, rapport mensuel, September 1909, 1EE 45(2).
Poste d'Assikasso, rapport agricole, the fourth trimester 1914, XI–43–426.
Présidence de la Chambre des Députés, Réponse à une pétition à M.K. Kanga, à Agnebilekrou, 1 June 1917, VI–23/6, MM69.

ANF-DOM: Archives Nationales de France–Section Outre-Mer, Aix-en-Provence.
Deane, administrator of Indénié and Bondoukou to the governor of the Ivory Coast, 10 April 1899, C.I. VI–3.
Minister of colonies Maginot to the president of the Chamber of Deputies, 7 August 1917, C.I. 1–15.

ANS-AOF: Archives Nationales du Sénégal, Gouvernement de l'Afrique Occidentale Française, Dakar.
Lieutenant-governor Lapalud to Governor-general Clozel, 6 December 1917, 5 G 73.

Other

Asiwaju, A. I. 1976. "Migrations as revolt: The example of the Ivory Coast and Upper Volta before 1945." *Journal of African History* 17:577–94.
———. 1979. "Control through coercion, a study of the indigenat regime in French West African administration, 1887–1946." *Bulletin de l'I.F.A.N.* 41, série B: 35–71.
Breton, A. 1982. *Leçons de droit civil.* 4ème Tome, vol. II, 4th ed. Paris: Editions Monchrestien.
Buell, Raymond Leslie. 1928. *The native problem in Africa,* vol. I. New York: Macmillan.
Chandra, Bipan. 1985. "The long-term dynamics of the Indian National Congress." Presidential Address, Indian History Congress.
Chanock, Martin. 1982. "Making customary law: Men, women, and courts in colonial Northern Rhodesia." In *African women and the law: Historical perspectives,* ed. Margaret Jean Hay and Marcia Wright, 53–67. Boston: Boston University African Studies Center.
———. 1985. *Law, custom, and social order: The colonial experience in Malawi and Zambia.* Cambridge: Cambridge University Press.
Fatton, Robert, Jr. 1987. *The making of a liberal democracy: Senegal's passive revolution, 1975–1985.* Boulder, Colo.: Lynne Rienner.
Groff, David H. 1980. "The development of capitalism in the Ivory Coast: The case of Assikasso, 1880–1940." Ph.D. dissertation, Stanford University.
———. 1987. "Carrots, sticks, and cocoa pods: African and colonial initiatives in the spread of cocoa cultivation in Assikasso, Ivory Coast, 1908–1920." *The International Journal of African Historical Studies* 20:401–16.
———. 1989. "The 'revolt of Assikasso': An episode in the colonial reconstruction of an African regional economy." *African Economic History* 18:1–24.

Lemarchand, René. 1977. "Political clientelism and ethnicity in tropical Africa." In *Friends, followers and factions*, ed. S. Schmidt, J. Scott, C. Landé, and L. Guasti, 100–123. Berkeley: University of California Press.

Michellet, E., and J. Clement. 1906. *La Côte d'Ivoire: Organisation administrative, financière, judiciaire, régime minier, domanial, forestier, foncier*. Paris: Challamel.

Perrot, Claude Hélène. 1976. "De la richesse au pouvoir: Les origines d'une chefferie du Ndényé (Côte d'Ivoire)." *Cahiers d'Etudes Africaines* 61–62:173–87.

Robinson, Ronald. 1972. "Non-European foundations of European imperialism: Sketch for a theory of collaboration." In *Studies in the theory of imperialism*, ed. R. Owen and B. Sutcliffe, 117–42. London: Longman.

Snyder, Francis J. 1982. "Colonialism and legal form: The creation of 'customary law' in Senegal." In *Crime, justice and underdevelopment*, ed. C. Sumner, 90–121. London: Heinemann.

Weiskel, Timothy C. 1980. *French colonial rule and the Baule peoples: Resistance and collaboration, 1889–1911*. Oxford: Clarendon.

7

Tswana Government and Law in the Time of Seepapitso, 1910–1916

Simon Roberts

I. Introduction

Upon their earliest contact with the Tswana, European intruders found men who appeared to be the rulers of their people. Relations with the Tswana were conducted through these figures; and they were ultimately absorbed as "the Tswana chiefs" into the local administration of the Bechuanaland Protectorate. That much is perhaps uncontroversial; and the Tswana case provides just one example of something that was then happening right across the British colonial world, the establishment of "traditional authorities" within a governmental process which came to be known as "indirect rule." What remains insufficiently explored is the part actually played by such figures as the Tswana chiefs, who found themselves at the point of contact between the various agents of colonial intrusion and Africans in the localities. Many of the details of what went on in those early years are now irrecoverable; they were not at the time closely observed or recorded, and few of the actors themselves left their own accounts in any durable form.

Seepapitso of the Ngwaketse provides us with an important exception to this general loss, enabling us to reconstruct something of what rule in the localities was like in those now-shadowy years between the establishment of the Bechuanaland Protectorate and attempts to formalize local government in the 1930s. Shortly before the death of his father Bathoen in 1910, Seepapitso began to keep a written record, in his own hand, of some of the meetings which took place at the central *kgotla* (open meeting place) in the village of Kanye. He continued to maintain these records when he himself became *kgosi* (chief) later in the same year, and they were kept continuously until his assassination in 1916. These records survive, thanks to the care of Seepapitso's son Bathoen II and to the exemplary scholarship of I. Schapera, doyen of Tswana anthropologists and historians.[1]

The survival of a contemporary account of Ngwaketse public affairs by one of those principally involved makes it possible to seek answers to some important questions about government and law in the localities at that time:

1. What did a Tswana kgosi do, and what was he for his people in the early years of this century?

This may seem a mundane, even unnecessary, question but it is a neglected one. Under Weber's influence we have tended to take for granted what people in apical positions actually "do" — it is assumed that they occupy "command" roles — and regard as problematic and interesting how such people acquire, maintain, and lose legitimacy. While it would be absurd to underplay the importance of the latter kind of question, it must be remembered that they were formulated in the Europe of the nineteenth and early twentieth centuries, resting on particular understandings of what rulers at that time and place "were," and what they were trying to do. These understandings are not necessarily very helpful to us when we move outside that context. An important lesson of modern political anthropology, conveyed in work such as Geertz's studies of Balinese kingship (1980), is that we must be extremely cautious when we try to characterize apical figures in other cultures.

This caution is all the more necessary when we are confronted with actors in positions of prominence, such as Seepapitso of the Ngwaketse, who look to us very much like "kings." The Protectorate authorities certainly saw the Tswana *dikgosi* (chiefs, plural) as acting in "command" roles, and it is all too easy to invest the kgosi with the attributes of a medieval king, seeing the business of rule as a matter of "sovereign power," of command. It may well be that they correctly assessed this office; the point is we cannot make that assumption.

As well as providing us with an understanding of what one kgosi actually did, Seepapitso's records also enable us to measure that against what Tswana have said a kgosi *should* be and do. When Tswana speak of the role of the kgosi, they almost invariably draw on the image of the herdsman, *modisa*. The management of men is likened to the husbandry of cattle. Hence, a broad, managerial, "steering" role is contemplated. How significant is it that this idea of overall general care is stressed rather than the focussed, directive, urgent role of the commander in battle? Perhaps something of the latter is suggested in the saying, *lentswe lakgosi kemolao* (the chief's word is law). But his power was seen to be subject to normative constraint, exercised within the framework of *mekgwa le melao ya Setswana* (literally, Tswana custom and law). The flavor of this Tswana "legalism" is well conveyed by the striking saying, *molao sefofu, obile otle oje mong waone*, which Schapera translates as "the law is blind, it eats even its owner" (Schapera 1966:121–34).

2. **To what extent does the Tswana evidence help us to delineate with more confidence an opposition between "traditional" and "modern" government and law?**

A persistent feature of modern social theory, linking the work of Marx, Tönnies, Durkheim, and Weber with such contemporary scholars as Habermas (1976), Luhmann (1982), Giddens (1985), and Mann (1986) is an opposition, variously formulated, and put to use in a number of different ways, between "traditional" and "modern" forms of society and government. Does the Tswana case provide any support for such generalizations? What could it mean to describe Seepapitso as a creature of tradition or of modernity? Before attempting any such speculation, we must note an immediate caveat. Although Seepapitso's writings cover a period early in the Protectorate, they cannot be treated as speaking unambiguously of some precolonial past, and the extent to which they can enable us to guess at the nature of such a past is problematic.

3. **How far, and in what ways, at the time of Seepapitso, had the Tswana chiefs become implicated in the processes of colonial rule and in European economic operations? What, in other words, had colonial encapsulation and intrusion come to mean for the Ngwaketse at this early stage in the Protectorate?**

The "truth" about the colonial encounter in Africa, as elsewhere, had inevitably been contested strongly. Clearly, we have to see it in terms of coercive domination, even if we allow some space for benign, disinterested rule. The economic side of the story must include exploitation and disruption, even if advantageous "development" can be identified here and there. There is also room for disagreement as to the extent to which we can see elements of continuity between the precolonial world and what we find in the localities today. Again, there are arguments as to whether "custom" was co-opted, even invented, in the process of colonial domination, or whether it offered means of escape and resistance for the ruled. (See e.g. Snyder 1981; Hobsbawm and Ranger 1983; Chanock 1985; and Roberts 1984, 1985.) The general lines of argument have been delineated and the various corners vigorously defended. What is now needed is much more empirical material, indicating both local detail and regional differences, before further general assessments can be made.

Looking at local government in the Bechuanaland Protectorate before 1940, two moments stand out in purely formal terms: the declaration of the Protectorate in 1885, and the attempt to put local government arrangements on a more systematic footing, which Colonel C. F. Rey had been working on since his appointment as resident commissioner in 1929 and which crystalized with the enactment of the Native Administration and Native Tribunals Proclamations in 1934 (Rey 1988). The question which Seepapitso's records can help us to answer is: How profound were the changes which actually took place in the localities in the early period of the Protectorate prior to 1934? In terms of personnel, an important element of continuity existed over the original transition. Following the declaration of the Protectorate in 1885, the Tswana dikgosi, including Seepapitso's grandfather, remained in place, and the understanding at the beginning was that they should do so with minimal interference from the Protectorate administration (Sillery, 1965). The agents of government at the local level were the same in the years after the declaration of the Protectorate as they were before that event, but how far were their activities transformed?

II. The Records and Their Maker

What were these writings, and why should Seepapitso have decided to keep them? The writings consist of a series of manuscript notebooks and some unbound typed sheets to which manuscript additions were made. Their form and content indicate that Seepapitso must have seen them as an official record of the public affairs of the *morafe* (nation), rather than as a private diary. The manuscript notebooks contain a chronological list of public meetings, with a terse summary of what happened at each one, while the unbound sheets contain a list of rules comprising both long-established customs and more recent legislative pronouncements. There is no private material in the records, or anything in the way of commentary on the business recorded. It all has the air of a formal record of what had been done in public.

Why Seepapitso should have maintained these records at a moment in history long before the Protectorate government was encouraging or even insisting on such a practice is an interesting question. On one level, the answer seems straightforward. Seepapitso had received a Western education from missionaries. Schapera writes that after receiving the "rudiments of a literary education at home from two evangelists of the London Missionary Society...he was sent in 1897 to Lovedale, perhaps the best known school for Natives in Southern Africa. He studied there until the end of 1903 and passed the Junior Certificate examination" (Schapera, 1947b:9). Beyond that, those at Lovedale must have known that he was destined to rule a large Tswana group within the overarching embrace of the Protectorate government; they would therefore have made sure that he would know how to conduct and record official business in a proper bureaucratic way. Seepapitso, for his part, the same argument would suggest, absorbed this lesson well and put this training into practice when he came to power. In this sense we must see him as a creature of "modern" government, embued with the ethic that Weber was theorizing so comprehensively in Germany at the same time. But such an answer leaves unresolved the more difficult question of the extent to which Ngwaketse government was transformed through its proceedings being written down. Was what Seepapitso did in his kgotla fundamentally different from what his predecessors had done? Something of an answer to this emerges from the substantive content of the records, considered below.

The same question is posed when we begin to examine the way in which Seepapitso classified his own work. This is revealed in the form his written records took. One set of notebooks record "tribunal assemblies" in which a wide range of matters are dealt with, while the other is limited to judicial "cases." It seems that he went further to draw what we would see as a distinction between judicial, executive, and legislative functions, as there is reference in the minutes of tribal assemblies to a "Book of Laws." This document has never been found, but he prepared a typed list of laws in January 1913, on unbound sheets and made subsequent additions to it in manuscript (Schapera, 1943b:1947b). Items of legislation are also recorded among other business in the minute books.

It is important that Seepapitso saw his role in settling disputes brought to him by members of the tribe as sufficiently different from the other kinds of business entrusted to him that he wrote down this judicial business in a separate set of notebooks. It is difficult now to be certain why he did this: was this a distinction embedded in Tswana culture, or had he simply absorbed in the course of his education at Lovedale an alien idea that "the legal" and "the political" are best kept apart?

To answer that Seepapitso had been properly schooled in the doctrine of the separation of powers would be an over-simplification. It is beyond argument that at the time of their first contact with Europeans, members of the Tswana merafe saw the regularities of everyday life *and* the activities of those in power as subject to a normative repertoire labelled *mekgwa le melao ya Setswana* (Schapera 1938; Comaroff and Roberts 1981). But as Comaroff and I have argued, this was an undifferentiated repertoire which did not separate out legal rules from other normative prescriptions. At the same time, a thread of legalism is certainly revealed in the maxim quoted on page 168. It is also clear that Tswana had long made a distinction between set-piece public assemblies, called by the kgosi to transact public business which he felt needed to be dealt with, and the meetings held when individual tribesmen in dispute brought a case (*tsheko*) before the kgosi to be decided by him. To keep this latter business separate from the former does not necessarily imply that Seepapitso was seeking to put into practice some notion of the separation of powers formed in the course of his "European" education.

Before considering the detail of Seepapitso's records, it is important to recognize the limits of what we can hope to learn from them. They cannot tell us the whole "truth" about the Tswana world, or even about what one Tswana kgosi did. They represent what that one kgosi chose to record; they tell us how he classified the various meetings he recorded, and the kinds of business that seems to have been dealt with in those meetings. They do not purport to constitute a full "minute" of what was said, but are rather a terse summary of conclusions on each item of business recorded. This glimpse is nonetheless very instructive, revealing clearly the kinds of matter brought to the meetings recorded and how Seepapitso chose to present the outcome.

It must also be emphasized at the outset that these records deal only with the "set-pieces" of Ngwaketse public life, meetings formally summoned by the kgosi and held either in the open central meeting place (kgotla) at Kanye, or in an agreed location in the bush outside the village. The meetings in the kgotla were known as *lebatla*, those in the veld as *letsholo*. The former, much more numerous, assemblies were generally used for routine business; the latter for ceremonial occasions, such as the opening of the ploughing season, or for matters to which Seepapitso attached special importance. Both of these types of meeting need to be distinguished from those called to discuss specific disputes, which Seepapitso recorded separately. All of these moments have to be seen as small, apical points in a much larger continuum, the general features of which are known to us, but whose details, at least for the 1910–1916 period, can never be recovered now.

We must assume that Seepapitso did and said a lot in private. Most Tswana chiefs seem to have relied heavily on small, shifting groups of intimates made up of trusted kinsmen and associates; not a specialized bureaucracy, more a group of kin and cronies including men of particular experience and ability. While kinship provides a formal guide to hierarchy in the Tswana world, genealogy is notoriously manipulable, leaving plenty of room for achieved ascendancy (see especially Comaroff 1978). So it may be that we learn nothing at all of some aspects of Seepapitso's "business" from the records. It is also probable, indeed almost certain, that the business that surfaced at recorded meetings was known to and had already been discussed by an inner group of associates in private.

Further, these recorded meetings constituted only a tiny part of what happened in public. Every morning Ngwaketse men were up before dawn, sitting and talking around a fire in the kgotla, the central meeting place of any Tswana ward (see Schapera 1938). This was naturally the case at the chief's kgotla too, which constituted both the meeting place of his own agnatic segment, and the central point of tribal public life at which formal meetings were held. This kgotla was also inevitably the center of the Ngwaketse network of communications, the point to which information was brought and from which it circulated outwards within the tribe as a whole. So every morning in the central meeting place of the tribe people were talking in public. Today these are occasions at which matters of public concern are aired in a preliminary way; this must have been the case in Seepapitso's time too.

III. Seepapitso and Ngwaketse Public Affairs

In assessing the nature of Ngwaketse public affairs in the early years of the Protectorate and the role in them played by Seepapitso, we look first at the records of the tribal assemblies, then at the judicial records. In examining both types of meeting, two general questions need to be asked. First, what was the range of business dealt with? Second, what were the means, the "techniques of power," used to dispose of it?

A.   The Work of the Tribal Assemblies

One immediate and striking feature of the minutes of tribal assemblies Seepapitso kept is the broad sweep of business these covered. In general terms it ranged over internal Ngwaketse administration, Protectorate government business, and relations with European commercial interests. The relative amount of business in these three categories can be illustrated if we take the profile of a single year. I have chosen 1912 at random. In 1912 Seepapitso summoned thirty-nine ordinary assemblies and two veld assemblies. At these meetings one hundred and twenty-six separate items are minuted. These fall into three principal categories:

Ngwaketse internal administration	— 63 items (50 percent)
Protectorate government business	— 47 items (37 percent)
European commercial and agricultural interests	— 16 items (13 percent)

Business was thus split into roughly equal parts represented by internal matters on the one hand, and that arising out of contact with central government and European commercial interests on the other.

Business generated internally was of a varied character. Topics minuted include ceremonial announcements relating to the agricultural cycle; control over access to arable land; the regulation of population densities in residential areas; the regulation of family life; the management of education; the organization of public works, such as road or dam construction, and the eradication of noxious weeds; attempts to control Christian sects; regulation of the activities of Ngwaketse medico-religious specialists (*dinaka*); control of money-lending; and the management of stray cattle. It can be seen from this summary of "internal" business that even its categories were already influenced by contact with the outside world.

Of business associated with the activities of the Protectorate government, the largest single subject was the hut tax, which in 1912, for example, accounted for twenty of the forty-seven items recorded. The remainder of this business largely concerned announcement of proclamations and government notices. Business connected with European commercial and agricultural operations was largely made up of announcements concerning the availability of work in the South African mines, reminders to pay debts to traders within the territory, notifications of opportunities to trade with outsiders, and warnings about cattle straying onto the European-held farms to the East.

If the range of business covered was wide, the same can be said of the modes of intervention employed. Here it is noticeable at once that while Seepapitso had available a command role, he used it rather unobtrusively. If these minutes are safe evidence, Seepapitso spent a limited time in ad hoc command, in telling the Ngwaketse what to do, and in rule-making. His most extensive roles seem to have been what I shall describe as informative, memorial, homiletic, and permissive. In the first of these roles he acted as a channel of communication, passing messages between tribesmen, and between tribesmen and the outside world (in the shape of the Protectorate government and European commercial interests). In the second, he was drawing the attention of the Ngwaketse to things they had to do, providing reminders. In the third he was handing out lectures about how Ngwaketse ought to behave, what they should and should not be doing. In the last he was granting permission, in most cases putting in motion the cyclical processes of the Ngwaketse farming and hunting calendar.

i. *The informative role*

Seepapitso's kgotla, as was the case with the kgotla of any Tswana chief, was the communications hub of tribal life. To it came information from the wards and outlying villages of the tribe. To this point also came information from the outside world. Some of this latter was official; whenever the government of the Protectorate wished to communicate with the Ngwaketse people, whether it was about the collection of tax, the spread of cattle diseases, or the outbreak of war with Germany, word came to the chief's kgotla. Sometimes whole assemblies were given up to communication. The minute for 23 August 1912, begins: "I have summoned you merely in order to advise you...." A string of messages then follows.

I have already noted what a large proportion of tribal assembly time was given up to transmitting messages from the central government, and that Seepapitso fulfilled a similar role in unofficial matters. If laborers were wanted for the gold mines of the Transvaal, or if Europeans wanted to purchase wood or cattle, or if Christian evangelists wanted to settle, or traders establish stores, word was brought to the kgotla. And from the kgotla this information passed outwards across the tribal territory. So an important part of Seepapitso's role was telling the Ngwaketse what was happening; this is reflected in the very numerous minutes recording matters that he had simply brought to the attention of the tribe.

ii. *The memorial role*

Related to this role in the transmission of information was a memorial one. The minutes of the assemblies also reveal that Seepapitso spent much of his time *reminding* the Ngwaketse of things they had to do. This role cut across the internal/external classification of business that I have suggested. One persistent theme was the hut tax, in respect of which Seepapitso acted as an intermediary between central government and the Ngwaketse. The minutes contain repeated reminders as the time of year approached when this levy had to be paid (e.g., "Remember to seek that little matter known as hut tax..." 14 February 1912). Other reminders drew the attention of the Ngwaketse to their own traditional rules or to domestic legislation. For example, in 1912 ten of the sixty-three items relating to internal administration concerned reminders about compliance with existing "laws," or mekgwa le melao.

iii. *The homiletic role*

Obviously, the boundary between informing, reminding, exhorting, and commanding is an uncertain one, especially when the communication comes from a political superior. Yet again and again entries in the minutes have the flavor of homily and are pedagogic or didactic in tone, encouraging particular courses of conduct, either traditional or innovative:

> Why are your cattle going about with testicles? Let them be castrated while they are still calves (14 February 1910; see also 1 March 1912).
> Where are the children? They do not go to school (4 April 1910; see also 24 November 1911, 21 February 1912, 23 August 1912, 4 September 1912).
> Let the village be cleansed of the dirt that is in it, and henceforth be tidy (3 August 1911).
> It is very disgusting to see the "white" children of Europeans in our midst (15 August 1912).

One preoccupation, touching the very heart of Tswana "government," was with the maintenance of traditional ward organization. This involved effort at two levels: first, ensuring the presence of ward heads within their wards and their readiness to attend to local business. Second, there was a constant struggle to make sure that people maintained their homes within the approved administrative divisions of the central village, instead of dispersing to live out at arable lands or the cattle posts. Seepapitso worked hard at maintaining ward organization. For example:

> You are indeed abandoning our traditional usages. Now you no longer light the fires at [your] council places. This should not be. And truly, you ward heads, it is you who are spoiling [the custom], because if their

seniors do not frequent the council place the people will also become tired of it (31 July 1913).

iv. *The permissive role*

All accounts of mekgwa le melao ya Setswana portray the kgosi as coordinating the cycle of the agricultural year, announcing the commencement of ploughing, reaping, and ultimately the opening up of the arable lands for cattle to eat the discarded stalks of the corn. Similarly, permission was given for hunts of larger game animals and the seasonal cutting of certain timber. These traditional norms are clearly reflected in the minutes, and such permissions were normally granted at a veld assembly called specifically for the purpose.

> [I declare the opening of] the sowing season. The corn that will be reaped must be brought home, and not, as in the past, threshed at the fields (2 November 1911).
> I give you permission to go to your fields to reap..." (18 May 1915).

See also minutes of 2 June 1910, 15 June 1911, 2 November 1911, 14 August 1912, 22 June 1913, 1 September 1913, 2 June 1913, 18 May 1915, and 16 August 1915.

v. *The orchestration of decision-making*

Quite numerous entries in the minutes appear in the form of question and response, in which Seepapitso asks the assembled tribesmen what they want done about a particular matter he has put to them. These concern a wide range of matters, such as whether a particular European trader should be allowed to keep a store in the territory (20, 21 January 1913); the price at which loads of firewood should be sold to Europeans from outside the territory (15 March, 16 April 1913); the administrative arrangements for the handling of revenue collected for educational purposes (20 January 1913); and as to whether female children should be able to participate in the distribution of cattle from their father's estate (16 March 1913).

At this distance it is impossible to understand why some matters were put to the tribesmen for their decision, while others appear as a decision by Seepapitso himself. Again, it is not clear how far the ground was prepared for these decisions in advance, or to what extent the outcome was "arranged." What is important in this context is the fact that these matters are *presented* as questions for joint decision-making by tribesmen, rather than the imposed decision of a ruler.

vi. *Rule-making*

The rule-making activities of Tswana chiefs have been fully described by Schapera in his path-breaking work *Tribal Legislation among the Tswana of the Bechuanaland Protectorate* (London, 1943). Numerous laws were enacted during the period of Seepapitso's incumbency, and it is clear that Seepapitso saw rule-making as a distinct aspect of the business of government, for in addition to cryptic references to a "Book of Laws," he prepared in January 1913 a typed list of the laws which he and his predecessors had made (Schapera 1947b:11, 68). The list was subsequently added to as other laws were made. Numerous references to these laws appear in the minutes of tribal assemblies. From these and other sources, it seems that the procedure for making laws was variable: sometimes Seepapitso simply announced a new rule unilaterally; sometimes he posed a problem to the assembly, asked what rule those present wished to make, and recorded a response.

These laws contained both restatements of traditional customs and explicit innovations. They covered a considerable range of matters, indicating the very wide reach of Ngwaketse government. Rules existed covering aspects of public health, cruelty to animals, the preservation of woodland and grazing, veterinary matters, public security (e.g. the reporting to strangers), attendance at public meetings, the consumption of alcohol, traffic regulation, the branding of livestock, the lending of arable land, cattle sales and cattle theft, family life (including marriage, bridewealth, inheritance, and divorce), debt management, compensation for defamation, the trial of assault cases, and the registration and control of traditional medico-religious specialists (dinaka).

vii. *Command*

All accounts of Ngwaketse public affairs confirm that a facet of Seepapitso's role was one of command, telling people what to do. In part this role was exercised through rule-making (see above), in part through ad hoc command: "Pay your tax now"; "I want the harvest tribute delivered on Wednesday next"; "Dancing at night must cease"; or "Bring me the strays." In the minutes coercive threats backing up such commands, such as threats to fine people ignoring commands, are rare. So also is other direct action, but instances can be found. When some people refused to move their houses in the course of ward reorganization, he announced: "I am going to pull down the huts of Leburu today" (19 August 1912).

The kgosi's traditional arm in executive action was the age-regiment (see Schapera 1938). The minutes reveal that Seepapitso made extensive use of the regiments: "The maLau will make bricks, the other regiments will work on the roads" (8 July 1912); "MaYakapula (regiment), go to look for horses in the veld" (23 September 1912. cf. 24 February 1913); "The regiments working on the dam must go today to help build up the walls on the south" (6 September 1913); "Let the women bring me water" (25 August 1913); "MaYakathata, maYakapula, maTshelaphala, and maLau, go to dig out the *mogau* (a small poisonous bush) on the outskirts of the town" (29 September 1915).

Overall the impression gained is not of some precariously established strong-man, uttering ad hoc commands in the struggle to maintain a following and pursue private aims such as the assembly of wealth and the destruction of rival potentates. Rather, we see a constitutional figure with a predominantly "steering" function extending across the whole field of Ngwaketse life. The minutes thus confirm the Tswana image of modisa, the chief as the herdsman of a flock. Obviously, this self-portrait has limitations, and must be treated with caution in any general evaluation of Seepapitso's rule. It inevitably tells us nothing of how his subjects saw him, or of action he chose not to record.

B.   Adjudication in Seepapitso's Time

The notebooks of "cases" maintained by Seepapitso show that his role in dealing with disputes was unambiguously one of adjudication, of third-party decision. Disputes came before him and he decided them. But the separation of this aspect of public affairs from others, which the different series of notebooks implies, raises difficult problems. How far does it reveal an indigenous distinction between executive action and adjudication, between "government" and "law," even the local development of a differentiated legal system? How far do we see instead a move to reproduce nineteenth-century European constitutions, filtered through missionary education?

Certainly there is for the Tswana a conception of a cause, a matter brought to an authority to be decided (tsheko), distinct from regulatory action indicated by the chief himself. But it may be that the idea of isolating the "judicial" side of government in separate records was something which Seepapitso had absorbed in the course of his education at Lovedale or through his contacts with colonial government. However that may have been, cases were dealt with in the chief's kgotla in the mornings and among the people who would have been there anyway. There were no specialist personnel, no courthouse with its own spatial organization, and no distinctive procedures. Adjudication was in that sense an undifferentiated activity.

The records show that in this part of his business Seepapitso was effectively doing two different things: he was both actively seeking to enforce regulations that he and his predecessors had introduced, and passively waiting in his kgotla to deal with matters which Ngwaketse chose to bring before him. The enforcement of regulations, which generally involved the payment of a fine or more rarely corporal punishment, made up by far the smaller part of his judicial business. Of over four hundred and fifty cases heard between 1910 and 1916, fewer than 15 percent were initiated by Seepapitso himself for the enforcement of regulations (see Schapera 1943a). Most of the cases he heard were brought before him by individual complainants. These covered a wide range of matters across the areas of family, property, and wrong. As Schapera had noted, there does not seem to have been a fully differentiated "criminal" law. Certainly there was a narrow range of regulations through which Seepapitso actively required specific behavioral patterns, and which he enforced through the sanction of fine or corporal punishment. But beyond that there was a category of "wrongs" he dealt with as complainants brought them to his attention, and which he generally handled through orders of a compensatory kind.

This undifferentiated character of Seepapitso's adjudicatory role is well illustrated in his handling of complaints of interpersonal violence and wrongful taking — instances in respect of which "modern" government has generally been prepared to intervene on its own behalf to impose criminal penalties for "assault" and "theft," quite apart from the civil implications of the matter. Seepapitso almost invariably left it to the aggrieved party to bring the wrongdoer to the kgotla, where an assault or wrongful taking was complained of; and where such a wrong was found to have taken place, it was generally dealt with by compensation or restitution.

While wrongs against property and assaults constituted a very considerable portion of the business that Seepapitso dealt with in the years 1910–1916, corporal punishment and fines were seldom imposed. Of forty-two assault (*tlhaselo*) cases over this period, only four were dealt with by corporal punishment and one by a fine (see cases 1/11; 65/12; 69/15; 9/12, thrashings; 38/11, fine). Out of sixty-four cases of theft (*bogodu*), the great majority were disposed of by an order for restitution or compensation where any order was made. In only five cases were there fines (27/11, 9/13, 10/13, 18/14, 30/15). In two cases, there were orders to repay, with thrashing in the event of failure (10/12, 9/15). In one case immediate imprisonment was ordered (45/15). In two cases imprisonment was ordered for failure to pay compensation (11/15, 46/15). But in both assault and theft cases the hearings were entirely undifferentiated, with compensatory and penal aspects dealt with together, and only on motion of a complainant. There was no sense of civil and criminal aspects being dealt with separately, as in Western courts.

IV. The Impact of Colonial Government in the Localities

Although Seepapitso's records cover a period early on in the Protectorate, at a time when Ngwaketse public affairs were carried on with limited direct intervention by central government, long before efforts were made to formalize "local government" under the Native Authority and Native Tribunals Proclamations of 1934, important formal changes had already taken place. The boundaries of the tribal territories had been defined; the powers of the chiefs to try cases of murder and culpable homicide had been removed; an annual hut tax had been levied, which Tswana chiefs were required to administer; a central government police force was stationed in each tribal capital; and, perhaps most important, the chiefs were seen by central government as the channel through which it communicated with its subjects.

Just as important, potentially, as explicit governmental intrusion was the continuous presence of missionaries and traders within the territory of the Ngwaketse, which stretched far back into the nineteenth century. Already by 1910 also, Ngwaketse were leaving the tribal territory in considerable numbers to work in the gold mines of the Transvaal and the diamond mines of the Northern Cape (see Schapera 1947a).

How far had these changes transformed the activities of the kgosi on the ground, and hence penetrated Tswana life? In how much of his work was he an intermediary between the Ngwaketse people and the colonial power?

A.   Seepapitso and Central Government

By 1916 a consistent and very substantial part of the business dealt with at tribal assemblies was generated by central government. Some of the time this business seems to have dominated the meetings, and only at a minority of them are central government matters unrecorded. For example, of the thirty-nine meetings recorded in 1912, at only eleven was there nothing touching directly upon central government. In some cases an assembly would be convened for the sole purpose of dealing with central government matters (that was so, for example, with the meeting recorded on 12 January 1912).

In respect of much of this business the role of the kgosi did not extend beyond informing tribesmen of recent government proclamations and notices. Prominent among these were matters concerning game, veterinary regulation, stock trading, firearms and ammunition, tobacco, and labor recruiting. In many of these matters, revenue collection and regulation were closely linked, and it was in the area of taxation that the Tswana chiefs were made to play their most active role in colonial government.

Here the central device was the hut tax, collected with the help of an annual cycle of reminders, exhortations, and threats on the part of Seepapitso. Throughout the 1910–1916 period, hut tax is minuted in the records of Ngwaketse assemblies more often than any other subject. In 1912, for example, it features in the minutes of eighteen out of thirty-nine meetings. The same entries appear again and again: "Where is the hut tax?"; "Let the tax money come"; "Pay your tax, you who are still in arrear"; "Ward heads, report those who have not paid tax"; "Where is the tax money, BaNgwaketse?"; "Remember to seek that little matter known as hut-tax." Seepapitso was directly implicated in this process, collecting the money at Kanye, issuing receipts, and sending the proceeds to Gaberones. He was allowed a 10 percent commission upon these proceeds. Those who failed to pay were identified and made to stand forward at tribal assemblies, and then sent to the European magistrate for punishment (see minutes of 18 and 25 February 1911). Initially, the nearest resident magistrate was at Gaberones, some sixty miles away, but a resident was stationed at Kanye from May 1913.

The administration of the hut tax represented one side of the role played by Seepapitso as an intermediary between central government and the BaNgwaketse. But it would be wrong to see Seepapitso or other Tswana dikgosi simply as agents of colonial domination, as part of the top-down exercise of power. There was a flow in the other direction. Seepapitso energetically forwarded complaints, protests, and petitions, and when agents of central government visited Kanye, matters worrying the Ngwaketse were drawn vigorously to their attention. Notably, Seepapitso, like his father Bathoen I and his son Bathoen II, played a central part in the local protests against the proposed incorporation of the Protectorate within the Union of South Africa. (See, for example, the report of a meeting with the resident commissioner of the Protectorate minuted at the meeting of 27 June 1912). This project was, of course, ultimately abandoned; the implacable opposition of the Tswana chiefs was an important element in that outcome.

B. Seepapitso and European Commercial Interests

Seepapitso's role also involved him with several categories of outsiders from the commercial world. First, there were employers outside the Ngwaketse terri-tory who wanted to draw on this reservoir of labor. Considerable numbers of BaNgwaketse were already migrating to work in the South African mines, labor recruiters coming into the territory required Seepapitso's permission to recruit, and when complaints were made by tribesmen, he investigated. In addition, there were traders who wished to buy cattle and other natural resources for sale outside the territory, and others who wanted to sell things to tribesmen within the territory. Traders wishing to operate in the territory required his permission, and he similarly sought to regulate trade with outsiders. Such a list is of course not exhaustive, and omits the role Seepapitso played between the Ngwaketse and the missions.

V. Conclusions

At the outset of this essay some very general questions were posed about the nature of Seepapitso's role in the public affairs of the Ngwaketse in those early years of the Bechuanaland Protectorate; about whether we can sensibly describe him as a creature of tradition or of modernity; and about the manner in which, and extent to which, his role had been transformed by his incorporation into the government of the Protectorate. We are now in a position to address these questions further, concentrating upon the last one given its immediate relevance to the concerns of this volume.

1. What was Seepapitso?

As the grandson of a man who was already the ruler of the Ngwaketse at the time the Protectorate was formed, Seepapitso was a "traditional authority" in the narrow sense. The Tswana had a well established conception of "kingship" at that time, and it was with that package of ideas about what a kgosi was that Gaseitsiwe and his fellow Tswana chiefs were incorporated in the Protectorate. So Seepapitso could not in any way be seen as an "invention" of the colonial authorities, however much his role might have been transformed through his implication in their projects. From the perspective of the administration Seepapitso's provenance had both advantages and disadvantages; it was useful that his legitimacy could not initially be challenged, but at the same time the established nature of his position potentially gave rise to conflict over what his proper role in the administration of the Protectorate ought to be.

The local role Seepapitso played in Ngwaketse public life appears clearly through the records we have examined, however cautiously we feel obliged to read them. Two general points only need to be made here in summary. The first concerns the wide-ranging nature of the kgosi's role. Seepapitso shows himself to have been concerned with most aspects of Ngwaketse life. The implication of this broad sweep of involvement is considered further below. The second special feature of his activity was the great diversity of the *ways* in which he intervened. As we have seen, "command" was by no means the dominant mode. Notable is the extent to which Seepapitso's role was primarily reactive; a persistent image is of the kgosi waiting—for messages from central government to transmit to the people, waiting for the Ngwaketse themselves to bring him their disputes for a hearing. We now need to know whether the breadth of Seepapitso's involvement in Ngwaketse affairs, and the diversity of his modes of intervention, were typical of comparable "traditional authorities" at this period.

2. Creature of the "past" or the "present"?

These records inevitably raise questions as to which aspect of Ngwaketse public life must be seen as residues of a precolonial past, and which the product of that colonial present in which Seepapitso found himself when he became chief in 1910. On one level, the answers seem straightforward; individual items of business sort themselves readily enough into those generated through contact with the outside world and those arising internally. But it is much more difficult to characterize Seepapitso's general style of government in these terms. It might be argued that his broad, steering role, involving plural modes of intervention, was attributable in part to his interstitial location between colonial rulers and their indigenous subjects; indeed, that his wide-ranging involvement was explicable solely in terms of that predicament. My own assessment would be that while this style was well-suited to the demands which the Protectorate government was then making on traditional authorities, it had in origin nothing to do with the colonial encounter. That does not necessarily mean that we should see in Seepapitso's almost parental involvement with his subjects a glimpse of the moment at which essentially familial structures give way to those transcending kinship (cf. Fried 1967). Indeed, there is something eerily modern about his concern with the spatial arrangements of his capital at Kanye, about his anxiety that ward heads should be at their posts, and about his reluctance to let Ngwaketse live "out of sight" at the lands rather than under his surveillance in the capital. This almost "disciplinary" intervention has features that have generally been identified as attributes of "modern" government. Yet there is no evidence that he did not inherit these concerns from his ancestors of the precolonial period.

Overall, the Tswana case points to the difficulty of drawing any generalized distinction between traditional and modern forms of authority. While the "household" rather than "bureaucratic" character of Seepapitso's rule fits well with Weber's pure type of "traditional authority" (Weber 1967:226), as does the generally undifferentiated nature of Tswana government, features such as those mentioned in the previous paragraph do not conform to that model. Consider also the kgosi's self-conscious involvement in a "governmental" project, the clarity of the Tswana normative repertoire, the kgosi's explicit subjection to it, and his acknowledged rule-making capability (Schapera 1938; Comaroff and Roberts 1981). It is very doubtful whether much of this can be attributed to the colonial encounter.

In connection with this general project of trying to characterize "traditional" society and authority, the records of Seepapitso's judicial business provide further empirical evidence that Durkheim (1893) overstated the role of repressive law in preindustrial societies (see Lukes 1973). The records reveal that by far the greater part of his judicial role involved availability to adjudicate in quarrels between subjects, rather than the active enforcement of regulations. Further, the normal form of order was one of compensation or restitution. Thus the Ngwaketse case seems to provide confirmation that the Durkheimian hypothesis of an evolutionary movement from "repressive" sanctions towards "restitutory" sanctions, and of the association of "repressive" sanctions with "tradition" rather than "modernity," is increasingly hard to sustain.

3. The impact of colonial intrusion on the Ngwaketse world

Seepapitso's records provide important evidence on the detail and timetable of colonial intrusion at a local level in Bechuanaland. They show unambiguously the considerable extent to which the business of central government had impressed itself on Ngwaketse public affairs even at the relatively early date in the Protectorate when Seepapitso became chief. By 1910 a major part of the kgosi's work was as an intermediary between the Ngwaketse people and the Protectorate government and European commercial interests. Most notable was Seepapitso's implication in the process of revenue collection; by the time of his death in 1916, this had become the dominant item in the recorded business of the tribal assemblies.

In comparative terms Seepapitso's records are important because they enable us to delineate with some confidence one type of traditional authority found at the meeting point of colonial intruders and their subjects, at that critical moment before local arrangements of rule had become formalized. At first sight, Seepapitso appears strikingly different from such figures as Kangah and Mademba, whose activities form the subject of other chapters. He enjoyed a firmly ascribed status, and an established role that, with rather limited modification, fitted well the demands of central government. He thus provides an instructive contrast with the achieved positions of Kangah and Mademba, who seem largely to have made up their roles as they went along, enjoyed a much less well defined relationship to the colonial power, and who invoked "tradition" as well as the machinery of the received legal order *ex post facto*, by way of justification. But it was not just that they were entrepreneurs by nature; the cognitive and normative universe within which Seepapitso operated was more clearly marked out. It is difficult to imagine a Kangah in the Kalahari in Seepapitso's time. While we are beginning to know something about the kinds of people who came to prominence in these early years, we still need to know much more about their provenance, and the various ways in which their relationships developed with central government on the one side and those in the localities on the other, before even a rough typology of "traditional authorities" can be constructed.

NOTES

1. The minutes of Ngwaketse public assemblies maintained by Seepapitso have been published in translation, with an introduction and notes, by I. Schapera in *The Political Annals of a Tswana Tribe* (Cape Town, 1947). That work together with unpublished translations of Seepapitso's judicial notebooks which Schapera has generously made available to me, provides the principal source for the present paper. Ngwaketse legislation is discussed in detail by Schapera in his important monograph *Tribal Legislation among the Tswana of the Bechuanaland Protectorate* (London, 1943); see also, I. Schapera, *Tribal Innovators: Tswana Chiefs and Social Change 1795–1940* (London, 1970). For a general account of Seepapitso's judicial work, see I. Schapera, "The Work of Tribal Courts in the Bechuanaland Protectorate", (1943) 2 *African Studies* 27).

SOURCES

Chanock, M. 1985. *Law, custom, and social order.* Cambridge: Cambridge University Press.

Comaroff, J. L. 1978. "Rules and rulers: Political processes in a Tswana chiefdom." *Man* 13: 1–20.

Comaroff, J. L., and S. A. Roberts. 1981. *Rules and processes.* Chicago: University of Chicago Press.

Durkheim, E. 1893. *De la division du travail social.* Paris: Alcan.

Fried, M. 1967. *The political evolution of society.* New York: Random House.

Geertz, C. 1980. *Negara: The theatre state in nineteenth century Bali.* Princeton, N.J.: Princeton University Press.

Giddens, A. 1985. *The nation-state and violence.* Cambridge: Polity Press.

Habermas, J. 1976. *Legitimation crisis.* Trans. by Thomas McCarthy. London: Heinemann.

Hobsbawm, E. J., and T. O. Ranger, eds. 1983. *The invention of tradition.* Cambridge: Cambridge University Press.

Luhmann, N. 1982. *The differentiation of society.* Trans. by S. Holmes and C. Larmore. New York: Columbia University Press.

Lukes, S. 1973. *Emil Durkheim.* Oxford: Oxford University Press.

Mann, M. 1986. *The sources of social power,* Vol. 1. Cambridge: Cambridge University Press.

Rey, C. F. 1988. *Monarch of all I survey,* ed. N. Parsons and M. Crowder. London: The Botswana Society.

Roberts, S. A. 1984. "Some notes on 'African customary law.'" *Journal of African Law* 28:1–5.

———. 1985. "The Tswana polity and 'Tswana law and custom' reconsidered." *Journal of Southern African Studies* 12:75–87.

Schapera, I. 1938. *A handbook of Tswana law and custom.* London: International African Institute.

———. 1943a. "The work of tribal courts in the Bechuanaland Protectorate." *African Studies* 2:27–40.

———. 1943b. *Tribal legislation among the Tswana of Bechuanaland Protectorate.* London: LSE Monographs in Social Anthropology.

———. 1947a. *Migrant labour and tribal life: A study of conditions in the Bechuanaland Protectorate.* London: LSE Monographs in Social Anthropology.

———. 1947b. *The political annals of a Tswana tribe.* Cape Town: University of Capetown.

———. 1966. "Tswana legal maxims." *Africa* 36:121–34.

———. 1970. *Tribal innovators: Tswana chiefs and social change 1795–1940.* London: LSE Monographs in Social Anthropology.

Sillery, A. 1965. *Founding a protectorate.* The Hague: Mouton.

Snyder, F. G. 1981. "Colonialism and legal form: The creation of 'customary law' in Senegal." *Journal of Legal Pluralism* 19:149–90.

Weber, M. 1978. *Economy and society.* Trans. edited by G. Roth and C. Wittich. Berkeley: University of California Press.

8

The Case of Faama Mademba Sy and the Ambiguities of Legal Jurisdiction in Early Colonial French Soudan

RICHARD ROBERTS

In 1899 Faama Mademba Sy, king of Sansanding, was charged with abuse of power and administrative malfeasance.[1] His case was heard in Kayes, the temporary headquarters of the colonial administration of the French Soudan. Mademba was interned during the course of his hearing and for several months thereafter. He returned to his kingdom late in 1900, neither clearly vindicated nor punished (Suret-Canale 1971:74).[2]

Mademba's defense rested on his claims that he acted as befitted an African king. The prosecuting authority, the Corps of Colonial Inspectors — a semi-autonomous service under the direct authority of the Ministry of Colonies — argued that Mademba owed his crown to the actions of French conquest and his continued position to being an agent of the colonial administration. Moreover, the prosecution pointed out that Mademba was a French citizen who must be held accountable to French law and could not therefore justify his actions according to customary African law and practice. The prosecution could also have added that Mademba had interpreted these laws and practices himself (ANS-AOF Mademba 1897). Charging Mademba with administrative misconduct, therefore, confronted a vague and sensitive area in colonial legal practice, because it touched at the heart of French efforts to build colonial rule on precolonial institutions.

Mademba's fellow administrators came to his defense. They argued that the peculiar situation in the French Soudan warranted certain kinds of administrative practices. And if these practices exceeded legal and administrative decorum expected in metropolitan France, then the fault lay in the colonial situation and not with the individual administrator.

The case against Mademba raised important issues of legal jurisdiction. Even though Inspector-general Danel of the Corps of Colonial Inspectors assembled evidence of civil crimes, the case against Mademba was limited to the jurisdiction of the *loi administratif*, which was concerned only with infractions committed in the course of administrative service. After a flurry of correspondence running up and down the administrative ladder, the case apparently just faded away without resolving the issues of legal jurisdiction and administrative propriety. The case against Mademba did not result in reforms, guidelines concerning administrative and legal practices, or regularization of the position of Africans in French colonial service. Nor did the case receive more than superficial attention on the ministerial level.

Nonetheless, the case against Mademba allows us to interpret colonial legal policy as part of the larger cultural project of colonialism. French colonial policy — and in particular French native policy — vacillated between an ideological commitment to make Africans into Frenchmen and a profound worry about the implications of assimilating people at such different stages of "civilization." French colonial policy thus contained competing models of colonialism, which enabled both colonial officials and Africans serving the French to implement different cultural projects. The case against Mademba crystallizes these competing models of colonialism and the place of African and colonial law in them.

At least three competing models of colonialism are represented in the case against Mademba. First, there was Louis Archinard's version of indirect rule. Colonel Archinard, the architect of military conquest in the French Soudan, applied a policy of building colonialism on incorporating indigenous authority into colonial institutions. Second, there was what Robert Delavignette (1968:6–11ff) has called the "vrais chefs de l'empire," the virtually uncontrolled local military (and later civilian) administrators, who ruled more or less as they pleased. And third, there was the recently started centralization of colonial organization and authority represented in the founding of the government-general of French West Africa in 1895 (Newbury 1960). Within this model, colonialism was represented by the regularization of the patchwork of legal jurisdictions and the implementation of procedures to control free-wheeling administrations. This effort to centralize and control colonialism resulted in the promulgation of a colonial legal system in 1903. The 1903 legal system was based on discussions and debates dating from 1895, thus coinciding with the case against Mademba. Moreover, the peculiarities of the 1899 case against Mademba and the discrepancies between the evidence Inspector-general Danel collected and what was used in the case are suggestive of a cultural project of colonialism which was still being debated and conceived. Thus, the ambiguities surrounding the legal jurisdictions of the case must be understood within the context of competing conceptions of colonialism and the place of colonial law within them.[3]

From the conquest of Segu in 1890 to the sack of Sikasso and the capture of Samori in 1898, the French conquered an immense area of the interior of continental

West Africa. Conquering the region was merely the preliminary phase of much more ambitious and ambiguous processes of transforming African societies, building a colonial state, and shaping the economy and productive social relations. A crucial but as yet little examined aspect of these processes was the development and operation of a new and explicitly colonial legal system.

The judicial field of colonial French West Africa was a hybrid, composed of metropolitan French, military, customary, and Muslim components. The shape of the judicial system was directly linked to the maturation of the colonial state and the colonial economy. Colonial legal systems, however, never developed in a neat and tidy manner. Especially where there were powerful or populous precolonial social entities, colonial rulers recognized or were forced to recognize precolonial legal systems. Throughout Africa, the new colonial rulers sought to use, occasionally to incorporate, and sometimes to manufacture precolonial legal systems as part of their efforts to control subject populations.[4] No matter how carefully and assiduously colonial administrators sought to retain indigenous legal institutions, conquest transformed them. Conquest created opportunities for both Africans and Frenchmen to implement different cultural projects. For our purposes, the case against Mademba pitted Archinard's model of an indigenous king against the government-general model of colonialism. Although the case against Mademba preceded the promulgation of the 1903 colonial legal system, the role of the Corps of Colonial Inspectors and the case itself must be understood as part of the government-general's efforts to control both indigenous chiefs and French administrators. This chapter examines an episode in the formative period of fashioning a colonial legal order in the French Soudan.

I

Mademba Sy was born in 1852, probably in or near Saint Louis, son of M'Baye Sy (Mademba 1931:9; Terrier 1918:169). According to Mademba's son and biographer, Abd-el Kader Mademba, his grandfather was a Futanke of clerical origins, who fled to Saint Louis following Al-hajj Umar's stormy visit to Futa Toro in the 1840s because he did not believe in the militancy of Umar's message. According to contemporary Europeans, who may have wanted to impute royal or aristocratic lineage to Mademba, M'Baye was a Waalo chief or married to a Dagana princess (Dubois 1897:88; Terrier 1918:169). We do know, however, that Mademba studied at Governor Faidherbe's *Ecole des Otages*, where sons of African chiefs were trained as interpreters, political agents, and clerks. In 1869 Mademba entered French colonial service as a *commis auxiliaire*, a temporary clerk, in the post and telegraph system. Between 1869 and 1880 Mademba served in Senegal until he was promoted to *commis deuxième classe*, transferred to the upper Senegal river, and charged with constructing the telegraph line from Salde to Bakel. During the 1882–83 Soudan campaign, Mademba's African crew pushed the telegraph line from Kayes to Kita. On the first of April 1883 a band of Samori's cavalry attacked Mademba's crew and made off with reels of copper telegraph wire. Mademba directed his first military operation as he led a brigade to retrieve the stolen wire. For his actions, Mademba was promoted to *commis première classe* and sent to telegraph school in Mont Valerien, France. Sometime between 1869 and 1886,

Mademba became a naturalized French citizen, which was possible under the restrictive and limited opportunities offered by the colonial policy of assimilation. Because of French "Islamic" policy, there was considerable imprecision over the boundaries between French civil status and Muslim personal status: Muslims who held legal and electoral rights in the four communes of Senegal also exercised the privilege of having some conflicts adjudicated according to Muslim law (Sarr, Ch. 5; Christelow 1985).

Mademba's fortunes in the colonial service rose directly with the expansion of French conquest. Gallieni, the senior military officer in the French Soudan, appointed Mademba to head his political bureau in 1886. Gallieni's political bureau was charged with propaganda and intelligence-gathering missions. Mademba was thus the primary intermediary between the French command and local populations. Because of the scarcity of trained personnel, Mademba continued to direct the telegraph operations as well. In recognition of his contributions to the conquest, Mademba received in 1886 the honorific rank of *chevalier* in the French Legion of Honor. In the 1887 campaign, Mademba was given command of a cavalry division (Chandoné 1906:189–90). Throughout the French military conquest of the Soudan, Mademba improved his political position and demonstrated his loyalty to the French.

In 1890, Louis Archinard, who replaced Gallieni as the senior military commander, captured Segu and rewarded his African troops with captured women. Mademba was given Jenuba Umar Tall, daughter of Shehu Amadu, the ruler of the crumbling Umarian empire. Mademba also participated in the conquest of Nioro, where he was in charge of mopping-up operations. He assembled 2,000 prisoners of war, mostly Bambara who had served as Umarian soldiers, together with their families and their slaves. In late 1890 or early 1891 he led them back to the Middle Niger valley (Mademba 1931:34–39, 55–56; Gallieni 1891:327).

Even before the capture of Segu, Archinard had negotiated with the Bambara rebels about resurrecting the Segu Bambara dynasty, which had been toppled by the Umarians thirty years earlier. He thus recognized Mari Jara, who was the leading, although far from unanimous, candidate for the Jara throne, as the new *faama* (Bambara: king or ruler) of the Segu kingdom. Within a few months, however, the French accused Mari Jara of conspiring against them and executed him and twenty other leading Bambara chiefs (Roberts 1987a:154–58).[5]

Mari Jara's alleged conspiracy worried Archinard. If he were to continue using African intermediaries as central players in establishing French colonialism, then he would appoint only those whose loyalty to the French was unquestioned. He therefore appointed Bojan, a loyal chief of Archinard's African auxiliaries, who was also a son of the rival Kaarta Kulubali line, as successor to Mari Jara. Archinard was aware that Bojan had little claim to Segu kingship, and he worried that this choice, too, would lead to political turmoil. With this in mind he wrote to Etienne, the powerful under-secretary of state for colonies in Paris, that Bojan's kingdom was much too large for a black to govern. Large black empires, he argued, constantly produced revolts that required force and therefore expense to quell. "I have thought that it would be good to establish a second kingdom next to that of Segu, a kingdom that will be powerful and devoted. . . ." Archinard concluded that the problem was to find a suitable candidate. He then suggested that Mademba was such a person, whose devotion to France and whose leadership were proven (ANF-DOM Archinard 1891). Archinard did not seem to worry that Mademba had no legitimate claim to kingship and that Sinsani, where the new king was to reside, had never had a tradition of kingship.

On 7 March 1891 Archinard made Mademba faama in a letter of investiture. Mademba was given all the territory on the left bank not actually in the district of Bamako or in the kingdom of Segu. Mademba was to be the "advance sentinel" against the remaining Umarian state in Masina and was to convince the African forces of the region to join with him and the French. Archinard planned that before long Mademba would reign over the entire expanse of the Niger from Segu to Timbuktu. He instructed Mademba "to work with all your force for the development in the land of French influence, of our ideas of civilization, and of our commerce" (ANS-AOF Perignon 1900). Mademba was also instructed to render justice between natives following customary rules, subject, however, to the intervention of the commandant of Segu if one of the parties were an inhabitant of another district. In case of divergent judgments, the case was to be forwarded to the senior military commander. Moreover, Mademba was to have no rights over cases involving Europeans (ANS-AOF Perignon 1900). In recognition of his subordination to the French, Mademba was obligated to send twenty service-quality horses each year to the administrative command of the French Soudan.

Archinard was not alone in his praise for Mademba. Felix Dubois referred to Mademba as *"un français noir,* whose government was impregnated with our manner of living, thinking, and was entirely devoted to us and to our ideas" (Dubois 1897:88). Mademba extended hospitality to any Frenchman who passed through Sinsani. His table was covered with fine linen and crystal imported directly from the best shops in France. He also served excellent wines and champagnes to accompany desserts made by a pastry chef in Sinsani. After dinner, Mademba served coffee and cigars, and conversation was invariably about France. One French traveler wrote that "it was easy to forget that we are in the middle of the Soudan, in a lost corner of Africa, thousands of kilometers from civilization" (Thiriet 1932:77−78).

To his African subjects, Mademba presented a very different image. On 15 March 1891 Mademba arrived in Sinsani at the head of nearly 7,000 people who accompanied him from Nioro. Preceding Mademba were his praise singers and flute players.[6] In a letter dated 16 March 1891 Mademba wrote: "I have taken over the functions of faama conforming to the customs of the land" (ANM Mademba 16 March 1891). This statement, his regal entrance into Sinsani, and his description of the region's judicial process point to Mademba's new sense of identity. In his description of customary law, Mademba wrote that the powers of kings over their subjects rested on the right of conquest (ANS-AOF Mademba 1897).[7] Mademba's subsequent actions were clearly founded on the conception of himself as conqueror and king.[8]

In his early correspondence with the French commandant of Segu, Mademba claimed the largest amount of territory for his kingdom. Since Archinard had not clearly delimited Mademba's domain, it was in his interests to claim areas not yet included in neighboring jurisdictions. Thus, Mademba claimed all of Sarro east of Kaminiadugu and Nyamina, which empowered him to collect taxes and to establish customs stations. Both, he argued, were rights of conquest.[9]

Rather than encouraging the inhabitants between Segu and Masina to join with him in furthering France's colonial agenda, Mademba's actions contributed to widespread revolts against colonial rule in 1891–92. The details need not concern us here. The important aspects were that Mademba had alienated the regional chiefs in his domain, his ruthless behavior towards his military sub-ordinates (composed largely of prisoners of war) undercut his command over them, and that he had been unable to suppress the revolt once it began. By early 1892 Mademba was a prisoner in Sinsani and had to be rescued by a division commanded by Captain Bonnier.

During the course of suppressing the revolt, Bonnier uncovered evidence which pointed to Mademba's role in instigating the revolt. Mademba was accused of demeaning the region's warlords by making them supplicate before him. He was also accused of beheading a number of prisoners of war under his jurisdiction who formed the bulk of his military capacity, thereby jeopardizing his own military command. Mademba responded to French criticism by arguing that these actions were the custom of African kings. Refusal to obey the king's orders, he argued, constituted a threat to his authority. Bonnier noted that Mademba used a "very heavy hand" in dealing with administrative and political problems.[10]

On his return from the 1892–93 campaign in Bandiagara, Archinard passed through Sinsani and reorganized Mademba's domain (ANF-DOM Archinard 1893). Archinard noted that all the inhabitants feared for their lives. He did not, however, depose Mademba. "The small amount of success you have had, the desertions of your *sofa* (Bambara: cavalry, soldiers), and the measures you have taken to create order and discipline indicate that I have given you a task that was too heavy. I have abandoned the idea of seeing you command one day in Bandiagara" (quoted in Mademba 1931:87–89; Kanya-Forstner 1969:201). Instead, Archinard dramatically reduced the size of Mademba's kingdom. In contrast, Archinard deposed Bojan and dismantled the Segu kingdom.

Archinard's 1893 reorganization of the Middle Niger Valley's administration was paradoxical. It indicated his deep ambivalence about the place of precolonial kingship within the new French colonial state, but he was also not ready to renounce his reliance on loyal intermediaries and the fiction, at least, of the royal legitimacy of the African kings he had made. He had, after all, just crowned Aguibu king of Bandiagara (De Loppinot 1919; Méniaud 1931). Although ruler of a diminished domain, Mademba was again given a free hand to run his own affairs. He was only obliged to send monthly reports to the Segu resident, now burdened with the complete administration of the Segu district.

Mademba turned his attention to constructing his palace, to his harem, and to his experimental fields of tobacco, wheat, and cotton. Mademba's palace was built in the local Sudanese style: it had a wall twelve meters high but only one door. The palace obviously isolated Mademba in his splendor and prevented his harem from leaving (Baillaud 1902:84). The construction of this massive palace involved extensive corvée labor, which is still remembered in Sinsani. Mademba also used his position to enlarge his harem by taking whomever he desired.[11] While Mademba was interned in Kayes during his hearing in 1900, Captain Lambert opened the palace door and many of his more than one hundred "wives" fled (ANS-AOF Mademba March 1900; interview Musa Keita 1976). The 1899 legal challenge to Mademba's authority empowered Sinsani inhabitants to challenge him as well.

In contrast to his local style of rule, which led to his 1899 case, Mademba's interest in the agricultural side of colonialism earned him the respect of the senior administration. Mademba experimented with wheat, tobacco, and rice (ANM Mademba 1894; ANM Mademba 1896), but his most enduring contribution came with cotton. In 1897 Mademba's experiments with long staple cotton were so successful that it promoted metropolitan interest in the Middle Niger valley as a potential cotton-exporting region. His success with imported cotton seed occurred precisely during a crisis in the world supply of raw cotton and when French industrialists were eagerly searching for more secure colonial sources (Roberts 1987b). In recognition of his continued service to French colonialism, Mademba was named an officer of the Legion of Honor in 1897 (ANF-DOM Grand 1895; ANS-AOF lieutenant-governor 1918). Mademba's agricultural innovations were possible because he stood at the head of a large army of unpaid and coerced labor.

II

In 1897 griot Jali Garé Kouyaté fled Sinsani and complained to the Segu commandant that Mademba had kidnapped his daughter and his wife, and had threatened his life (ANM lieutenant-governor Sept. 1897). The Segu commandant investigated Kouyaté's charges. Mademba did not deny the charges; instead, he justified his actions as pre-emptive moves against Kouyaté's plan to murder him. The commandant sent a report to Colonel Trentinian, the lieutenant-governor, who in turn wrote to Mademba. He accused Mademba of fabricating this story: "you have imagined and pretended a plot [on your life] which allowed you to pronounce a verdict as justification, *ex post facto*, for your barbarous acts" (ANM lieutenant-governor January 1898). Apparently Trentinian considered the reprimand sufficient for no further action was taken.

Again in 1899 Mademba brought critical attention upon himself. He sold a large quantity of local cotton to the *service administratif* and retained the profits for himself (ANS-AOF Lambert October 1899; ANM Affaire 1899). Complaints against Mademba reached Captain Lambert, the commandant of the Segu district, who inquired into the matter. Villagers in Mademba's domain accused him of expropriating cotton and of arbitrarily setting exorbitant demands on several villages under his jurisdiction: the village of Jalsusu, population of twenty-five, had to deliver 100 kilograms of millet, 240 kilograms of peanuts, and 1020 kilograms of cotton, the village of Medine had to fill twenty large baskets of cotton. It could fill only three, so Mademba demanded an indemnity of 240,000 cowries (ANS-AOF Danel January 1900; Lambert 31 October 1899; Veil, 27 November 1899). Inhabitants of Sinsani complained to Captain Lambert of a whole series of brutal acts, from rape to ritual murder, allegedly committed by Mademba.[12] Mademba was accused of killing between twenty-five and thirty children since he arrived in 1891 (ANS-AOF Lambert October 1899). Captain Lambert collected depositions testifying to the disappearance of the latest one, Kamla Jakité, last seen entering Mademba's palace (ANS-AOF depositions 1899; ANS-AOF Lambert October 1899).

In 1899, Inspector-general Danel of the Corps of Colonial Inspectors conducted an investigation into the charges of Mademba's misconduct involving the cotton deal. As an inspector of the colonial administrative services, Danel's specific instructions limited his jurisdiction to administrative matters, especially the cotton affair. The investigation into Mademba's alleged malfeasance coincided with debates surrounding the reorganization of the colonial legal system. Both the case against Mademba and reorganization of the colonial legal system were aspects of efforts by the government-general in Dakar and by the Ministry of Colonies in Paris to constrain free-wheeling administrators in the field. Both can be considered challenges to the power and authority of Archinard's model of colonialism.

Danel assembled sufficient evidence to prove that Mademba had expropriated the cotton under the pretense that the French had demanded a surplus tax.[13] In addition, but beyond the jurisdiction of his investigation, Danel attached thirty-five written depositions testifying to Mademba's administrative malfeasance and to other crimes. He argued:

> Mademba had by his [previous] services, perhaps earned the consideration and appreciation of the Commandant Supérieur of the Soudan in 1891. But, it was certainly imprudent to elevate the modest employee of the Post and Telegraph, for which he was qualified, to the possibility of founding a royal dynasty under the shelter of the Republic of France... Once in possession of power granted by the letter of investiture of 7 March 1891, Mademba quickly forgot his promises and violated his instructions.

Danel concluded that "Mademba considered the territory of Sansanding as his personal property. The best solution is to rapidly terminate the functions of the faama of Sansanding...which have no more reason to exist" (ANS-AOF Danel 1900). Danel's proposals for dealing with Mademba contained two parts: first, Mademba's position as "king" had outlived whatever administrative validity it may have had, and to continue it under the auspices of the Third Republic was incongruous; and second, Mademba's abuses of power demanded his recall from the French colonial service and further punitive action.

Jean-Baptist Chaudié, the governor-general of French West Africa, quickly responded to Danel's assessment and suggestions.

> The Mademba affair is at once more delicate and more serious than [Danel] makes out. If this colony were a colony constituted in the normal way, nothing could be easier than to repress the functions of a functionary. But is Mademba really a functionary when he exercises the authority of faama of Sansanding?

Chaudié further tried to minimize the gravity of Danel's accusations and his suggestions by advancing an *ad homonim* defense: since France had awarded Mademba the prestigious rank of officer in the Legion of Honor after careful consideration, these accusations made by African subjects must be wrong. He concluded that "for an officer [like Danel, without sufficient field experience] it was impossible to appreciate the exact gravity of a situation usually exaggerated by fatally jealous intermediaries" (ANS-AOF Chaudié 1900). To further bolster this argument, Chaudié commissioned reports from the administrators of two neighboring districts, Captains Chenard and Perignon. Both reiterated Chaudié's claim that the accusations were blown all out of proportion with the actual events (ANS-AOF Chenard 1900; Perignon March 1900).

It is worth examining Chaudié's position in Mademba's case further. His major arguments were also twofold: first, that Mademba was really not an employee of the French and therefore not subject to French laws; and second, that the peculiar conditions of Soudanic administrative justified whatever means were necessary. The first point was countered by Danel in a telegram sent in response to Chaudié's comments. He wrote that Mademba was receiving a salary, which made him a functionary, and that as a French citizen, Mademba must be accountable to French law, just like any other French colonial administrator (ANS-AOF Danel February 1900). Interpreting Chaudié's second argument, however, is more problematical in light of the government-general model of colonialism. As the first governor-general of French West Africa, Chaudié oversaw a transitional period in which the goals of the new federation were not yet fully articulated. Indeed, elaboration of the government-general model awaited the more forceful leadership of governor-general Ernest Roume in 1902. On the other hand, Chaudié's interest in reforming the colonial legal system may have stemmed from his senior position within the Corps of Colonial Inspectors (Cohen 1978:21–22). In his response to Danel, however, Chaudié seemed to back down from confrontation with local administrators and therefore with Archinard's model of colonialism. Essentially Chaudié argued that administrators had the right to transcend the rule of law if the conditions warranted. The conditions of administration in the French Soudan, which spread a handful of French administrators over a vast territory, created special conditions which permitted excesses. The fact that Danel did not have either military or administrative experience in the region was the cause of his inability to understand these special conditions. The letters in support of Mademba's actions from his fellow administrators suggest a closing of the ranks of the old Soudanese hands, perhaps because they understood what the legal challenge to Mademba meant.[14]

At this stage in my research, I am uncertain about William Ponty's role. The establishment of the government-general of French West Africa in 1895 and the appointment of Ponty as civilian governor in 1899 signalled important changes in colonial policy. The case against Mademba must be examined within the context of decisions to impose greater control over free-wheeling administrators and African collaborators. Certainly the debates surrounding the 1903 decree suggest this. However, Ponty either was not yet ready to challenge the military or he missed an opportunity to use the Mademba case more widely because he wrote to the minister of colonies in Paris that the evidence against Mademba was inconclusive and that Mademba had promised to reimburse the residents for the cotton. The minister replied that Mademba's general attitude could not remain unsanctioned, but did not specify what steps should be taken (ANS-AOF Ponty 1900; Minister of Colonies 1900).

While in Kayes Mademba refused to acknowledge even the accusations of his malfeasance. He wrote to the governor-general that "I am still ignorant of the motives which prevent me from returning to Sansanding" (ANS-AOF Mademba March 1900). Mademba apparently tempered his ways because in his history of Sinsani written in 1903 he described the judicial process there and his role: justice is rendered by a tribunal composed of the cadi [Islamic judge] and six notables and in the last resort by the Faama assisted by six chiefs of villages or notables. Penalties include fines and prison terms" (ANS-AOF Mademba 1903). The faama's traditional right of life and death and the right of conquest were now conspicuously absent.

Mademba spent three months in detention in Kayes before returning to his kingdom. In order to insure no further misconduct, Louis Corviaux, a civil administrator in the department of Native Affairs, was appointed resident of Sinsani. He remained in Sinsani for slightly over a year and was not replaced. Mademba reigned as faama of Sinsani until his death in 1918.

III

Faama Mademba justified his rule by arguing that he only acted as befitted African kings. The very fact of having to justify his actions suggests that Mademba was a peculiar kind of African king. Mademba was not disingenuous in his defense; he was, after all, a "king." Mademba's efforts to draw on precedent failed because he could lay claim only to Archinard's model of colonialism.

Mademba's case provides a glimpse into the ways power was conceived and expressed on the colonial frontier of the French Soudan. The French needed the active collaboration of those in positions of authority, but the very act of participation transformed their authority. Although collaboration was the acceptance of subordination, it often resulted in an enhanced opportunity for the application of power and the accumulation of wealth. Mademba might not have consciously collaborated with French authorities in making customary law and in defining traditional authority, but Mademba was the beneficiary of the ways Archinard and his followers conceived traditional Soudanese kingship. As the colonial state eliminated challenges to its power, the recourse to customary practices as a legitimation for the power of collaborators became progressively untenable for Africans such as Mademba.

Specifically, Mademba was undone as an African king because of the French metropolitan legal tradition called loi administratif. Loi administratif, as a separate judicial field including case law and courts, was born of the French Revolution. The loi administratif shielded administrators from the jurisdiction of civil courts and allowed the revolutionary forces to proceed with the reconstruction of the state. The enactment of the loi administratif in August 1790 effectively prohibited judges from interfering with the workings of administrative bodies and from summoning administrators before them in connection with the exercise of their functions (Schwartz 1954; Brown, Garner, and Galabert 1983). The administration, however, was aware of the potential for abuses of power, and therefore established a mechanism for internal review. Already in 1806, a separate section of the administration was empowered to deal with disputes involving administrative action. In 1873, the Third Republic formally separated the internal review process into an "autonomous" system of administrative justice.[15] This accounts both for the presence of the Corps of Colonial Inspectors, which led the investigation into the accusations of Mademba's malfeasance, and for its limited jurisdictional mandate.

The Mademba case and Inspector-general Danel's investigation fell, however, into a vague area between administrative malfeasance and *voie de fait*, which occurred when an administrator took the law into his own hands. "French legal theory," wrote Bernard Schwartz, has assumed that individual administrative acts are susceptible to varying degrees of illegality...and can attain such flagrant proportions that it destroys the very administrative quality of the affected act...When this is the fact, it follows that French [civil] law courts, not the administrative courts, have jurisdiction over cases brought by those adversely affected by the act, for it is no longer an act of administration in question (Schwartz 1954:72).

Danel's mandate only to inquire into Mademba's role in the cotton scandal reflected the administrative quality of that action. Danel's failure to pursue the accusations of Mademba's civil crimes, despite the depositions he collected to that effect, pointed to the vague middle ground between administrative law, French civil law, and customary law into which Mademba fit. That the accusations of Mademba's civil crimes were not pursued at all indicated the limited jurisdiction of the civil courts for cases brought by Africans against French citizens.

Conclusion

The crimes Mademba was accused of—extortion, abuse of power, kidnapping, rape, and murder—were not exceptional on the colonial frontier of French West Africa. More exceptional was that the case against Mademba went as far as it did. Most complaints of malfeasance and abuse of power against colonial administrators were quickly and quietly disposed of (Cohen 1971:79–83; Klein 1988). Administrators were often reprimanded and reassigned, but only rarely were they severely disciplined or imprisoned.

The Mademba affair was exceptional because it was the object of a formal administrative review and because of the ambiguities of legal jurisdiction it raised. At issue was Archinard's blueprint for a colonial society which rested upon an invented tradition of Soudanese kingship and Mademba's defense of himself in terms of the prerogatives of that office. Nobody questioned Archinard's right to establish African kingdoms. Inspector-general Danel only questioned whether this invention had outlived it usefulness and whether Mademba had exceeded his prerogatives to the point where his actions had tarnished the operation of the colonial administration.

Had we access to actual transcripts of the 1899 hearing in Kayes, we might better be able to flesh out the gaps and silences that hinder the analysis at this stage in my research. Transcripts of French colonial legal hearings, which often appear as stylized and truncated minutes recorded by the convening authority (for example, ANS-AOF M 201), might have yielded more detail on the strategies pursued by the defendant and the prosecution, their sense of the importance of this case, and their arguments concerning the boundaries of jurisdiction in complex legal settings.

Even without these transcripts, but relying on the administrative inspection of Mademba and the dialogues it contained,[16] the case against Mademba indicates ambiguities over jurisdiction in legal spheres in French West Africa during the early colonial era, when conquerors confronted societies with well established legal traditions. Conquest and the subsequent establishment of colonial rule skewed the legitimacy of these legal spheres, without clarifying the limits of jurisdiction between them.

Mademba acted as he thought befitted an African king. Archinard empowered him to act that way because he had constructed a political environment in which Africans like Mademba, with real or fictive claims of precolonial kingship, culled what they wanted from the received and invented traditions of precolonial and metropolitan sources of authority and power. On the colonial frontier, what constituted power and authority was being determined by actions of men and women in the field.

The maturation of the colonial state in the French Soudan manifested itself in efforts to control free-wheeling military commanders and district commandants. This took the form of replacing military commanders with civilian governors like Alfred Grodet in 1893 and William Ponty in 1902, and in the application of internal review processes, such as those conducted by the inspectors of colonial administration.

Many ambiguities remained concerning the application of power and authority, however. Not the least were the ambiguities of legal jurisdiction, highlighted by the case against Mademba. Despite evidence of civil crimes, Inspector-general Danel was limited to pursuing a case against the crimes committed in the course of administrative service. The case against Mademba refracted the legal and political opportunities and challenges facing both Africans and Europeans in the formative era of colonialism in Africa.

NOTES

1. I first came in contact with Mademba during research in Mali in 1976. I was initially confused by the French policy that made Mademba a king, because the mercantile community of Sinsani (Sansanding in the French sources), which I was studying, had traditionally eschewed the political realm in their long history with Segu. I wish to thank The Canada Council, the Social Science Research Council, and the National Endowment for the Humanities for research funds, although directed to other projects, which enabled me to collect data on Mademba whenever I came across any. I also wish to thank Martin Klein and James Mokhiber for their comments and their suggestions for further research.
2. Suret-Canale argues that Mademba was deposed in 1900.
3. The 1903 decree reorganized the legal system in French West Africa. It was one of the first significant efforts to regularize the mosaic of overlapping jurisdictions established in the flurry of institution-building following conquest. But the 1903 reorganization must also be seen as part of the efforts by the new government-general of French West Africa to control its free-wheeling administrators. The new code established legal guidelines for cases involving Africans. They would not have been applied to Mademba, who was a colonial administrator and a French citizen. For a sampling of the discussions surrounding the drafting of the 1903 code, see ANS-AOF Justice 1900–1903. For a suggestive study of this interpretation, see Mokhiber 1990.
4. Chanock 1982, 1985; Moore 1986; Hobsbawm and Ranger 1983.
5. Martin Klein suggests some refinement of this part of the story. First, Mari Jara was already faama before Archinard's recognition, because of his place within dynastic succession. Mari Jara was not, however, the uncontested successor. Second, immediately after the conquest of Segu Archinard established the domains of both Bojan and Mademba, although Mademba was not formally "appointed" until March 1891. Personal communication, April 1990.
6. ANF-DOM Archinard 1890–91; ANS-AOF Mademba 1903; interviews with Majum Sy 1977; Baba Kuma 1976; Binke Baba Kuma 1976. Binke Baba Kuma noted that Mademba's entourage was larger than the city's population. In the Soudan, 7,000 is a magical number.
7. This document reveals more about Mademba's orientation than it is an accurate description of Sinsani's judicial process.
8. Mademba's self-perception may not have differed greatly from that of many French officers at the time. See Kanya-Forstner 1969:273.
9. ANM Mademba June-July 1891; Mademba 21 March 1891; Segu Resident April 1891; Segu Rapport politique Sept 1893.
10. Bonnier 1897:80. See also interviews with Sidi Ba, 30 Dec 1976, Markala; Seydou Diane, 4 Jan 1977, Sinsani; Moussa Keita, 12 Dec 1976 and 30 Dec 1976, Sinsani; Baba Kuma, 4 Aug 1982, Sinsani; Binke Baba Kuma, 28 Dec 1976, Segu; Majuma Sy, 10 Mar 1977, Kirango.
11. Interviews with Santa Kulubali 1977; Baba Kuma 1976; Sidi Ba 1976; Kalil Konaté 1977. See also ANM Lieutenant-governor September 1897. Mademba was accused of kidnapping Fatimata, daughter of griot Jali Garé Kouyaté. Mademba kidnapped Fatimata's mother the next year.

12. Abd-el Kader Mademba (Mademba 1931:10) argued that the 1899 incident and the accusations of misconduct were a product of a personal vendetta Captain Lambert had against his father, Faama Mademba.
13. ANS-AOF Danel January 1900; ANM Affaire 1899. Fasidiki Kuma, the chief of Sinsani at the time, captured the nature of the cotton affair: "Mademba betrayed the French and stole from us," quoted in ANS-AOF Danel January 1900.
14. Captain Lambert, who was instrumental in bringing attention to Mademba's abuses was not a member of the Marine infantry or artillery to which most administrators belonged. Instead, he was an officer of the Infantry of the Line. Lambert was quickly replaced by Perignon as commandant of Segu in 1900, ANS-AOF Perignon 1900.
15. Exactly how autonomous this separate administrative justice was is unclear. An analogy may be that of the police investigating citizens' charges of police brutality.
16. Administrative inspections at this time were written on large folio paper with separate columns providing the opportunity for the various parties involved to respond to the data, commentary, and conclusions raised in the document. While this document is not a transcript of a dialogue, its format contains the voices of the parties subjected to the review and the senior officials of the divisions concerned with the review.

SOURCES

Interviews

All interviews were taped and have been deposited at the Institut des Sciences Humaines, Bamako, Mali, and at the Archives of Traditional Music, Indiana University. French translations of the tapes are available at the Institut des Sciences Humaines and at Green Library, Stanford University.

Sidi Ba, 30 December 1976, Markala.
Seydou Diane, 4 January 1977, Sinsani.
Musa Keita, 12 December 1976, Sinsani.
Musa Keita, 30 December 1976, Sinsani.
Kalil Konaté, 8 March 1977, Sinsani.
Baba Kuma, 28 December 1976, Segu.
Baba Kuma, 4 August 1982, Sinsani.
Binké Baba Kuma, 19 December 1976, Sinsani.
Santa Kulubali, 21 March 1977, Sinsani.
Majuma Sy, 10 March 1977, Kirango.

Archival

ANM: Archives Nationales, République du Mali (Kouluba, Mali)
Affaire du coton, Sansanding, 1899, 1 E 220.
Lieutenant-governor, letter to Segu commandant, 8 September 1897, Kayes, 1 E 220.
Lieutenant-governor, letter to Mademba, 13 January 1898, Kayes, 1 E 220.
Mademba, letter to Segu resident, 16 March 1891, Sinsani, 1 E 220.
Mademba, letter to Segu resident, 21 March 1891, 1 E 220.
Mademba, letter to Segu resident, 20 April 1891, Sinsani, 1 E 220.
Mademba, letter to Segu resident, date unclear (probably between June or July 1891), Sinsani, 1 E 220.
Mademba, letter to Segu resident, 4 January 1894, Sinsani, 1 E 220.
Mademba, letter to Segu resident, 1 October 1896, Sinsani, 1 E 220.
Rapport politique, 23 September 1892, Segu, 1 E 71.
ANS-AOF: Archives Nationales, République du Sénégal, Section Afrique Occidentale Française (Dakar, Senegal)
Governor-general Chaudié, Notes attached to Danel, Rapport, 1 February 1900, 15 G 176.
Captain Chenard, commandant of Gumbu, letter to governor, 2 March 1900, 15 G 176.
Danel, Inspecteur-général des Colonies, Rapport, Inspection générale concernant la verification du service de Mademba, Fama Sansanding, 14 January 1900, 15 G 176.
Danel, telegram to governor-general, 17 February 1900, Saint Louis, 15 G 176.
Depositions by Alalé Karaba, 30 September 1899, and Mamdi Traoré 30 October 1899, 15 G 176.

Discours de lieutenant-governeur, 17 August 1918, *Journal officiel du Haut-Sénégal-Niger*, 1918, 15 G 176.
Captain Lambert, letter, 4 October 1899, Segu, Affaire Mademba, 15 G 176.
Captain Lambert, 31 October 1899, 15 G 176.
Lettre d'investiture de M. Mademba, 7 March 1891, Nyamina, quoted in Captain Perignon, Généralités sur Haut-Sénégal et Moyen-Niger, 1900, 1 G 248.
Lieutenant Veil, 27 November 1899, 15 G 176.
Minister of Colonies, letter 18 May 1900, Paris, 15 G 176.
Organisation de la justice indigène, 1900–1903, M 79.
Captain Perignon, commandant of Segu, letter to governor, 15 March 1900, 15 G 176.
William Ponty, letter to minister of colonies, 31 March 1900, 15 G 176.
Mademba, Coutumes juridiques, #15, Etats de Sansanding, 30 March 1897, 1 G 229.
Mademba, letter to governor-general, 5 March 1900, Medine, 15 G 176.
Mademba, no title, 9 December 1903, 1 G 319.

ANF-DOM, Archives Nationales, République de France, Dépôt d'Outre-Mer (Aix-en-Provence, France)
Archinard, Renseignements sur la situation des colonies, Campagne 1890–91, Soudan V 1 a.
Archinard, letter to under secretary of state for colonies, 9 January 1891, Nioro, Soudan I 1 a.
Archinard, telegram, 5 May 1893, Soudan I 2 bis.
Commandant Grand, Etat de proposition pour grade Officier Légion d' Honneur, 1895, Segu, Soudan XI 6 b.

Printed

Baillaud, Emile. 1902. *Sur les routes du Soudan*. Toulouse: Edouard Privat.
Bonnier, Chef d'Escadron. 1897. *Mission au pays de Ségou: Campagne dans le Gueniekalary et le Sansanding en 1892*. Paris: Imprimerie Nationale.
Brown, L. Neville, F. Garner, and Jean-Michel Galabert, 1983. *French administrative law*. London: Butterworths.
Chandoné, Paul. 1906. "Mademba, Fama de Sansanding." *Revue Indigène* I(7):189–92.
Chanock, Martin. 1982. "Making customary law: Men, women and the courts in colonial Northern Rhodesia." In *African women and the law: Historical perspectives*, eds. Margaret Jean Hay and Marcia Wright, 53–67. Boston: Boston University.
———. 1985. *Law, custom and social order: The colonial experience in Malawi and Zambia*. Cambridge: Cambridge University Press.
Christelow, Allan. 1985. *Muslim law courts and the French colonial state in Algeria*. Princeton: Princeton University Press.
Cohen, William B. 1971. *Rulers of empire: The French colonial service in Africa*. Stanford: Hoover Institution Press.
———. 1978. "The French governors." In *African Procounsuls: European governors in Africa*, eds. L. H. Gann and Peter Duignan, 19–50. New York: Free Press.
Crowder, Michael. 1967. *Senegal: A study of French assimilation policy*.
Delavignette, Robert. 1968. *Freedom and authority in French West Africa*. London: Frank Cass.
De Loppinot, A. 1919. "Souvenirs d'Aguibou." *Bulletin du Comité d'Etudes historiques et scientifiques de l'Afrique occidentale française* 1:24–64.
Dubois, Felix. 1897. *Tombouctou, la mystèrieuse*. Paris: Flammarion.
Gallieni, Joseph Simone. 1891. *Deux campagnes au Soudan Français 1886–1888*. Paris: Hachette.
Hobsbawm, Eric, and Terrence Ranger, eds. 1983. *The invention of tradition*. Cambridge: Cambridge University Press.

Johnson, G. Wesley. 1978. "William Ponty and Republican Paternalism in French West
Africa (1866–1915)." In *African Procounsuls: European governors in Africa*, eds. L. H.
Gann and Peter Duignan, 127–56. New York: Free Press.

Kanya-Forstner, Sidney. 1969. *Conquest of the western Sudan: A study in French military
imperialism*. Cambridge: Cambridge University Press.

Klein, Martin. 1988. "The rule of law and the abuse of power in colonial French Guinea: The
Hubert-Noiret affair." Paper presented at the Stanford-Emory "Law in Colonial Africa"
Conference, Stanford University.

Mademba, Abd el Kader. 1931. *Au Senégal et au Soudan*. Paris: Larose.

Méniaud, Jacques. 1931. *Le pionniers du Soudan, avant et après Archinard, 1878–1894*. Paris:
Société des Publications Modernes.

Mokhiber, James. 1990. "Forms of authority and the ordernig of empire: The native justice
system in colonial Senegal 1903–1912." Unpublished B.A. honors thesis, History
Department, Stanford University.

Moore, Sally Falk. 1986. *Social facts and fabrications: "Customary" law on Kilimanjaro,
1880–1980*. Cambridge: Cambridge University Press.

Newbury, Colin. 1960. "The formation of the government general in French West Africa."
Journal of African History I (1):111–28.

Roberts, Richard. 1987a. *Warriors, merchants, and slaves: The state and the economy in the
Middle Niger Valley, 1700–1914*. Stanford: Stanford University Press.

———. 1987b. "French colonialism, imported technology, and the handicraft textile
industry in the Western Sudan, 1898–1918." *Journal of Econonomic History*, 47(2):461–72.

Schwartz, Bernard. 1954. *French administrative law and the common law world*. New York:
New York University Press.

Suret-Canale, Jean. 1971. *French colonialism in tropical Africa, 1900–1945*, trans. by Till
Gottheiner. London: Hurst.

Terrier, A. 1918. "Fama Mademba." *Bulletin du comité de l'Afrique Française*: 168–70. 1918.

Thiriet, E. 1932. *Au Soudan, souvenirs, 1892–1914: Macina-Tombouctou*. Paris: Andre Lesot.

PART IV

LITIGANTS, COURTS, AND
LEGAL STRATEGIES

9

Theft, Homicide, and Oath in Early Twentieth-Century Kano

ALLAN CHRISTELOW

Introduction

The city of Kano lies at the heart of a densely populated agricultural district in what is now northern Nigeria, and at the junction of trade routes extending north through the Sahara and to the Mediterranean, and south to the forest. When the British captured Kano in 1903, it could boast an urban tradition as a political capital, commercial hub, and Islamic cultural center reaching back more than five hundred years.

In the brief period between the arrival of the British and the First World War, Kano underwent a remarkable economic reorientation. It had been a center for the exchange of locally produced craft goods and slaves, salt from the desert, kola from the forest, and manufactured goods from the Mediterranean or Europe brought across the desert by caravan. By 1912, the railroad from Lagos had reached Kano, and almost overnight, the city became a center for the export of groundnuts to the European market, and the distribution of European manufactured consumer goods into local commercial channels (Hogendorn 1978). In 1913–14, a serious drought hit the region and the ensuing famine was aggravated by the fact that traditional precautions against food shortage had been eroded by the advent of the colonial cash economy and new taxation practices (Watts 1983).

While there was marked economic change, there was substantial political and social continuity. The emir and the royal office holders, descendants of the *jihad* leaders of the early nineteenth century, adapted themselves to British demands for administrative reform (Paden 1973; Fika 1978). With the one major exception of the gradual abolition of slavery—the impact of which is yet to be fully understood by scholars (Christelow 1988; Lovejoy 1983; Miers and Roberts 1988)—the British did little directly to change the established social order.

These two themes of economic change and political continuity intersect in a key institution, the judicial council of the emir of Kano. In the records of this institution, one can see the response of Kano's traditional ruler both to the direct interference of the British, in matters of slavery, and to the indirect effects of the British presence, especially the reorientation of commercial patterns, and a wave of thefts that accompanied it (Christelow 1986, 1987). The council's cases only began to be recorded in 1910, apparently at the instruction of the then British Resident, Charles Temple. The records which form the basis of this study, which include over 2,000 cases, cover the period Jumada II 1331/May 1913 to Muharram 1333/November 1914.[1] The council was presided over by Emir Abbas, who had been appointed by the British in 1903, and included the *waziri*, the top Islamic legal official of the emirate, and a number of Islamic legal scholars. It heard a wide variety of cases, some quite trivial, others serious. Most cases could be classed under the rubrics of theft, violence, land disputes, slavery, and administrative cases involving taxes or the abuse of authority by local officials. Those cases which involved family matters or disputes arising from business agreements were heard by the *alkali* or Muslim judge.

The records were kept in Arabic, not in the romanized Hausa used by the colonial administration. Since few British officials knew Arabic, its use diminished the possibility of their interference in legal matters. The vast majority of cases were recorded in very brief form, a sure sign that no further action was expected on the case. Most cases ran from two to six lines, and not even the longest — invariably homicide cases — ran more than one foolscap page. This stands in contrast with the voluminous legal dossiers assembled on occasion by European colonial administrators in Africa.

While the council applied Islamic law, especially in the treatment of evidence, many decisions were made on the basis of *hukm*, or administrative rule, or *hukm zamanna*, "the rule of our times." Hukm referred to long-standing aspects of secular legislation in such matters as land rights. Hukm zamanna designated legislation originating in the colonial period, whether at the instigation of the British, as in slavery matters, or at the initiative of the council. The term implies that all new legislation, regardless of origin, was still made by authority of the emir, that what distinguished it was not an alien origin, but rather its relationship to a clearly perceived historical transformation. It also connotes awareness of some earlier legal principle that had been superceded. The term *qanun*, which usually designates customary law that has been formalized in writing (Repp 1988), does not occur in the council's records.

Secular legislation has been a long-standing feature of the Muslim world, but because it has seldom been systematized or codified, it has been little studied by Western scholars. Colonial administrators in Africa were so preoccupied with discovering established custom that they too have neglected the question of legislation. In the Muslim and African colonial worlds alike, Europeans have seen traditional rulers as the guardians of time-honored custom, while they have assumed secular legislation to be the purview of modern government institutions run by, or under the guidance of, Europeans. Local custom, bequeathed by an earlier sovereign, could be accepted by a colonial or national administration, but local powers to legislate could not be recognized unless specifically delegated by the current sovereign power. The hukm of the Kano judicial council seems to fall in a gap between the European concepts of custom and legislation.

In northern Nigeria, the role of hukm has been obscured because conservative northern politicians in the 1940s and 1950s defended the autonomy of their judicial system on the grounds of its religious character. As a written law, the shari'a easily overshadowed hukm. And because it was theoretically unchangeable, it could be defended against all interference. But in Kano emirate, because of the railroad and the groundnut export economy, there were a good many pressures for legal change from early in the colonial period. Given the conservative and non-interventionist tenor of the British administration in the north, legal innovation outside such sensitive areas as slavery and taxation, was largely up to the emir's judicial council.[2]

A critical problem is how a particular principle of hukm comes into being. It is not issued in the form of a decree cast in precise legal terminology and published in a government gazette. Nor does it represent the real or supposed extension of a customary legal principle by a body whose sole function is simply to apply and interpret custom. What seems to have happened is that the council would set forth a new principle in an actual case, and further refine it in subsequent cases.

The council's chief innovation, a law on compensation for theft victims, involved not simply an innovation in law, but a major deviation from the normal Islamic judicial procedure, which required proof by the testimony of witnesses. The need for innovation in the first place came from the scarcity of witnesses in these cases. A procedural device was still necessary for the validation of claims. The device chosen was the oath of affirmation — as opposed to the oath of denial, a common element of Islamic legal procedure. Such an oath is found in an aspect of shari'a law, the yamin al-qasama, or oath of compurgation, which arose in certain homicide cases. It is possible that the theft compensation law was grounded in a conscious analogy to qasama. But there is a more important connection between the two: both were used in cases stemming from pressing social and economic conflicts, and both were used in socially discriminatory fashion. In both theft compensation and homicide cases, the council effectively honored the claims of certain categories of people while denying those of others. The discrimination could be direct, resulting from the council's decision on whether or not to allow the oath, or indirect, a product of the individual plaintiff's internalized sense of a religiously sanctioned social order — which guided his decision as to whether or not to take the oath.

To understand the pivotal importance of oath-taking, we need to situate it first within the general picture of Kano legal procedures, and then to consider what elements of the legal, economic, and political contexts accentuated the importance of the types of case where oaths were taken.

The Legal Process

In the records, the legal process is distilled to one or more of these nodal points: the raising of a complaint; the testimony of witnesses; the oath of denial, or, more rarely, of affirmation; forgiveness by the plaintiff; imprisonment and release from prison. Prison, while used occasionally to punish, was quite often an extension of the legal process, a sort of intermission (which could last more than a year) between the raising of the complaint and the conclusive event of testimony, oath, or forgiveness. In some cases, the emir or his representative would carry out an investigation (Arabic: *bahth*), only the result of which was reported.

For most cases, testimony and oath lie at the heart of the legal process. Thus we need to consider their implications. A basic principle of Islamic legal procedure is that one who affirms a point must prove it by the testimony of at least two legally acceptable witnesses; one who denies a point must back up his denial by an oath, normally taken before the *minbar* (or pulpit) of a mosque. Socially confirmed truth, then, took precedence over the individual's affirmation of a truth before Allah — and truth deduced from evidence by human reason had no place at all. This means that the sort of people who lack witnesses to their claims cannot back up their claims. The solitary person or stranger is likely to have trouble in court — in Kano, particularly the itinerant trader. Also, cases of violence are often difficult to prosecute, either because they occur in isolated areas, or because they occur within the home and the victim is a socially dependent individual, for whose sake one cannot find any willing, legally capable individuals to testify (for example: household head kills wife). The defendant, too, would sometimes have to call upon his social resources, particularly in allegations of theft or cooperation with thieves.

Witnesses were perforce friends or neighbors, patrons or clients, since neither immediate kin nor slaves could serve this function. Thus it was non-kinship bonds which came into play in court (except in the oath of compurgation, discussed below). Occasionally, no doubt, bribes prevailed where the bonds of friendship or clientship did not, though this was a risky business, as the following case suggests:

> Habu of Gorondoma [ward] complained to the emir of Kano that Adamu and Maikano came to him as swindlers. They said to him that Maigoron called to us, and he said to us, "I am complaining against Habu to the emir, and so I called you two to give you two pounds as a bribe to testify between myself and Habu." They agreed to that. Then they went to Habu and had many words, and said "We will not give false testimony of deception." He did not understand their meaning. Habu was in good spirits, so that he gave them a blanket [Hausa: *bargo*] to make them happy. Later, the matter came to the emir of Kano, and [this account] was confirmed. So he put them in prison and took the blanket from them and returned it to Habu (EKJC 167 D, 20 Dhu al-Qa'da 1332).

The records give one the sense that there was a difference between testifying for someone and testifying against someone. It was one matter to testify that one's friend was indeed the owner of such-and-such an animal, or of such-and-such a plot of land. It was quite another to testify that someone stole something or assaulted someone. Part of the problem of course was that few people saw these acts, but one can also suspect that such testimony was reckoned to be a hostile act into which one should not venture lightly. It is especially rare in Kano to find someone taking on the role of second (and thus key) witness in homicide cases.

Oath-taking was a more important matter than merely offering testimony in court, and it lies at the heart of the most serious and interesting cases. Oaths sometimes were taken to defend against an accusation when the plaintiff had not been able to produce two valid witnesses. But in such situations, the plaintiff would often abandon the case before administration of the oath, or even just as the would-be oath-taker approached the minbar in the mosque (EKJC 101 F, Jumada I 1332). The taking of an oath before Allah imparted a certain kind of finality to a dispute which a frustrated plaintiff might have wanted to avoid. The plaintiff could magnanimously withdraw the complaint before the court while muttering under his breath that on the final day Allah would surely decide the matter a different way.

In the judicial council records, one finds two instances where oaths were taken not to deny an accusation, but to affirm one. In certain homicide cases, two male agnatic relatives of the victim might be allowed to share in taking a fifty-fold yamin al-qasama or oath of compurgation (literally "oath of division"), affirming that the accused had indeed been responsible for causing the death of their relative. Such an oath could be invoked only where grave presumption (Arabic: *lawth*) existed as to the guilt of the accused. This legal device is a part of Islamic shari'a law. In practice, the judicial council used this device primarily in cases involving the killing of food thieves.

The second type of case involved complaints by victims of theft. Such a person, by virtue not of the shari'a but of a legal innovation of the judicial council, under the rubric of hukm zamanna, could take an oath that goods equivalent to a certain value in currency had been stolen, and would have the right to compensation from the person responsible for law and order—in Kano city, the police chief, outside it the district or village head. The right to take this oath might be denied on certain technical grounds, such as an itinerant merchant's failure to report to the relevant authority, which invalidated his or her claim to that person's protection (Arabic: *dhimma*). Some theft victims availed themselves of the opportunity to take the oath and recoup their avowed losses. Others declined to take the oath, in which case the emir usually invoked Allah's help in their continuing search for the missing items.

There is no evidence that this law was instituted at British prompting. The only reference to the problem of theft in Abbas's time in an historical study comes in Abubakar Dokaji's Hausa-language *Kano ta Dabo Cigari* (The Kano of Dabo Cigari) (1958:66–67), which is based largely on oral tradition. The silence of the British archives on this issue suggests that theft was largely a "native" concern, and the compensation law a response to domestic political pressure from the big traders of Kano city.

In both the theft compensation and the qasama cases, one finds a certain subjective element in the legal process. Often the council's decision on whether or not to allow an oath in a homicide case was not explained. In no case does one find a direct explanation for a theft victim's decision on oath-taking. In each situation, however, one finds evidence that might explain the decisions. It will be suggested that the subjective aspect of these cases stems from the difficulty of making explicit the rules involved in decision making, especially because the decisions ultimately involved political judgments about an individual's power or the public's view of the case. Ironically, while oath-taking suggests the resort to divine mediation, it was precisely those cases where oaths were forsaken in which Allah was invoked—as final judge between homicide victim and killer, as guide to the retrieval of stolen property.

It is significant that the two types of case in which oath-taking played the most prominent role were also distinctly related to newly arisen social and economic problems resulting from changing trade patterns and the drought. Routine cases, such as disputes over land rights, could be handled by the more or less mechanical application of rules. But new or unusual cases with an important political or moral dimension required a device which allowed for the weighing of certain factors outside the normal framework of procedural discussion. This device was the oath of affirmation.

Changes in the Context of Theft and Homicide

In the years 1913–14, theft of goods from traders and the killing of food thieves were especially acute problems. What made them so were several important changes in the legal, economic, and political context of Kano emirate. These changes are especially important in understanding the issue of theft compensation.

Legal Change

Unfortunately, legal records in Kano began to be kept only in 1910. Thus we do not know the extent to which the British imposed changes of legal policy in the first years of occupation. Certainly the British did outlaw the use of mutilation as a punishment for theft. In a 1906 memo, Governor Lugard claimed that mutilation had "probably" been the primary punishment for theft (Brooke 1952:7), but there is no evidence to support his contention.[3] Moreover, Islamic law sets exacting requirements, concerning the value of items stolen and the circumstances of the theft, for the application of this punishment. And, since the records demonstrate the difficulty of finding witnesses to theft, it seems likely that mutilation was rarely applied. One British source mentions that in cases of theft, where the victim was of equal status to the thief, the thief would have a long piece of wood tied to his head—presumably as much a source of public humiliation as of physical discomfort (Tremearne 1913:457). Prisons had existed in precolonial Kano emirate, but they seem to have been few and small, and mainly used for incarcerating the emir's political foes, not for meting out standardized punishments for crime.

It is likely that in the precolonial period potential theft victims did not rely on legal recourse to deter theft, but rather took measures of self-help. A person whose house had been broken into would summon neighbors by letting out a hue and cry. Traders organized themselves into caravans for protection.

After their initial conquest, the British sent European-officered colonial police to some northern cities, but these were withdrawn in 1907 out of concern that they did more to arouse local resentment than to maintain order. In line with a policy of bolstering emiral authority, the *dogarai*, or emir's (unarmed) police were reinforced within Kano city. At the same time, the British encouraged the native authorities to build prisons. They did not, however, define how these new legal instruments should fit into the policies of courts which had previously worked, for the most part, without either. The judicial council was left on its own to define their roles. In requiring the police chief to make restitution for losses from theft, the council did so in a markedly original manner.

Economic Change

With the "Pax Britannica," traders no longer felt the need to band together in caravans, and began to move about individually (Hopen 1958:50). By 1912, the advent of an agricultural export economy began to transform the trading patterns of Kano Emirate as European manufactured goods were distributed from the railhead at Kano, and export produce collected there (Hogendorn 1978). Both of these factors helped augment the possibilities for theft. The replacement of bulky cowrie shell currency with coins also contributed, for coins could be easily concealed. Traders connected with the new commercial economy acutely sensed the inadequacy of traditional security measures.

The coming of the railway and the growth of the colonial administrative aparatus in Kano city created a growing market for foodstuffs. When famine hit Kano, public discontent naturally focused on grain horders, and that discontent turned to outrage when grain horders killed famished food thieves.

The Role of Office Holders

Theft in Hausaland at this time often had political overtones. Those who held or aspired to office in the native authority structure were known to use theft, and the evident need to control it, to achieve political ends — such as the creation of the autonomous Hausa community at Sabo in Ibadan. They might also sponsor theft in order to line their own pockets and victimize their enemies, as was done by a new royal office holder in Daura. Thieves were recruited from a floating population of young, single men, known as *'yan iska*, or sons of the spirit, who were involved in all the pursuits typical of an urban underworld — gambling, theft, and prostitution (Cohen 1969:103–113; Smith 1978:326–29). It is conceivable that a good many of such men were recruited from the large number of male slaves who deserted their masters after the conquest but, lacking land and families, had not been able to settle as farmers.

Groups of *'yan iska* might be mobilized for political ends, but might also operate on their own account. It is unlikely that they would have accounted for all theft, but they probably had a major role in certain types — especially those where the resale of items was involved, such as would be the case with trade goods, and with riding and pack animals. Those who stole out of their own individual desperate need were more likely to be interested in cattle, or especially in basic foodstuffs such as grain or cassava.

It is clear from the records that victims of goods theft often suspected the collusion of authorities in facilitating both the theft and the resale of stolen items. Certainly this widespread suspicion was a principal reason for instituting a law requiring local authorities to compensate theft victims. It is likewise clear that food thieves who were killed were regarded as innocent martyrs by the public. Under the shari'a, those who needed food to survive had the right to it, and the fault lay with those who denied it to them.

Procedure, Testimony, and Oaths in Theft Cases

The significance of oaths of affirmation in specific types of theft cases needs to be understood against the background of the role of procedure, testimony, and oaths in a wide variety of cases.

Animal Theft

The theft of goods and money and the theft of animals involved different problems and tended to be treated differently. Most complaints about animal theft turned up only when the beast had been recovered — sometimes right after the theft, but often months or even years later. In contrast to the theft of goods, there were almost never any reports of violence associated with the theft of animals. As a rule, animal thieves were imprisoned only when they had sold or disposed of the animal in question. A man who had returned only two of three stolen cows was imprisoned, and then released when he promised to pay for the third one (EKJC 69 F, 2 Safar 1331). A thief who had passed on a stolen mare to another person was imprisoned (EKJC 36 A, Shawwal 1331). A man who had stolen a goat and sold it, and could not reimburse the buyer, was imprisoned (EKJC 3 B, 27 Jumada II 1331). When a thief had slaughtered a steer himself (and presumably not in the proper ritual fashion), and taken the best meat and the hide, the emir ordered a house-to-house search (EKJC 111 A, Jumada II 1332). In only two or three of twelve cases in which animal thieves were sent to prison does prison appear to have been used simply as a punishment. By contrast, there were twenty-nine cases in which animal thieves confessed, or did not deny, that they had stolen the animal. If the animal was then returned to the owner, they were not imprisoned. There were over forty other cases in which the accusation could not be proven, or no accusation was made, or where the suspect was released on the basis of oath or character witnesses. There were nine instances in which animal thieves escaped their captors, in one case with the aid of the *sarkin sati*, the chief of a "guild" of thieves (EKJC 43 F, 26 Shawwal 1331).

When the animal was not recovered and the thief not caught, complaints were sometimes made against a lodging house owner (generally by those travelling to a market with their beast) or a village head (usually in a nearby village to which the stolen beast had been traced from the victim's home). As will be seen, in cases of theft of goods from itinerant merchants, complaints against these parties were generally rejected outright. But in matters of animal theft, the lodging house owner (Hausa: *fatoma*) or village head was required to produce character witnesses (Arabic: *shuhud al-tazkiya*), usually neighbors who would testify that one was neither a thief nor one who collaborated with thieves. Out of eleven such cases, six involved equine stock (out of twenty-four equine cases), but only two bovine stock (out of thirty-five bovine cases). There are two possible interpretations of this. First, the council may have taken the complaints of the well-to-do, as the owner of such a luxury as a horse necessarily was, more seriously than those of humbler plaintiffs. Second, stolen horses were usually resold at a point some distance from the owner's home, and this complex operation probably required protection and coordination by important figures. The existence of networks for the resale of stolen horses made accusations against local office holders in these cases plausible.

One might class animal theft cases at a point intermediate between land disputes and cases of goods or money theft. In animal theft, the chief objective was to secure return of the beast, and to prove that it was one's property. Taking an animal for its use value was not much different than say, taking over the farming plot of an absent neighbor. It was a wrong which could be easily righted by return of the item in question. Only when the animal was sold or slaughtered did the case take on a different complexion — i.e., when the animal was treated as exchange value. One should note that the integrity of butchers was crucial to preventing the theft of large animals. A group of Maguzawa, or pagan Hausa, were found consuming the meat of a camel in the bush. They claimed that they had found it dead. Muslims who made such a claim could have been punished for eating impure meat — or else for both stealing the beast and lying about it. But non-Muslims were not held to Islamic ritual law, so their story was accepted and they were let off (EKJC 146 E, Sha'ban 1332).

A further characteristic that distinguished animal theft from goods theft is that the victim was usually the owner rather than a trader. Also, it was common (though not quite to the same degree), that the theft occurred on the owner's home turf rather than en route to market. Because of these factors, and because animals, unlike goods, were often recovered, one finds far less involvement of third parties in animal theft than in goods theft.

Goods Theft

The most common sort of complaint over goods theft involved an individual itinerant trader who came with his goods to a village or town or city and spent the night at a lodging house. He or she went to sleep and later woke up to find the goods stolen, or was robbed on a trail through the bush the next day. There was little likelihood of finding a witness who would lead one to the thief and testify in court. One could of course look around in likely places — the market place, or the *samsar's* (broker's) shop. But this seldom led to satisfaction. The plaintiff's frustration naturally turned to the lodging house owner or to the village head.

A few words need to be said about these "third party" roles. In Hausaland, the commercial lodging house was a small affair compared to the North African caravanserai (Geertz 1979). The latter was often a large institution accommodating dozens of traders and offering secure storage facilities for their goods. Often it was constituted as a religious endowment (*waqf*). In Hausaland, traders away from home stayed at the house of a fatoma, or lodging house owner,[4] who provided a room to stay in, and often arranged commercial contacts as well. *Fatomai* (plural) and traders were thus often linked by a strong shared commercial interest. But such relations could develop simply from a casual encounter in the market. In one case, for instance, a trader met a woman at the market at sundown, and went with his goods to her house. That night a thief entered her house and stole goods from both of them — and then they went out together and caught the thief (EKJC 46 A, 17 Dhu al-Qa'da 1331). The anonymity of the relationship was most intense for traders in transit, stopping in a village on their way from Kano city to an outlying market. Such relations were bound to be uneasy. In one case, a trader was refused entry at sundown to a house which had earlier agreed to take him. When he tried to force his way in, he was beaten to death (EKJC 45 F, Dhu al-Qa'da 1331). With the groundnut boom, such uneasy relationships proliferated as new trade routes were established, and new manufactured trade goods and coins appeared.

The aggrieved trader could make two possible complaints: either that the owner of the house in which he stayed or the local headman (Arabic: *'arif*) had somehow been involved in the theft; or that the house owner or more likely the headman was responsible for the security of his goods and thus owed him compensation. The former would have to be established by witnesses, but the latter could, in principle, be established by oath. The report of the complaint seldom specified which sort of complaint was intended, but most often it seems to have been the latter.

Compensation for Stolen Goods

Within Kano city, the emir's judicial council established the principle of the liability of police authorities in the event of goods being stolen within their jurisdiction. There, the city had gates to close at night, police patrols circulated, and there was a new prison in which to deposit suspicious characters rounded up by the patrols. As the system developed, responsibility for reimbursing the value of stolen goods passed from the ward patrol to the city police chief (*sarkin dogarai*). This shift may have been a result of the fact that wealthy merchants began to make sizeable claims. When such judgments were rendered, they were clearly labeled as being on the basis of hukm zamanna. One can discern a two-fold rationale behind the measure: to spur the dogarai to diligence in catching thieves, and to dissuade them from stealing themselves, either on their own account or at the behest of some prominent official. And presumably it helped to attract merchants and their capital to Kano. Certainly, the compensation law could prove an expensive proposition for the sarkin dogarai, but he could balance his books by taking advantage of the right to confiscate from suspected thieves any property they could not account for (EKJC 168 F, Dhu al-Qa'da 1332).

The first major compensation case provides us with some intriguing clues about the changing nature of theft litigation. It involved a sum of £12 claimed by one Muhammad Gaja of Gorondoma ward (EKJC 86 E, Rabi' II 1332). He had travelled — no doubt for business — before the compensation could be paid, leaving his brother, Isa, to collect the money from the sarkin dogarai. The judgment is recorded as being according to the "legislation of this time of ours." In the very next case, five theft victims from different wards of the city (Dawasi, Dala, Jingo, Kabuga, and Adakawa) came forward with complaints but declined to take the oath, saying that "We are patient as Allah decrees" (EKJC 86 F, 2 Rabi II 1332). It is likely that these five individuals had heard about Muhammad Gaja's compensation case, and had come to the council hoping to avail themselves of the same right. In the council, they would have been informed of the necessity of taking an oath, and they might have been reminded of the dangers one incurred in taking an oath before Allah on unsound grounds. Intimidation occurred, but in a subtle way, not through a direct threat, but by using the oath as a cue to set off internalized fears of retribution. Before this point, some relatively small claims had been made — for £1 5sh, and for £1 13sh 6p (38 D, 20 Ramadan 1331; 85 G, Rabi' I 1332). Afterwards, out of seven claims for which oaths were taken, all were over £3, five were over £8, and it was the *sarkin dogarai*, rather than the ward patrol, who was held responsible. Petty claimants declined to take the oath. Thus the £12 case, followed by the five oath decliners, seems to have established that compensation was only available to big traders. In principle, there was legal equality. In practice, there was self-selecting privilege, based on whether or not one had the gumption to take the oath.

Was Emir Abbas opposed to the very principle of compensation? This does not seem likely. It is probable that he wanted to attract merchants and their capital to Kano. The theft problem also offered the occasion to strengthen his administrative control over the city, concentrating power in the hands of the police chief, a slave official. In effect, Emir Abbas was able to adapt pressures for theft control to his own purposes by, as it were, publicizing the advisability of declining the oath—unless one were well equipped to cope with the dangers, magical and otherwise, which it entailed.

In the countryside, the same basic rules on oath and compensation applied in principle, but in this context, the results were different. The compensation rule was hedged by conditions: that one be staying at a lodging house and not in the open, and that one report one's presence to the administration. Within the walled city of Kano, these conditions were usually met, since one could be arrested for sleeping in the market and one had to report overnight guests to the ward head. But itinerant traders in the countryside often stayed in market places or simply under a convenient tree. Even staying in the entry-hut (*zaure*) to a compound, rather than within the compound proper disqualified one's claim (EKJC 80 H, Rabi I 1332).[5] Also, the council did not consider local authorities responsible for robberies which took place in the bush outside of settlements. As for reporting to the authorities, it did not seem to be a common practice for itinerant traders to report their presence to village heads. Between these two factors, there was almost always grounds for dismissing the complaint without offering the possibility of taking the oath.

There was, however, one case where an itinerant trader got compensation:

'Umar of Laraba Gida came to Harbu in the territory of Kano with his goods and he settled in the house of the Wazirin Harbu. When he had prayed his evening prayer, the Wazirin Harbu came to him and said to him, "Leave my house, you don't have a place to stay here." So he ejected him forcefully, and he got up and went to the market and settled there. During the night, a thief came to him and stole goods from him, and so he complains against the one who ejected him at night. It was investigated, and it was confirmed that he ejected him, so ten shillings is taken from the Wazirin Harbu and given to 'Umar, on the basis of *hukm* (92 A, 28 Rabi II 1332).

Here the verdict seems to have been based on the Wazirin Harbu's breaking of an oral contract to shelter the trader, and thus it did not involve the new compensation rule or the taking of an oath of affirmation. Also note that the record not only tells us that an injustice has been committed, but that it has been committed against a good Muslim who carried out his ritual obligations.

Itinerant traders seldom had the satisfaction even of having the defendant required to produce character witnesses, although this was a common procedure in animal theft cases, and in cases where a local official or group of people accused some individual of being a habitual thief. It seems that character witnesses were ordered when the plaintiff(s) had some degree of influence and respectability, and itinerant traders on the road seem to have had little of either. Given these obstacles to protecting themselves against theft, it is not surprising that two itinerant traders who had been robbed and were rebuffed when they asked the local headman for help in finding the thieves took the extraordinary step of appealing to a British district officer for help. In this case, Emir Abbas was clearly vexed to have to order compensation, and he noted that neither oath nor testimony had been taken to back up the claim of the theft victims (EKJC 118 A, Rajib 1332; Christelow 1987:238–39). In avoiding both testimony and oath, the two traders had escaped from the normal constraints of social relationships and Islamic religious culture which played such crucial roles in the judicial council's procedures. To avoid having it constitute a precedent, the emir had to make it clear that this case of compensation resulting from intervention of the district officer represented only arbitrary administrative fiat, and not law of any sort. The factor that distinguished administrative fiat from law in the council's eyes was the absence, in the former, of any means of validating the claim made.

Theft and Violence

When a thief was not caught, as we have seen, it was often assumed that he benefitted from the protection of a local power holder. But when a thief was caught, the question of his connections to a power holder was never raised. Once a thief was caught, or at least physically encountered, the critical legal issues became, first, whether violence against the thief was permissible, and second, whether and how to punish the thief.

Virtually the only instances in which theft was punished judicially were when the thief himself confessed his crime, and this was likely to occur when the thief had been caught during or soon after the act. Prison was not automatic: in nine cases confession led to prison, in two to sentences of five lashes, and in five, no punishment is mentioned, and presumably there was none.

Why was the petty theft of goods punished, even when the goods were returned? And why did this not happen in cases of animal theft? Part of the answer may lie in the very paltriness of the objects concerned—some garments; five shirts; a satchel; 3 sh. 6 p.; some millet from a field; some groundnuts from a field.[6] Such minor thefts reflect desperation and poverty. And the desperate and poor were likely to be seen as suitable candidates for the sort of work prisoners did—cleaning Kano's sewage channels.

As to why a thief would confess, there may be a simple answer: to save his life. Theft of the breaking-and-entering or highway robbery varieties was a violent affair. Twelve goods thieves were killed in the period in question; six food thieves were also killed. And the violence was hardly one-sided. Thieves killed ten people, and injured ten others. Where the question was raised, those who killed thieves were generally exonerated of claims to blood payment, except where food thieves had been killed (see below). I doubt whether the violence associated with goods theft reflected the monetary values involved, since animal theft so seldom led to violence. Rather, the violence may have stemmed from a sense of outrage at a violation of the sacred boundary of the *gida*, the family compound. It might also have been that house-breaking goods thieves were assumed to belong to a different social category than animal thieves. The latter frequently seem to have come from neighboring settlements, and could be presumed to have families. Killing an animal thief thus might poison relations with neighbors, and it certainly raised the possibility of liability for blood payment. It would be of interest to know if goods thieves tended to be escaped or redeemed slaves (and for men, escape would be more likely), since this would greatly reduce the fear of liability. Slaves and ex-slaves were less likely to have family, above all agnatic male kin who would be required for the yamin al-qasama. In one case where a thief had been killed, the question of the slave status of the dead man was indeed raised because of its legal relevance (EKJC, 19 Muharram 1332). It was decided that the dead man in question was a free Muslim, but his relatives were not found.

Homicide and Oaths

The records under study cover both the tail end of the initial groundnut boom and the great famine of 1913–1914: both led to an upsurge in the theft of goods, and an upsurge in the theft of food. According to Islamic law, it was not a crime for a hungry person to take food, and on the few occasions where food thieves were brought before the council, this was pointed out. Nevertheless, food thieves, as well as goods thieves, were sometimes beaten by crowds.

It has been mentioned that homicide cases often lacked witnesses. Islamic legists had long been aware of this problem, and thus made a provision for it in the form of the yamin al-qasama, literally, the oath of division, usually rendered as "fifty-fold oath" or "oath of compurgation." Western Orientalists such as J. N. D. Anderson and Joseph Schacht have criticized this oath as irrational or archaic (Anderson 1955:202; Schacht 1964:202–203). Where there was incomplete proof, but a grave presumption of guilt (*lawth*) existed, the blood-writ executors (*awliya al-damm*) could take a fifty-fold oath to have the right to retribution or blood payment (in the case of intentional homicide) or simply blood payment (in the case of accidental homicide). In the killing of food thieves, the problem was not a lack of witnesses, or their reluctance to testify, but rather establishing a link between cause and result. If goods thieves were often assaulted with lethal weapons such as bows or knives and died fairly promptly, this was seldom the case with food theft, where the victim was simply beaten—or, in one case, castrated as well. In two cases, the victim took as long as nineteen days to die (EKJC 161 A, 26 Shawwal 1332; 164 B, 11 Dhu al-Qa'da 1332). The question, then, was to establish that the beating was indeed what led to death, and this was achieved by having two male agnates of the deceased share a fifty-fold oath. In the case of the castration, there was also a question of whether the granary owner at whose behest a mob had acted should be held accountable. In no case did a food thief turn out to lack the required two male agnates—he was a "family man," unlike the marginal 'yan iska, who, I have suggested, were more likely to go after resaleable items.

Like beauty, grave presumption of guilt is in the eye of the beholder. While some seventy-one cases of violent death came before the council, in only ten was the yamin al-qasama invoked, and fully half of those involved food theft. And nearly all food thief killings led to this oath. In one case, the killers had simply disappeared on news of the victim's death. A great many of the violent deaths in Kano emirate were accidental, and these were usually forgiven. Most others lacked witnesses, or else the culprit had fled before he could be brought to court.

There was one case where clearly the plaintiffs expected the yamin al-qasama to be invoked, since two male agnates of the deceased appeared in court. This involved a woman from a prominent family in Kano city:

> There came to us Sarki Maiaduwa, of whom it is said that he killed his wife, Hafsa. We asked them for *wali al-damm* [executor of the blood-writ],

and the Sarkin Yaki Ibrahim, her father's brother was mentioned. We called him, with her mother, Hajja, and Muhammad, the son of her [Hafsa's] father's father's brother. We asked Ibrahim about the matter. He said that her husband, Maiaduwa hit her, and she died after six days. We asked, "Did you see the blow?" and he said "No," and that he had not heard [directly about it from Hafsa]. We asked her mother. She said that [Hafsa's] husband struck her. [Hafsa] came to [her mother] crying, and she asked her why, and she said that her husband had taken her bed and given it to his concubine, and that she had not agreed. Then he struck her with his hands on her side and neck and chest. [Having told her mother about this,] she went back to her husband's house for one night. Then she returned to her mother's. [Her mother] asked her why she came back. She said that the blows on her neck and side hurt her, and she died six days later. Maiaduwa denies the blow and the quarrel, and says she was sick from an attack of *jinn* [evil spirits] for twenty-four days at his house. We asked her mother for witnesses and none were found who saw the blow or heard from her mouth that her husband struck her with three blows, the first on her neck, the second on her side, the third on her chest. Thus we rule that there is nothing against the defendant, that is Maiaduwa. He is now set free and his path is cleared. When he explained his words to us previously, he had not said that she suffered from an attack of jinn, but rather that she was violently ill. Now when they come back to the line [of writing], he mentions that an attack of jinn was the cause of her sickness and all that evil.

And also the mother says, when she comes back to the line [about] the evidence of the concealment of the matter, that Hafsa, the dead woman, had adjured her by Allah and the Prophet not to complain against her husband Maiaduwa and to leave him, and that Allah would judge between them on the day of reckoning. Thus she did not inform anyone of the matter and thus it was not made known to the *wali al-damm*, and thus he did not see any way of intervening in it, due to the lack of hearing or presence (EKJC 54 A, 1 Dhu al-Hijja 1331).

Is this simply a matter of the council deferring to a man? There are clear indications that the council believed him guilty, but could not muster the legal arguments to prove him so. At the end, Maiaduwa was simply "set free" (*atlaq*) and "his path" was "cleared." The council neither exonerated (*bar'*) him nor cleared him of blame (*zakka*). Maiaduwa appears to have engaged in a clever legal maneuver in what seems to have been the second reading of the record, claiming that his wife had been suffering from an attack of *jinn* for twenty-four days — since well before the alleged argument and beating. This might have weakened the mother's report, or at least have been intended to do so.

Hafsa's mother's postscript to the record should be seen in light of the legal factors at work. Clearly the plaintiffs did expect the council to permit them to take the yamin al-qasama. The mother's report would have been expected to establish the grounds for grave presumption. The paternal uncle certainly knew that Hajja was prepared to relate what her daughter had said, and one can presume that she had indeed told him. But when the council released Maiaduwa, in spite of what seemed like overwhelming suspicion, Hajja had to cover for herself, and invent the story about her daughter's injunction to leave the matter to Allah. If that indeed had been Hafsa's wish, one could argue, she would not have told her mother about the beating, for it was common knowledge that the words of a dying person could be used to establish grave presumption in the court.

I have elaborated on this final case in order to underscore the importance of looking closely at legal procedure, and to demonstrate the subjective character of the decision to allow the taking of an oath of affirmation. One needs to see the pattern of yamin al-qasama cases in order to see that this case was expected to be one, and thus decipher the maneuvers that occur, and to evaluate the decision of the council. The council was certainly not indifferent to Hafsa's plight, but it did not have the certainty to invoke the oath. The councilors and the public did, after all, believe in jinns, and in their proclivity to affect women, even if they were skeptical of Maiaduwa's story. On the other hand, there was a widespread consensus, based on Islamic values, that the hungry had a right to food, and that a granary owner, above all when he was a food merchant living in the newly established settlement for Southern wage workers, Sabon Gari, had no right to stop a man from taking food let alone to have his toughs beat and mutilate him.

Conclusion

The early phase of British colonial rule in Kano, as seen through the judicial council records, did not bring new laws, but rather a new "time," a new political and economic context in which traditional authority, laws, and legal mechanisms had to operate. The most significant element of the new context was the railroad-based export economy, which contributed to the increased theft of goods. Famine came soon after the arrival of the railway, producing an upsurge of food theft.

The problem of theft was closely related to that of homicide, since a considerable proportion of intentional homicide cases were theft-related. Here it is important to understand how the council judged different sorts of theft, and to have an idea of what kinds of people were involved in theft. Housebreakers, I have suggested, were drawn from marginal groups — probably young, unmarried males, ex-slaves, criminal fugitives, and assorted social drop-outs and misfits. Not only were they widely disdained; they were also unlikely to have male agnates who would care to come before the council to claim blood compensation. Their character may help explain both the violence and the frequency of prison sentences.

Food thieves were quite a different matter. The taking of food, to begin with, was not considered a crime. Grain hoarders in this time of famine were scarcely likely to be popular figures. Thus when food thieves were beaten and died as a result, the emir was quite willing to cut through legal barriers and invoke the yamin al-qasama, or shared oath. Food thieves were likely to be "family men," and their act would not be regarded as dishonorable. Thus it was no problem to find the two male agnates required for the oath. Where public reprobation of the alleged killer was not so strong — as with the wife slayer — the council was more likely to hesitate from invoking the yamin al-qasama. Since the qasama oath could only be taken at the discretion of the council, it allowed for the weighing of such factors as the political influence of litigants, and public opinion on the case.

In the theft of goods, a roughly parallel situation arose. It involved not the killing of thieves, but rather the question of compensation by authorities for goods stolen. Here, there was no established device in shari'a law that would allow the council to assuage the grievances of traders. Thus it resorted to the emir's traditional authority to establish new rules under the rubric of hukm. The council intended the rule to apply only to big traders in Kano city, but could not justifiably announce this as a legal principle. At the same time, a procedural device was needed to validate claims for compensation. The oath of affirmation, which was analogous to the qasama oath in homicide cases, served both of these purposes. The oath eliminated the claims of poorer, less influential plaintiffs, who were reluctant to risk incurring divine or royal wrath by taking it, at the same time as it validated the claims of big traders. British authorities could not intervene to set new legal precedents of their own precisely because they did not have a means of validating claims, for they could neither order nor administer Islamic oaths. Conditions regarding when the oath could be taken eliminated the claims of most itinerant traders who had been robbed outside of Kano city.

While the council upheld the rights of wealthy traders within the overall economic order of the emirate, it also defended the rights of dominant members of the domestic order, the *masu gida* or household heads. They were, in effect, permitted to use violence in defense of their households against thieves; their deaths at the hands of granary owners were avenged; and they could escape punishment for violence against subordinate members of their households. By contrast, the floating population of ex-slaves and rootless youths and at least the less willful of itinerant small traders had at best precarious legal protection for their lives and goods; and so did a household head's wives and concubines. The power of the emir, then, may be seen as both supporting and resting on two different orders within society: the economic order dominated by big traders, and the domestic order controlled by household heads. It should be noted that the council made few decisions concerning the political order, except in the lower ranks of village heads, and these cases are so sparse in detail as to be difficult to exploit. Conflicts within the upper ranks of the office-holding elite were evidently not deemed fitting for such a public forum as the emir's judicial council.

NOTES

1. This register is held in the Kano Native Authority Series at the National Archives, Kaduna, Nigeria. Others remain at the emir's palace in Kano. The pages of the register are not numbered, and many cases are dated only by month or not at all. Case numbers referred to in the text are ones I have assigned to the cases.
2. In the 1920s and 1930s, as pressure built to have the Northern Nigeria court system subordinated directly to the Nigeria Supreme Court, British administrators in the north supported the idea of modernizing the emirate legal systems through the development of native authority "regulations" (Brooke 1952).
3. Walter Miller, an early missionary in northern Nigeria, refers to the Jakara, a stream which runs through Kano city, as a place where "for centuries criminals had their hands and feet cut off and finally their heads and their bodies thrown into the foul stagnant water" (Miller 1952:31). Adamu Fika reports that there were two prisons in Kano in the precolonial period. One, for the free-born, was run by the Sankurmi, the official in charge of Kasuwar Kurmi, Kano's principal market. This suggests that its' function was related to commercial conflicts, probably to debt problems—cases in which a person would be held in lieu of goods or money he or she owed someone else. The other prison, for slaves, was run by the *sarkin yari*, the head of the unmarried male slaves, and was adjacent to the residence of the *ma'ajin watari*, the emir's treasurer. Whether this was used for the discipline of recalcitrant slaves, or for some other purpose, is not clear (Fika 1978:36). Captain Abadie, who took part in the capture of Kano, reported that one of these prisons held up to 200 prisoners in extremely cramped conditions (Muffet 1964:99).
4. The terms *fatoma* and *zangoma* seldom appear in the records. Rather the term used is *rabb manzil*, a literal Arabic translation of the Hausa *mai gida*, master of the dwelling. I use the term fatoma here for the sake of convenience.
5. For a merchant in transit, to stay in a house would of course have increased his costs. Lodging in a commercial center was usually part of a business relationship, since the lodging house owner arranged commercial contacts for his clients. In transit, however, this aspect of the relationship was probably absent, hence there was little basis for shared interest. Traders themselves were sometimes suspected of theft or of having designs on the women of the house.
6. EKJC 46A, 17 Dhu al-Qa'da 1331; 28A, 8 Ramadan 1331; 34 B, Ramadan 1331; 13B, Rajib 1331; 153F, Ramadan 1332; 160 G, Shawwal 1332.

SOURCES

Archival

EKJC — Records of the Emir of Kano's Judicial Council, Jumada II 1331/May 1913 to Muharram 1333/November 1914. Kano Native Authority Series. Nigerian National Archives, Kaduna.

Published

Anderson, J. N. D. 1955. *Islamic law in Africa*. London: Frank Cass.

Brooke, Neville. 1952. *Report of the Native Courts (Northern Provinces) Commission*. Lagos: Government Printer.

Christelow, Allan. 1985. "Slavery in Kano, 1913–1914: Evidence from the judicial records." *African Economic History* 14: 57–74.

———. 1987. "Property and theft in Kano at the dawn of the groundnut boom, 1912–1914." *International Journal of African Historical Studies* 20:225–43.

———. 1988. "A fugitive institution: The strange disappearence of slavery in Northern Nigeria." Paper presented at The African Studies Association annual meeting, Chicago.

Cohen, Abner. 1969. *Custom and politics in urban Africa: A study of Hausa migrants in Yoruba towns*. Berkeley: University of California Press.

Dokaji, Alhaji Abubakar. 1958. *Kano ta Dabo Cigari* (The Kano of Dabo Cigari). Zaria: Northern Nigeria Publishing Company.

Fika, Adamu. 1978. *The Kano civil war and British overrule. 1862–1940*. Ibadan: Oxford University Press.

Geertz, Clifford. 1979. "Suq: The bazaar economy of Sefrou." In *Meaning and order in Moroccan society*. Clifford Geertz, Hildred Geertz, and Lawrence Rosen. Cambridge: Cambridge University Press.

Hogendorn, Jan. 1978. *Nigerian groundnut exports: Origins and early development*. Zaria: Ahmadu Bello University Press.

Hopen, C. Edward. 1958. *The pastoral Fulbe family in Gwandu*. Oxford: Oxford University Press.

Lovejoy, Paul. 1983. *Transformations in slavery: A history of slavery in Africa*. Cambridge: Cambridge University Press.

Miers, Suzanne, and Richard Roberts, eds. 1988. *The end of slavery in Africa*. Madison: University of Wisconsin Press.

Miller, Walter. 1952. *An autobiography*. Zaria: Gaskiya Press.

Muffet, D. J. M. 1964. *Concerning brave captains*. London: Andre Deutsch.

Paden, John. 1973. *Religion and political authority in Kano*. Berkeley: University of California Press.

Repp, Richard. 1988. "Qanun and shari'a in the Ottoman context." In *Islamic law: Social and historical contexts*. Aziz al-Azmeh, ed., London: Routledge.

Schacht, Joseph. 1964. *An introduction to Islamic law*. Oxford: Oxford University Press.

Smith, M. G. 1978. *The affairs of Daura: History and change in a Hausa state, 1800–1958*. Berkeley: University of California Press.

Tremearne, A. J. N. 1913. *Hausa superstitions and customs: Introduction to the folklore and the folk*. London: John Bale and Daniellson.

Watts, Michael. 1983. *A silent violence: Food, famine, and peasantry in Northern Nigeria*. Berkeley: University of California Press.

10

Law in African Borderlands: The Lived Experience of the Yoruba Astride the Nigeria-Dahomey Border

A. I. ASIWAJU

I

Borderlands—the lands and local communities lying in close proximity to, and directly affected by an international boundary—are well known for the peculiar problems posed for state control. Arising directly from their nature and character as bifurcated constituencies, border regions pose intractable problems primarily because they are ill adapted to the application of nationally determined laws (Furnish 1983; Carter 1978, 1980; and Asiwaju 1984b). In Africa, where the history of international boundaries is none other than the history of originally super-imposed European colonial borders, there are two immediate dimensions of conflict of law: (i) that between the precolonial system and the new order imposed by colonialism as such, and (ii) that between distinct Metropolitan traditions where, in West Africa and elsewhere, different European powers exercised control on different sides of the borders. The borderlands, especially of decentralized colonial state systems such as those in British controlled territories, also had to face the challenge of convergence and divergence between the demands of legis-lation by different levels of government—central, regional and local. To these general considerations must be added border specific regulations and procedures that govern the passage of persons, goods and services.

This paper discusses the experience of the Yoruba-speaking people who straddled the border between Nigeria and Dahomey (now Bénin) as an example of the several hundreds of other similarly partitioned African peoples (Asiwaju 1984b). It begins with a brief discussion of shared Yoruba law, and it goes on to examine the subsequent imposition of divergent legal systems based on French civil law on the one side of the border and the British common law on the other side. The emphasis is on the responses of Yoruba residents of the border areas during the colonial era to these legal changes. The paper discusses actors' movements between indigenous and colonial, and between French and British systems of authority. It looks at the problems posed and opportunities offered by the overlapping of indigenous and colonial, and of French and British legal systems, as the Yoruba inhabitants of the border regions struggled to cope with conflict and resolve their disputes with kin and outsiders.

In these accounts, emphasis is placed on the role of the border not only as a pole of attraction for those seeking asylum from one or the other of the opposing colonial regulatory systems, but also as a major challenge to nationally oriented law-enforcement agencies and procedures operating in the inherently internationalized localities along the border. The distance of the borderlands from the colonial (and later national) seats of government (Porto Novo in the case of French Dahomey and Lagos in the case of British Nigeria) gave its residents the advantage of relative autonomy, and it helped to convert conflicting national laws and procedures into locally workable processes.

Finally, advantage is taken of the Nigeria-Dahomey border as an Anglo-French configuration to attempt a generalization for a wider area of Africa where, as in West Africa, most intercolonial (now international) boundaries were lines of demarcation between divergent European metropolitan political, legal, and cultural traditions. The challenge posed to regional integration efforts and to law research in postcolonial Africa is then evaluated.

II

Before examining the Dahomey-Nigeria borderland as a laboratory for the study of colonial legal history, it is imperative to look briefly at the colonial situation (Asiwaju 1976a, 1986a). Two fundamentally important points emerge: (1) the Dahomey-Nigeria border was a purely colonial creation, and (2) in the precolonial period ethnic and political boundaries defined two interlocking social systems within which African community life was organized.

The 770-kilometer border from the Kwemẹ Beach near Badagry to the Nigeria-Bénin-Niger tripartite point on the Niger River has a typical coast-to-the-interior alignment that runs through changing climatic and vegetational zones. More significantly, the border divides not only the culture areas of the Yoruba and such closely related peoples as the Aja to the south and west and the Borgu to the north, but also the territories of specific sub-groups of these peoples that often corresponded to distinct precolonial states. This paper need only enumerate the major Yoruba sub-groups and states affected. They are easily divided into three main conglomerations. The northern-most of these includes the Ṣabẹ and the closely related Onko, Idesa, and Ibarapa dialectal communities in the area of present-day Kajọla, Ifedapo, and Ibarapa local government areas of Ọyọ State on the Nigerian side, and Ṣabẹ (rendered "Save" in French) rural district on the Bénin side. South of Ṣabẹ was Ketu, another historically renowned western Yoruba kingdom that stretched from the Wemẹ (Ouémé) River to the Ogun River (Parrinder 1967; Asiwaju 1970). Ketu embraced the present-day Ẹgbado North local government area of Ogun State in Nigeria and adjacent Ketu and Ipobe (rendered "Kétou" and "Pobé" in French) rural districts in Bénin. Over this area, the *Alaketu* of Ketu exercised either direct authority or widespread political and moral influence. The remainder of the Yoruba border region to the south is inhabited by the culturally and politically related communities of the Anago and Awori sub-groups of the Yoruba in modern-day Egbado South local government area of Ogun State in Nigeria and Ifọnyin and Itakete (rendered "Ifangni" and "Sakété" in French) rural districts in Bénin. The dominant precolonial state in this area was the Yoruba kingdom of Ifọnyin with the *Ẹlẹhin odo* as titular ruler. (Johnson 1973; Asiwaju 1970).

These conglomerations of Yoruba-speakers belonged to a large cultural complex of peoples that inhabited territory bounded by the Ouémé or Opara River to the west, the Niger River to the north and east, and the Atlantic Ocean to the south. The peoples of this whole area spoke dialects of the same language, and they practiced the same economy, based on peasant agriculture and trade. The ruling elites traced their origins to Ile-Ifẹ and regarded Oduduwa as a common culture hero. The autonomous kingdoms, centered on ancestral cities which served as the capitals, developed identical social and political institutions. Their inhabitants shared the same religion, philosophy, and values. More directly relevant to this essay, the western Yoruba sub-groups that came to be split by the Anglo-French colonial border between Nigeria and Dahomey were indisputably at one with the rest of the culture area on issues of indigenous law.

The first point to make about indigenous law is that, unlike later French and British impositions, it developed with society itself: the one blended and harmonized with the other so much that the history of law is the history of society as well. Produced by a non-literate culture, Yoruba law was and remains unwritten. Adewoye has observed that local law was "latent in the breasts of the community's ruling elite or of the court of remembrance, and was given expression only when...called for" (Adewoye 1977:3). Nevertheless, it was as much "a functional element" or "a means of practical action" as law in literate societies.

The purpose of Yoruba law has been aptly stated as "peace-keeping and the maintenance of the social equilibrium" (Adewoye 1977:3). Reconciliation of parties to a dispute was the ultimate objective of the judicial process. In striking contrast to the essentially adversarial or winner-takes-all perspective of the French inquisitorial or the British accusatorial systems, which were eventually imposed on the Yoruba, the primary goal of law in precolonial society was "to assuage injured feelings, to restore peace, to reach a compromise acceptable to both disputants" (p. 4). T. O. Elias, one of Africa's most prolific jurists, has noted that "parties to a suit left Yoruba courts neither puffed up nor cast down—for each a crumb of right, for neither of them the whole loaf" (quoted on p. 4). Because of the adherence to the principle of conciliation, the practice of restitution was greatly stressed. Except for willful murder, which was invariably punished by death, most other offenses were settled on the principle of restitution.

Precolonial Yoruba society was a corporate entity, and law was viewed in holistic terms. The principles of separation of powers, central to modern French and British law and government, had no place in Yorubaland. The kings (*ǫba*) and councils of title holders constituted the highest authorities and combined both executive and judicial functions. Since the emphasis was on the community as a corporate entity, the administration of law was directed as much to the offender's lineage as to the offender himself. Families took collective responsibility for the conduct of their members. The obligation of restitution, for example, often involved the entire lineage of the individual offender.

Indigenous religion greatly influenced Yoruba legal theory and practice. Faith in departed ancestors as guardians and supervisors of the affairs of society helped ensure fairness on the part of ruling elites. Oaths were taken seriously because they were based on rites and rituals that involved invocation of supernatural forces believed to be capable of retribution. Police duties, both to apprehend and punish criminals, were vested in essentially religious bodies, notably the Oro cult. Ritual experts administered various types of ordeals.

III

Legal differences began to develop in western Yorubaland when the area was partitioned by France and Britain. In the era of informal empire the colonial governments of Porto Novo and Lagos recognized and enforced a border between their respective spheres of influence (Newbury 1961; Aderibigbe 1959). The Anglo-French agreements of 10 August 1889 and 14 June 1898 formally defined the boundary between Dahomey and Nigeria from the coast to the Niger River, and successive boundary commissions between 1895 and 1960 attempted to survey and demarcate it (Brownlie 1979; Mondjannagni 1964; Abiodun 1983). To date, the work remains incomplete and unsatisfactory (Asiwaju 1988c).

The Dahomey-Nigeria border is physically invisible for almost its entire course, owing to the absence of demarcation and the blurring effects of local geography and ethnography. For this reason, it is sometimes argued that an international boundary does not exist in the area. Nothing could be further from the truth. No sooner does one cross from Nigeria into Benin or vice-versa than one encounters an unmistakably different official culture, which makes it quite clear that a border has been crossed. Signposts, uniforms, language, and orthography are all very different, as are town planning, architecture, and vehicles. *Gendarmes* comport themselves quite differently than policemen. These symbols make apparent that the reality of an international boundary, as a line of demarcation between sovereign jurisdictions, is less a function of its visibility on the ground than of the effectiveness of the administration on either side.

The British and French colonial administrations lost no time ensuring the functional reality of their border. Their initial understanding was not to make a barrier of the Dahomey-Nigeria boundary. The 1889 agreement guaranteed freedom of trade for all European nationals and freedom of movement for African peoples. However, subsequent agreements, the product of traditional Anglo-French rivalry, imposed protective tariffs and quickly a mercantile border-maintenance culture developed. The rapid creation of rival customs and immigration services and the establishment of control posts along the border contradicted the earlier guarantees of freedom of movement for partitioned peoples (Udochu 1987; Dioka 1987; Ajayi 1986; Mondjannagni, 1964).

IV

It is no longer seriously disputed that the Yoruba on the different sides of the Nigeria-Dahomey colonial boundary experienced very different systems of colonial control (Asiwaju 1970, 1976a, 1976b, 1984a, 1984b). In spite of the similarity in their overall objectives, French and British colonialism differed substantially in method, content, and impact. The purpose of the present essay is to explore differences in French and British colonial law, a subject overlooked in most comparative studies of the two systems of colonial rule.

Before beginning the comparison, it is helpful to remember Lord Hailey's observation that "colonial policy...projected into overseas areas...certain domestic characteristics and philosophies of life (Hailey 1938:542). William B. Cohen restated the point when he asserted that both France and Britain "attempted to establish overseas an administrative pattern similar to that existing in their homelands" (Cohen 1971, Chapter V). Members of the French and British colonial services were products of their respective metropolitan cultures. Training programs at Oxford and Cambridge for the British and at the *Ecole Coloniale* in Paris for the French might teach the value of allowing for local conditions when administering in the colonies, but once in Africa, French and British officials tended to fall back on the institutions and practices that they knew best. For the Yoruba on opposite sides of the Nigeria-Dahomey border, this led to a fundamental divergence in systems of law and government. In both colonies, law was the "handmaiden of colonialism," as Adewoye has argued. However, the character and role of the servant differed substantially from the French to the British side. The great advantage of examining law in a borderland is that it throws the characteristics of the two systems into unusually bold relief (Asiwaju 1976a; Asiwaju 1983; Stoddard 1982).

Before focusing on the differences, it is useful to highlight the similarities in the French and British colonial legal systems encountered by Yoruba on different sides of the border. Both colonial powers abrogated the sovereignty of the indigenous precolonial states, which undermined the political and legal autonomy of the local rulers. Inter and intracolonial boundaries divided the territories and jurisdictions of such kingdoms as Sabe, Ketu, and Ifonyin. The *Onisabe* of Sabe, the Alaketu of Ketu, and the Elehin Odo of Ifonyin, the leading Western Yoruba potentates of precolonial times, found themselves on the French side of the border and the bulk of their subjects on the British side. These three rulers did not exercise colonially sanctioned authority over most of the inhabitants of their kingdoms. Unable to deal with the obas of the indigenous states but eager to govern through local authorities, the British appointed formerly dependent chiefs rulers. These new men took advantage of the situation to increase their power. The rise of Western-educated elites in Dahomey and Nigeria sealed the fate of the precolonial rulers. On the French side, the position of the oba suffered near-total eclipse as an institution (Asiwaju 1970 and 1976a: Ch. 4).

The objectives of Yoruba customary law underwent a revolutionary change in both Nigeria and Dahomey. In the context of European rule, law did not serve as a means of arriving at social equilibrium, as in the precolonial period. Gone was the conciliatory focus of local law, replaced by the adversarial tradition of both French civil law and British common law. In sharp contrast to the situation in the precolonial period, when parties to a suit would leave the court "nor puffed up nor cast down," the winner took all under the French and British colonial systems. Yoruba on both sides of the border expressed their clear awareness of the change in a new proverb to the effect that parties to a suit in a European court did not return as friends. Finally, both the French and British declared the role of chiefs and ordeals in law to be repugnant and tried to abolish it.

V

Against this general background, it is now possible to examine more specifically the French and British colonial legal systems. Latin-based civil law and Anglo-Saxon common law differ fundamentally. In a brilliant lecture delivered at the University of Lagos in March 1966, Kwame T. Opoku outlined the differences as they were manifested in the geographically contiguous Francophone and Anglophone countries of West Africa (Opoku 1967).

Civil law is derived primarily, if not solely, from statutes and doctrines, prior court decisions being an exception to this general rule only in situations where they point to "*jurisdiction constantes*". Common law, on the other hand, is based primarily on the decisions of earlier courts with statutes playing a secondary role. Civil law rests on well defined codes which date back to the nineteenth century; common law on much earlier decisions of the Chancery and of the royal courts at Westminster.

The style of operation in the two systems also differs substantially. While in civil law the inquisitional model prevails, the accused presumed guilty until proved innocent; in common law, the accusatorial mode predominates: the accused is presumed innocent until proved guilty. Both systems are procedure-oriented, but civil law is far less dilatory and far less protracted (critics would say less thorough) than the common law. The format of judgment in the one situation is characteristically terse and precise; in the other, it is personal and extensive with little or no demand for brevity and compromise. While judges in French courts generally remain anonymous, this is not the case in English courts. Since the statute is the primary source of the civil law, the appointment of a judge is based on proven knowledge of the legal codes garnered from university study. It is therefore quite usual to recruit judges directly from among professors of law faculties. Under the procedure-oriented English common law, professional lawyers with substantial experience at the Bar are appointed to the bench. Until relatively recently, university-level training was unnecessary.

Two such clearly dissimilar bodies of law could not but have different effects on colonized peoples. This point emerges with real force in situations such as that on the Nigeria-Dahomey border where a single African people was subjected to both legal traditions. The French introduced three legal sub-systems: the *statut civil français*; *statut personnel*, and *côde d'indigénat*. While the *statut civil français* (based on French metropolitan laws for the benefit of French citizens and African "assimilés") and the statut personnel (based on indigenous law for the benefit of African subject peoples) operated through systems of regular courts, the côde d'indigénat (everywhere the most dominant for both the subject peoples and colonial rulers) empowered colonial administrators to impose penal sanctions for a wide range of mostly political infractions without recourse to any of the regular courts of law.

Discussion of the impact of French colonial law on the Yoruba, as on other subject populations, must cover both the statut civil français and the statut personnel. The Yoruba of Dahomey had the legal status of subjects, not citizens, but provisions of the statut civil sometimes applied to them even so. French law, as Opoku has argued, was the general law of the state, whether in France or the colonies (Opoku 1967). All other laws, including African customary law, were treated as subordinate. French law was the choice wherever and whenever customary law conflicted with it. French law also applied when (1) French citizens were involved in a legal transaction; (2) parties to a dispute who were of statut personnel elected statut civil; (3) customary law proved inadequate, as in claims relative to insurance law; or (4) customary law ran atoul of *ordre public*, translated in ordinary language as "French civilization," or *ordre public colonial*, which referred to rules and legislation aimed at fulfilling France's *mission civilisatrice*. The statut personnel operated under the overarching influence of the assimilationist statut civil français.

In the Yoruba communities on the French side of the Nigeria-Dahomey border — as elsewhere in France's African empire outside the Four Communes of Dakar, Rufisque, Gorée, and St. Louis, where French metropolitan law applied — the statut personnel was administered within the framework of *justice indigène* (Chabas 1954). Introduced in French West Africa by a decree of 1903, justice indigène created a system of local-level courts presided over by a European administrator (*the commandant du cercle* or *chef de subdivision*, as the case might be), assisted by two indigenous assessors. These courts exercised full civil and criminal jurisdiction, subject to the statutory control of the attorney-general of the specific colonial territory and the Chambre d'Homologation in Dakar. Justice indigène paid no regard to Yoruba political or legal institutions that survived below the colonial superstructure and continued to exercise palpable moral and legal authority outside officially recognized institutional frameworks.

The French justice indigène was far less important both to the colonial administration and the local subject populations than the much older, more established, and more dominant côde d'indigénat (Asiwaju 1977, 1979; Aissi 1978). Based on a decree dated 30 September 1887 and described in relevant official documentation as *sanctions de police administrative*, the indigénat derived from the French criminal code, which gave colonial administrators the power to impose on subjects, as distinct from citizens and "assimilés," summary penalties without reference to any court of law, whether French or customary. While local administrators could impose fines on individual offenders, governors of territories had the power in situations of grave crisis to impose communal fines and pronounce sentences of deportation and banishment. The essence of the code was to punish very swiftly a wide range of offenses, mostly political and administrative in nature, which could threaten French authority or obstruct colonial public order.

I have discussed the code in considerable detail in a separate study (Asiwaju 1979b) and will confine myself here to mention of its most salient characteristics. In spite of its summary nature, the indigénat was not an arbitrary regime. It was founded on the same type of statutes as formed the basis for the statut civil and statut personnel and, with them, it comprised a unitary legal system (Asiwaju 1979). The connections between the indigénat and the two statutes were especially clear vis-a-vis justice indigène: the local European officer administered the three and prisoners committed by each method served their terms in the same local gaols. Although the indigénat co-existed with other French colonial legal procedures, it was by far the most dominant. The *sanctions simples de police administrative* were used far more than other judicial procedures to enforce demands for taxes, labor, and conscription — the cornerstone of the French ordre public colonial. The indigénat made French rule extraordinarily oppressive. This oppression stemmed from both the summary way that the code was applied and the nature of the obligations that it was used to impose.

French legal writers have neglected the indigénat, probably owing to the official view that it was a temporary measure that would be eliminated ultimately once subject peoples developed to the point that they were ready for other forms of justice. Rather than decline, however, as France's West African colonies evolved, the indigénat was applied with increasing vigor, to the neglect of the alternative modes, particularly justice indigène. By the time the code was abolished in 1946, it had become so deeply entrenched that its impact continued to be felt.

VI

Development of colonial laws and courts in British Yorubaland began with the annexation of Lagos in 1861. Following the amalgamation of Northern and Southern Nigeria in 1914, a legal system was created that remained more or less the same until independence, despite subsequent reforms (Adewoye 1977). The British system, like the French, rested on multiple bodies of law and a distinct hierarchy of courts. However, this basic resemblance should not obscure the fundamental differences in form and content between the two. The highest legal authority in British Nigeria was the Supreme Court, based in Lagos. A functionally equivalent court, based in Dakar, was established for French West Africa in 1904. The Nigerian Supreme Court administered the doctrines of equity, British common law, and statutes of general application in force in England on 1 January 1900. It exercised appellate jurisdiction over lower courts in cases tried under either common law or customary law. Originally restricted to Lagos, jurisdiction of the Supreme Court in Nigeria was gradually extended to other urban centers along the coast, owing to the presence of substantial numbers of Europeans in these communities.

Immediately below the Supreme Court were the provincial courts, which had two express purposes. The first was to complement the powers of the political officers who administered them. The second, in the words of Sir Frederick Lugard, chief architect of the amalgamation, was to curb the tendency for "useless litigation without good results" that characterized the Supreme Court. Political officers were encouraged to hasten the judicial process in the provincial courts by not being overly concerned with "technicalities of law or procedure," consistent with the "requirements of native administration in its simplicity, cheapness and rapidity" (Adewoye 1977:139).

Tribunals similar to the provincial courts operated throughout most of French West Africa (Sarr, Ch. 5), except in the Four Communes of Senegal and in the territorial capitals and coastal cities designated as "mixed communes," where the presence of a substantial number of Europeans and African "assimiliés" justified the application of the statut civil français. European officials responsible for administering particular provinces presided over the French courts, just as British officials did over the provincial courts. In rendering their judgments, officials in British Nigeria or French Dahomey could apply as they saw fit either the metropolitan law or customary law (Asiwaju 1977, 1979b; and Chabas 1954).

At the lowest level of the judicial system of Nigeria were the so-called *native courts*. These tribunals touched most directly the non-literate and primarily rural African masses. The origins of the native courts stretched back to the Native Advisory Councils of the late nineteenth century. However, the courts took lasting form following the administrative reorganization of 1914 which divided them into four grades — A, B, C, and D — and replaced European administrators with traditional African rulers as the presiding judges.

Grade A native courts were reserved for "paramount chiefs": rulers of large centralized states such as Ọyọ, Abeokuta, and Ijẹbu Ode, whose territories consituted major colonial administrative units. In the less highly centralized societies of western and eastern Yorubaland, Grade B and C courts predominated (Asiwaju 1970, 1976; Akintoye 1970). These courts were presided over by traditional African rulers whom British officials had designated as "Native Authorities." Grade D courts operated at the village level and were staffed by village or ward heads, also recognized by the British. While appeals from the two lower grades of the native court system could be made to the A or B levels, all four grades were subject to review by the provincial courts.

Ilaro (later Egbado) Division of Abeokuta Province, located immediately to the east of the Nigeria-Dahomey border, lacked a traditionally accepted paramount ruler. Here the British colonial government created twelve administrative districts, each headed by a chief designated as the local "native authority." These officially recognized "native authorities" presided over Grade C courts. All twelve district native authorities constituted the divisional native authority and formed a Grade B court. The operation of the native courts in Ilaro Division greatly enhanced the power and prestige of the Yoruba rulers on the British side of the border. On the French side, where similar institutions did not exist, the power of the indigenous rulers declined (Asiwaju 1976a).

The functioning of the three tiers of the legal system of British Nigeria, established as a result of the administrative reorganization of 1914, received frequent criticism during the colonial era. Critics focused on the excessive politicization of judicial processes, the wide-spread corruption of Native Courts, the complete exclusion of European litigants from provincial courts, and the severe limitations on processes of appeal and legal representation. The significant point for the purposes of this essay is that these and other criticisms of the Nigerian legal system have been advanced without benefit of insights derived from comparative study of other colonial legal systems, most particularly the French West African.

In addition to being subject to the laws and law enforcement procedures of general application throughout Nigeria or Dahomey, Yoruba residing astride the border demarcating the British and the French colonial states were affected by border-specific laws and enforcement procedures. Restricted in the early colonial period to matters affecting customs and excise, these gradually proliferated until they encompassed immigration, health, agriculture, and security as well. Whatever their purview, these border laws were formulated by distant central authorities without consideration of their implications for border communities.

VII

Along the Nigeria-Dahomey border, the French and British colonial legal systems intersected and overlapped. The two may have had similar ultimate objectives and institutional frameworks, but they were experienced very differently by the local population. Yoruba living astride the border were sensitive to the complexities of their legal world, and they developed strategies to ignore, accommodate, and exploit French and British laws and courts as well as border-specific regulations. A brief look at some common strategies will illuminate both the legal perceptions and responses of Yoruba borderlanders.

Borderland Yoruba completely ignored French and British laws and courts when issues of land tenure, matrimony, and inheritance affected persons on both sides of the border. When such matters arose, claims and disputes were settled in accordance with customary law without any reference to colonial laws and courts. With regard to land tenure, for example, it was not uncommon for elders or other Yoruba authorities capable of judging a dispute to live on one side of the border while the land and disputants in question lay on the other side. Elders also supervised customary rituals — marriage, naming ceremonies, and funerals of lineage members — without paying heed to the border separating kin.

Borderland Yoruba pursued a strategy of accommodation in situations where conflicts arose between the interests of the local peoples and the laws of the colonial governments promulgated to maintain the border. Specific examples include all forms of customs and immigration regulations. It has been observed among border communities elsewhere that conflicts between the will and interest of the state and those of a borderland constituency are frequently resolved in favor of the latter (Furnish 1985). Accommodation enabled borderland Yoruba to soften somewhat the impact of border-specific laws that ran contrary to Yoruba aspirations. This strategy enabled local people to achieve a measure of autonomy, because it won them the sympathy of customs and immigration personnel responsible for enforcing border regulations.

The third strategy used by borderland Yoruba — the exploitation of their geographic position — reflected an awareness of the asylum value of the Nigeria-Dahomey border (Asiwaju 1976a). Proximity to a foreign jurisdiction facilitated quick escape not only for criminals but also for political protestors. During the colonial period, Yoruba often "voted with their feet." This was particularly the case with Yoruba residing in French Dahomey. That Yoruba perceived French rule to be harsher than that of the British is demonstrated by the massive movement of entire Yoruba settlements from French Dahomey into British Nigeria (Asiwaju 1976a: Chs. 5–6). Emigration was clearly a response to the more onerous impositions of French colonial rule: excessive taxation, forced labor, and compulsory conscription. It was also a response to the authoritarianism engendered by rigid French adherence to the indigénat (Asiwaju 1976b).

VIII

The three strategies adopted by Yoruba to handle the problems posed by their borderland legal situation point to certain policy options for postcolonial Africa. The strategy of ignoring the legal impositions of colonial rule draws attention to the persistence and survival of customary law throughout the colonial period into independence (Ajayi 1988). It is necessary to study further the contemporary domain of informal but effective customary legal sanctions with a view toward formalization of customary legal tenets.

There are precedents for the formalization of customary law, especially in regard to disputes occurring across borders. S. W. Boggs, in his examination of litigation between inhabitants of the Sudan and the Belgian Congo (today's Zaïre) during the early years of the colonial period, wrote:

A boundary court for the settlement of disputes between litigants from the Sudan and the Belgian Congo has continued to hold successful periodic sessions...arranged jointly by the District Commissioner of Yei (Sudan) and the Administrateur of Faradje (Congo)...(Boggs 1940:173).

A. C. McEwen describes similar frontier tribunals operating along the boundaries of Ruanda and Burundi in relation to Uganda and Tanzania. According to McEwen:

These tribunals, composed of chiefs of tribes living on opposite sides of the border, settled disputes concerning the ownership of cattle and other livestock that strayed or were carried across the line. They also decided matters relating to customary family law, such as marriage, and the handing over or restitution, of dowries. Although it was alleged...that the tribunals did not function as courts in a strict (i.e., European) sense since they had neither an authority granted by the territorial government nor the power to impose penalties, it appears that their decisions were regarded as binding by customary law and were invariably heeded by the litigants. Occasionally, the tribunals would perform an extraordinary function by returning refugees to the appropriate administrative territory. The system appears to operate successfully mainly owing to the fact that the imposition of arbitrary boundaries means that in many cases the applicable customary law on each side of the frontier, in the particular areas concerned, was similar, if not identical (McEwen 1971:40–41).

As the above examples illustrate, the experience of Yoruba along the Nigeria-Dahomey border is by no means unique. The existence of identical culture areas on both side of an international border offers possibilities for regional integration, cooperation and official recognition of the customary laws that comprise a major facet of the cultural linkages binding peoples in spite of their being divided by a border. Customary law could thus serve as an instrument for the promotion of trans-border cooperation.

The chances for trans-border cooperation based on the shared customary law of identical ethnic communities residing on either side of an international boundary are particularly bright on the African continent, where the concept of the nation-state is still inchoate and where trans-border ethnic, cultural and socioeconomic affinities remain powerful. One specific reform that merits consideration is the possibility of permitting border communities to serve as mediators of relations between geographically contiguous nation-states. Putting this reform into effect, however, would require radical structural adjustment of the laws imposed under colonialism, for these were originally created in order to maintain intercolony boundaries as barriers to, not as bridges for the free flow of people, ideas, goods, and services.

There is an urgent need for further systematic study of border regions by experts in African law. Without such study, efforts at regional integration will ultimately be frustrated by conflicts engendered by the laws African nations have inherited from their colonial past. Along borders which divide Anglophone from Francophone West African countries, the existence of a shared corpus of customary laws linking peoples across international boundaries is particularly valuable, given the operation at the national level of inherently irreconcilable legal systems based on English common law on the one side and French civil law on the other.

SOURCES

Abiodun, T. A. 1983. "Demarcation and survey of Nigeria's frontiers: An aspect of national security." Paper presented at the XVIII Annual Conference of the Nigerian Institution of Surveyors.

Aderibigbe, A. B. 1959. "The expansion of the Lagos Protectorate frontier, 1863–1900." Ph.D. dissertation, University of London.

Adewoye, Omoniyi. 1977. *The judicial system in southern Nigeria, 1854–1954.* London: Longman.

Aissi, A. 1978. "La justice et la vie Congolaise." Doctorat de 3ème cycle, Toulouse.

Ajayi, J. F. A. 1988. "Resilience of African institutions and cultures." In *African unity: The cultural foundations,* ed. A. I. Asiwaju and B. O. Oloruntimehin. Lagos: Centre for Black and African Arts and Civilisation.

Ajayi, Samuel Adelakun. 1986. *The true customs-man: An outline history of Nigeria's Department of Customs and Excise.* Lagos: Delly-Lead.

Ajomo, M. A. 1989. "The legal perspectives." In *Borderlands in Africa: A multi-disciplinary and comparative focus on Nigeria and West Africa.* ed. A. I. Asiwaju and P. O. Adeniyi. Lagos: University of Lagos Press.

Akintoye, S. A. 1970. "*Ọbas* of the Ekiti Confederacy since the advent of the British." In *West African chiefs*: their changing status under colonial rule and independence. ed. Michael Crowder and Obaro Ikime, 255–70. Ife: University of Ife Press.

Asiwaju, A. I. 1970. "The Alaketu of Ketu and the Onimeko of Meko: The changing status of two Yoruba rulers under French and British rule." In *West African chiefs: Their changing status under colonial rule and independence,* ed. M. Crowder and O. Ikime. 134–61. Ife: University of Ife Press.

———. 1973. "A note on the history of Ṣabẹ." *Lagos Notes and Records,* 17–29.

———. 1974. "Anti-French resistance movement in Ọhọri-Ije (Dahomey), 1895–1960." *Journal of the Historical Society of Nigeria* 8(2):255–70.

———. 1975a. "Formal education in western Yorubaland, 1889–1945: A comparison of the French and British colonial systems." *Comparative Education Review* 19(3):434–50.

———. 1975b. "The colonial education heritage and the problem of nation-building in Dahomey." *Bulletin de l'IFAN* 37(2):340–57.

———. 1976a. *Western Yorubaland under European rule, 1889–1945: A comparative analysis of French and British colonialism.* London: Longman.

———. 1976b. "Migration as revolt: The example of the Ivory Coast and the Upper Volta before 1945." *Journal of African History* 18(4):577–94.

———. 1978. "The socio-economic integration of the West African sub-region in the historical context: Focus on the colonial period." *Bulletin de l'IFAN* 40(1):160–78.

———. 1979a. "The Aja-speaking peoples in Nigeria: A note on their origin, settlement and cultural adaptation up to 1945." *Africa* 49(1):15–28.

———. 1979b. "Control through coercion: A study of the indigénat regime in French West African administration, 1887–1946." *Bulletin de l'IFAN* 41(1):35–75.

————. 1983. *Borderlands research: Comparative perspectives*. Border Perspective Monograph Series No. 6. El Paso: Center for Inter-American and Border Studies, The University of Texas at El Paso.

————. 1984a. *Partitioned Africans: Ethnic relations across Africa's international boundaries, 1884–1984*. London: C. Hurst.

————. 1984b. *Artificial boundaries*. Inaugural lecture series. Lagos: University of Lagos.

————. 1984c. Towards an ethnohistory of African state boundaries. In *The methodology of contemporary African history*, 91–110. Paris: UNESCO.

————. 1985. *Border impact: Notes on a comparative study of the Nigeria, U.S.-Mexico and Western European international boundaries*. End-of-research project report. Lagos: University of Lagos.

————. 1986a. "Problem-solving along African borders: The Nigeria-Benin case since 1889." In *Across boundaries: Transborder interaction in comparative perspective*, ed. O. J. Martinez, 159–90. El Paso: Texas Western Press.

————. 1986b. "Borderlands as regions: Lessons of the European transboundary planning experience for international economic integration efforts in Africa." In *Towards an African economic community: Lessons of the experience from ECOWAS*, ed. A. A. Owosekun. Ibadan: Nigerian Institute of Social and Economic Research.

————. 1986c. "Report on the Nigeria-Benin border up to Kwara State: A comparative history and policy analysis." A contribution to the research project on Nigeria's border defense and security. Kuru: National Institute.

Bertho, J. 1949. "La parenté des Yoruba aux peuplades du Dahomey et du Togo." *Africa* 19:121–32.

Boggs, Samuel Whitmore. 1940. *International boundaries: A study of boundary functions*. New York: Columbia University Press.

Brownlie, Ian. 1979. *African international boundaries: A legal and diplomatic encyclopedia*. London: C. Hurst.

Carter, Marshall. 1978. "Law-enforcement and federalism: Bordering on trouble." *Policy Studies Journal* 7(5):413–18.

————. 1980. "Agency fragmentation and its effects on impact: A borderlands case." *Policy Studies Journal* 8(6):862–70.

Chabas, J. 1954. "La justice indigène en Afrique Occidentale Française." *Annales Africaines*.

Cohen, William B. 1971. *Rulers of empire: The French colonial service in Africa*. Stanford: Hoover Institution.

Crowder, Michael. 1964. "Indirect rule: French and British styles." *Africa* 34:197–205.

Deschamps, H. 1963. "Et maintenant, Lord Lugard?" *Africa* 33:293–306.

Dioka, L. 1987. "Badagry since 1841: Urbanisation in a Nigerian border region." M. Phil. thesis, University of Lagos.

Eguntola, J. A. 1984. "Ifonyin and Ifonyintendo: A case history of Yoruba twin towns on the Nigeria-Benin border." B. A. History Original Essay, University of Lagos.

Elias, Taslim O. 1958. *The impact of English law on Nigerian customary law*. Lagos: Ministry of Education.

Fadipe, N. 1978. *The sociology of the Yoruba*. Ibadan: Ibadan University Press.

Forde, Cyril Daryll. 1951. *The Yoruba-speaking peoples of south-western Nigeria*. London: International African Institute.

Furnish, D. B. 1985. "Border laws and other artificial constraints." In *Rules of the game and games without rules in border life. Symposium of Mexican and United States Universities, 23–25 Oct. 1983, Tijuana, Baja California, Mexico*, ed. M. Miranda and J. W. Wilkie, 73–95. Tijuana: Anvies.

Gann, Lewis, and Duignan, Peter. 1979. *African proconsuls*. New York: Free Press.

Hailey, Lord. 1938. *An African survey* Oxford: Oxford University Press.

Heussler, Robert. 1963. *Yesterday's rulers: The making of the British colonial service.* Syracuse: Syracuse University.

Igue, Ogunsola J. P. 1983. "L'Officiel, la parallèle et le clandestin: Commerce et intégration en Afrique de l'Ouest." *Politique Africaine* 9:29–51.

Johnson, Samuel. 1973. *The history of the Yoruba.* Lagos: C.M.S. Bookshop.

Kouassigan, Guy A. 1974. *Quelle est ma loi? Tradition et modernisme dans le droit privé de la famille en Afrique noire francophone.* Paris: A Pedone.

Lloyd, Peter C. 1954. "The traditional political system of the Yoruba." *South-western Journal of Anthropology* 10(4):366–84.

———. 1962. *Yoruba land law.* Oxford: Oxford University Press.

Martinez, Oscar J. 1985. "Commentary on Milton H. Jamail, De Facto rules along the United States-Mexican border, and Jorge A. Bustamantes, La migracion Mexicana a Estados Unidos: Reglas de facto." In *Rules of the game and games without rules in border life. Symposium of Mexican and United States Universities, 23–25 Oct. 1983, Tijuana, Baja California, Mexico,* ed. M. Miranda and J. W. Wilkie. Tijuana: Anvies.

McEwen, A. C. 1971. *The international boundaries of East Africa.* Oxford: Oxford University Press.

Mondjannagni, Alfred. 1964. "Quelques aspects historiques, économiques et politiques de la frontier Nigeria-Dahomey." *Etudes dahoméenes,* n.s., 2:51–63.

Moulero, T. 1964. "Histoire et légendes de chabe." *Etudes Dahoméenes* 2:51–63.

Newbury, C. W. 1961. *The western slave coast and its rulers.* Oxford: Oxford University Press.

Opoku, K. T. 1967. "Our civil law neighbours." *University of Ghana Law Journal* 4(1):40–53.

———. 1970. "L'évolution du droit traditionnel dans les pays francophone et anglophones de l'Afrique occidentale." Thesis, Doctorat en droit, Aix-Marseille.

———. 1974. "Traditional law under French colonial rule." In *Verfassung und recht in Ubersee* 7:139–53.

Parrinder, Edward G. 1947. "The Yoruba-speaking people in Dahomey." *Africa* 17(2):122–28.

———. 1967. *The Story of Ketu.* Ibadan: Ibadan University Press.

Prescott, John R. V. 1971. *The evolution of Nigeria's international and regional boundaries, 1861–1961.* Vancouver: Tantalus Research.

Solanke, L. 1931. *The Egba-Yoruba constitutional law and its historical development.* Abeokuta.

———. 1932. "Yoruba (or Aku) constitutional law and its historical development." *West African Students Union Journal* 9.

Stoddard, E. 1982. "Local and regional incongruities in binational diplomacy: Policy for the U.S.-Mexico border." *Policy Perspective Journal* 2(1).

Udochu, K. A. K. 1987. "A History of customs administration in Southern Nigeria, 1861–1960" M.A. history dissertation, Nigeria: University of Lagos.

11

"A Case for the Basoga": Lloyd Fallers and the Construction of an African Legal System

DAVID WILLIAM COHEN

In 1969, Lloyd A. Fallers published his *Law Without Precedent: Legal Ideas in Action in the Courts of Colonial Busoga*, based on fieldwork in Uganda between 1950 and 1953. In introducing his work, Fallers located his study of law in Busoga in a broad, comparative tradition of studies of "the historically recurrent phenomenon to which the term 'customary law' has usually been attached" (Fallers 1969:3). Seeking to free his inquiry of African law from a notion of a natural jural order, Fallers defined customary law generally, and particularly in respect to Busoga, as

> not so much a kind of law as a kind of legal situation which develops in imperial or quasi-imperial contexts, contexts in which dominant legal systems recognize and support the local law of politically subordinate communities...customary law is folk law in the process of reception (Fallers 1969:3).

Fallers's method in *Law Without Precedent* was to apply a case method to the study of the courts of colonial Busoga. He ordered a large number of case records into a series of fields of civil litigation: marriage, divorce, and adultery; landholding; inheritance and succession; and tenancy.[1] Focusing on these fields, Fallers examined the social wells of litigation in Busoga, the nature of argumentation, the work of the courts in fact-finding and recording witnesses, and the patterns of decision, resolution, and appeal. His definitive achievement lies probably not so much in his larger interest in the "process of reception" of local concepts and practices of law by a dominant colonial legal system but rather in detailing "the courtroom encounter" through the recording, presentation, and analysis of a group of distinctive cases which he read or observed during his field work in Busoga.

Fallers began his research in Busoga at a time when the relations between chiefs and local officials of the Protectorate were generally cordial and constructive. The Busoga chiefs had been effective in the immediate post-war period in squelching economic unrest among peasant farmers and laborers; the Europeans in the Protectorate service held an informed and positive view of the capabilities of African chiefs. On both sides, greater training and experience were reflected in the work of the Protectorate civil service, both African and European. Fallers was in Busoga at a time when African chiefs were toning down their rhetoric, and their rhetorical claims to domination, as a way of establishing stronger associations with those groups actively opposing colonial rule.

This particular, and short-lived, context may be part of an explanation of Fallers's construction of a harmonic world in Busoga in the early 1950s. But there is certainly a larger context for Fallers's work, and this is in his formation as a scholar. In a 1973 essay, Fallers reflected on his training under Marion J. Levy, Edward Shils, and William Lloyd Warner at the University of Chicago, and of the catharsis experienced in the field in Busoga in the early 1950s when he discovered that what he had learned about classes and strata did not work. Instead, Max Weber was encountered:

> one of the first things I discovered was that in the African kingdoms the hierarchy of chiefs, despite their great wealth and authority vis-à-vis their people, and despite the elaborate deference granted them, was very fluid. Except for the kings and a few princes, most persons in authority were "socially mobile": they were not in hereditary positions but instead were appointed by rulers on the basis of ability and personal loyalty. I had read Max Weber and I thought: Aha! I had found "patrimonial authority" in the flesh (Fallers 1973:4).

In his subsequent work on Busoga (*Bantu Bureaucracy*, [1956]) and also on Buganda (*The King's Men*, 1964), Fallers was concerned to demonstrate the ways in which status and wealth differentiation were mediated and a working polity organized through such mediation. In *Bantu Bureaucracy*, Fallers sought to show how chiefs mediated the tensions that surrounded and defined their multiple responsibilities — to their administrative overseers, to their kin, and to their clients and subjects.

Beyond this, Fallers sought to evaluate how these new political roles and practices, shaped through the mediation of tensions and conflicts, were being integrated into the larger political systems of the "new states"; indeed, he demonstrated how the observations of smaller political units in practice could reveal process in the larger units. Fallers saw the Busoga courts as the locus and means of important integration between "traditional ideas and practices" and the larger overlay of regional administration and national state. This was, in simpler terms, the study of the modernization of traditional and neotraditional political institutions in colonial and postcolonial institutions and was reflected, for Fallers, in the very hierarchy of justice in the Uganda Protectorate. The officially recognized sub-county (*ggombolola*) in Busoga stood above informal and continuing local "courts" unrecognized by the colonial administration. Appeals from the sub-county courts traveled to the county (*ssaza*) court, then to the Busoga Lukiiko, the recognized district council of senior chiefs, then to the magistrate's court in Jinja and finally to the High Court of Uganda, the latter two the only courts — at the time of Fallers's research — in which Europeans served as judges.

In *Law Without Precedent*, Fallers joined the study of the integrative process to the close examination of the "case" in Busoga practice. Fallers's definition of "a case for the Basoga" fits this intellectual formation, of a modeling of local ideas and practices in a process of integration, and in some respects unification, within an expanding "modern" state apparatus. For Fallers, this state was itself marked, affected, by "patrimonial tendencies" incorporated within the administration of justice in the formal apparatus of the courts.

Fallers defined a "case for the Basoga" as

> a proceeding to decide whether or not a particular set of "facts" falls within the reach of one particular concept of wrong. All sorts of other issues may be raised in argument but only those relevant to the reach of the particular concept of wrong enter into the decision; and the latter is delivered quite unilaterally, with little attempt to elicit consent (Fallers 1969:327).

This definition is extraordinarily arresting and demands close scrutiny. The passage captures Lloyd Fallers's method precisely and offers at least three critical entry points to the examination of Fallers' work, and to the work of others who have deployed a similarly constructed case method in the study of colonial African law.

I. "All Sorts of Other Issues..."

In declaiming that "All sorts of other issues may be raised in argument but only those relevant to the reach of the particular concept of wrong enter into the decision," Fallers indicates that litigants raise a broader range of arguments — and, as the previous sentence suggests, "facts" — than those which will enter into the decision of the court. What is implicated is that there is a remarkable distinction between what the courts see as appropriate, relevant, and correct facts and arguments and what the litigants see as appropriate, relevant, and correct. By the time Fallers began his studies in Busoga in 1950, the colonial courts had been in operation for about a half-century. The distinction observed here between two forms of discourse in the same location — the colonial court — has, clearly, its own long history. Still, Fallers does not himself lead us to attach significance to this observation of the distinctive discursive intentions and activities among the "players" in the Busoga court setting. If this is the meaning of "a case for the Basoga," as Fallers argues, how does one explain the persistence of broader, alternative, and "irrelevant" discourses within the proceedings of the Soga courts?

II. "Only Those Relevant to the Reach..."

Fallers suggests here a legal sieve through which are sifted "issues raised in argument." One may ask what sort of mechanism of authority drives this process of selection, determining relevance, limiting what information and what arguments are to enter into "the decision"? What are the frames of knowledge and what are the expectations of litigants concerning the nature of information and argument that will enter into the decision? Do litigants share a vision of what enters into a decision that is distinctive from those who make the decision? How do litigants perceive the place of information and argumentation which they bring in respect to the decisions which the court will produce? What is the relationship between anticipation and result?

III. "With Little Attempt to Elicit Consent."

What is the form and effect of court decisions and opinions in respect to the consent of litigants and observers? How do litigants perceive the form and voice of the court as it produces its decisions and opinions? What is the motor of consent in the processes of litigation in a colonial setting such as Busoga?

When we look for answers to these questions from within *Law Without Precedent*, we find that Fallers closed off the possibilities of making certain fresh observations from his text. Fallers systematically used ellipses in his presentation of court testimony, omitting from the reader's view some of the "facts" and arguments presented to the court. Most critically, Fallers deleted, by use of ellipses, all testimony that he evidently viewed as not relevant to the "reach of the particular concept of wrong," or that did not "enter into the decision," thereby producing in the end a record of the nature of "what the court heard." Fallers's compact representation of case records resembles the abstracted and abbreviated documentary records of other courts in which an administrative routine, or a technology, of full inscription is not available. So, in closing off from view "that which was presented" as opposed to "what the court heard," Fallers positioned himself and his own act of discerning relevant and appropriate argumentation between the setting of the court and a possible audience's intentions to read directly and closely the litigants' presentations to the court.

In their introduction to *The Disputing Process: Law in Ten Societies*, Laura Nader and Harry F. Todd, Jr., argue for a recognition of the significance of alternative and multiple intentions in a courtroom.

> There is a special importance to be derived from treating the participants in the disputing process as deserving of equal sociological attention. People who write about the judicial process and the judicial decision as if the outcome were solely the product of a third party, a judge, miss the sociological relevance of the courtroom as an interactive arena (Nader and Todd 1978:22).

The practices of elision in the recording and reporting of court testimony, whether from Fallers's emphasis on the receptive mode of the colonial court or from imperfect or selective practices of court reportage, have the power to close off from inspection these alternative agendas and complex intentions to which Nader and Todd draw our attention.

The questions raised concerning Fallers's definition of "a case for the Basoga" suggest the incomplete nature of colonial judicial practice in Busoga. In Busoga, there may indeed be alternative agendas and complex interactions operating beneath the dominant and recorded official practice of the court. But, moreover, these alternative practices may constitute, on the one hand, practices of resistance to further "integration" and, on the other, practices that establish the facts and modes of domination, extending and refining the receptive process even where the receptive mode (in *its* practice and in its scholarly examination) closes off access to these alternative voices.

Through the close reading of a single piece of litigation, it is possible to examine more closely the field of difference between a case as it is heard by a colonial court (in Fallers's receptive mode) and recorded imperfectly or selectively (in the manner of many court records) and the case as it is presented by the litigants, informed here by both a close reading of the case record and by material drawn from the neighborhood in which the case, *Namuluta v. Kazibwe*, originated. The case selected comes from the period of Fallers's field work (though he does not refer to it in his study) so as to illuminate better the risks and opportunities associated with the narrow and broad conceptualizations of "a case for the Basoga" which one might choose to implement.

In April 1950, Saida Namuluta stood before the chief of Sabagabo ggombolola (sub-county), Butembe-Bunya County in Busoga and declared:

> I accuse Varantini Kazibwe for claiming my hereditary *mutala* [village] Nakati which belonged to my grandfather, Gumula. When Gumula died it was taken over by Mwegambi; when Mwegambi died it was taken by Kyemba; after Kyemba's death Babaire took it; after Babaire's death Kagoma took it; after Kagoma the *mitala* [villages, plural form] remained vacant, and became uninhabited. The defendant is charged with having claimed the mutala Nakati which is Namuluta's mutala.[2]

And so began nearly a year of litigation over the claims of a woman Saida Namuluta and a man Valantini Kazibwe for recognition as holder or owner (*ow'omutala*) of a section of land close by the developing Kakira sugar estate operated by the Madhvani family.

When Saida completed her charge in the Sabagabo ggombolola court, the chief turned to Valantini and asked, "Do you agree to the charge or have you got something to say to defend yourself?" Valantini responded,

> I am not guilty of the charge for the following reasons: The mutala Namasiga which she claims is mine, it is hereditary. As to the mutala Nakati which she says that I claim I have never claimed such a mutala for Nakati is only a *kisoko* [sub-village] within my mutala Namasiga; and that same kisoko is called Itala, but Nakati which she is talking about is neither a mutala nor a kisoko but only a well. This mutala Namasiga was given by my grandfather, Bamba, to Kirimuta Nkoma who was his assistant. Magaya Mulema and Magaya Alabike first settled at Namasiga and it is where they were buried. After their death Bamba Musumba, their son, changed his home [official residence] and built it at Kasozi, Bugaya, and he gave the mutala to Kirimuta Nkoma. In 1928, on August

26th the mutala Namasiga was given to me and I was confirmed in it by Kitawo Biwero. Musumba Biwero son of Nawaguma gave me his son Munaba to escort me to the mutala Namasiga together with the following emissaries: (i) Kasia Kasiba, representative of the gombolola chief; (ii) Bakonte was representative of the *muluka* [parish] chief. There were other representatives too.

The following are the people who ruled Namasiga: (i) Kirimuta Nkoma; (ii) Nkoma; (iii) Mulyansime; (iv) Ikanka; (v) Ikanka Kisibo; (vi) myself, V. Kazibwe, the present ruler. I have ruled the mutala for 22 years now. To prove that the mutala Namasiga is definitely mine Nsaiga the clan head of Namuluta's clan accused Biwero in 1922 and he [Bandi] lost the case in the gombolola court at Bugaya, and in the saza court at Kiyunga in the same year. Then in 1929 Namuluta's kinsman, Enosi Byansi, accused me; he called my mutala Namasiga another name, Bukasa. He lost the case in the gombolola court at Bugaya before L. Muwanika who was the gombolola chief. The case was left at that. In 1940 Aloni Kanyika accused me; he claimed my mutala Namasiga and he called at Bulondo. He lost the case in the court at Bugaya when Eria Waiswa was the gombolola chief. On the other three occasions Bandi and Bakikuya gave evidence in 1929 and in 1940 but they lost the case. From that Namuluta accuses me that I claim her mutala Nakati whereas my mutala is Namasiga but not Nakati as she says and Nakati which she is talking about is merely a well; and the mutala which Namuluta says that it was ruled by six ancestors of hers, those people have never ruled Namasiga.

Following several questions to clarify Valantini's statement, the ggombolola chief then turned to "The Plaintiff, Namuluta", who was given the opportunity to restate her claim:

I accuse Valantini because of claiming my hereditary mutala Nakati which belonged to my grandfather Gumula. After Gumula's death, Mwegambi took the mutala; after Mwegambi's death Kyemba took it and the following ruled in that mutala in succession: Babaire, Kagoma Mpalageni, Mugimba; after Mugimba the mutala remained without a ruler. At that time I was taken out of Busoga by my husband; then I came back to settle in my mitala. On my arrival I accused the clan leader and he sent me to higher powers to accuse V. Kazibwe who claims my mutala Nakati. There is a boundary between Nakati and Bugaya and also a hill called Luwuga on the upper side. The "baiseMugaya" who, he said, gave him the mutala, used to stop in [settle up to the edge of] the boundary between Bugaya and Nakati, but I am claiming my mutala Nakati. His statement that I claimed three mitala: Nakati, Namasiga, and Ntala is untrue, the clerk made a mistake. The name Namasiga is a misnomer and the boundary between Nakati and Bugaya passes through that mutala. That mutala belonged to my uncle Nsaiga Kibwa and Kibwa gave it to my father Gumula.

Following Saida's statement, the chief then directed a series of clarifying questions to her. After completing the examination of the testimony of Saida and her witnesses, the chief rendered his ruling. In his judgment, 4 April 1950, the ggombolola chief stated,

The defendant, Varantini Kazibwe, has lost the case, for he claimed the mutala Nakati, calling it a kisoko or the boundary of Namasiga; he made it a part of Namasiga. That mutala Nakati belonged to the forefathers of Namuluta. Nsaiga Kibwa gave it to Gumula son of Nsaiga; on Gumula's death Kyemba took it and it was ruled by other rulers in successions until people evacuated on account of sleeping sickness. But the defendant says that there is no mutala called Nakati, that Nakati is merely a well, but in that part the kisoko is called Ntala. He says that Namasiga is his hereditary mutala; his grandfather Bamba Musumba gave it to him. The witnesses of the plaintiff have given evidence proving that Nakati is a mutala and it belongs to Namuluta, it belonged to her grandfather Gumula son of Nsaiga; in the end it became uninhabited, at that time Varantini took it. The witnesses of Varantini said that they do not know the mutala Nakati; they know Namasiga which is Varantini's mutala; but the plaintiff does not claim Namasiga; therefore the mutala Nakati has been given to Namuluta and Varantini will pay shs 10/- court fee.

Saida won her case in the ggombolola court, but then Valantini appealed and the decision for Saida was reversed in the ssaza (county) court. Saida appealed and won in the Busoga District Court (Lukiiko). Valantini again appealed and won in the Magistrate's Court, Jinja. Saida then appealed to the High Court of Uganda, the last court of appeal in the Protectorate, which dismissed her claim. The High Court declared that

> Here is a woman who for half a life time has been absent from her place of origin, returned to claim not land, nor rights over land, nor the right to receive profits from land, nor the right to exact services or tribute from persons living on land, but merely the right to be known as Mutala chief, a right which carries with it, so far as I can see, only a few ill defined and partially recognized executive duties and a certain standing in the community.
>
> This scarcely seems a claim triable by Court of law. If however I must adjudicate in the matter I would say that the decision of the Saza Court and of the Magistrate seems preferable to that of the Central Native Court [Busoga Lukiiko]. If the Mutalla of Nakati ever existed, the community ruled by the petitioners ancestors had disappeared. There has been no continuity of rule. Part of the land where the old community lived has been peopled by a fresh group of families who have acknowledged the respondents rule for many years. The petitioner does not claim the land on which they live as her land — she cannot do so, they do not hold the land from her. If her claim is granted she cannot eject them. There seems absurdity in saying that they must at this stage in history fall under her rule because long ago an earlier community in the same spot was ruled by her ancestors.
>
> Though I avoid the term "Prescriptive Right" used by the Magistrate, I think the long settled order of things should not be broken upon by this lady with her contentions of a pre-existing mutalla in this area. If one went back in history the whole map of mutalas and kisokos [sub-villages] could no doubt be disrupted and a complete re-deal of these headmanships could be effected. I make no order, and the decision of the Magistrate will stand.

And so the case of "Saidi Namuluta, Petitioner, versus Valantini Kazibwe, Respondent" concluded. Saida Namuluta had lost her claim.

Namuluta v. Kazibwe was a familiar case, though the High Court does not reiterate what it had declared in an earlier order concerning "these tiresome

Busoga headmanship cases." Fallers himself discussed seven of such cases among the fifty-one cases cited in *Law Without Precedent*. Fallers's citations developed the central issues in each of these cases as they were introduced in the court; he then reported the decisions of the courts and the rationale in each; and he finally discussed that logic of the rulings which was seen to straddle the several cases within this category of "possession of sub-village or village." Fallers was concerned to show the ways in which persisting concepts of sovereignty in Busoga — the capacity of existing authorities and executives to continue to command authority over such rights and offices as sub-villages and villages — were supported by, or in conflict with, the concerns, interests, and existing policies of Protectorate administration.

How does one read a series of texts, so incomplete in the sense discussed earlier, from a single judicial case? Do we, as Fallers has done, examine the testimony, arguments, and facts, to see what constitute relevant matter for the judges in making their rulings, as a way of understanding the process of reception of local ideas and practices by the overlying judicial administration? Here, immediately, we face a conundrum created by the very different reading of the litigation by the two judges whose rulings are presented above (not to speak of the three intervening judgments). What, in this sense, is "a case for the Basoga"?

In discussing his method, Fallers noted that he fell short of his own objectives in broadening his knowledge of each case.

> The case records provide, I believe, excellent data on what takes place in Soga courtrooms, and my ethnographic inquiries make it possible to relate these data to their general sociocultural setting. But for far too many cases, I know only what the case records tell and what I can infer from my knowledge of the society. In too few cases do I know what happened before and after and I have too few interviews with judges and litigants about particular cases and about law in general. More of such material would have made possible a richer analysis of Soga legal culture and of the relationship between the legal institution and society than I am able to provide (Fallers 1969:38).

The present agenda is to explore but one case, not so much to discern the relationship between the legal institution and society, but rather to examine the broader range and deeper meanings of the voices of individuals in the practice of litigation. The several texts produced within *Namuluta v. Kazibwe* in this one court proceeding at the ggombolola level could be read in a number of different ways; the direction taken here is to look at the *silences, allusions,* and *indirections* in the light of a much thicker body of material relating to the dispute than that which the parties brought into the court; and, finally and briefly, to discuss the implications in recognizing the distinctions among (a) what the judges chose to *hear,* (b) what the litigants chose to *say,* and (c) what broader knowledge the court players held concerning the material detail of the dispute.[3]

Indirections

In Valantini's rejoinder to Saida's first statement of claim, the very logic of Saida's claim is not recognized. Where she asserted a claim to a mutala she called Nakati,

Valantini responded with a defense of his title to a mutala he called Namasiga. And far from implying that this is one place, or one office, or title, with two different names, Valantini insisted that Nakati is not a mutala but a well. And he noted that the place she claimed as Nakati was a kisoko (sub-village) known as Itala and that this lay within the mutala Namasiga which he owned. He had thus multiply confounded Saida's claim through the implication that he was holding expert knowledge of the essential meaning of the name Nakati (a "well") and of the materiality of the place which Saida claimed (the kisoko Itala), as well as concerning his own authority (over Namasiga).

In recording Saida's first statement, the clerk of the ggombolola court noted that "after Kagoma the mitala remained vacant, and became uninhabited." The clerk used the plural form, i.e. "villages," giving the implication that Saida is concerned with more than one mutala. In her second statement, Saida attempted to correct what she remarked was an error in the record of previous court testimony, an error she attributed to the clerk: the notion that she was claiming "three mitala: Nakati, Namasiga, and Ntala." It is possible that this "error" was introduced to the record by a clerk who did not readily recognize the incongruity of the claim and the response: Saida claiming Nakati from Valantini and Valantini defending Namasiga, of which he claimed "Ntala" or "Itala" as a part, from Saida. But there is possibly another edge to the question of the number of mitala under discussion, for Saida's lineage were recognized to be the "owners" of two other mitala in the area. To succeed in the case against Valantini would have made three.

Elsewhere in the court testimony, Saida argued, under questioning from the chief, that "Namasiga is not a mutala but only the name of a spirit [*musambwa*]", though Valantini responded, "Namasiga is a mutala and it is where the spirit is." In giving his ruling, the ggombolola chief worked within the "logic" of the asymmetrical debate: "the plaintiff does not claim Namasiga; therefore the mutala Nakati has been given to Namuluta and Varantini will pay shs 10/- court fee." He left open, however, the critical question: if Saida can be given Nakati and Valantini can be left with Namasiga, then what were the essential grounds for Saida's original claim against Valantini? Indeed, from a distant perspective, Valantini could have looked upon the chief's decision as the fourth occasion upon which a court vindicated his ownership of Namasiga. But if this were the case, why did Valantini appeal his case to the next level court? What is suggested is that both Saida and Valantini recognized that a claim for Nakati was a claim for Namasiga, but perhaps Saida recognized that this direct assault on Valantini's title would not work, as it had not when members of her lineage brought cases against Valantini earlier. For Saida to assail Valantini's control over Namasiga was for Saida to assault a well-defended turf, so she perhaps consequently moved forward into the litigation by indirection. The ggombolola chief saw an opportunity for a resolution not in adjudicating the actual material claims of the two parties but through moving into the spaces opened in their incongruent discourse.

In the ruling of the judge in the High Court of Uganda, the issue is much simplified into a debate between two parties to a single title, office, mutala. It is as if Saida's claim and Valantini's response are, essentially, reciprocal, predictable, commonplace, and reducible to the statement of a principle (the judge's reference to "prescriptive right"). In looking at the presentations Saida and Valantini made to the court, one might say that they agreed in a powerful way on the primacy of factual detail in settling differences, rather than on the bases of which party held the stronger claim to an acknowledged principle. Indeed, they agreed on the larger principles that the High Court judge found objectionable: that these headships mattered and that one's rights in them could be substantiated by fact and force of argument. For them, a facility to control the outcome of the litigation lay in their control of distinct sets of "facts" concerning, of a first order, grants, appointments, and legacies, and of a second order, the names, locations, and meanings of places. If the grammar of each of the rulings of the ggombolola court and the High Court of Uganda were distinctive, so also was the grammar of presentation of argument to the ggombolola court different from that of each of the rulings. What was offered to the courts was substantially different from what was received by them.

Allusions

In his presentation to the court, Valantini brought attention to what he alleged to have been a series of prior cases brought by members of Saida's lineage against his ownership of Namasiga mutala. Beyond giving further depth to his gambit of opposing Saida's claim to Nakati by defending his ownership of Namasiga, his testimony suggests an implication that Saida's claim against Valantini for Nakati was simply a further invention, E. Byansi having "called my mutala Namasiga another name, Bukasa..." and A. Kanyika having "claimed my mutala Namasiga and he called it Bulondo." Moreover, in alluding to these cases, Valantini evidently sought to establish a long judicial record behind his defense of Namasiga, extending back twenty-eight years to 1922.

Valantini went one step further. In reviewing what he presented as a series of vindicating cases he was at the same time appropriating status and authority to two individuals who he would later call as witnesses to his ownership of Namasiga: Lameka Muwanika and Eria Waiswa, who had long periods of service in different parts of Busoga as ggombolola chiefs, eventually leaving government service in good standing. Later, Saida's witnesses challenged the status of Muwanika's and Waiswa's knowledge of such local details, saying that they were not in the area long enough to know the details concerning ownership of mitala. Saida's witnesses, with Saida, were, in this counter-testimony, alluding to general understandings concerning the effects of practices of frequent rotation in the African civil service in Busoga, that responsible office did not translate as authoritative knowledge. In his statement, Valantini impugned the testimony of one of Saida's initial three witnesses, Bakikuya, by stating that Bakikuya had been the losing party in cases in which he gave evidence in 1929 and 1940. Before Bakikuya testified, Valantini was suggesting that, if his evidence were not to be believed ten and twenty years before, why was it to be believed in 1950?

Saida, in turn, introduced in her second statement two new issues: one in the admission of a delay in her initiating her claim to Nakati mutala; and a second in bringing attention to a "boundary between Bugaya and Nakati." In the first, she was anticipating what would be at a major concern of the High Court judge in his ruling; in a sense predicting the judicial reasoning of an appellate court four courts removed from the one in which she was testifying. In the second, she placed before the court the concept of a "Bugaya" as a territorial entity sharing a boundary with Nakati. Though Valantini mentioned Bugaya at three points in his formal presentations to the ggombolola court, it was his adversary, Saida, who sought to place Valantini's claims and rights within the history of settlement and administration of the small Bugaya state in south-west Busoga, a state ruled by a lineage of the abaiseMagaya. The implication of Saida's reference to "boundary" is that there was a historical limit to the extension of the authority of the Bugaya state and therefore of its capacity to turn over estates (bisoko and mitala) to clients and kin of the members of the ruling house of Bugaya, the authority of which in this area was still recognizable through the 1960s. Saida's reference to boundaries in her second statement carried an additional power in the debate before the court, for just previously Valantini and two of his witnesses had admitted that they could not find or discover, and did not mark, boundaries when they first were sent to set up Valantini as head of Namasiga. In an important sense the coteries or networks of witnesses in both sides represented the present (1950) form of old territorial expansionist and defensive practices of the ruling houses, and their clienteles, of the Soga states.

In her second statement, Saida alluded to still another development:

> I came back to settle in my mitala. On my arrival I accused the clan leader and he sent me to higher powers to accuse V. Kazibwe who claims my mutala Nakati.

Saida was giving her own claims a special legitimacy, that they exceeded other claims to Nakati, or against Kazibwe, which had been festering in her lineage; and also that she appeared in court with the blessing of the leader of the clan. Here we see the first indication of what is later revealed through questions posed to Saida and her witnesses that there was a struggle within her own lineage and clan for precedence in going forward with a case against Kazibwe. This was the little case before the big one.

Relatively few of the allusive gambits of either party were recognized in the rulings of the ggombolola court and the High Court. They were, however, recognizable because again and again the transcripts of the proceedings show the witnesses checking and counter-checking on such points and they show the very standing of the witnesses in the court rising and falling with the play of allusion within the testimony presented to the court. If the testimony of *indirection* was about the valorization of "factuality" as opposed to principles, the *allusions* in testimony were about the character and values of participants in the case and, in turn, about the credence to be given to particular claims of fact.

Silences

There are critical silences and suppressions throughout the formal statements to the court given by Saida and Valantini. In his statement, Valantini mentioned Kirimuta Nkoma as preceding him as "owner" of the mutala of Namasiga. He gave Kirimuta's name as part of a "genealogy" of recognized office-holders. But under questioning, Valantini revealed first that Kirimuta Nkoma was removed from the Namasiga post by the local government for, we learn, incompetence. The opening of this oyster produced a succession of difficulties requiring Valantini's explanations. Did he receive the title to Namasiga from the local government, that is from the representatives of the district administration, or from the hereditary "rulers" of the neighborhood in which Namasiga was located? Who then actually appointed him to his title or office and what was that person's standing at the time? Under further questioning, Valantini and his witnesses were pressed to reveal that Kirimuta Nkoma actually held Namasiga not as ow'omutala but rather as the representative or surrogate of another ow'omutala. When therefore, if ever, did that ow'omutala turn over ownership of the mutala to Valantini? In the county (ssaza) court proceedings, we find two of Valantini's expanded array of witnesses claiming that Valantini did not hold the title of ow'omutala but was himself a surrogate or representative of the actual owner, who was recognized to be a member of the royal house of Bugaya.

A second suppression is a jointly enacted one (though it is slightly breached by Saida in her second statement). This concerns the evocation in court of the expansionist programs of two old and residual political corporations: neighboring Bukasa and Bugaya in southwest Busoga. Saida and her lineage were closely affiliated with the ruling house of Bukasa, while Valantini was part of the "ruling" establishment of the Bugaya state. The suppression of argument based on the legacies of the small states drew on a recognition that the courts, from top to bottom in Busoga, were considerably suspicious of claims that came out of the ancient political and social histories of states in the district. It was anachronistic to establish or support claims on grounds, on histories, that *were not supported* by the colonial state. And so Saida and Valantini and their witnesses contended over boundaries to polities that did not, in their constructions of the court's "mind," exist; yet the ebb and flow of state expansion in the neighborhood in the nineteenth century, in the early twentieth century, and indeed in the cases before the local courts, constituted the very motor of the dispute between Saida and Valantini.

A third suppression or silence is opened slightly when, in her second statement, Saida mentioned that she "accused the clan leader and he sent me to higher powers." This is a most important element in the development of the case, for, as the record of responses to questions placed by the ggombolola chief indicates, Saida had to establish her claim to Nakati within her own clan against the prior claims of several individuals. This is tender ground, for Saida would not have wanted to make too evident the embattled nature, and therefore fragility, of her claims to Nakati. Yet at the same time the critical evidence she would have wanted to bring before the court lay within these struggles within her clan for rights to the Nakati title, the "little case before the big case." For Saida to build a picture for the court of her success in struggles among her peers was to introduce discordant voices and disputed evidence from within her own family. On the other side, for Valantini the history of the struggles within Saida's lineage for control of the rights to Nakati contained both opportunities and risks; he had already claimed to have defeated three members of her lineage — Bandi, E. Byansi, and A. Kanyika — in previous legal assaults on his title. To make too much of a sustained claim by a single lineage would possibly have jeopardized his own history of his title. And, again, to raise this history of litigation in its fullest and roundest way would, possibly, have given status to the notion of Nakati as a mutala, something which was obviously not in his interest to do.

Through the silences and suppressions, small and large, of both parties and their witnesses, the court players, litigants and witnesses, were identifying issues for which there were substantial risks in bringing them forward in too great detail, or at all—risks for both the case at hand and for broader concerns. They were, through considerable selectivity in argumentation and fact-bringing, gathering control over what it was that the court should know, even in a setting in which the procedures of the court were such that the judge could delve into practically any matter through his own examination of plaintiff, respondent, and witnesses.

Namuluta v. Kazibwe was a narrow thread of organized dispute within a broad lattice of contention concerning the ownership of titles, offices, and estates in the neighborhood of Namasiga/Nakati. There was, in 1950, a long history in and of the various contentions that inflected this single case, and the contentions spread out through the various coteries of witnesses and supporters on both sides. The very form and meaning of the contest—as the reproduction of an old pattern of territorial aggression across an indistinct political boundary between the remnants of the Bukasa and Bugaya polities—was withheld from the view of the court. In each of the rulings that have been examined here—the lowest and highest courts of the organized Protectorate judiciary—the judges picked through what was placed before them for a handle on a complex case. The ggombolola chief saw the possibility of preserving both claims, and in the process he ignored the meaningful interests being asserted and defended by the two parties. The High Court judge simply saw the case as one in which a new party was attempting to swipe the office of an old one. Neither articulated the older, historic issue at the base of the dispute.

What is finally revealed in this discordance between the "case" as presented by the litigants in all its indirections, allusions, and silences, and the "case" as it is "heard" by the judges? Here we may begin to see some of the distinctions between an approach to litigation and legal ideas in colonial Africa oriented around the "receptive mode" of a developing colonial judicial system, and an approach that brings into focus the ways in which facts, arguments, practices, and ideas are offered by those participating in the courts.

The close reading of this one case suggests that there are two rather different discourses or programs present in the setting of the colonial court in Busoga. In the program of the judiciary there is an economy of practice, a selectivity in hearing the participants.[4] As noted earlier, Fallers argued that "a case for the Basoga...[is] a proceeding to decide whether or not a particular set of 'facts' falls within a particular concept of wrong" (Fallers 1969:327). Reading *Namuluta v. Kazibwe*, one would turn the emphasis from the "whether or not" to the question of particularization: how judges *hear* certain "facts" from a broad webbing of fact-bringing and argument and how judges particularize a specific "concept of wrong" from the dispute context constituted by the "facts" heard.

In the second program or discourse, the litigants and witnesses work upon their own criteria of what "facts" and arguments are to be voiced, and how strongly they are to be voiced. They are not simply attempting to make "their best case": bringing forward all the facts and arguments that will empower their claims and defenses. They are evaluating the risks of bringing certain information before the court and the dangers of opening certain points too broadly. They are introducing material, by allusion, that holds the power to depose the adversary's witnesses and arguments. They are, through silences, constituting argument, containing risks, and gathering control over what the courts should learn. They are, as well, attempting to predict what material might be "heard" and be effective among the broad arrays of knowledge which they have the capacity to muster. In *Namuluta v. Kazibwe*, the litigants appear to agree that there are certain boundaries in producing testimony across which one should not venture. There is in this an indication of some undefined, unvoiced rules evolved by litigants as they experience the practice of courts, which, at times, are confirmed by subsequent judicial rulings. Yet, as we compare the readings of the rulings of the judges to the readings of the testimony brought before them, we recognize immediately that the litigants nevertheless bring substantial evidence and argument before the court that will, subsequently, hold no interest for the judges producing their rulings.

These "discordant voices," which Fallers removed from his renderings of cases through the use of ellipses, perhaps had several important resonances. First, such discordant testimony was epiphenomenal to broader, continuing, and often irresolvable tensions outside the courts; it also gave sustenance to particular claims and rights even where courts had ruled against them (witness the series of claims brought by members of Saida's lineage against Kazibwe). Second, the presentation of discordant testimony within a formalized court setting, as opposed to a market, a bar, or a feast, accorded status to particular speech and to particular issues. An argument over an ancient boundary between two small precolonial states in a court in 1950, even where the litigants were embarrassed from explicating the historical dimensions of the boundary issue, provided a means of reproducing the ideas of long-enduring local sovereignties and statuses unrecognized by the colonial authority. Third, and following on these first two points, discordant testimony of such kind was the means of establishing consent. Where Fallers looked for consent in the rulings of the court, and did not find it, we might look for the motors of consent in the very patterns of introducing discordant voices — the stuff that Fallers has elided. The litigants and witnesses were, through their voices, discordant and otherwise, establishing the very facts and modes of domination, consenting to the administrative and judicial functions of the courts while organizing therein the reproduction and defense of an underlying system of domination. Fourth, and still more speculatively, the discordant voices — the far broader realms of testimony brought to the courts than that which the judges "heard" — may have induced the formation, in the practice of the courts, of an economy of judgement in which judges were distanced from the deep contours of facts and argumentation and pressed into patterns of narrow and specious judgement, simply to get on with the system of governing.

This approach to the study of litigation in colonial Africa reveals a critical arena of tension and discord between an instituted and evolved system of justice — the colonial courts of Busoga — and a sociology of participation. These overlying and underlying fields of litigation practice are inextricably involved, each operating in the context of the other, yet critical aspects of each field are undisclosed to the other.

Most studies of African colonial law have focused on the overlying field of litigation practice. Such an orientation of legal research in Africa may be explained, variously, by the relatively privileged survival of documentation in the overlying field, by applied concerns of many researchers concerned with the evaluation and improvement of overlying judicial practice, and through the political silencing of the underlying field in the more general "work" of authority formation of judges, jurists, and administrators operating in the overlying field.

Lloyd Fallers, like many observers of African and colonial legal systems, used the case method. He drew his material from courtroom observations and court and appellate proceedings. While his observations of litigation were brilliantly contextualized in the anthropological study of Soga society and culture, his perspective of law as the *work of courts* subordinated, and effectively closed off from view, the broader and elongated aspects of ideas and action relating to specific disputes and conflicts. Fallers's definition of "a case for the Basoga" was likewise quite restrictive; and the manner in which he operationalized this definition in his presentation of testimony worked to suppress discordant voices in his reports on the practices of litigation. Fallers's concentration on the work within the courts, his suppression of discordant voices through the use of ellipses in the presentation of testimony, and his search for the integrative mechanism in colonial litigation lead us away from a comprehension of the discursive intentions of the players in the Busoga court setting and away from an understanding of the constructive power located in such discursive practices. In a certain way, Fallers has become part of the process of elaboration of a distanced and selective authority in the colonial courts of Busoga, establishing in our domain of study further rules of what is "heard" and how meaning is to be attached to it.

Acknowledgments

This paper was originally prepared for The Stanford–Emory conference on Law in Colonial Africa, sponsored by the Social Science Research Council, which was held at Stanford in April 1988. In discussion, conference participants stimulated a good deal of further thinking on colonial litigation. George Martin provided extensive and valuable assistance in developing an approach to the subject, a method of reading Fallers, and a way of giving a fresh perspective to the reading of *Namuluta v. Kazibwe*. Ashraf Ghani, Alf Lüdtke, Hans Medick, and Gabrielle Siegel provided sounding boards during the development of the project. The John Simon Guggenheim Foundation and the Dean of Arts and Sciences at Johns Hopkins made possible a second year of field work in Busoga in 1971–72, which made possible this present reading of litigation in Busoga. Students in my Johns Hopkins African history seminar in the second semester, 1988, contributed in important ways to my thinking on "customary" and colonial law.

NOTES

1. In selecting cases for his study, Fallers eliminated a large number of proceedings that individuals brought against their chiefs and headmen (derelection of duty and abuse of office), as well as cases which the government brought against common people (for tax avoidance and disobedience).
2. The case record of *Namuluta v. Kazibwe* is a handwritten English translation of the proceeding, which was rendered from the original Luganda or Lusoga transcriptions when they were readied for presentation to the Jinja magistrate in the next-to-last court of appeal. The orthography has been left in the form written. There are companion records for the county (ssaza) and district (lukiiko) proceedings, though not for the magistrate's and High Court pleadings. However, the rulings are available from all five courts. *Namuluta v. Kazibwe* was selected from notes, microfilms, and xeroxes of some twenty cases collected in Busoga in 1971 and 1972.
3. This broader knowledge comes from records of examination of witnesses, plaintiff, and respondent in the ggombolola, ssaza, and district courts; from research by the present author on this area of Busoga, done before the case record was discovered; from the records of interviews done by the author in 1966–67 and 1971–72 with a number of the parties to the case, also before the physical record of the case was found; and from the records of a survey of mitala and bisoko histories done by the author in 1971–72.
4. It is in relation to this "program of the judiciary" that one might find the conventional description of courts and court practices focusing on the authority of the judges and the rules of jurisprudence.

SOURCES

A microfilm copy of the original Lusoga and Luganda transcripts and the English translations of the interviews undertaken by the author during research in Busoga in 1966–67 was presented to the Makerere University Library under the title *Collected texts, Busoga traditional history*. A limited xerox edition of some of these texts, and of additional texts recorded in 1971–72, *Selected texts, Busoga traditional history* (3 vols.), 1969, 1970, 1973 was deposited in the CAMP collection at Evanston, in the Library of the School of Oriental and African Studies, University of London, and in the Makerere University Library. A smaller selection of texts was published in 1986 as *Towards a reconstructed past* (Cohen 1986).

Cohen, David William. 1986. *Towards a reconstructed past: Historical texts from Busoga, Uganda*. London: The British Academy and Oxford University Press.

Fallers, Lloyd A. [1956] 1965. *Bantu bureaucracy: A century of political evolution among the Basoga of Uganda*. Chicago: University of Chicago Press.

———. ed. 1964. *The king's men: Leadership and status in Buganda on the eve of independence*. Chicago: University of Chicago Press.

———. 1969. *Law without precedent: Legal ideas in action in the courts of colonial Busoga*. Chicago: University of Chicago Press.

———. 1973. *Inequality: Social stratification reconsidered*. Chicago: University of Chicago Press.

Foner, Laura, and Harry H. Todd, Jr., eds. 1978. *The disputing process—Law in ten societies*. New York: Columbia University Press.

Namuluta v. Kazibwe, Busoga District Native Court, Civil Case no. 159 of 1950.

INDEX

Abandoned land, legal status of, 125
Aba women's war, 21, 23
Abbas, Emir, 206, 209, 214–16
Abolitionists, 28. *See also* Anti-slavery
Aborigines Protection Society, 65
Adewoye, Omoniyi, 228
Adjudication, in Seepapitso's time, 176–78
Administrative law, Faama Mademba Sy
  and, 194–195
Administrative misconduct, Faama
  Mademba Sy and, 185–86
Administrative rule (hukm), 206, 207
Administrators
  African collaborators and, 148, 150, 194
  control of, 186
  indigénat, 17
  indigenato, 17–18
  law and, 6
  loi administratif and, 194
Adoption, legal status and, 116–18
Afahene, defined, 10
L'affaire Kanga. See also Kangah, Kwame
  development of, 151–53
  impacts of, 158–60
  origins of, 148–51
  resolution of, 153–58
Affirmation, oath of, 207, 210, 219, 220
African collaborators, 148, 150, 194
African kings. *See* Chiefs; Tswana chiefs
African legal systems, 8–9
  anthropological study of, 6–8
  colonialism and, 5
  courts, legitimacy of, 13
  disputes and, 3–4
  European conflicts with, 10, 11
  as evolutionary paradigm, 6
  historical study of, 5–9
  in precolonial era, 4, 8, 9–10
  rule-oriented approach and, 6
Africans
  intermarriage with Europeans, 9
  use of European lawyers by, 155
Africans of Southern Rhodesia, 65
Agnatic consent rule, 118–20, 125
Agnatic inheritance, 109, 110, 113–24
Agricultural trade. *See also* Trade
  labor and, 30
  production, 191
  property pledges and, 11
  as replacement for slave trade, 86
Ajasa, Taiwo Olowo and, 98–99
Akilogun, Brimah, 39
Alkali, 206
Allah, oath-taking and, 208, 209

Allocation of land, in Malawi, 81
Allott, Anthony, 6, 68, 78
Allusions, in Basoga colonial courts, 246–48
Anderson, J. N. D., 217
Angola, forced labor in, 30
Angoulvant, Lieutenant-governor, 152
Animal theft
  attitudes toward, 216
  legal process and, 212–13
Anthropology
  land tenure and, 66–68
  legal, 6–8
  "time-oriented," 7
Anti-slavery. *See also* Slavery *entries*
  colonial courts and, 39
  labor and, 28–30
  proclamations, 29
Anyi-Juablin social system, 148
Apical figures, 168
Appeals Court, Dakar, 136–40
Arbitrariness, of colonial legal systems, 36
Archinard, Louis, 186, 188–90, 194, 195
Asiwaju, A. I., 23, 44
Bahht, 208
Bantu Bureaucracy (Fallers), 240
Barber, Karin, 90
Barotse, 3, 6
Barotse *kuta*, 41
Basoga courts, 19, 38–39, 41, 42, 46, 239–53
  allusions in, 248–49
  consent and, 242–53
  incompleteness of records, 242–43
  indirections in, 246–48
  issues considered relevant in, 241–42,
    246–48
  issues raised in, 241, 248–49
  Namulta v. Kazibwe and, 243–52
  silences in, 249–51
Baudin, Governor, 133
Bechuanaland Protectorate
  local government in, 169–70
  Seepapitso's records of activities of, 173
  Tswana chiefs and, 167
Benin, 225, 227
Bennett, W. Lance, 43
Bentham, Jeremy, 62
Berry, Sara, 20, 25–26, 31, 91
Beurdeley, E., 21
Blanc-Jouvan, Xavier, 80
Boahen A. Adu, 68
Boggs, S. W., 234
Bohannan, Paul, 38, 69
Bojan, 188, 190
Bonnichon, A., 140

Bonnier, Captain, 190
Borderlands. *See also* Dahomey-Nigeria
  border
  control of, 224
  customary law development and, 23
  French and British legal systems and, 225
  resolving disputes across, 234–35
Botswana, dispute management in, 6–7
Bradford, Helen, 31
Brew, Harry, 40
Brew, Henry, 40
Brew, Richard, 40
Brew, Samuel (Kanto), 40
Bribes, 208
Bridewealth. *See also* Marriage
  cadi jurisdiction regarding, 140
  Chagga, 117
  as collateral, 114–15
Brière de l'Isle, Governor, 16
British colonial administration. *See also*
  Great Britain
  Dahomey-Nigeria border and, 227 28,
    233–34
  Kano theft and homicide context and,
    210–11, 219
  in Kilimanjaro, 110, 111
British colonial law
  in colonial India, 37–38
  compared with French colonial
    administration, 228–29
  customary land law, 24–27
  dispute management under, 13–14
  indirect rule, 19–23, 33–34, 64, 167
  land policy, 64–66
  legal jurisdiction, 18–19
  prohibition of ordeals, 33
  property ownership, 24–27
  slave-owner disputes and, 39
  in Yorubaland, 231–33
British common law, 229
British maritime law, 11
British Nigeria, court system, 232
British South Africa Company, 15, 65
Buganda, 19. *See also* Basoga courts
Bush land, as collateral, 116
Business operations, credit and, 95–98
Buxton, T. F., 28
Cadis, 14
  French courts and, 133
  1903 French legal code and, 135–36
  jurisdiction of, 131, 140
  restrictions on, 131, 140
Cahier de doléances, by French citizens in
  Senegal, 132
Campbell, Robert, 94
Caravanserai, 213
Case method. *See also* Court records
  colonial Basoga courts and, 46, 239, 241,
    243–53

problems inherent in, 44–46
Castration, of food thieves, 217
Cattle, as economic property, 113
Cattle loans, collateral for, 114–15
Central Africa, customary land law in,
  74–77
Chagga
  coffee cultivation, 116
  colonial courts, 38–39, 42
  court records, 46
  customary law, 7
  economy of, 111–12
  gender-related attitudes, 113, 115–18
  historical background of, 110–12
  inheritance to adopted sons, 116–18
  inheritance to sons-in-law, 118–20
  land shortage, 112, 113, 123
  loaned land, 120–23
  patrilineage, 109, 110, 112, 113, 118–20
  patrimonial property disputes, 109–10,
    113, 117–20, 124–25
  property ownership and, 26–27, 108–25
Chanock, Martin, 7, 8, 14, 15, 22, 24–27,
  32–33, 44, 45, 91, 147, 153
Chartered companies, legal powers of, 15
Chaudié, Jean-Baptist, 192, 193
Cheater, Angela, 66
Cheruy, commandant de cercle, 150
Chewa, witchcraft and ordeal, 32–33
Chiefs. *See also* Tswana chiefs
  administrative law and, 194–96
  behavior befitting, 185, 194, 195–96
  claims of, 4
  communal land ownership and, 75
  land ownership accorded to, 64
  land transactions and, 113–14
  as lenders of capital, 114
  paramount, 232
  political authority of, 86
Childhood betrothal, 41
Children, as collateral, 114–15
Christelow, Allan, 7, 20, 43, 45–46
Christianity, 89
Christian missions, 9, 14–15
Civil law, 229–31
Class
  customary land law and, 72–73
  rule of law and, 35
Clément-Thomas, Governor, 131
Clerc, Louis, 146, 151–54, 156, 157
Clifford, James, 47
Clozel, Governor-General François-Joseph,
  149, 150, 153, 155–58
Côde d'indigénat, 229–30
Coffee cultivation, Chagga, 116
Cohen, David William, 8, 19, 22, 42, 43, 44,
  45, 46
Cohen, William B., 228
Coins, theft and, 211

Collaboration, 148, 150, 194
Collateral, 113
  bush land as, 116
  children as, 114–15
  land as, 123–24
Collective land ownership, 24. *See also* Land
  ownership
Collier, Jane F., 7–8, 21
Colonial courts
  conflict resolution and, 38–43
  in India, 37, 43
  Lagos, 88
  rules or traditions of, 41–42
  slave-owner disputes and, 39–41
Colonialism, 3–5
  models of, 186
Colonial legal systems
  arbitrariness of, 36
  authority and, 32–36
  company rule and, 14–15
  conflict resolution and, 38–43
  control and, 3
  Crown Colonies and, 11–14
  culture and, 24
  customary law and, 19–23
  development of, 9–23
  empire expansion and, 17–19
  Four Communes and, 11–14
  historical study of, 7–8
  indirect rule and, 19–23
  labor and, 27–32
  missionary influence on, 14–15
  native administration and, 19–23
  property ownership and, 24–27
  social order and, 6
  study of, 5–9
  Tswana chiefs and, 178–82
Colson, Elizabeth, 38, 61, 77
Comaroff, John L., 6–7, 45, 171
Command, Tswana chief's role in, 176
Common law, 229–31
Communal land ownership, 24–27, 63, 65–
  68, 74–79. *See also* Land ownership
Communal rights, customary, 73
Communication, Tswana chiefs and,
  173–74, 178
Communism, land ownership and, 67
Company of Merchants Trading to Africa,
  11
Compensation for theft, 207, 209, 219–20
  legal process and, 214–16
  Tswana chief's role in, 177–78
  validation of claims for, 220
Compurgation, oath of, 207, 209, 217
Conflict. *See* Disputes
Conqueror, African king as, 188
Conrad, Daniel, 93. *See also* Taiwo Olowoba
Consent, Basoga colonial courts and,
  242–53

Contracts, property pledges, 11
Corps of Colonial Inspectors, 185, 186, 187,
  193, 194
Corviaux, Louis, 194
Côte d'Ivoire, 35
Councils of Reconciliation, 12
Court records, 43–48. *See also* Case method;
  Legal records
  analyzing, 46–47
  historical context of, 45–46
  limitations of, 47, 90–91
  oral testimony and, 47
  Seepapitso and, 176–78
  as sources, 43–48
  Taiwo Olowo life history and, 90
  trouble cases, 46
Courts
  African, 13
  European establishment of, 11
  French reorganization of, 12
  native, 232
  Portuguese colonial, 12–13
  provincial, 231–32
  recovery of debts through, 96–98
  Supreme Court, 231
Courts of Equity, in Niger Delta, 11
Cowrie shell currency, 211
Credit. *See also* Debt
  business operations and, 95–97
  interest rates and, 87
  international trade and, 87, 88–89
  recovery of debts through courts, 96–98
Crespin, Georges, 138
Crown Colonies, 11–14, 16, 39
Culture
  law and, 24
  legal conflicts and, 4–5
  prejudice and, 28–29
  religious conversion and, 15
  research on, 8
Currency, coins for, 211
Customary communal rights, 73
Customary economic behavior, 63
Customary land law. *See also* Land *entries*
  in British Africa, 24–27
  in Central Africa, 74–77
  class and, 72–73
  colonial land policies and, 62
  development and, 78–80
  gender and, 73–74
  land registries and, 77–78
  land sales and, 74–77
  land surveys and, 77
  political institutions and, 64–66
  postcolonial states and, 80–82
  women and, 73–74
Customary law, 19–23
  L'affaire Kanga and, 152–53
  borderlands and, 23, 234–35

codification of, 22
colonial rule and, 7
defined, 239
development of, 21–22, 153
economic conflicts and, 23–24
evolution of, 4, 7
formalization of, 234
French law and, 230
indigenous law and, 8, 21
indirect rule and, 21–22
of land tenure, 61–82
Muslim court jurisdiction and, 137
Native Authorities and, 22, 23
permanent rights and, 70
property rights and, 71–74
qanun, 206
use of by subordinate groups, 22–23
transformation of, 109
Yoruba, 229
Dahomey-Nigeria border. *See also*
    Borderlands
Anglo-French rivalry and, 227–28
cultural differences and, 227
emigration across, 233–34
law and, 224–35
strategies dealing with French and British
    law in, 233–34
Dakar, 11
courts, 42, 136–40
French citizenship in 133
jurisdiction of Muslim tribunals in,
    131–41
Dakar Appeals Court, 136–40
Danel, Inspector-general, 186, 191–96
Debt. *See also* Credit
business operations and, 96–98
as mechanism of subordination, 98
transfer of land for repayment of, 122
Delavignett, Robert, 186
Denial, oath of, 207
Development, customary land tenure and,
    78–80
Dhimma, 209
Dikgosi. *See* Tswana chiefs (kgosi/dikgosi)
Dinaka, 173
Diouf, Galandou, 138
Disputes
African law and, 8
between Africans, 4–5
between Africans and Europeans, 4–5
British colonial judicial system and,
    13–14
colonial legal systems and, 38–43
credit, 87
cultural change and, 4–5
customary law and, 23–24
French colonial judicial system and, 12, 14
labor, 31
land ownership and, 27

Native Administration and, 21
over labor and resources, 23–24
over sale of land, 68
patrimonial property, 109–10, 113,
    117–20, 124–25
Portuguese colonial judicial system and,
    12–13
in postcolonial period, 6–7
violence and, 38
Disputing Process: Law in Ten Societies, The
    (Nader and Todd), 242
Division, oath of, 209, 217
Dogarai, 210
Dokaji, Abubakar, 209
Dubois, Felix, 189
Durkheim, E., 169, 181
Earnshaw, Justice, 40–41
Economic behavior, 63
Economic control, 3
Economic systems, Lagos, 85–89
Ehua, Nana, 148–50, 152–55, 157
Elifatio, 42, 43
Emirs, 20, 210
Enforcement, Tswana chief's role in, 177
Equality under the law, 37
Estates of administration, 67
Etienne, 188
Europeans
intermarriage with Africans, 9
shift in balance of power to, 10–11
Evidence, Islamic law and, 206
Evolutionary paradigm, of African law, 6
Faidherbe, Governor Louis, 12, 16, 132, 134,
    136
Faji, Chief, 93, 94
Faliyi, 39
Fallers, Lloyd, 19, 38–39, 41, 46, 239–53
Family property, ownership of, 70–73
Fardet, commandant de cercle, 152, 159
Fatoma, 213
Feldman, Martha S., 43
Fifty-fold oath (yamin al-qasama), 207, 209,
    217–19
Food thieves, 210–11
attitudes toward, 211, 216, 217, 219
killing of, 216, 217, 219
Forced labor, 30
Four Communes, 11–14, 16, 36, 131–41
France
colonial development of Senegal by,
    132–35
expansion of control by, 15–16
Four Communes, 11–14, 16, 36, 131–41
1903 legal code, 135–37
Muslim tribunals and, 131–41
"native policy," 16
recognition of Muslim tribunals by,
    133–34
Senegalese commerce, 132

Freehold land tenure, 79
Freeman, Governor, 93
Freetown, 12, 13–14
French citizenship
  Mademba Sy and, 185, 193
  Muslim personal status and, 188
  status of Africans, 186
French civil law, 229–31
French colonial administration compared
    with British colonial administration,
    228–29
  Dahomey-Nigeria border and, 227–28
  indigénat, 17
  indigenous authorities and, 33, 34–35
  "Islamic" policy, 188
  models of, 186
  revolts against, 190
French colonial legal system
  civil law, 229–31
  customary law and, 230
  development of, 186–87
  dispute management under, 12, 14
  harshness of, 17–18, 231, 233–34
  Mademba Sy and, 185
  Muslim legal disputes and, 139–40
  native policy, status of Africans and, 186
  Nigeria-Dahomey border and, 233–34
  overlapping legal jurisdictions in, 16
  reform of, 192–93
  rule of law and, 147
  slave-owner disputes and, 39–40
  sub-systems, 229–30
French Company of Senegal, 15
French Soudan
  conception of power in, 194
  legal jurisdiction in, 185–96
French West Africa
  colonialism model in, 186
  colonial legal code revision in, 135
  governor-general of, 16
  indigénat in, 230, 231
  legal jurisdiction in, 17
  rule of law in, 35–36, 146–60
  tribunals in, 232
Gaiser, G. L., 64, 93
Gallieni, Joseph Simone, 188
Gambia, 12, 13
Geetz, C., 168
Gender. *See also* Women
  agnatic inheritance and, 117
  Chagga attitudes toward, 113
  customary property rights and, 73–74
  labor conflicts and, 30
Genovese, Eugene, 35
German colonialism, in Kilimanjaro, 110–11
German East Africa Company, 15
Ghani, Ashraf, 253
Gida, 216
Giddens, A., 169

Glover, Lieutenant-Governor, 93, 94
Gluckman, Max, 3–4, 6, 41, 44–45, 67, 69,
    75, 76, 91
Gold Coast, 12, 13
  19th-century legal changes, 11
  1874 ordinances to abolish slavery, 29
  property rights, 73
Goldie-Taubman, George, 15
Goods theft
  compensation for, 177–78, 207, 209,
    214–16, 219–20
  from traders, 210–11
  legal process and, 213–14
  lodging house owners and, 213
  punishment for, 216
Goody, Jack, 5
Gorée, 11, 12
  French citizenship in, 133, 134, 135
  jurisdiction of Muslim tribunals in,
    131–41
Governor-general, French West Africa, 16
Great Britain. *See also* British colonial
    administration
  chartered companies, 15
  Crown Colonies, 11–14, 16, 39
  expansion of control by, 16
  Kano and, 205
  Lagos and, 85–86
  Native Administration and, 20–21
Grodet, Alfred, 196
Groff, David, 34, 36, 44, 45
Guilt, Christian and legal concepts of, 15
Gutmann, Bruno, 114
Habermas, Jurgen, 110, 169
Hailey, Lord, 228
Haldane, Lord, 65
Hansen, Karen, 31
Hausaland, theft by office-holders, 211
Hay, Douglas, 32, 35
Hay, Margaret Jean, 7
High Court of Uganda, 4
Historical research, 7–8
Homicide, Kano
  British colonial rule and, 210–211, 219
  oaths and, 207, 209, 217–19
  witnesses and, 208, 217
Hopkins, Anthony G., 11
Housebreakers, Kano, 216, 219
Household heads, violence by, 220
Hukm, 206, 207
Hukm zamanna, 206, 209, 214
Hut tax, 173, 174, 178–79
Ifonyin, 228
Igboo Native Administration, 21
Iliffe, John, 63
Imperial British East Africa Company, 15
Imprisonment. *See* Prison
Indian colonial legal system, 37–38, 43
Indigenas, 17–18

Indigénat, 17
  Yoruba and, 230–31
Indigenato, 17–18
Indigenous law, 8
  British judicial system influence on, 13–14
  customary law and, 21
  French colonialism and, 33, 34–35
  land tenure, 64, 82
Indirections, in Basoga colonial courts, 246–48
Indirect rule, 19–23, 34
  defined, 20
  land ownership and, 64
  Tswana chiefs and, 167
Individual rights
  communal and ownership and, 74–79
  land ownership and, 24–27, 65, 66–71
  opposition to, 70–71
  vs. tribal rights, 67–68
Inheritance
  to adopted sons, 116–18
  agnatic, 109, 110, 113–25
  cadi jurisdiction in, 140
  Chagga and, 108–109
  family property ownership and, 72–73
  permanence of, 69–70
  to sons-in-law, 118–20
Institutional research, for study of law, 8
Interactional research, for study of law, 8
Interest rates, 87
Intermarriage, 9
International trade. See also Agricultural trade; Trade
  after abolition of slavery, 86–87
  credit and, 87–89
  development of, 87–89
Islam, in Lagos, 89
Islamic (shari'a) law, 8
  evidence and, 206
  hukm and, 207
  incompatibility with French civil code, 133
  punishment and, 207–208, 210
  recognition of, 14
  secular legislation and, 206
  theft and, 206–207, 211, 220
Islamic legal process, 207–210. See also Muslim law
  legal officials, 206
  oaths and, 208–210
  testimony and, 208
  witnesses and, 208
  "Islamic policy," Senegalese Muslim tribunals and, 131–32, 134
James, Roden William, 81
Johnson, Bishop James, 101
Johnston, Sir Harry, 111, 116
Judicial Process among the Barotse of Northern

Rhodesia, 44–45
Justice, as blind, 37, 38
Justice indigène, 230
Kabaka, protectorate rule and, 19
Kandawire, J. A. K., 66
Kangah, Kwame, 16–17, 34–36, 146–60
Kangah, M'Bea, 151, 154
Kano, 205–220
  economic transformation in, 205–207
  emir of, 206
  political and social continuity in, 205–207
Kano ta Dabo Cigari, 209
Kaolack, Muslim tribunal in, 141
Kayes, Muslim tribunal in, 141
Kenya, 29, 67
Ketu, 228
Kgosi. See Tswana chiefs (kgosi/dikgosi)
Kgotla, 167, 171, 172, 173, 174, 177
Kidder, Robert L., 37–38, 43
Kihamba, compensation for, 116, 121–124
Kilimanjaro
  historical background of, 110–12
  property transactions, 108–25
Kinship, property transfer and, 109–10, 113, 117–20, 124–25
Kouyaté, Jali Garé, 191
Labor
  agriculture and, 30
  colonial law and, 27–32
  control of, 27–28, 31
  forced, 30
  international trade and, 88
  laws relating to, 31
  mobilization of, 27–28
  slave trade and, 86
Lagos, 12, 13–14, 85–102
  colonial court system, 88
  economy of, 85–89
  international trade, 86–89
  land grants, 86, 87
  Marriage Ordinance, 41
  property ownership, 26, 27
  real estate investment, 88
  rental property development, 88
  Yorubaland and, 227
Lambert, 155, 157
Lambert, Captain, 190, 191
Lambert, H. E., 70
Land
  abandoned, 125
  chief's role in transactions of, 113–14
  as collateral, 87, 115–16, 123–24
  commercialization of, 79
  compensation for improvements to, 120–23
  development of, 78–80
  as economic property, 113
  government control of, 80
  grants, in Lagos, 86–87

individual rights to, 67–71, 74–77
loaned, 120–23
purchase and sale of, 68, 69, 82, 101–25
rental of, 88
Taiwo Olowo's investment in, 100–101
Land allocation, in Malawi, 81
Land concessions, property rights and, 74
Land disputes, litigation over in Basoga colonial courts, 243–52
Land law, *See* Customary land law
Land loss, fear of, 66–67, 76–77
Land ownership
  African concept of, 64
  British control of, 64–66
  Chagga and, 108–25
  chief and, 64–65
  colonial law and, 24–27
  communal, 24–27, 63, 65–68, 74–79
  individual rights and, 67–71, 74–77
  private, 24–27, 65–66
  state trustee, 24, 26
  taxation and, 67
Land policy
  customary law of land tenure and, 62
  Privy Council and, 64–65
Land registries, customary land tenure and, 77–78
Land shortages, Chagga, 112, 113, 123
Land surveys, customary land tenure and, 77
Land tenure
  anthropological study of, 66–68
  customary law of, 61–82
  dominant features of, 68
  freehold, 79
  indigenous sytem of, 82
Lapalud, Lieutenant-governor, 155, 156
Law-making, Tswana chief's role in, 175–176
Lawth, 209
Law Without Precedent: Legal Ideas in Action in the Courts of Colonial Busoga (Fallers), 239, 241, 242, 246
Lawyers
  administrators, 6
  European, use of by Africans, 155
Lebatla, 171
Legal anthropology, 7–8
Legal records. *See also* Court records
  information provided by, 4–5, 91
  limitations of, 90–91
  Taiwo Olowo life history and, 90
Letsholo, 171
Levy, marion J., 240
Life histories, 90–92
Life world, 110
Lineage
  individual property rights and, 70–71, 77
  matrilineal, 73–74
  patrilineal, 109–13, 118–20

Linguists, role of, 149
Literacy, impacts of, 89
Litigation
  Basoga courts, 243–53
  conflicts among Africans, 3–4
Livingstone, David, 28
Loans
  collateral for, 113, 114–16, 123–24
  of land, Chagga, 120–23
  land as collateral for, 87, 123–24
Lobengula, 64–65
Lodging house owners, 212, 213
Loi administratif, 186, 194
Loi bureaucratique, 34 .
Lozi, property rights and, 69
Lüdtke, Alf, 253
Lugard, Sir Frederick, 19–20, 210, 231
Luhmann, N., 169
Macdonald, Claude, 19, 21
McEwen, A. C., 234
Macmillan, W. M., 78–79
Mademba, Abd-el Kader, 187
Mademba Sy, Faama, 16, 33–35, 185–96
  background of, 187–91
  charges against, 185, 191–92, 195
  as conqueror, 189–90
  cotton production and, 191–92
  defense of, 185–86, 192–93
  French citizenship of, 185, 193
  punishment of, 193–94
  revolts against colonial rule and, 190
Maine, Henry, 62
Mair, Lucy, 75
Malawi, 30, 81–82
Malinowski, Bronislaw, 6
Mandala, Elias, 30
Mandara, 111, 116–17
Mann, Kristin, 22, 26, 31, 45, 46–47
Mann, M., 169
Maria, Euuca, 40
Mari Jara, 188
Marriage. *See also* Bridewealth
  cadi jurisdiction in, 140
  colonial ordinances, 15
  forced, 41
  invention of customary rules for, 22
  property rights and, 73–74
  women and, 41
Marriage Ordinance, Lagos, 41
Martin, George, 253
Marx, Karl, 169
Mas, Joseph, 146, 151, 153–54, 157
Masters and Servants Ordinances, 31
Masu gida, 220
Matrilineal property rights, 73–74
Mavin Ovenja, 114
Medick, Hans, 253
Meek, Charles Kingsley, 6, 21, 61, 64, 67, 68, 70, 71, 73, 79

Mekgwa le melao, 174, 175
Men, property rights and, 73–74
Merlin, Governor-general, 16
Middle Niger Valley, 190, 191
Minbar, 208
Missionaries, 9, 14–15
Modisa, 168, 176
Moore, Sally Falk, 7, 8, 22, 26–27, 38–39, 42–44, 46–47
Moor, Ralph, 19, 21
Mortgages, business operations and, 95–96
Mozambique, forced labor in, 30
Muslim judge (alkali), 206
Muslim justice system, decrees defining, 139–140
Muslim personal status
  French civil status and, 133, 188
  French courts and, 139
Muslim tribunals, 12, 17. *See also* Islamic law; Islamic legal process
  jurisdiction of, 36, 131–41, 137–40
  1903 legal code and, 135 37
  recognition of by French, 133–34
Muslim Tribunal of Saint Louis, 132
Mutilation, 210
Nader, Laura, 242
Namulta v. Kazibwe, 243–52
Napoleon, Louis, 133
Native Administration, 19–23
  in British colonies, 18
  fundamentals of, 20
  instability and, 20–21
Native Administration Proclamation (1934), 169
Native Authorities, 20
  authority of, 22, 23
  Tswana kgosi as, 34–35
Native Authority Ordinances, 31
Native Authority Proclamation (1934), 178
Native Courts, 14, 20
  British Nigeria, 232
"Native policy," customary law and, 16
Native Treasuries, 20
Native Tribunals Proclamation (1934), 169, 178
Ndebele, land policy and, 64–65
Newman, Katherine S., 46
Ngoni, ordeals and, 33
Ngwaketse government
  colonial government and, 178–82
  judicial records, 176–78
  Seepapitso's records of, 171–82
  tribal assemblies, 172–76
Niger Coast Protectorate, 18–19
Niger Delta, 11
Nigeria. *See also* Dahomey-Nigeria border
  Kano, 205
  Native Administration in, 20–21
  native courts, 232

provincial courts, 232
  Supreme Court, 231
North Charterland Enquiry, 74
Northern Nigerian Lands Committee, 70
Northern Rhodesia
  land loss in, 67
  property rights, 74–75
Nyasaland
  property rights, 74
  witchcraft accusation and ordeal in, 32–33
Nyerere, Julius, 80
Oath of affirmation, 207, 210, 211, 219, 220
Oath of compurgation, 207, 209, 217
Oath of denial, 207
Oath of division, 209, 217
Oaths
  Allah and, 208, 209
  homicide and, 207, 217–19
  Islamic legal process and, 208–10
  theft and, 207
  Yoruba law and, 227
Oba, 227, 228
Occupation, permanence of, 69–70
Ogubote, Taiwo Olowo and, 99
Oil Rivers Protectorate, 18–19
Olowo, praise name given Taiwo Olowo, 94
Opoku, Kwame T., 229, 230
Oppression, French colonial law and, 231, 233–34
Oral testimony, court records and, 47
Ordeals, 32–33
Originaires, 12
  legal status of, 137–41
  Muslim tribunals and, 131, 132, 134
Oro cult, 227
Oswald, William, 94
Paramount chiefs, native couts and, 232
Patrilineage, Chagga, 109–13, 118–20
Patrimonial property, Chagga disputes involving, 109–10, 113, 117–20, 124–25
Pax Britannica, 69, 211
Peasant agriculture, transition from, 30
Permanence of inheritance, 69–70
Permanence of occupation, 69–70
Permanent rights, customary law and, 70
Planters Union, 70
Police
  colonial, 210
  emir's, 210
  liability of, for theft, 214–5
  Yoruba, 227
Polygyny, 41
Ponty, William, 193, 196
Pope-Hennessy, Sir John, 98
Porto Novo, Yorubaland and, 227
Portuguese colonies
  evasion of African laws in, 10
  forced labor in, 30

indigenato, 17–18
judicial system, dispute management
provisions, 12–13
legal jurisdiction in, 17–18
Postcolonial states, customary land tenure
and, 80–82
Precolonial Africa, 4, 9–10
Precontact native law, 21
Primitive societies, economic behavior in,
63
Prison
British colonial influence on, 210
Islamic law and, 207, 216
Tswana chiefs and, 177–78
Privy Council, land policy and, 64–65
Procureur général, 12
Property pledges, 11
Property rights. *See also* Customary land
law; Individual rights; Land *entries*
concept of, 62–63
customary law and, 71–74
gender and, 73–74
marriage and, 73–74
private, 24–27, 65, 67–68
Property transfer, kinship and, 109–10, 113,
117–20, 124–25
Protectorate rule, 18–19
Protectorates, legal jurisdiction and, 16
Provincial courts, British Nigeria, 231–32
Punishment
Islamic law and, 207–208, 210, 216
Tswana chiefs and, 177–78
Qanun, 206
Qasama cases, 209
Qasama oath, 220
Racial prejudice, abolition of slavery and,
28–29
Ranger, Terence, 7
Rattray, R. S., 6
Regis Aîné, 94, 100
Religious conversion, cultural conversion
and, 15
Rental property, Lagos, 88
Repatriated slaves, 86–87
Repressive law, 18, 231, 233–34
Repugnancy test, 13–14
Rey, Colonel C. F., 169
Rhodes, Cecil, 15
Rhodesia, land policy, 65–66
Roberts, Richard, 16, 17, 33, 34, 36, 41, 42, 44
Roberts, Simon, 6–8, 18, 33–34, 36, 45
Roger, Governor, 133
Rosen, Lawrence, 24
Roume, Governor, 136, 137
Royal Niger Company, 15
Rufisque, 11, 133
jurisdiction of Muslim tribunals in,
131–141
Rule of law

colonial rule and, 147–48
in French West Africa, 146–60
idealogy of, 35–36, 147
Kwame Kangah case and, 158–59
Rule-making, Tswana chief's role in,
175–76
Rule of our times (hukm zamanna), 206,
209, 214
Sabe, 228
Saint Louis, 11, 12
French citizenship in, 133, 134, 135
jurisdiction of Muslim tribunals in,
131–41
Salema, 114
Sarkin dogarai, 214
Sarkin sati, 212
Sarr, Dominique, 12, 17, 36, 43–44, 45
Schacht, Joseph, 217
Schapera, Isaac, 6, 168, 170, 175, 177
Schwartz, Bernard, 194
Seaepapitso, records of, 170–72
Secular legislation, Islamic law and, 206
Seepapitso
central government and, 178–79
European commercial interests and, 179
government style of, 180–81
Ngwaketse tribal assembly records,
172–78, 181–82
records of, 18, 33–34, 36, 43, 167, 167–82
role of, 179–81
Selemani, 108, 109
Senegal, 11–14, 17, 131–141
Senegal Company, 132
Shari'a law. *See* Islamic (shari'a) law
Sheddick, V., 67
Shils, Edward, 240
Siegel, Gabrielle, 253
Silences, in Basoga colonial courts, 246–48
Simpson, S. R., 78
Sin, concept of, 15
Sinsani, 34
Slavery. *See also* Anti-slavery
abolition of, 28–31, 86
slave-owner disputes, 39–41
Taiwo Olowo and, 92, 94
Slaves, former
credit disputes by, 87
land ownership by, 86–87
suits by and against, 29–30
as thieves, 216–17
Slave trade
abolition of, 10
Lagos and, 85–86
legal practices and, 9–10
Sofa, 190
Sons-in-law, inheritance to, 118–20
Sons of the spirit ('yan iska), 211
Southern Rhodesia
land loss in, 67

land policy and, 64–65
property ownership in, 25
Spheres of influence, competition for, 15
Starr, June, 7–8, 21
Status, equality under the law and, 37
Statut civil français, 229–30
Statute law, 22
Statut personnel, 229–30
Stoke, Lambert, 73
Subordination, debt and, 98
Supreme Court, British Nigeria, 231
Supreme Court Ordinance of 1876, 88
Suret-Canale, Jean, 17
Survey, customary land tenure and, 77
Taiwo, Albert Owolabi, 99
Taiwo Olowo, 26, 89–102
Tanganyika, 63
Tanzania, 80–81
Taxation, land ownership and, 67
Temple, Charles, 206
Testimony, Islamic legal process and, 208
Theft, Kano, 206–20
Thiers, President, 135
Thompson, Maud, 40
"Time-oriented" anthropology, 7
Tiv
    conflict resolution by, 38
    property rights and, 69
Todd, Harry F., Jr., 242
Tönnies, 169
Torres land registry system, 77
Trade
    international, 86–89
    precolonial, regulation of, 9–10
    Seepapitso and, 179
Traders
    compensation of, 220
    complaints by, 213–14, 220
    theft of goods from, 210–11, 213–14
Treaties, 16
Trentinian, Colonel, 191
*Tribal Legislation among the Tswana of the
    Bechuanaland Protectorate*, 175
Tribal rights, private rights and, 67–68
Tribunals. *See also* Muslim tribunals
    French reorganization of, 12
    role of, 232
Tribunaux de première instance, 12, 41, 42
Trouble cases, 46
Trustee ownership of land, 24, 26
Tsheko, 177
Tswana chiefs (kgosi/dikgosi), 167. *See also*
    Chiefs
    colonial government and, 169, 178–82
    as Native Authorities, 34–35
    protectorate agreement with Great
        Britain, 18
    roles of, 167–69, 173–78

Seepapitso and, 167–82
Tswana law, 6, 167–82
    nature of, 168
    property rights, 69
Uganda High Court, 4
Uganda Protectorate, 19
Vagrancy laws, 31
Van Zwanenberg, R., 31
Villagization, 69
Violence
    against thieves, 216–17
    prohibition of, 38
Vrais chefs de l'empire, 186
War captives, adoption of, 116–18
Warner, William Lloyd, 240
Waziri, 206
Wealth, conflict over, 23
Weber, Max, 168, 169, 170, 240
White, C. M., 67, 79
White, Luise, 75
Wilson, Godfrey, 75
Witchcraft accusation, 32–33
Witnesses
    homicide and, 217
    Islamic legal process and, 208
Women. *See also* Bridewealth; Gender
    customary law and, 22–23
    inheritance by, 117–18
    labor conflicts and, 30
    marriage and, 41
    property law and, 73–74
Wood, Sarah, 40, 41
Worger, William, 31
Wright, Marcia, 7, 22
Yam Fum, Nana, 148, 149
Yamin al-qasama, 207, 209
    food thieves and, 219
    homicide and, 217–19
'Yan iska, 211
Yeboua, Koffi, 152, 153, 158
Yoruba
    customary law, 226–27, 229
    ideals, Taiwo Olowo and, 90
    justice indigène and, 230
    legal status of under French colonial law,
        230
    in Nigeria-Dahomey borderlands, 224–35
    tribunals, court records and, 90–91
Yorubaland
    British colonial law in, 231–33
    partitioning of, 227
Zambia
    development policies, 80–81
    property rights, 77, 79
Zanzibar
    certificates of freedom for slaves in, 29
    property rights, 71